John Barber

John Barber

1893–1965
Selections from the Archive

Edited and Introduced
by David B. Lawall

Bayly Art Museum of the University of Virginia, Charlottesville

This publication was supported by
The John and Margaret D. Barber Fund and
the Bayly Art Museum.

Photography credits:
Photographs of the artist, his family, and friends are
from the John Barber Archive, on loan to the Bayly
Art Museum from Dr. Margaret De Ronde Barber.
Photographers are unknown unless cited. Photographs
of works by John Barber and the portrait of John
Barber by Jules Pascin are by William A. Faust II
unless otherwise noted.

Dimensions are given in inches; height precedes width.

Illustrated Cover:
John Barber, *Self Portrait, at a Café* (detail of Pl. 19)
Oil on canvas, 17 x 21
Collection of Dr. Margaret De Ronde Barber,
on loan to The John Barber Memorial Collection,
Bayly Art Museum of the University of Virginia

Library of Congress No. 92-072648
ISBN No. 0-8139-1395-0

Table of Contents

Preface

It is one of the privileges of assuming the directorship in an established institution that ambitious projects resulting from years of labor come to fruition with only the most insignificant contributions by the new incumbent. That is certainly the case in this instance. The Bayly Art Museum and Dr. Margaret De Ronde Barber first began to discuss the establishment of the John Barber Memorial Collection at the University of Virginia in 1983. Subsequently Dr. Barber made a gift of 23 paintings and one drawing by her husband and the splendid portrait of John Barber by his friend and colleague Jules Pascin. In addition, she very generously established the John and Margaret D. Barber Fund. She also lent scores of additional paintings to the Museum, as well as hundreds of drawings, and the artist's extensive personal archives. His library, originally on loan, was recently given to the Museum. Rarely has it been possible to study in one place such a comprehensive record of an artist's achievement.

A fascinating, complex portrait of the artist emerged from this extraordinary opportunity to examine closely the full range of Barber's work, methods, philosophy, and character.

At the Museum, an exhibition of works by John Barber was held in 1988, to a warm response from visitors. The present book, published during a second, larger show devoted to his legacy, will serve as enduring testimony to his involvement in the tumultuous course of American art in the twentieth century, and to his distinctive view of his role in it.

Many people deserve to be acknowledged for their efforts in making this publication a reality.

David Lawall, the Bayly Art Museum's long-time Director, spent many years tending to every aspect of the University of Virginia's involvement with John Barber. He prepared the text of the book, writing the introduction and selecting material from the archive. His efforts are responsible for making John Barber accessible to a wider public than the artist has heretofore enjoyed. When Professor Lawall returned to teaching in the McIntire Department of Art at the University after nineteen years of devoted service to the Museum, John Hightower, Director of Planning and Development for the Arts, acting in his capacity as Interim Director, insured the continued well-being of this project. Suzanne Foley, Curator of the Museum, dealt expertly with the myriad critical details involved in bringing the book to press. Sue Deter, formerly on the Museum staff, prepared the manuscript for the printer. Tana Berry, a graduate student in the art department, assisted in ways too numerous to recount here. Jean Collier, Museum Registrar, has coped cheerfully with the daunting task of keeping track of the hundreds of items in the Barber Collection. John De Ronde, the artist's nephew, and his wife Cheryl, have provided critical assistance and counsel; without them, the project would have taken even longer to complete. And, finally, I must thank Dr. Margaret De Ronde Barber without whose unflagging devotion to and enthusiasm for her late husband's work this book could not have been published. To all these people I extend my most profound thanks.

Anthony G. Hirschel, *Director*

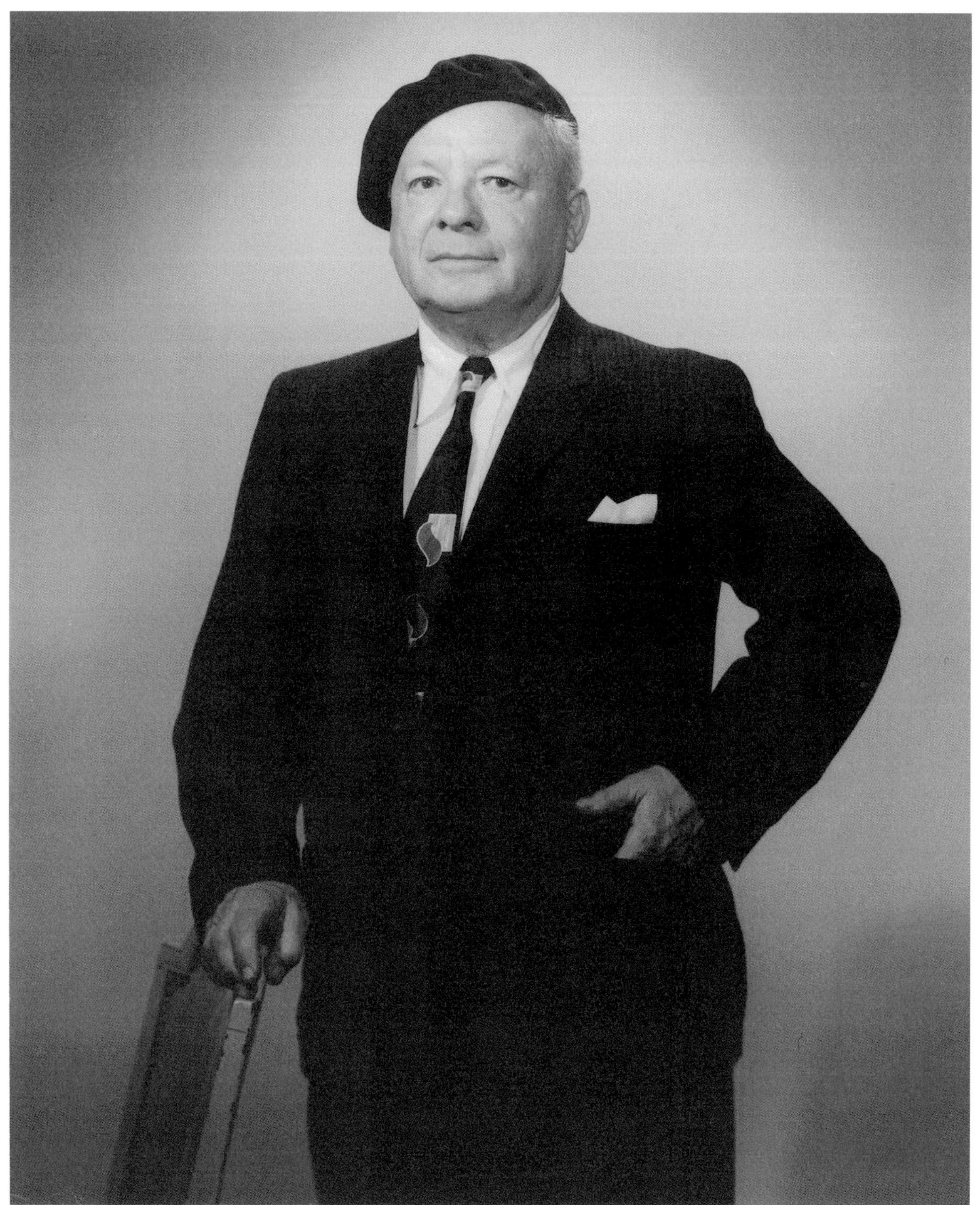

Fig. 1
John Barber,
September 1951

Introduction

The present volume celebrates the long, fruitful, and ongoing interest of the Bayly Art Museum of the University of Virginia in the art of John Barber. The artist's widow, Dr. Margaret De Ronde Barber (University of Virginia School of Medicine, '35), has generously shared with the Museum her comprehensive collection of his work. Including important donations to the Bayly as well as long-term loans, the material at the University comprises John Barber's library and personal papers—The John Barber Archive—and a significant selection of etchings, drawings, and paintings, representing the full range of his work. The collection will form the basis for further research on the life and work of an enigmatic, elusive, and intriguing painter who found his own voice among the cacophony of the international art world of the 1930s and the next two and a half decades.

Born in Galati, Romania in 1893—his father British, his mother Romanian—Barber arrived in the United States in time to launch his career as an illustrator on the staff of *The Masses,* to be inducted into the American army in 1917, and, after the war, to join the throng of American cultural exiles in France. To his profession, Barber brought an immense talent as a draughtsman, an insatiable curiosity about the world, and the firm resolve to live life on his own terms.

Around the year 1922, at the suggestion of his friend Jules Pascin, Barber paid a visit to the studio of Maurice Utrillo in Paris. According to Margaret Barber's report, "Utrillo showed considerable interest in the drawings and few canvases that John had taken with him. His chief comment, which he repeated several times, was an expression of amazement that John 'did figures,' while he was never able to do figures successfully." Doubtlessly Barber carried with him his own just-completed paintings of street scenes in Nice (Pl. 1; Fig. 18) that display crisp planes, plunging perspectives, and a tactile handling of paint not unlike Utrillo's own work. Yet where Utrillo's urban and suburban buildings diminish or absorb the human life of the city, the figures populating Barber's streets, by their concentration of attention or vigilance, diminish the importance of the buildings. Perhaps it is more than coincidence that, in the years following his meeting with Barber, Utrillo himself painted a few pictures in which figures became more numerous, prominent, and socially interactive.

From the picturesque of the Utrillo circle, Barber quickly moved on to the more theoretical cubism as taught in the atelier of André Lhote. Here Barber's instinct for cursive contour line came into conflict with a "learned" analysis of edge, angle, and plane in the interest of strong design and the illusion of sculptural form. A new monumentality is evident in the *Five Bathers* (Pl. 4)—each figure being the outcome of a preliminary pencil drawing (Fig. 27). Two portraits of the artist's father from this period mark an abrupt transition from a naturalist to a cubist-African idiom, from appearances to the abstract essence of forms (Pls. 3, 6).

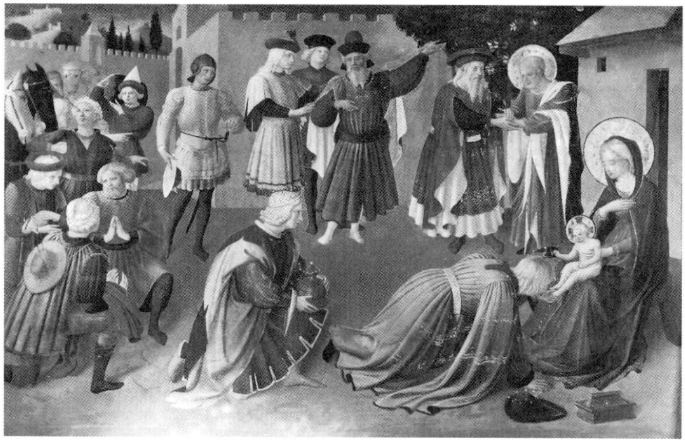

Fig. 2
Fra Angelico
Adoration of the Magi
Museo di S. Marco, Florence
Photograph: Alinari

As a student in the twenties Barber learned from Utrillo and Lhote without becoming attached to the essentially decorative aims of School of Paris painting. The influences that were to be decisive for his work came from his own study of the older paintings, frescoes, and mosaics in the museums and churches of Italy. The *Adoration of the Magi* by Fra Angelico, of which an old Alinari photograph is in the Barber Archive (Fig. 2; and see Figs. 20, 21), offers a paradigm of many important aspects of his mature style. In the work of quattrocento Italian masters, Barber found a tradition of painting that for all its abstraction accords centrality to human content. Each figure is shaped by aesthetic rather than descriptive ends. Each actor in a human drama performs his or her role through posture, gesture, and an awareness of and communication with others. The principal figures are composed above and beneath, to the left and right of one another in terms of the two dimensions of the picture-plane. A shallow depth of abstract space is controlled by the frontal and receding planes of make-believe architecture.

The example of Italian Renaissance art may also have reinforced Barber's innate tendency to see figures individually and in their integrity. The masterful drawing of ca. 1923 represents eight figures and three animals (Fig. 25). Each is seen separately in its full contour. Barber's typical first-draft from nature is a faint, hard-pencil delineation of the contour of the whole figure. At a second stage, he might heighten the line with ink—in a series of short pen strokes that often gives the figure a curiously hyphenated appearance. But the first draft reveals the artist's anxiety to meet an obligation to the wholeness of the figure with minimum evidence of the materials of art. The figures seem weightless, immaterial, transparent. They are a conscious rejection of the volume and density of the drawings made under the influence of Lhote and hark back to the early line drawings such as those for

The Masses (Fig. 8)—but with no easy charm.

We should dwell on these first-draft drawings, for they provide insight into Barber's artistic outlook. The drawings are plain, unembellished, direct. They have none of the decorative appeal of Art Deco style. They are imbued with the necessary and absolute, as though records of a metaphysically irreducible level of experience. If not directly influenced by, they clearly find a remarkable parallel in the Epicurean theory of vision.

> We must also consider that it is by the entrance of something coming from external objects that we see their shapes and think of them. For external things. . . stamp on us their own nature of colour and form. . . by the entrance into our eyes or minds, to whichever their size is suitable, of certain films coming from the things themselves, these films or outlines being of the same colour and shape as the external things themselves. (Epicurus, Letter to Herodotus, in Diogenes Laertins, *Lives of Eminent Philosophers*, x. 49, translated by R. D. Hicks, The Loeb Classical Library.)

Objects emit a steady stream of "films or outlines"— having precisely the faintness of the images that fill Barber's sketchbooks. The act of "seeing" engages both the eye and the mind, thereby reconciling the opposition between sensation and idea that plagued the Impressionists and Post-Impressionists.

There is additional evidence that Barber found explanations for large segments of experience in Epicurean philosophy. In a letter of September 11, 1948, he plainly confesses the central Epicurean criterion of judgement:

> For haven't I learned long ago—around the age of 18—that the symposium of the aim of life as conceived by all the Greek philosophers is as follows:
> "Pursuit of pleasure and avoidance of pain."

In another letter, three days later, he finds solace in a prodigious list of international comestibles. And what are the themes of his paintings but repose, the preparation (but not the antecedent agricultural labor) and consumption of food, the effortless motion of persons in horse-drawn vehicles, friendship and social intercourse, the community of man and animal, a delight in the way things always were? The old Greek philosophy mingles with the modern anarchist's confidence in the individual and celebration of personal freedom.

Yet for all of Barber's commitment to the pleasure principle, his work is not idyllic. The figures in the Fra Angelico possess another quality of which we should take note. A figure such as the kneeling king at the center foreground is not designed according to the canon of Greek sculpture, which Barber also rejected after painting the *Five Bathers* (Pl. 4). In place of the natural form of man, Fra Angelico creates the imaginative form of complex man. It is even a duality of personality that is visualized in the contrast between the boldly calibrated hem of the garment and the sweep of drapery that depends from the shoulder. In Barber's drawings and paintings, forms expand and contract unexpectedly, committing restless aggressions and retreating; heads may be set at awkward angles, and fingers or toes twist painfully (Pl. 17). The complexities of the figures are reminiscent of Soutine and El Greco. The anti-heroic repose of Barber's figures is belied by what they are. Their heroism lies not in their actions but in their peculiarly intricate and unpredictable modern identity. By their repose the figures ironically—and heroically—assent to the tensions which they live and fulfill in their forms.

Whatever elements of tone and color may be present as a separate mode of expression—and sometimes Barber added graphite shading or touches of watercolor to his line drawings—a drawing is essentially the movement of line across a sheet of paper,

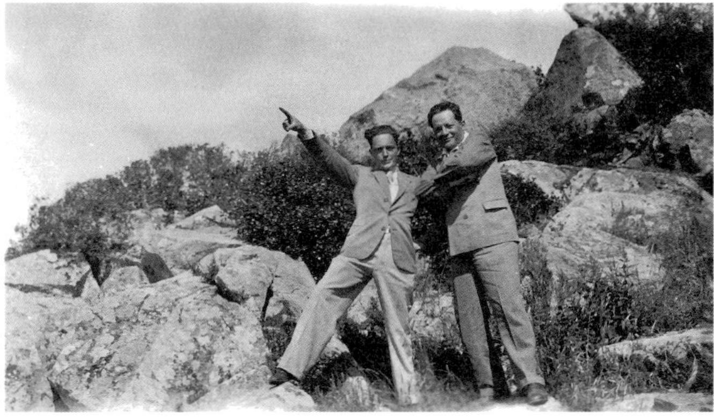

Fig. 3
John Barber (right) and Jules Pascin, ca. 1925

the intimate trace of inward impulse. Regardless of
what it represents, a drawing refers, in the first instance, to the character and state of the artist's mind.
Connoisseurship is a problem in psychology to which
the solution is given in the visible markings on the
paper. Both Barber and his comrade Jules Pascin
were master draughtsmen, but what a difference of
mind their drawings reveal! For Pascin, drawing was
an exercise in expression, provoked by experience.
What he saw released and diversified pent-up im-
pulses as the exposure of personal energies. The act
of drawing was the occasion of self-discovery. For
Barber, conversely, drawing was an exercise in the
receptivity to and criticism of experience. The line
hesitates as the mind ponders or exaggerates a new
twist of contour. Barber's more philosophical line is
not charged with emotional release but searches for
shapes, well crafted, that are at once vital and right in
the context of the design of the drawing as a whole.
Where Pascin stops with the self-revealing gesture,
Barber's equally personal line constructs an aesthetic
order out of experience in which none is given. It is
this invention of an aesthetic order, through which
the artist invents his own dignity—and many of
Barber's designs become astonishingly intricate
without loss of equilibrium—that places Barber's
draughtsmanship in the classic tradition of the
quattrocento masters, of Poussin, Cézanne, and the
Cubists. The drawing is the man, and the contrast of
temperament between Pascin and Barber could not be
better illustrated than by the photograph of the two
together in which the one expends energy through
gesture while the other, with folded arms, defines his
own structure (Fig. 3).

Despite his Epicureanism, Barber was acutely
aware of the of the anguish and sorrow of modern
experience. In the early etching, *French Tramps*
(Fig. 17), reality, as specified by the man, woman,
child, and horse, flatly turns its back. But out of the

center of individual isolation and collective indifference, the ferocious dog lunges directly at the viewer. The Barber Archive contains occasional but trenchant fragments of the litany of modern despair—

> Max Nordau. "Degenerates are not always criminals, prostitutes, anarchists, and pronounced lunatics; they are often authors and artists."

> Anatole France. "In all the universe the most unhappy creature is man."

> Epitaph on Oscar Wilde's tomb, Pérè Lachaise Cemetery, Paris. Copied November 1, 1923. "And alien tears will fill for him/Pity's long broken urn, /For his mourners will be outcast men/And outcasts always mourn."

> H. L. Mencken, August 3, 1923. On the Russian revolution: "For the first time in modern history an actual effort is being made to reorganize society, and though I believe that it will fail I still believe that it is thoroughly worth making." And, on American politics: "The papers gurgle over Harding's honesty, thus escaping the need of discussing his intelligence. . . I doubt that any public man under democracy can be honest, and I am now at work on a book attempting to show why it is."

> From a marble plaque in the old ghetto of Venice. Copied August 20, 1950, and again August 31, 1961. "Six million Jews of Europe by the blind barbarous hatred in distant lands hunted, martyred, killed."

Then, however, there is the aphorism of Netzahualcozotl, copied into a Mexican sketchbook of 1941:

> Not even with a heap of treasures
> can you give life to your people,
> because treasures are smoke.
> Exalt only in the songbirds
> and the flowers that cover the earth,
> for they intoxicate your soul.

In circumstances the reader will shortly discover, at an early age Barber exempted "the inviolable sanctum of his own pure inner spiritual life" from the decision of public law and a court of law. At the same time, he set his idea of nature as "imbued with goodness and purity" over against "forces of evil, waiting for combat." Since the contrast poses a question to which there is no final answer, any answer—but not no answer—may be the ground for personal heroism and creativity, as imagination functions to certify a conviction that has no other foundation.

Because Barber invests the figure itself with "real" psychological complexity, he found it necessary to shift his quest for the "ideal" from the figure to its pictorial context of space, light, and color. The early paintings of street scenes position very solid figures firmly amid architectural rigidities that effectively block any glimpse of infinite space (Pl. 1). From Lhote and the cubist tradition, Barber borrowed the emotionally neutral and intellectual monochromatic palette of greys and browns, which subjects all of the forms to the unity of an ideal light (Pls. 7, 11). It is upon this unified field of light that the "films or outlines" emanating from objects inscribe themselves. Golden figures on a ground of gold, as in the Byzantine mosaics or icons, the imagery of the painting is cut off from the tangible world and participates in a higher realm of the artist's own choosing and creation.

As the mind matures through the critical evaluation of experience—a process that we can trace so clearly in Barber's letters of 1947–1948—the imagery of the paintings changes. In the major paintings of the 1930s, the figures are still firmly situated in the stable architectural environments borrowed from the Italian painters of the Renaissance (Pl. 12). The visit to Mexico in 1941 brought a new appreciation of color—thin glazes of rainbow hues that bring with them a new vitality. By the late-1940s light begins to dissolve the environment. A wedge of light, more aggressively brushed and with its own personality, becomes a protagonist and divides the figure groups (Pl. 27). Intense sunlight reflected from pavements cuts away the ground men and animals tread. The fountain in one of the later paintings on the laundress theme becomes a fountain of light in which the women bathe themselves by looking (Pl. 29). In a whole series comprised of what are probably very late paintings (ca. 1955–1965), figures on deck or in a park or garden or at the beach recline, converse, or almost sleep along the edges of an abyss of light which elevates a still inwardly restless humanity far above the mundane plane (Pls. 30, 33). The complex personalities of the Greek gods, conversing on the Parthenon frieze, come to mind as a parallel apotheosis of human nature.

The late painting, *Sunday in the Park* (Pl. 34), provides a suitable point at which to close a survey of Barber's work. The painting is clearly a reprise of the early drawing for *The Masses* entitled *Trying to Recover from Civilization* (Fig. 8). Perhaps this is an adequate summary of the agenda of Barber's work. In the early drawing, the upper left corner is occupied by two youths—Epicureans—at table beneath a canopy. In the later painting this position is occupied by the bemused, pipe-smoking, contemplative "philosopher," which figure reminds us of a little dialogue. In 1928, Barber's friend, the American writer Claude McKay, published his novel *Home to Harlem*. At page 274, McKay writes: "the more I learn the less I understand and love life." The novel itself is dedicated "To my friend Louise Bryant," but the copy in the Barber Archive bears the manuscript inscription: "Paris, March 1st, 1930/and to *my* friend/John Barber/who never knows/how to stop loving life./Louise Bryant."

. . .

The purpose of the present volume is to introduce John Barber to a wider public through selected passages from documents in the John Barber Archive. Preference has been given to items in which Barber speaks for himself about life, the world, and art. The materials that would be required for a full-scale "life" of John Barber probably do not exist. Yet among the papers that do survive, we find vivid specimens of the artist's perceptions and opinions. These are, like life and art themselves, necessarily fragmentary. It is as though we were to recall a series of meetings with a friend over the years. A few letters addressed to Barber have been included for their intrinsic interest. In general, orthography and syntax have been regularized. Three dots are used at points where the texts have been abridged. Information in brackets does not appear in the original document.

From the earlier years, little is preserved—brief recollections of childhood, military papers, and a few postcards from Europe in the 1920s. All of the notes and letters from Jules Pascin in the archive are included for the glimpse they afford of one of Barber's closest friends. The miscellaneous notes on art and artists were probably written in the 1940s when Barber lectured on art and served as president of Harcum Junior College in Bryn Mawr, Pennsylvania. The two essays on travel in Greece and Mexico are datable even though it is not clear for what purpose or occasion they were written.

Compensating for the scarcity of written documents from the earlier years, a substantial body of drawings and sketchbooks has survived. A liberal selection of drawings is included, for, as proposed above, the drawings are the central autobiographical data. Yet if we try to construct a life out of the drawings, etchings, and paintings, we are hampered by the fact that often the drawings and always the paintings are undated. Time and timeliness were not factors in Barber's work, which aimed at the timeless through the grasp and interpretation of the visual experience of the moment. We have tried to arrange illustrations of the drawings and paintings in an approximate rather than absolute chronological sequence.

The last two sections of the text mutually complement one another and invite a word of introduction. In the winter of 1946–1947, Barber met and painted a portrait of Dr. Margaret De Ronde, a psychiatrist on the staff of the Institute of the Pennsylvania Hospital, University of Pennsylvania. Romance quickly blossomed. Yet in September of 1947, Barber found it necessary to tend and escort his ailing mother, Betty Barber, to Tunis, where she could enjoy support and comfort in the home of her daughter's widower, Marcel Gozland. The stay in Tunis extended through the winter and was followed by a move to Copenhagen in June 1948. Throughout a separation that lasted more than a year, John wrote letters to Margaret almost daily. These letters, preserved in the archive, make up a full-length self-portrait of the artist—as he saw himself and as he wished to be seen by one who became his wife. With his departure from Paris on the morning of October 1, 1948, this self-portrait comes to an abrupt end.

For the period 1948 to 1965, we have recourse to the memoranda written by Margaret De Ronde Barber after her husband's death. These report some of John's memories of his earlier years but are primarily the record of a happy married life filled with work, learning, mutual esteem, and love. One is struck by the simplicity of sudden departures and the spontaneity of unpremeditated adventure. Marriage seems to have verified John's philosophy of life—

> . . . why try to be intelligent—it's a sheer waste of time and good grey matter. The only thing we helpless, buffeted, harassed mortals can do is just use a little good will, a *great deal of love*, and patience and things somehow straighten out by themselves.

Although Barber found himself out of sympathy with the mainstream of American painting in the 1950s, his faith in "a law of harmony and order that puts things straight just when they seem most chaotic" provides an illuminating parallel to the Abstract Expressionists' reliance on improvisation. In Barber's letters of 1947–1948, however, we find a sweeping critique of life that leaps prophetically across the formalist limits of Modernism to a vision of the frailty of the postmodern individual who awakes in his own dream.

David B. Lawall

I. Childhood in Romania

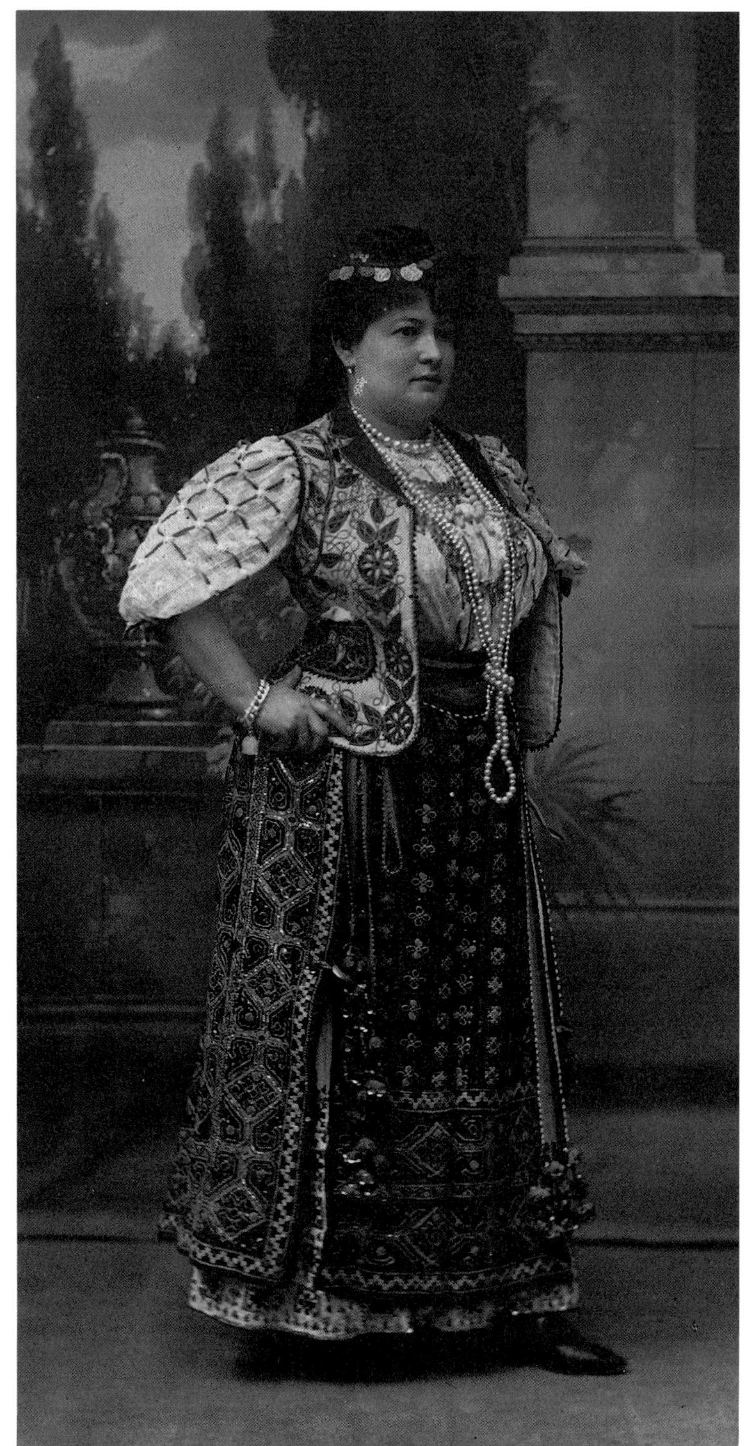

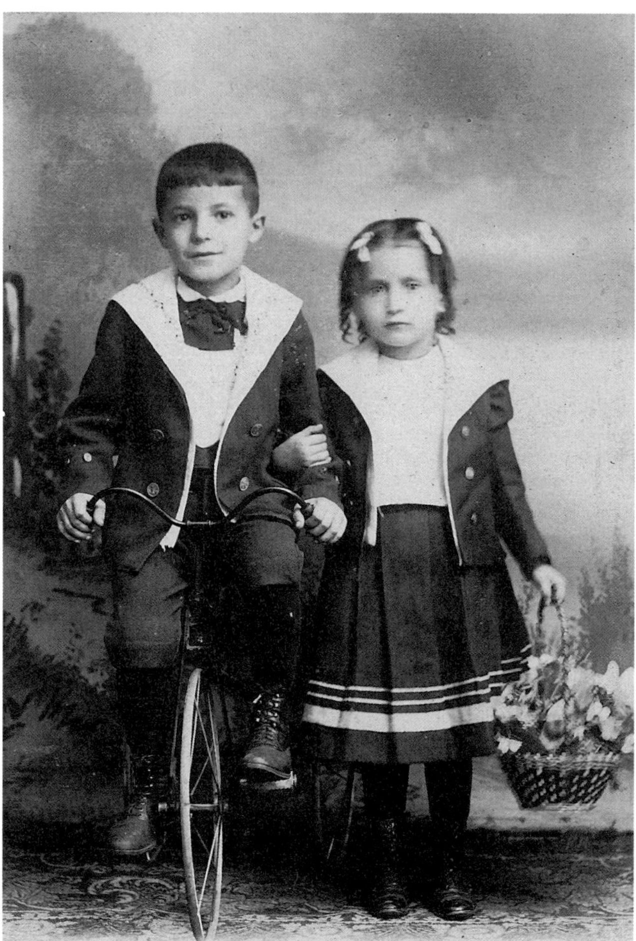

Fig. 5. *Above*, John Barber and his sister Riviere (Rita), Galati, Romania, ca. 1904

Fig. 4. *Left*, The artist's mother, Betty Barber, Galati, Romania

Childhood in Romania

Autobiographical fragment

My first childhood ambition was to become a great geographer—in that I learned to draw from memory maps of every country as an adjunct to my stamp collection. That perhaps accounts for twenty-five years of wanderings in Europe and North Africa and Mexico, and developing into a genre painter—painting the life and customs and all that seemed to me exotic and outlandish in the Western World.

Even as a child, I became fascinated with the freedom, the vastness, and the dynamism of the United States. I learned to draw maps of each state, read about the great and learned Americans of the past, while at the same time I kept abreast of its current events through every available source I could find. At last the day came when my father gave me a choice of going to the famous American Roberts College in Beirut, or going to the United States of America. The decision was very easy, and I came to New York.

A slightly edited version of this statement appears in American Artist, *June 1959, pp. 33–34.*

II. New York, 1911–1917

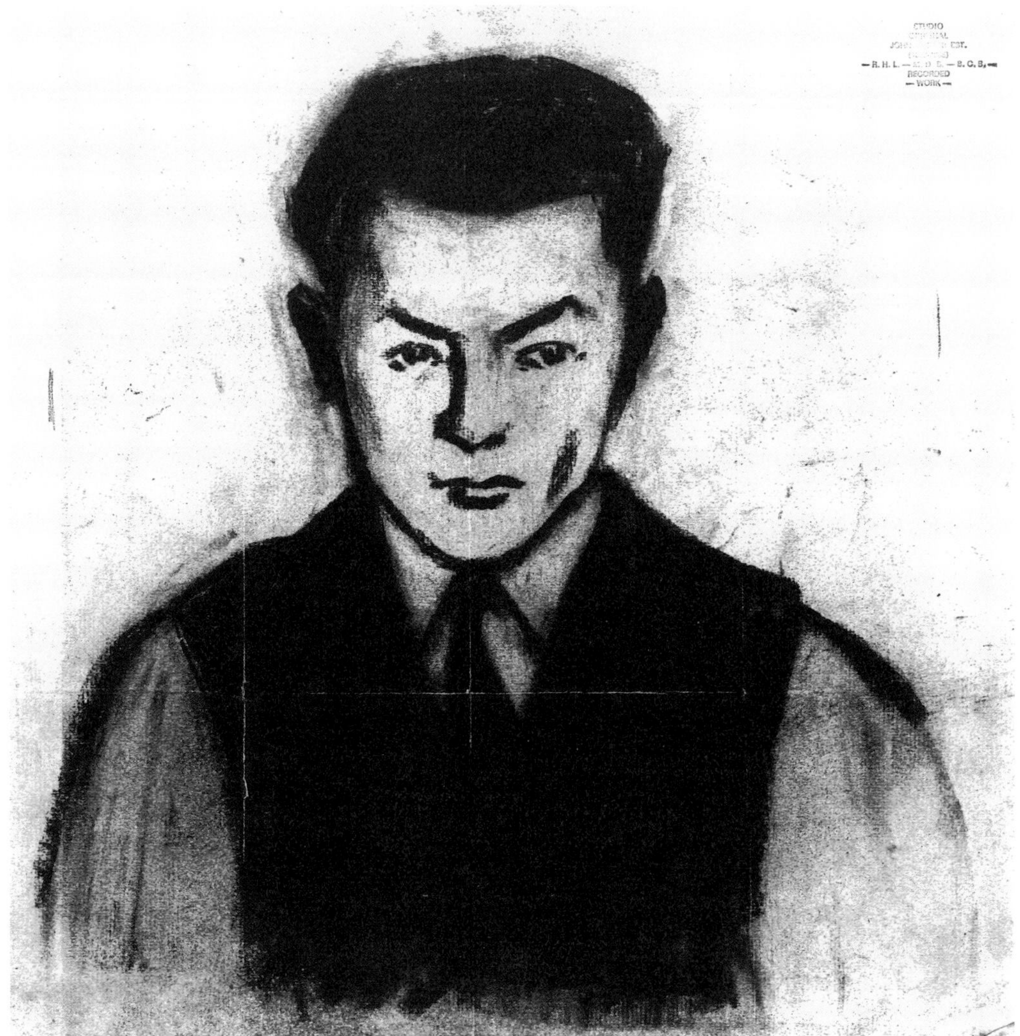

Fig. 6
John Barber
Self Portrait, New York, ca. 1915
Charcoal, 12 x 11 $5/8$
Collection of Dr. Margaret De Ronde Barber,
on loan to The John Barber Memorial Collection,
Bayly Art Museum of the University of Virginia

Autobiographical fragment

Practically upon arrival in New York I applied for citizenship, as I could not be happy until I identified myself completely with that Utopian ideal I had dreamed of so long. But, I also had to support myself, and found the best way through a job on a newspaper. Soon I was doing newspaper art reporting, as it was done in previous years, and contributing an occasional cartoon to periodicals. I got useful training that way in rapidity of observation and execution, which helped develop my style of work in painting.

Through these channels I had the good luck and happy destiny of meeting the famous Eight in American art—most of whom became my good friends and close colleagues for many years. John Sloan and William Glackens (who later joined me in a sketching trip in France) were perhaps my best friends as long as they lived.

A slightly edited version of this statement appears in American Artist, *June 1959, p. 35.*

Postcard

[New York
December 31, 1915]

John Barber
2140 Fifth Avenue
N.Y.C.

The Literary Meeting of THE MASSES will be held Monday Evening, January 3rd, at 9 o'clock, at the home of Floyd Dell, 135 MacDougal Street.

The Masses
Editorial Office
2 West 15th Street
New York
January 18, 1916

Mr. John Barber
2140 Fifth Ave., N.Y.

Dear Mr. Barber:

May I tell you how much I admire the picture you brought to the MASSES this month. I think it is a wonder, and lots of other people do too who have seen it.

I want to save it until warmer weather before I publish it, if you don't mind. Meanwhile, I hope you will keep on drawing for us. I think you have a very unique talent.

Yours sincerely,
Max Eastman

85 Hawthorne Avenue
East Orange, N.J.
Friday Dec. 15, 1916

Dear Barber,

It is our intention to have the cuts made and our magazine printed by the end of next week. In order to accomplish this it will be necessary to have $5.00 from you by Sunday night when we meet at MacKenna's.

And we also thought that you would be better represented and the variety of the paper helped out if you would print a composition instead of the nudes. We have a new man by the name of Goldberg who has not got anything else but nudes and so we are using one by him. Since you do compositional work we think it would be better if you would use one. Will expect to see you Sunday night.

Yours,
Stuart Davis

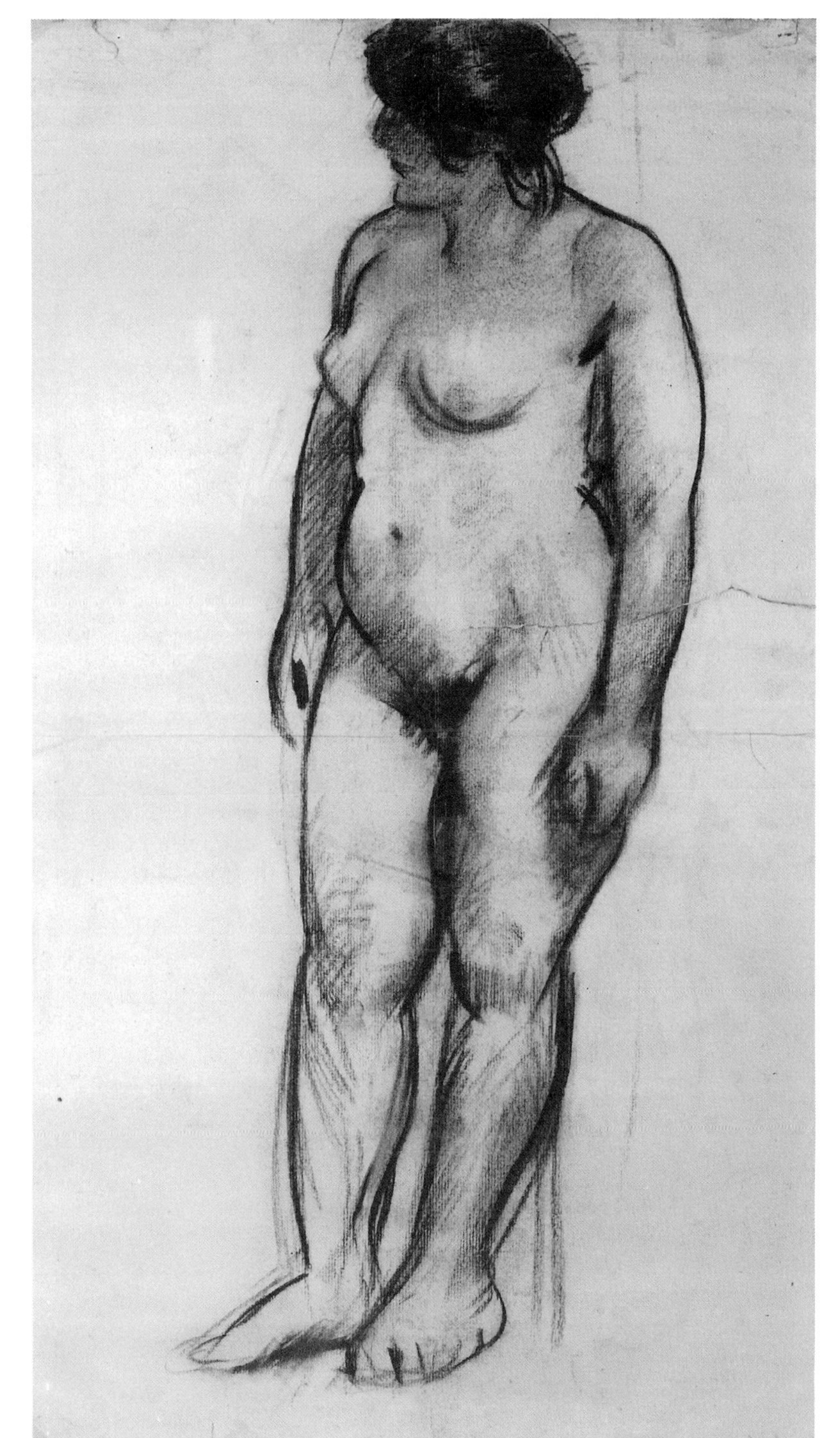

Fig. 7
John Barber
Standing Nude
Charcoal, 24 $^1/_2$ x 13 $^5/_8$
Collection of Dr. Margaret De Ronde Barber,
on loan to The John Barber Memorial Collection,
Bayly Art Museum of the University of Virginia

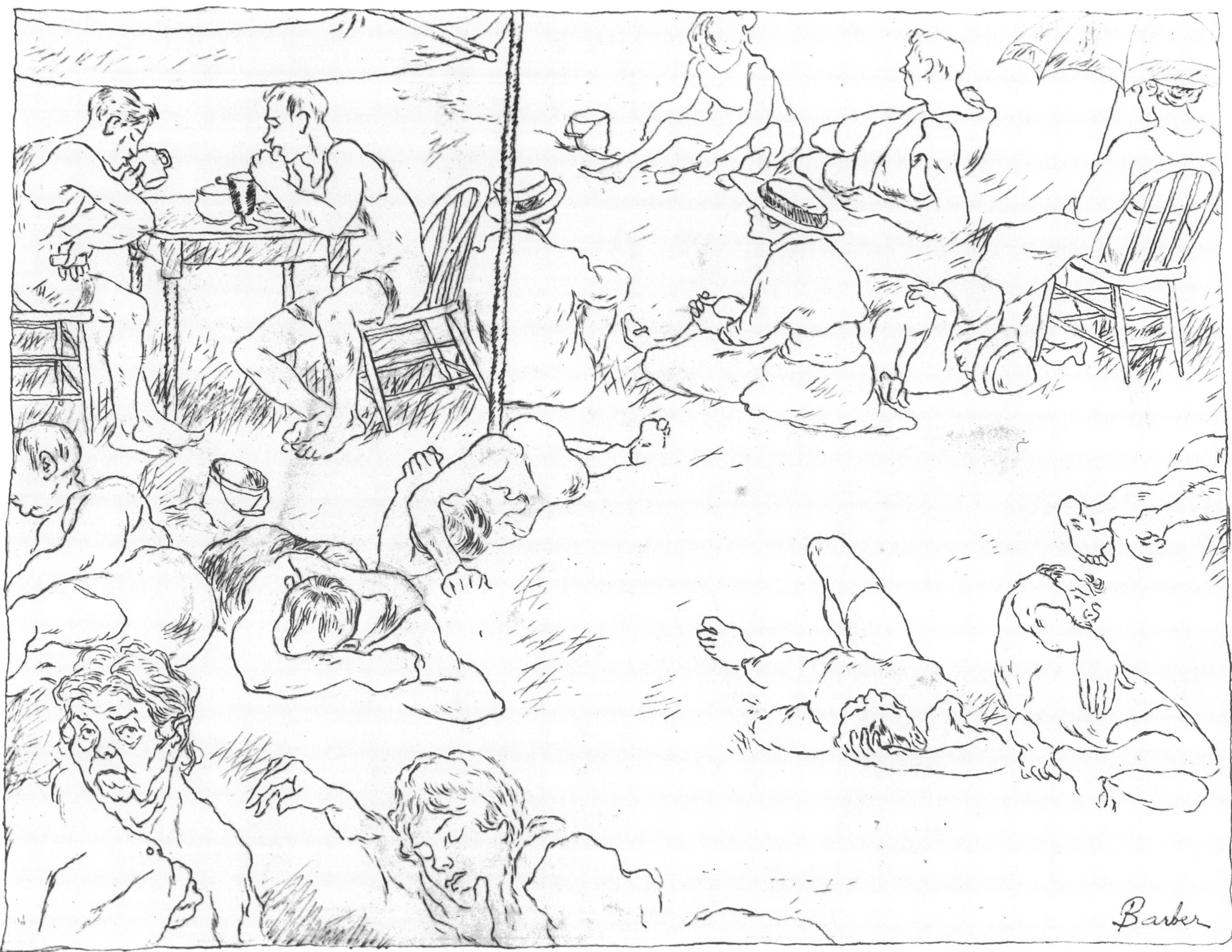
Barber

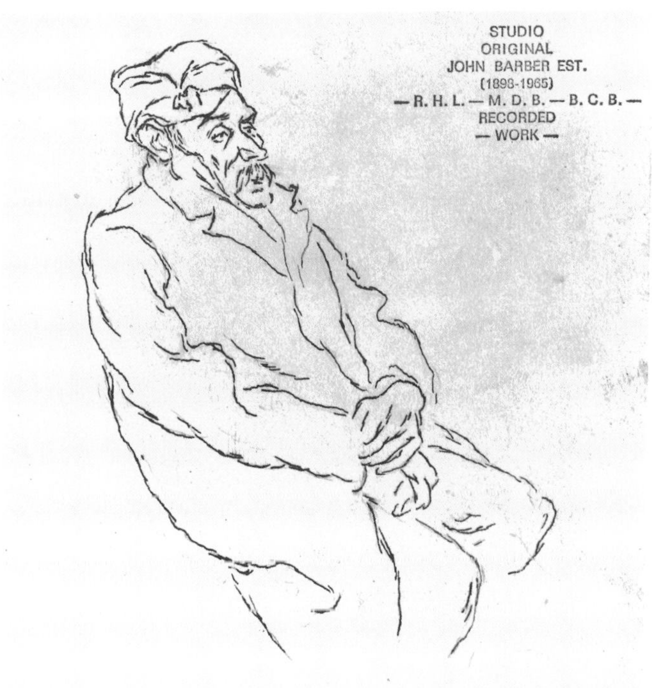

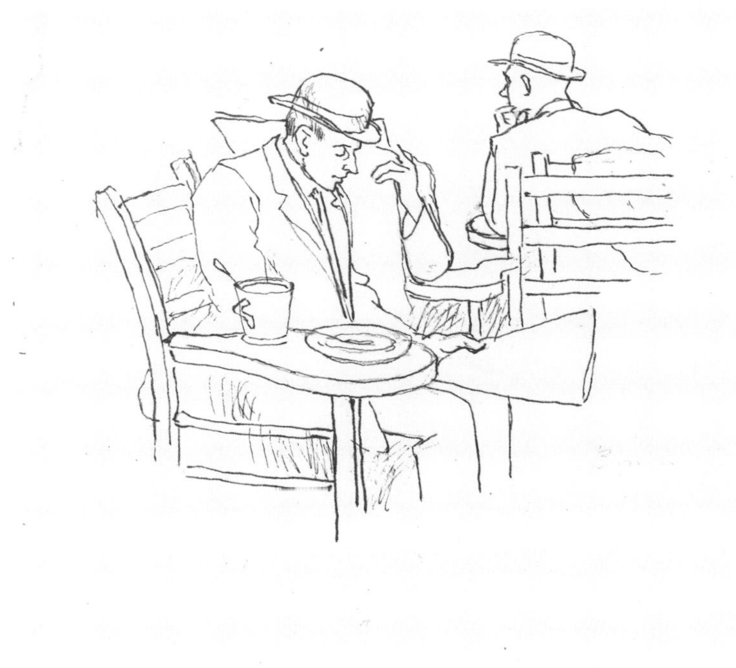

Fig. 9
John Barber
Study of a Man in an Overcoat
Graphite and ink, 4 3/8 x 4
Collection of Dr. Margaret De Ronde Barber,
on loan to The John Barber Memorial Collection,
Bayly Art Museum of the University of Virginia

Fig. 10
John Barber
Two Men at Lunch
Graphite and ink, 4 3/8 x 5 3/4
Collection of Dr. Margaret De Ronde Barber,
on loan to The John Barber Memorial Collection,
Bayly Art Museum of the University of Virginia

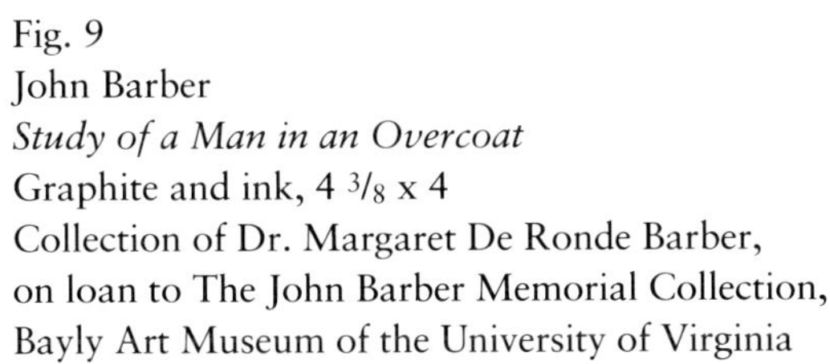

Fig. 8
Left, John Barber
Trying to Recover from Civilization, ca. 1916
A drawing for *The Masses, 8,* June 1916, page 15
Ink and graphite, 7 3/8 x 9 5/8
Gift of Dr. Margaret De Ronde Barber
to The John Barber Memorial Collection,
Bayly Art Museum of the University of Virginia, 1987.11

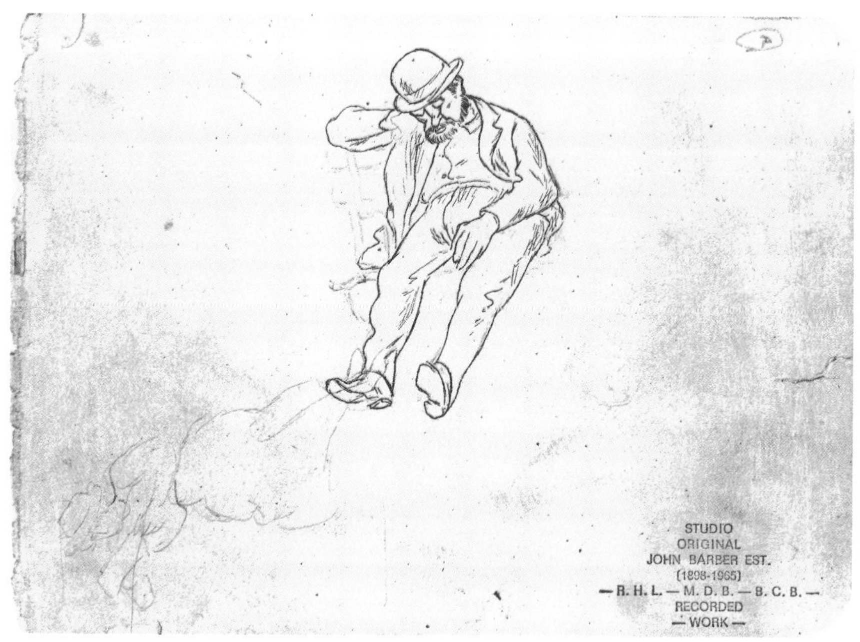

Fig. 11
John Barber
Man Asleep
Graphite and ink, 4 3/8 x 5 3/4
Collection of Dr. Margaret De Ronde Barber,
on loan to The John Barber Memorial Collection,
Bayly Art Museum of the University of Virginia

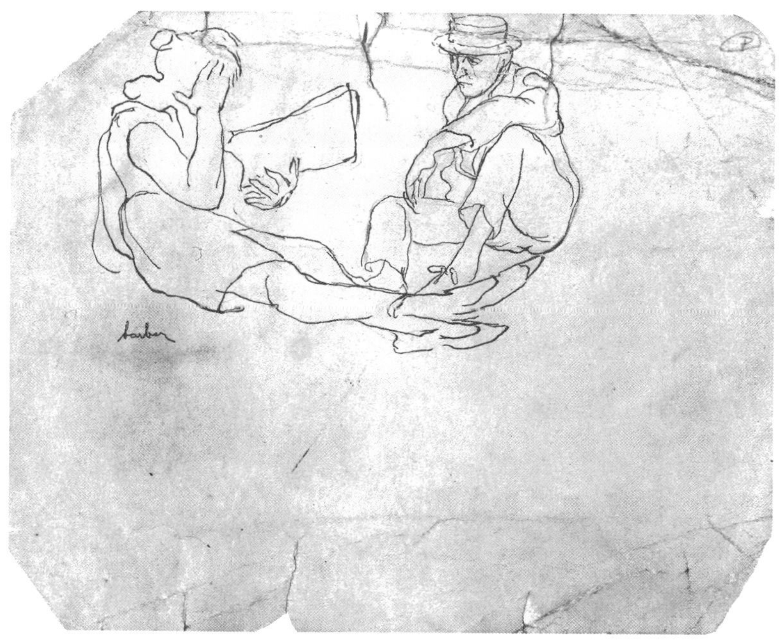

Fig. 12
John Barber
Woman and Man
Graphite and ink, 4 3/8 x 5 1/4
Collection of Dr. Margaret De Ronde Barber,
on loan to The John Barber Memorial Collection,
Bayly Art Museum of the University of Virginia

III. *War in France, 1917–1919*

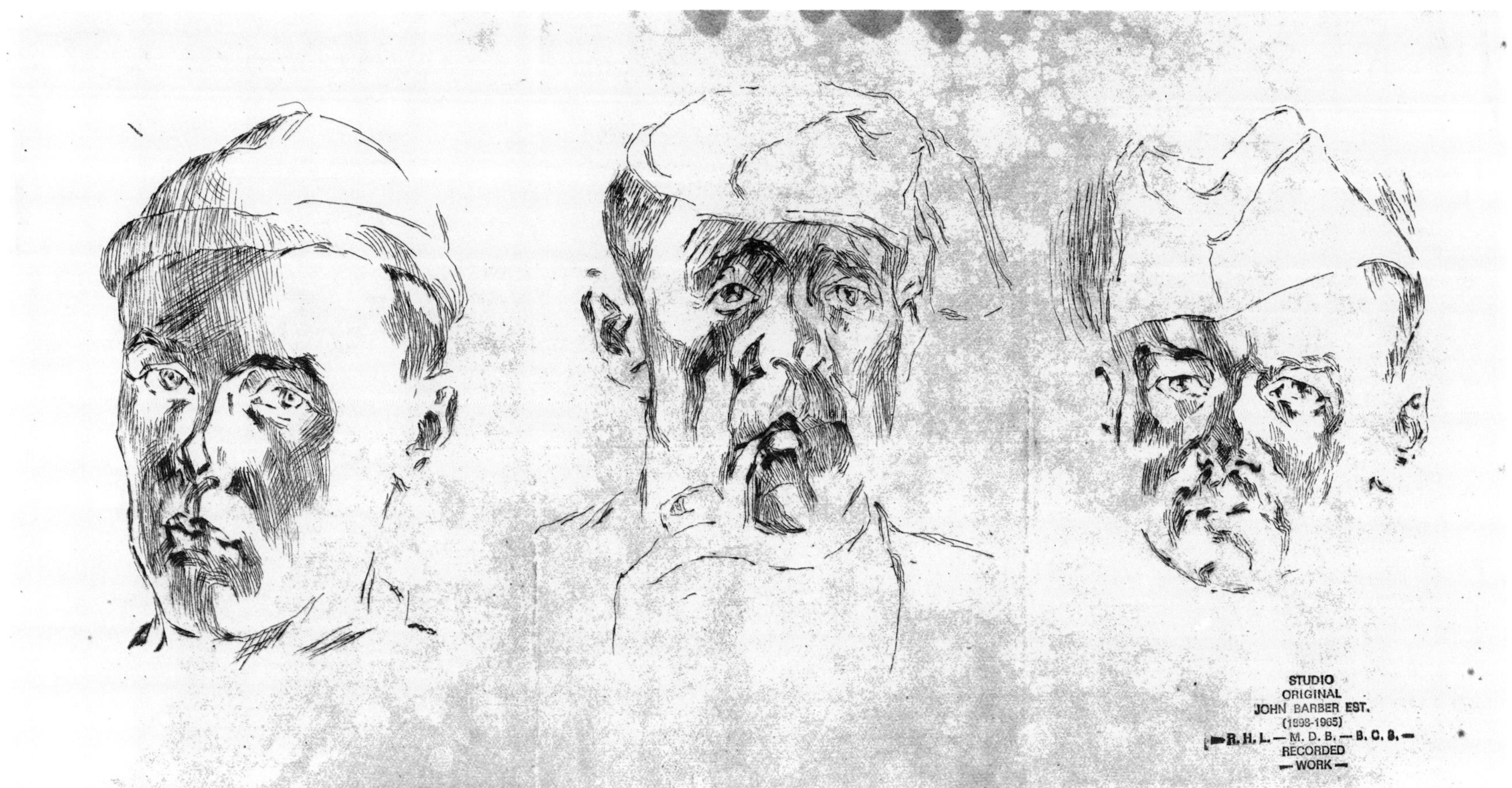

Fig. 13
John Barber
Three Heads, France, March 1918
Etching, 6 1/8 x 11 3/8
Collection of Dr. Margaret De Ronde Barber,
on loan to The John Barber Memorial Collection,
Bayly Art Museum of the University of Virginia

War Department
Local Board for Div. 139
Calvary Church
Cor. 129th St. & 7th Ave.

John J. Barber
34 West 129th Street
New York, N.Y.

Order No. 14
Red ink No. 2787

By direction of the Secretary of War, you are hereby ordered to report to the office of this Local Board at 7:30 A.M. on the 10 day of September, 1917, for military duty and for transportation to the Army mobilization camp at Camp Upton.

From the date herein specified for you to report, you will be in the military service of the United States and subject to military law. Failure to report or unpunctuality are grave military offenses punishable by court-martial. Willful failure to report with intention to evade military service constitutes desertion which is a capital offense in time of war. Present yourself at the precise hour specified in order that you may not begin your military record in the service of your country with delinquency.

You will be held under the orders of this board until the hour of departure of your train. During this period the Local Board will furnish you food and lodging. If you live within one hour's travel of the office of the Local Board, you may obtain permission to sleep and eat at home, but only if you fill out and forward to the office of the Local Board at once the printed application for this permission at the end of this sheet.

You will not be permitted to take with you on the train anything but hand baggage. You do not need bedding or changes of clothing except as specified below. You may take with you only the following articles: Soap; shaving accessories; comb and brush; toothbrush and tooth powder; towels; underclothing and socks; and if you desire, changes of collars and shirts, but you will have no use for these after arrival at the mobilization camp.

Since you will not be permitted to retain any trunks after your arrival at the railroad station, the articles listed above should be brought in a hand bundle.

If you desire to do so, you may return the civilian clothes you are wearing when you arrive at the mobilization camp to your home by express or otherwise, but if you desire to make no such arrangement, it will be better to appear in civilian clothes that you do not care to keep.

Sept. 5, 1917
Local Board for 139
City of New York
J. W. Savage
C. W. Andrews

War Department
General Office of the
Provost Marshal
General
Local Board No. 139
N. W. Cor. 129th St. &
Seventh Ave.
New York
September 27, 1917

John J. Barber
34 West 129th St.
New York City

Sir:

You are authorized to be present at the office of Local Board for Division #139, City of New York, Calvary Methodist Church, N. W. Corner of 129th Street & 7th Avenue at 7:30 A.M., Saturday, September 29th prepared to go to Camp Upton as an alternate.

Respectfully,
J. W. Savage
Chairman

RECORD OF TRIAL BY
GENERAL COURT MARTIAL OF
PRIVATE JOHN J. BARBER,
#189489, CO. D, 501ST
ENGINEERS.

. . .

Proceedings of a General Court Martial convened at Base Hospital No. 9, A.E.F., France, pursuant to the following order:

Headquarters Services of Supply
American Expeditionary Forces
France, April 18, 1918

Special Orders
No. 37

. . .

The members of the Court and the Judge Advocate were then sworn.

The accused was then arraigned upon the following charge and specification:

Charge 1: Violation of the 96th Article of War

Specification 1: In that Private John J. Barber, 189489, Co. D, 501st Engineers, having been found to be suffering from Varicocele (left) and having been advised by 1st Lieut. Frank E. Adair, M.C., U.S.R., that an operation consisting of the ligation and excision of these veins was necessary to enable him to perform properly his military duties, did, at Base Hospital No. 9, A.E.F., France, on or about the 6th day of April, 1918, refuse to submit to such operation; that after such refusal the said Private John J. Barber, 189489 was examined by a Board convened under authority of par. 2, G.O. 167 WF 1917: that the said Board found that the operation advised by the said 1st Lieut. Frank E. Adair, M.C., U.S.R., was necessary to enable the said Private John J. Barber, 189489 properly to perform his military duties: that the said Private John J. Barber, 189489 was at Base Hospital No. 9, A.E.F., France, on or about the 7th day of April 1918, notified of the finding of said Board, and that thereafter he persisted in his refusal up to the time when these charges were preferred to submit to such operation.

J. P. Erskins,
Captain, M.C., U.S.R.,
Adjutant.

To which the accused pleaded:
To the Specification, Charge 1: Guilty
To Charge 1: Guilty

The President of the Court then addressed the accused: "You, Private John J. Barber, have heard the charge, Violation of the 96th Article of War, the Charge and Specification thereunto for which the punishment may be dishonorable discharge from the Army, and in addition any punishment in time of War up to the death penalty. Now in pleading guilty to this charge you admit having committed all of the allegations of the crime or offense charged, and that you may be punished as stated. Understanding this, do you still plead guilty?"
To which the accused replied:
"I understand, and I desire that my plea of guilty shall stand."

. . .

1st Lieut. Frank E. Adair, M.C., U.S.R., Base Hospital No. 9, was sworn as a witness for the prosecution, and testified as follows:
Questions by prosecution:
Q. Do you know the accused, if so state who he is.
A. I do, Private John J. Barber, Co. D, 501st Engineers.
Q. On or about the 4th day of April, 1918, did you examine the accused?
A. I did.
Q. What was the accused's chief medical complaint?
A. His complaint was pain in the left testis, with resultant inability to perform his duties.
Q. What was your diagnosis?
A. Left Varicocele with atrophy of the left testis.
Q. What was your suggested treatment?
A. Surgical operation.
Q. What is the usual treatment?
A. Venectomy.
Q. You thought that a Surgical operation would remove the veins and the apparent disability?
A. I did.
Q. You think that if this patient were operated on he would be able to return to active duty?
A. I do.

Q. Ordinarily is the operation a simple one?
A. Ordinarily it is.
Q. How much risk to life?
A. Practically none.
Q. You have operated on many patients with Varicocele?
A. Yes.
Q. To an ordinarily healthy young man do you think there is much danger?
A. No.
Q. You have advised the accused of his condition, explained everything to him in detail, and he has refused to submit to the treatment offered?
A. I have.
Questions by defense:
Q. Did the accused give you any reason for refusing to submit to operation?
A. He did.
Q. What was his reason?
A. His religious beliefs.
Q. What were his religious beliefs?
A. He felt that he had sufficient faith in Christian Science and he would be cured without surgical operation.
Q. Can you put that in one word; what is his religious belief, what is his faith?
A. He says he belongs to the Christian Science Church.
Judge Advocate: There appear to be no further questions, the witness is excused.

. . .

Judge Advocate: The prosecution rests.
Defense: The defense has no further witnesses to submit, simply has a statement which was prepared by the accused, which I would like to read at this time. I had prepared another defense for him but today he opposed my wishes against my will and I have submitted to what he wants. This is what he has written, "I do not feel myself guilty of any crime,

therefore I have nothing to defend. An individual's faith and religious beliefs are sacred and belong to the inviolable sanctum of his own pure inner spiritual life. God and Christian Science cannot be threshed out in Court and, furthermore, a concrete decision cannot create an immortal right in the domain of the soul; while no obstacles can deviate the way of his intent on worshipping in his own way—he will uncomplainingly pay the price that would be exacted by those trying to hinder."

"Life to me is not worthwhile if I cannot pursue unhindered a higher form of existence—embracing all the spiritual grandeur of nature with the inevitable sublime forces of religious feeling that they create. I cannot afford to indulge in the pettiness of mortal mind and, therefore, will not defend any charge brought against me. I have consecrated my life to the delineation of the beauty that God has created—that would not have been possible if all things were not to my mind imbued with goodness and purity, therefore, I cannot but have the utmost confidence in the God-fearing qualities of those that will try me—defense could only signify that I consider them forces of evil, waiting for combat."

(Signed) John J. Barber

Judge Advocate:
Q. Has the accused any further testimony to offer or any statement to make?
A. He has not.

. . .

President: You, Private John J. Barber, understand that you have the right to be sworn as a witness in your own defense?
Counsel: I do.
President: Does the accused wish to be sworn?
Counsel: The accused does not wish to be sworn.
Judge Advocate: Has the accused anything further to offer?

Defense (Counsel): The accused has nothing further to offer.
President: Do you wish to make a statement of any kind as Counsel for the accused?
Counsel: The Counsel for the accused has made all the statements that he will make tonight.
Judge Advocate: The Judge Advocate submits the case without remark.

AMERICAN EXPEDITIONARY FORCES
HEADQUARTERS SERVICES OF SUPPLY
France, 20, June '18
GENERAL COURT MARTIAL
ORDERS No. 105

Before a general court-martial which convened at Base Hospital No......pursuant to Par.28, Special Orders No.37, Headquarters Services of Supply, American Expeditionary Forces, France, 18, April '18, was arraigned and tried:

Private John J. Barber, #189489, Company......Engineers.

Charge: Violation of the 96th Article of War.

Specification: In that Private John J. Barber, 189489, Company......Engineers having been found to be suffering from Varicocele (left) and having been advised by 1st Lieut. Frank E. Adair, M.C., U.S.R. that an operation consisting of the ligation and excision of these veins was necessary to enable him to perform properly his military duties, did, at Base Hospital No......, A.E.F., France, on or about the 6th day of April, 1918, refuse to submit to such operation; that after such refusal the said Private John J. Barber, 189489 was examined by a Board convened under authority of par 2, G.O.167, W.D.1917; that the said Board found that the operation advised by the said 1st Lieut. Frank E. Adair, M.C., U.S.R., was necessary to enable the said Private John J. Barber, 189489 properly to perform his military duties; that the said Private John J. Barber, 189489 was at Base Hospital No......, A.E.F., France, on or about the 7th day of April, 1918, notified of the finding of said Board, and that thereafter he persisted in his refusal up to the time when these charges were preferred to submit to such operation.

PLEAS: To the specification: "Guilty"
To the Charge: "Guilty"

FINDINGS:
Of the specification: "Guilty"
Of the Charge: "Guilty"

SENTENCE:
To be dishonorably discharged from the service and to be confined at hard labor at such place as the reviewing authority may direct for two (2) years.

In the foregoing case, the sentence is approved and will be duly executed as of 21, May '18.

The prison camp at General Intermediate Storage Depot, A.P.O. 713, is designated as the place of confinement, whither the prisoner will be sent under proper guard. (201-Barber, #John J., J.A., S.O.S.)

By command of Major
General Kernan:
Johnson Hagood,
Chief of Staff
Official:
L.H. Bash,
Adjutant General.

DISHONORABLE DISCHARGE FROM THE ARMY OF THE UNITED STATES

TO ALL WHOM IT MAY CONCERN:
This is to certify, that John J.-189489-Barber, Private, Company "D", 501st Engineers, National Army is hereby Dishonorably Discharged from the military service of the United States by reason of the sentence of a General Court-Martial, G.C.M.O., No. 105, Hq. S.O.S., June 20 1918.

Said John J.-189489-Barber was born in Galati, in the State of Roumania. When enlisted he was $23\,11/12$ years of age and by occupation an Illustrator. He had D. brown eyes, black hair, dark complexion, and was 5 feet, 7 1/4 inches in height.

Given under my hand at G.I.S.D., #APO.713, France this 13th day of Sept., one thousand nine hundred and eighteen, to date from June 20, 1918.

C.J. Symmonds
Colonel, Cavalry
Commanding.

ENLISTMENT RECORD:
Name: John J. -189489-Barber   Grade: Private
Enlisted: Sept. 29, 1917
at Board 139, New York City, N.Y.
Serving in First enlistment period at date of discharge.
Prior service: None
Noncommissioned officer: Never
Marksmanship, gunner qualification or rating: Not qualified
Horsemanship: Not mounted
Battles, engagements, skirmishes, expeditions: None
Knowledge of any vocation: Artist
Wounds received in service: None
Physical condition when discharged: Varicocele (left) testicle
Typhoid prophylaxis completed: Not completed
Paratyphoid prophylaxis completed: Not completed
Married or single: Single
Remarks: Sentenced to be dishonorably discharged the service, to forfeit all pay and allowances due or to become due, and to be confined at hard labor for two (2) years. Approved May 21, 1918.

John W. Breathed
1st. Lieut. Infantry

Base Hospital #9
A E F France
June 1, 1918

To Private Jn Barber;

We, the undersigned, desire to express to you our gratitude for your enthusiastic help in making the evening of May 28, '18, very pleasant to all who were so fortunate as to receive one of your delightful art souvenirs.

George W. Hawley, Major - M.R.C.
R. W. Bolling, 1st Lt. M.C.U.S.R.
F. W. Thim
Raymond S. Brown, Chaplain
A. H. Dugdah, Lt. M.C.U.S.R.
James W. Kent, Capt. M.C.U.S.R.
Frank E. Adair, 1st Lieut. M.C.U.S.R.
Al Busby, Capt. M.R.C.
P. D. Wilson, Capt. M.R.C.
Robt D. Schrock, Lieut. M.C.U.S.R.

Letters from a fellow soldier

October 22, 1918

Dear John,

It's raining cats and dogs outside this morning, and I've got to start on a twenty mile trip in about ten minutes—in a motorcycle. Add to the Horrors of War.

Life in Nevers is at least to be commended for its stability of character—always just the same. This darned Spanish fandango has become such an epidemic that it has closed all movies and churches. Really there is nothing left to do but work. And *sans doute* we are all doing that.

Last Sunday afternoon I went to the first Christian Science services held in Nevers. Two readers from Minneapolis have rented, renovated, and made holy a tailor shop. Awfully snug little place and quite a crowd of soldiers, considering the religious nature of the attraction.

I'm going in for French now quite diligently. My teacher is the patronne of a interesting little antique shop, a young girl, *très charmante*. Trust me to inject a bit of romance into our lessons. Each evening we read some Daudet, write a little, and drink tea brewed on the tiny porcelain stove in the back of her shop. A dull evening you say? Perhaps, judging it by our standards of pleasure; but I assure you that I enjoy myself immensely.

Here are some pictures of this quaint old place. I think they would look well hung in the blacksmith studio—say, just over the paint pots.

I'm still waiting to hear from you.

As ever,
Nick

Sunday, the 10th of November. [1918]

Dear John B.,

From now on whenever I want any fancy soothsaying or glimpses into the future taken I know just who to come to. It's been 'bout eight weeks now since you predicted a complete German defeat and probable peace before the end of the year. At the time, I confess, I couldn't see how it possibly could come about, but now that we are awaiting the result of the armistice proposition, and watching revolts and abdicating Emperors I, too, blind as I am, can see the end. I have utmost faith in your opinions on world subjects—as well as on art—and I would like very much to drop in to your workshop for a talk as I once did.

Now the next thing I want is word from you, and the meaning that it will carry along with it.

I thought for a while that I could get out of this police business, but it seems now impossible. We are getting busier every day. And Lord help us when the troops start coming back on their way home. They'll be so wild that we can't do a thing with them. Then there's always that fact staring me in the face, that even after it ends we'll be here until almost the last. As W.S.G[ilbert] has said "A Policeman's lot is not a happy one."

I've heard indirectly that Lts. Breatherd, Batchy, and Desjardins have all departed for the front. Any change?

As usual,
Nick

PASS   Hq. G.I.S.D., USAPO 713,
France, January 14, 1919.

Pvt. John J. Barber, 501st Engrs., has permission to be absent from his organization between the hours of 6 P.M. and 9 P.M. This pass GOOD UNTIL REVOKED.

By order of Colonel Symmonds:
EDW. R. DEWEY,
Captain A.G.D.
Acting Adjutant

GENERAL HEADQUARTERS, AMERICAN EXPEDITIONARY FORCES
Special Orders, No. 90. France, 31 March, 1919.
Extract.
Par. 87, General Prisoner John J. Barber (189489), now at Prison Camp, General Intermediate Storage Depot, A. P. O. 713, will be sent to the United States by the first available transportation sailing for the port of New York; and upon arrival of the prisoner in the United States all of the unexecuted confinement imposed upon him by the sentence published in G.C.M.O., No. 105, Headquarters, S.O.S., dated June 20, 1918, will stand remitted. (201 JAO)

Official: By Command of
ROBERT C. DAVIS, General Pershing:
Adjutant General   JAMES W. McANDREW
         Chief of Staff

Postcard to sister Rita

[France
April 4, 1919]

Miss Riviere Barber
34 West 129th Street
New York City
U.S.A.

Very happy because very soon with you.

John

IV. Europe, 1920s

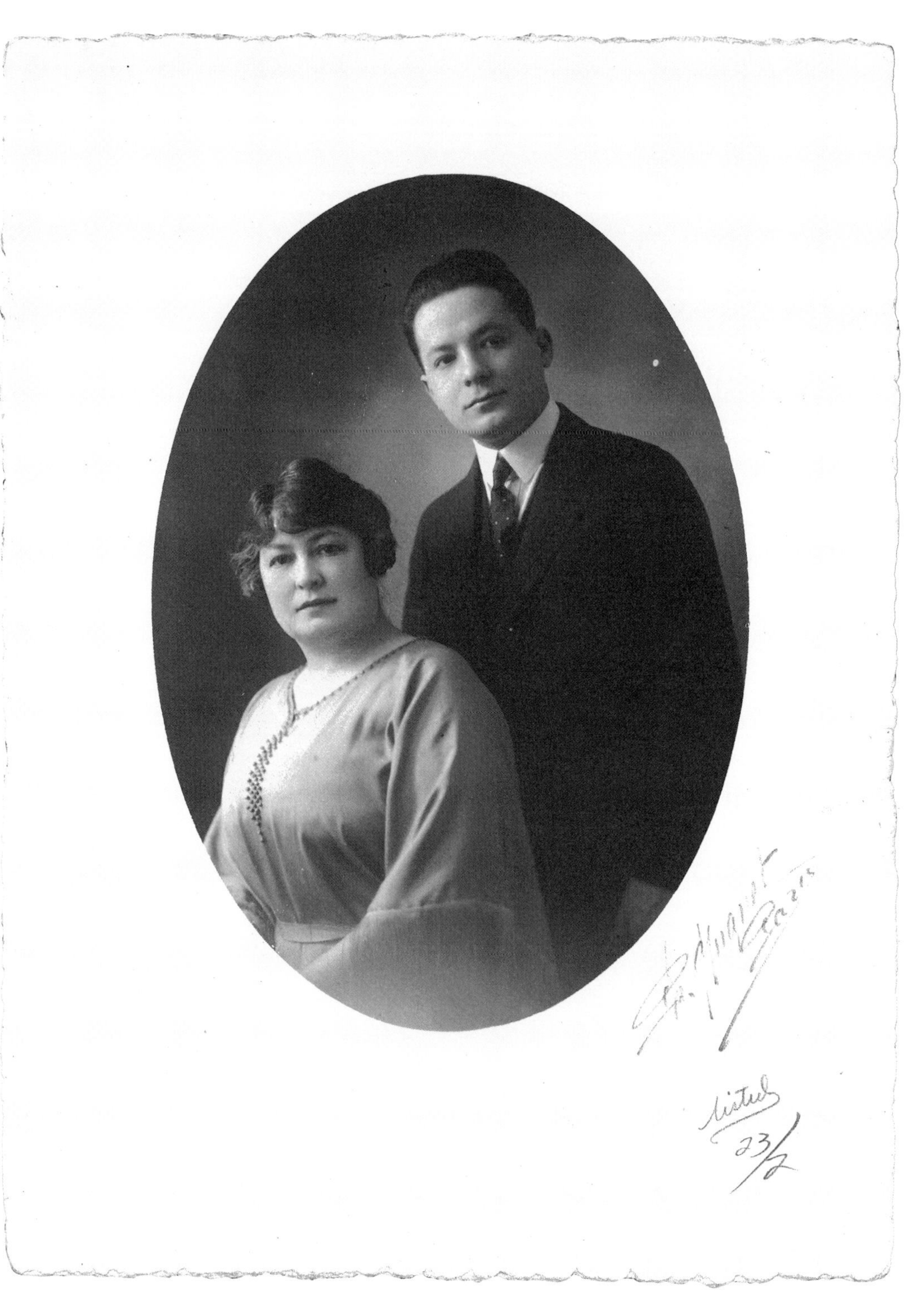

Fig. 14
John Barber and his Mother,
Betty Barber, Paris 1923
Photograph: Monquet

Europe, 1920s

Autobiographical fragments

It was just three years after the end of World War I, and the main arteries of Paris were still pockmarked here and there with small shell holes. As I stepped out of the Gare St. Lazare on my arrival from N.Y., a mob of students were celebrating in carnivalesque fashion the Mardi Gras through the streets of the city. It was late afternoon of the last day of February and the softer rays of the sun on the rooftops bespoke of that peculiar early Parisian springtime that fills one with a sense of nervous energy and desire for action. I came to Paris to study art. I was in my early twenties, and in those days one felt it was necessary to acquire the fundamentals of painting. Non-objective art and shortcuts to fame were still unknown. I had been painting portraits until then on the basis of reproducing faithfully what my eyesight told me—but the visits to museums told me there was more to it than that, so I came to try and make those mysteries my own. In technological America, I learned that if one is efficient one can do a lot in a short time, and I felt 6 months would be sufficient to make a successful practitioner out of me. In my youthful ignorance and enthusiasm I did not realize that portrait painting per se and art in the Grand Manner were not one and the same thing. The result was that my sojourn in France and the rest of Europe became a prolonged affair and only the jolt of World War II drove me back to these shores. . . .

The high standard of living fetishism plus the idea of "the best is none too good" would make even a young student feel he would lose caste, even in his own eyes, if he did not get first class reservations. My desire to take my mother along naturally defeated any doubts on that score. So, then, we find ourselves sailing on the ill-fated S. S. Paris in the company of the Italian Prime Minister and delegation from the Washington Disarmament Conference—and other notables. After that we naturally had to stop at the Grand Hotel in Paris where the accommodations were on a ratio with the American equivalents. When trying to wash up for our first dinner in Paris, great was my surprise at not finding any soap in the bathroom. A few moments after phoning the desk about it, a knock at the door ushered in a pompous personage in full dress holding a tray in a very elevated position with a piece of soap and a bill of 50 cents for it. This last item brought me back to realities, and I decided then and there to move the next day to Montparnasse or the left bank quarter of the Seine which could be compared to the classic other side of the tracks in the American social jungle.

• • •

As a mere youth I was one of André Lhote's first pupils, and soon after my paintings were being accepted at the Salon d'Automne, where they found several purchasers. My love of drawing in line made me do a number of drypoint etchings. My enthusiasm for that medium impelled me to insist that my friend, Jules Pascin, do some also—and of course with wonderful results. Pascin, who was my dear friend, reciprocated with great encouragement in honoring me to exhibit with him together.

In the Summer of 1927 we shared a cabin on the old S. S. Leviathan in what turned out to be Pascin's last trip to America. We sketched together during the entire trip as it was in the month of August and the ship was packed with returning tourists. Pascin insisted that I draw my entire compositions on one page, instead of in detail with single figures. That training was the best I ever had—and since then all my paintings are the result of such efforts. From then on I started to do the painting from memory, as each detail on the canvas was already based on life, and I felt free in the selection of the color scheme and elimination of the superfluous. This last statement brings to memory one evening long ago on the Terrace of the Café du Dôme, in Paris, with Sinclair Lewis. To a question of mine he gave the reason for doing all his writing in Europe. It gave him a clearer perspective on his *Main Street* characters and locale uncluttered by details that would otherwise overwhelm him. I did a caricature of him, as his features lent themselves to it most temptingly. I still have this piece of work. Returning to my work—Pascin often expressed to me: "Light is the most wonderful thing in painting," as he saw that I always eliminate conventional shading out of my work and barely suggest three-dimensional form. By comparing Oriental paintings to Western Art, I came to realize that chiaroscuro kills color—I therefore always paint my subject matter in full light, and try to achieve a subtle modeling that does not interfere with the richness of chromatic play.

Two consecutive summers in Holland, where, because of a climate similar to the lagoon atmosphere of Venice, the light is strong and golden, completed my conversion to light per se. In the first summer there, in my early youth, I had the good fortune to meet and win the friendship of their leading painter of the time, who was also painting in that fishing village of Volendam. Mr. Tholen was the last of their four great artists of the late 19th and early 20th centuries. The others were Maris, Mauve (a relative of Vincent van Gogh), and Jozef Israels, the most prominent of them all, who died in 1911. Mr. Tholen, a highly cultured gentleman, though much advanced in years, became such a close friend that the following summer when I returned with my mother, he was waiting at the station, the early morning arrival of the train, the Paris-Hague Express. That very same evening we dined at his palatial home, then went upstairs to his studio to look at his portraits of Royalty. He was also the court painter of the House of Orange. I remember well the amused expression with which he told my mother that the most terrible side of portraiture is the moment of first glance at the painting by a husband. Their bourgeois minds and preconceived notions of how a wife should look in a painting are the deadliest part of it. I inherited the sketch book full of the drawings he did the summer I was in Volendam with him. Mme. Tholen, a Grande Dame of the Dutch nobility, sent it to me with a beautiful letter after he passed away and willed it to me. I treasure it.

But of all lands, Italy is a never-cooling magnet for me. Perhaps Goethe expressed it for all artists when he wrote: "Open my heart and you will find the word Italy in it." I have lived months at a time in Rome, and one entire year in Florence, not to speak of Siena, Perugia, Assisi, and Arezzo, where the world's most beautiful frescoes by Piero della Francesca are.

After my first Portugese trip, the Luxembourg Museum purchased the painting exhibited at my first one-man show in Paris. But most encouraging to me was that so many eminent French and German collectors began to buy. Quite a number of the French painters became my friends, especially Derain, a man of bulky proportions, a great heart, and generosity in his appraisal of others. Together we went one afternoon to see a special exhibition of Japanese Art at the Musée d'Arts Décoratifs. We stopped for a long time before a superb painting depicting a samurai cavalcade. The beauty of the drawing of the horses made us both breathless, and, as we left, Derain said, "*A côté de ça nous ne sommes que des enfants.*" How modest and unchauvinistic a statement from such a prominent French artist! Another example of that attitude. I remember how he once made a red crayon copy in my studio of one of my complicated Portuguese market scenes. He said, "Just to get the geometry of it."

Also during my Paris years I was the artist-correspondent for the great Swedish weekly *Vecko-Journalen* of Stockholm and did a regular series of drawings for them of Paris life.

The world depression of the 30s put a great pall on the art world of Paris, and I left in a general exodus to the Americas. In 1934 I arrived in New York and immediately did a show at the Ehrich-Newhouse Gallery. Less than a year later I returned to Portugal just to paint and think of nothing but my development. Just before the Second World War broke out, I took the Grand Tour beginning in Tunis, through Italy, Yugoslavia, then Greece and finally the island of Crete. Of all peoples I have ever met, I found the Greeks the most civilized in the sense of Biblical hospitality towards the *xenos* (foreigners). Their motto is that a stranger is under the protection of every Greek. I experienced fantastic gestures of their courtesy and kindness and respect that would require a volume to recount.

Again on my return to America, I stopped in Paris for a few months. Our Ambassador William Bullitt, my dear friend of long standing, had me stay at his Chateau de St. Firmin in Chantilly, 30 miles north of Paris. During my work there, I did his portrait, and had the pleasure to meet at his dinners all the political celebrities of France, with whom he was in constant contact during those impending days of catastrophe.

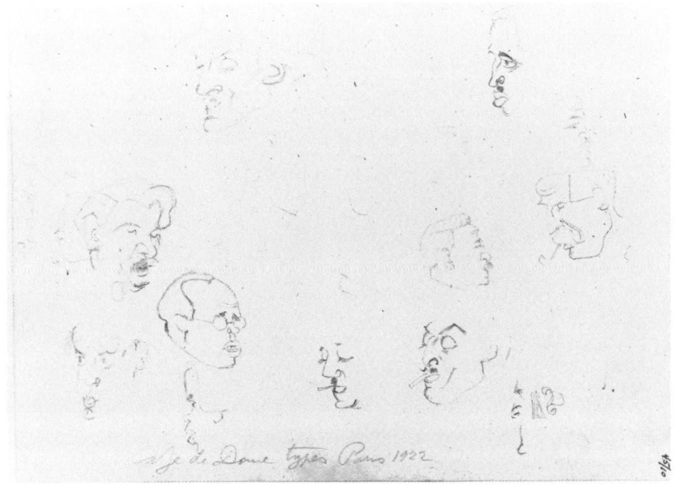

Fig. 15
John Barber
Café du Dôme Types, Paris, 1922
Graphite, 7 1/8 x 9 1/4
Collection of Dr. Margaret De Ronde Barber,
on loan to The John Barber Memorial Collection,
Bayly Art Museum of the University of Virginia

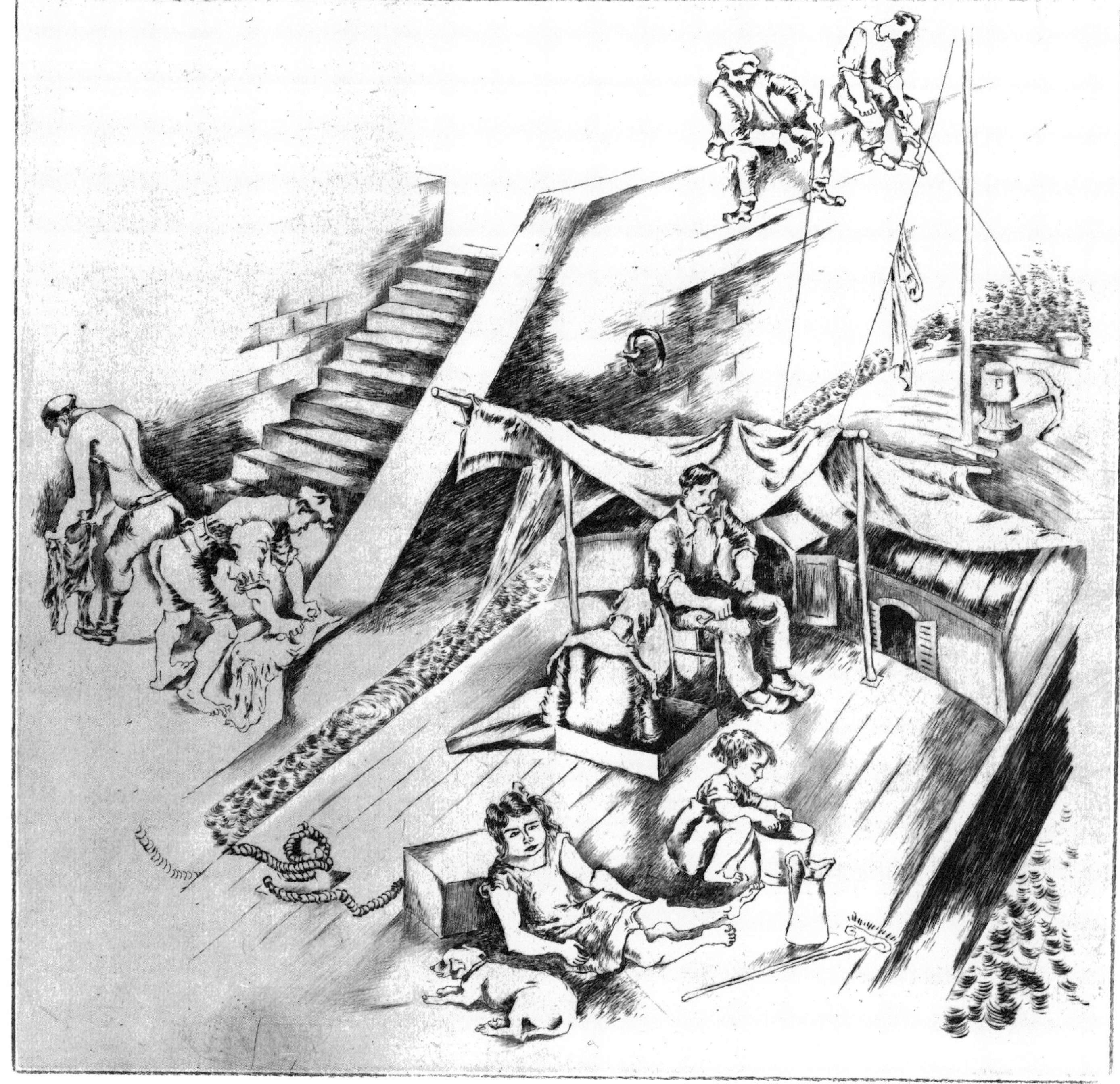

Fig. 16
John Barber
*Canal Boat on the Seine,
Paris*, ca. 1922
Etching, 11 x 11 $\frac{1}{8}$
Collection of Dr. Margaret
De Ronde Barber, on loan to
The John Barber Memorial
Collection, Bayly Art Museum
of the University of Virginia

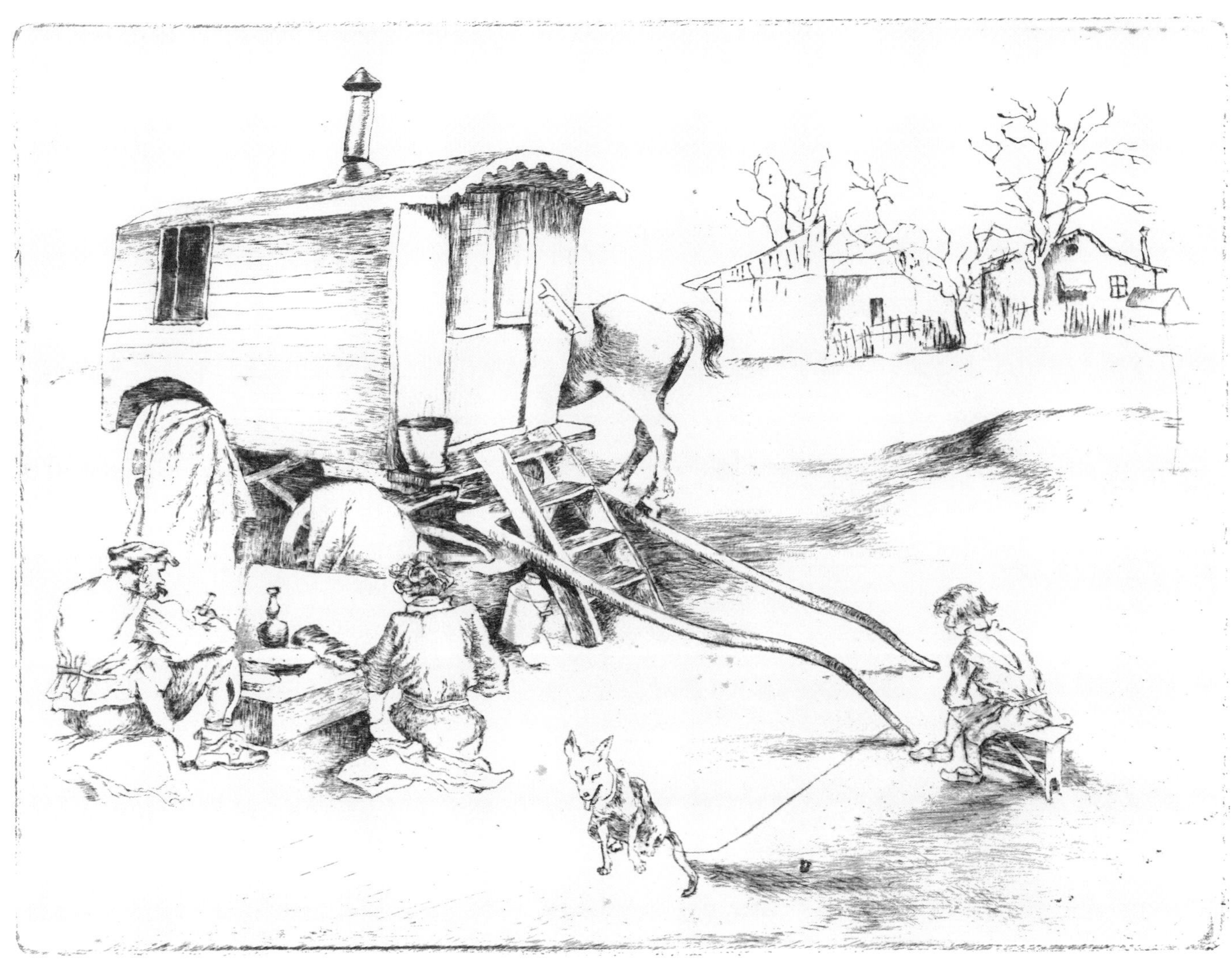

Fig. 17
John Barber
French Tramps, ca. 1922
Etching, 7 1/4 x 9 1/4
Collection of Dr. Margaret De Ronde Barber,
on loan to The John Barber Memorial Collection,
Bayly Art Museum of the University of Virginia

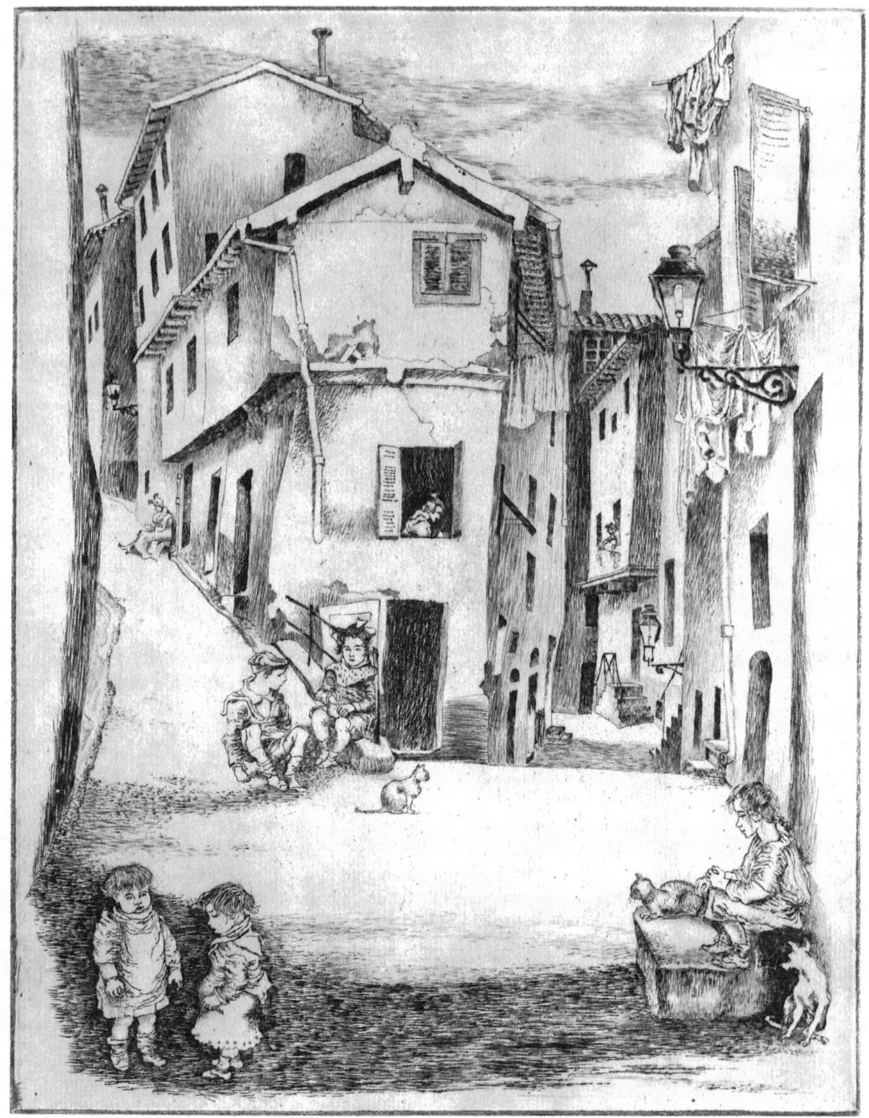

Fig. 18
John Barber
Vieux Nice, France, ca. 1922
Etching, 11 $7/8$ x 9
Collection of Dr. Margaret De Ronde Barber,
on loan to The John Barber Memorial Collection,
Bayly Art Museum of the University of Virginia

Fig. 19
John Barber
Wheelbarrow and Barrel
Graphite, 9 ¼ x 7 ¼
Collection of Dr. Margaret De Ronde Barber,
on loan to The John Barber Memorial Collection,
Bayly Art Museum of the University of Virginia

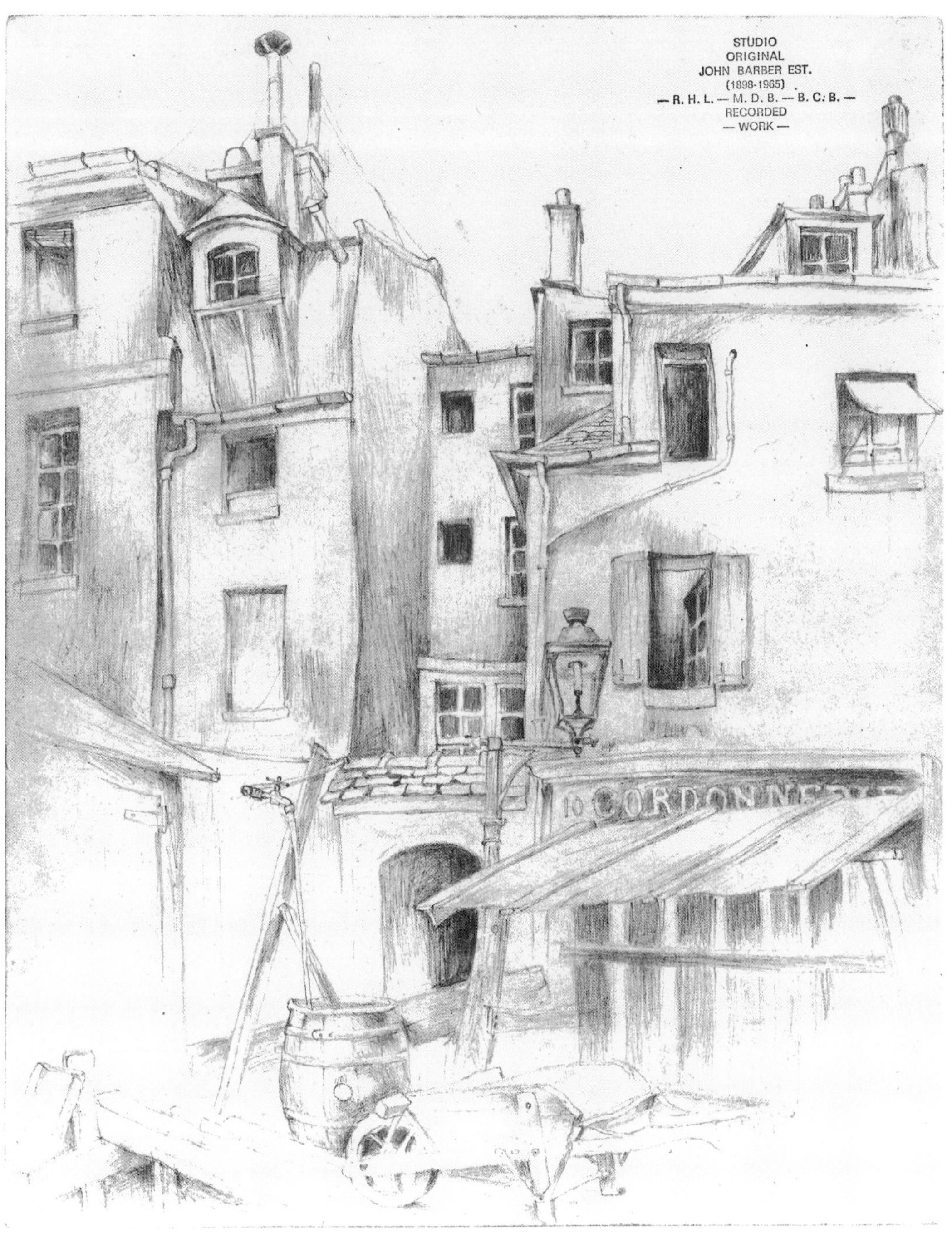

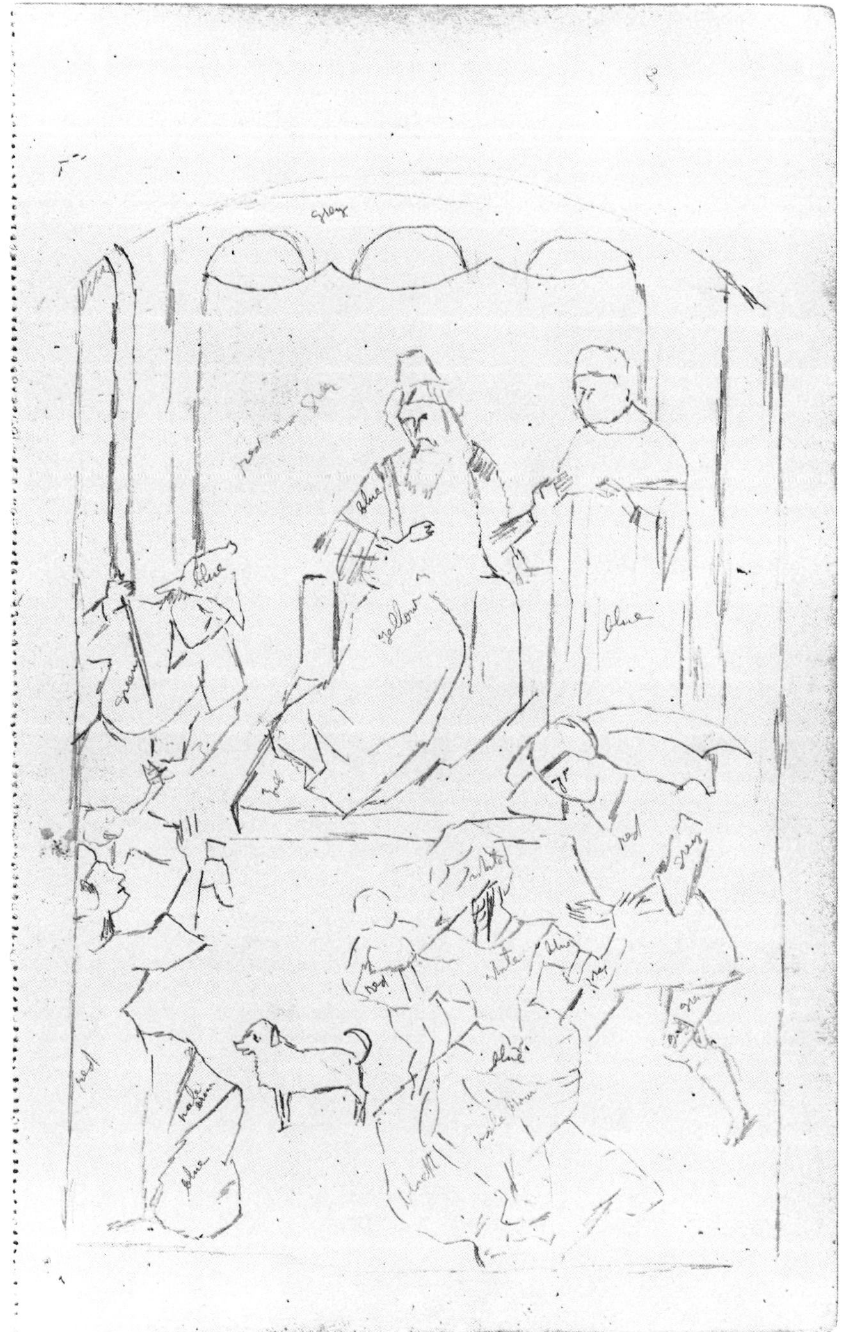

Fig. 20
John Barber
Massacre of the Innocents, After a Renaissance Painting
Graphite, 9 1/4 x 5 3/4
Collection of Dr. Margaret De Ronde Barber,
on loan to The John Barber Memorial Collection,
Bayly Art Museum of the University of Virginia

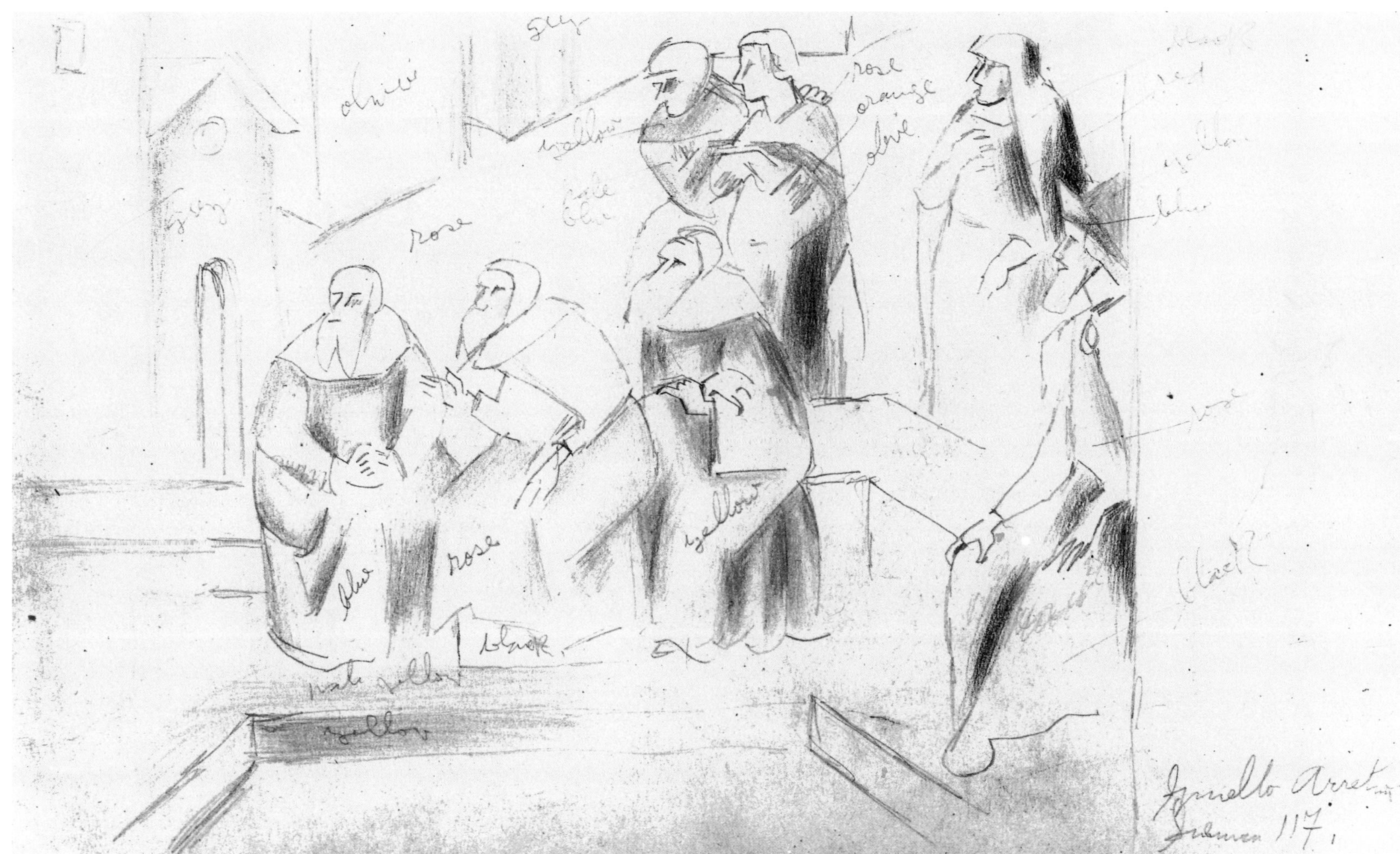

Fig. 21
John Barber
After Spinello Artino (Italian, late 14th century)
Graphite and colored pencils, 5 3/4 x 9 1/4
Collection of Dr. Margaret De Ronde Barber,
on loan to The John Barber Memorial Collection,
Bayly Art Museum of the University of Virginia

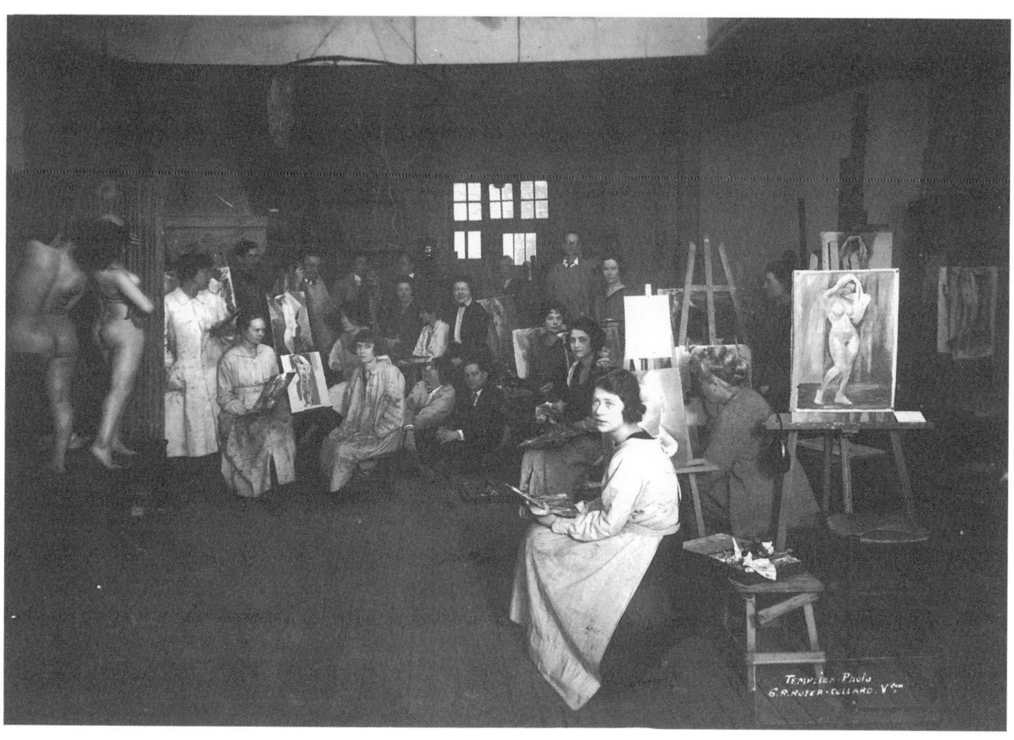

Fig. 22
Lhote School, Paris, June 1922
Photograph: Templier

The following statement on art is marked: "Written by André Lhote, 1923"

The essence of art is sensitivity. How does one retain the freshness of sensitivity? Answer: By working without worry, freely. How does one work freely? By possessing a technique which permits one to work spontaneously: it is necessary, therefore, to possess the elements of this technique. Meditation in front of the works of the masters puts one in possession of the eternal rules of art. Once these rules are learned there is nothing left but to know how to apply them to one's own temperament. Nowadays, everyone works with a feeling of unease. The old masters worked with peace of mind.
(structural)
The geometric spirit
(sensitive)
The spirit of refinement.

Translated by Beth Velimirovic

Fig. 23
John Barber
Nude Back, ca. 1922
Graphite and ink, 11 $^7/_8$ x 8 $^5/_8$
Collection of Dr. Margaret De Ronde Barber,
on loan to The John Barber Memorial Collection,
Bayly Art Museum of the University of Virginia

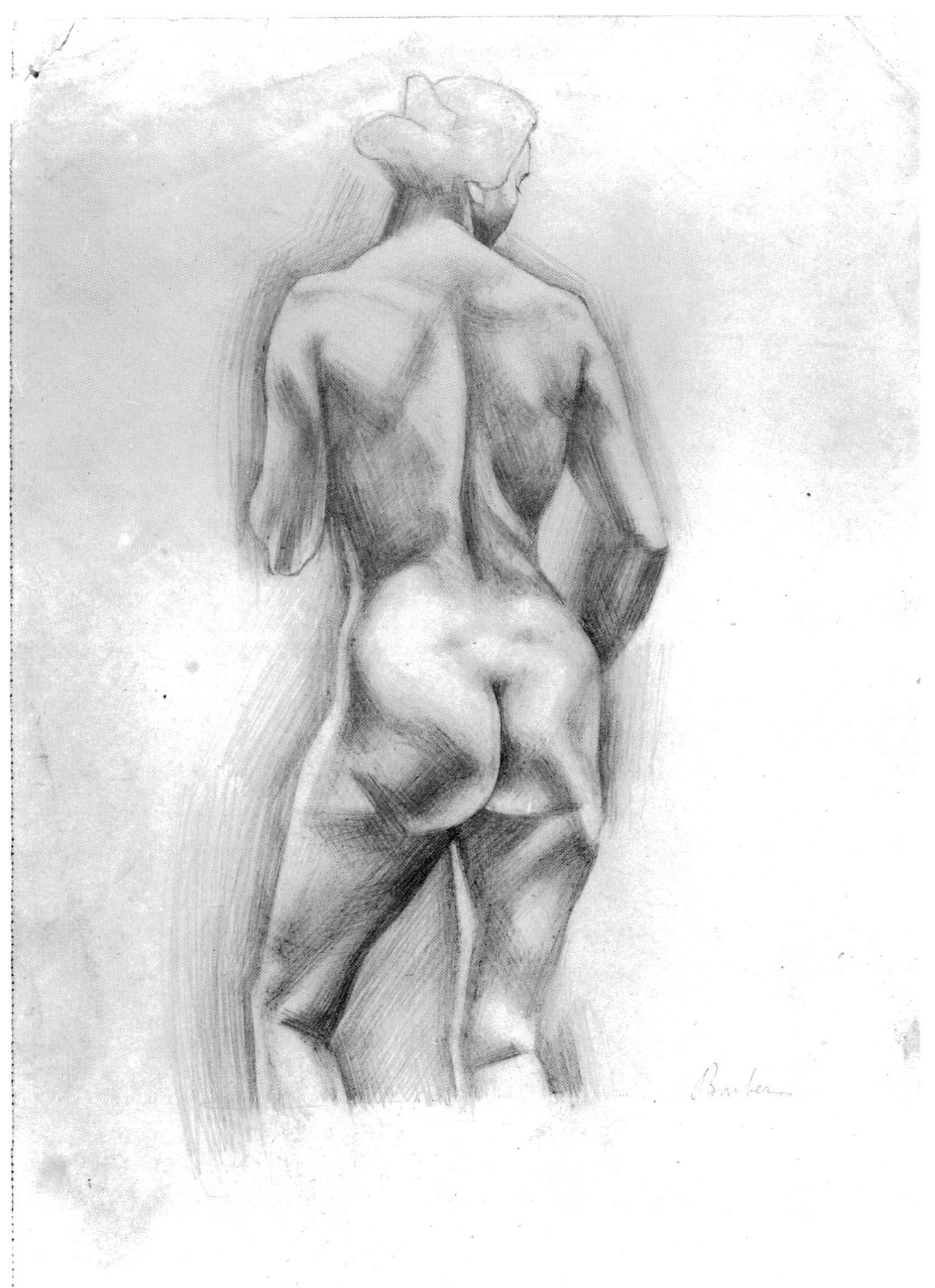

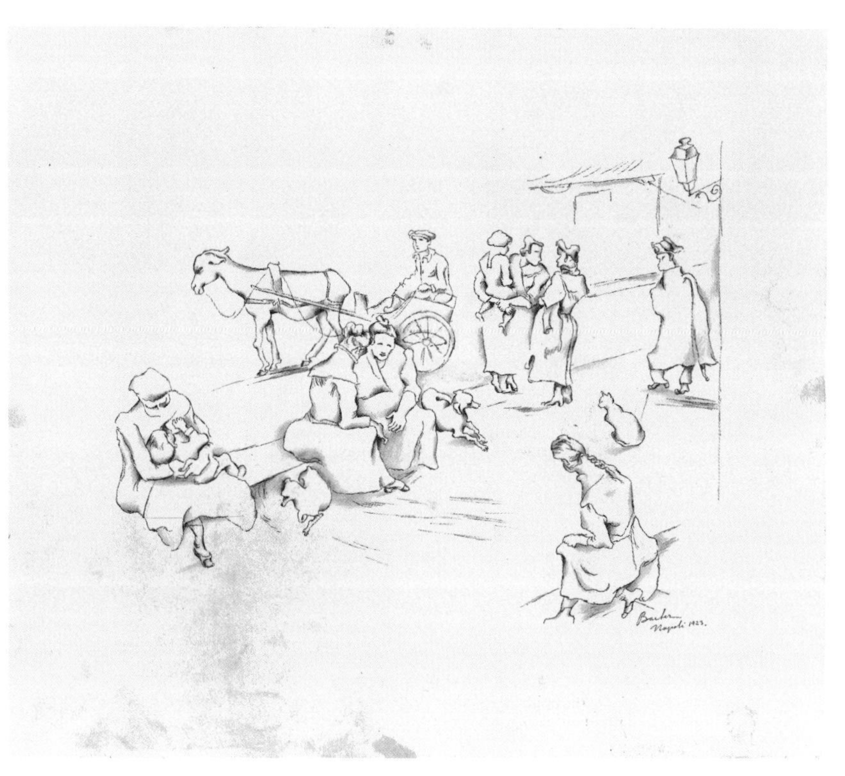

Fig. 24
John Barber
Conversations, Naples, 1923
Graphite and ink, 12 ³⁄₈ x 13 ¹⁄₄
Collection of Dr. Margaret De Ronde Barber,
on loan to The John Barber Memorial Collection,
Bayly Art Museum of the University of Virginia

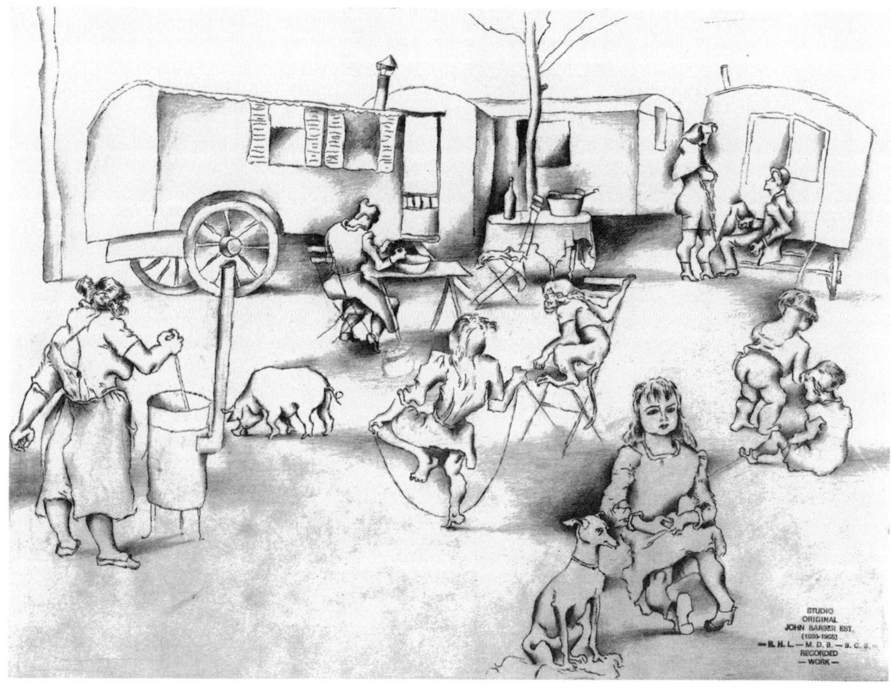

Fig. 25
John Barber
Encampment, ca. 1923
Graphite and ink, 8 ¹⁄₂ x 11
Collection of Dr. Margaret De Ronde Barber,
on loan to The John Barber Memorial Collection,
Bayly Art Museum of the University of Virginia

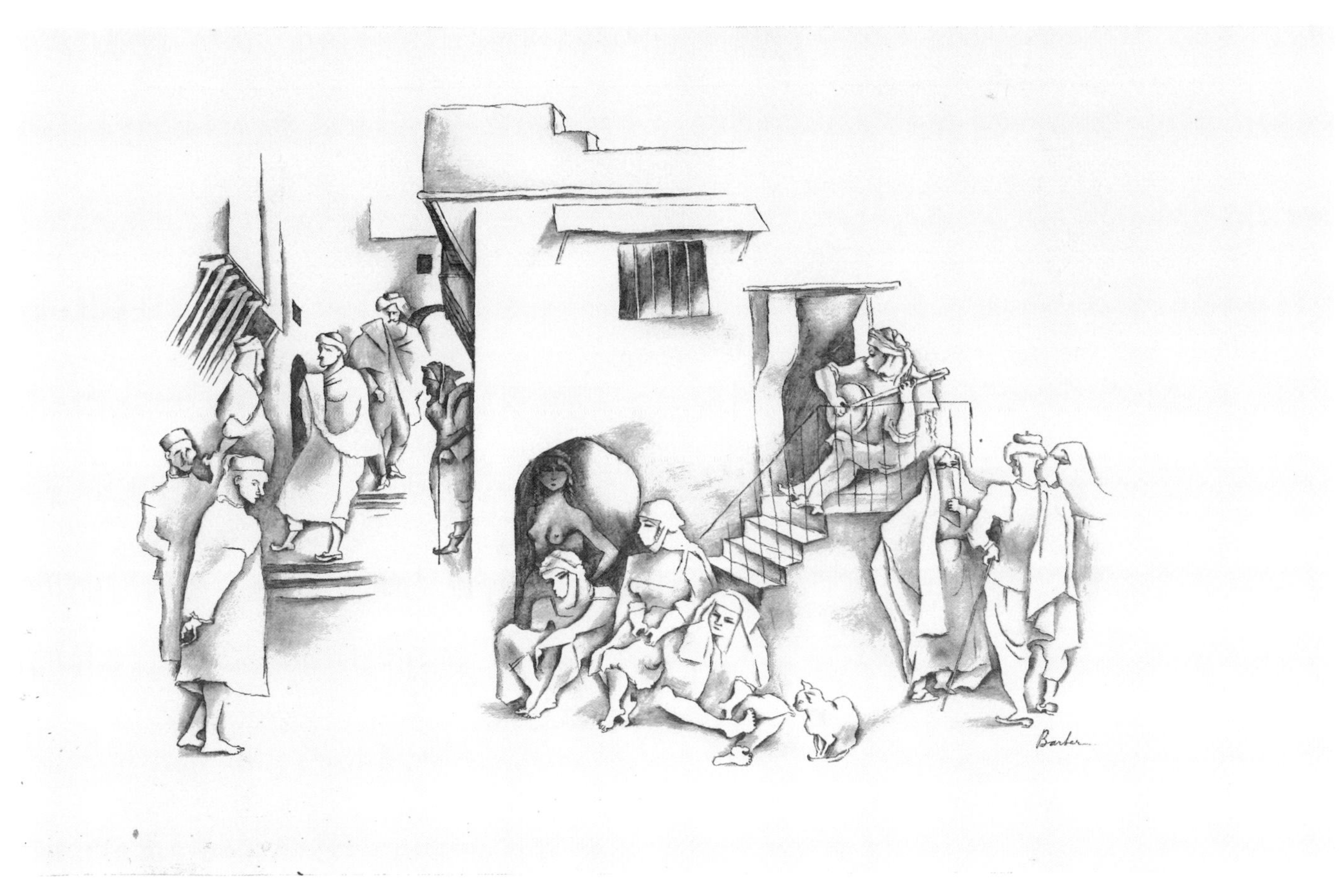

Fig. 26
John Barber
North Africa, ca. 1923
Graphite and ink, 12 1/4 x 18 3/4
Collection of Dr. Margaret De Ronde Barber,
on loan to The John Barber Memorial Collection,
Bayly Art Museum of the University of Virginia

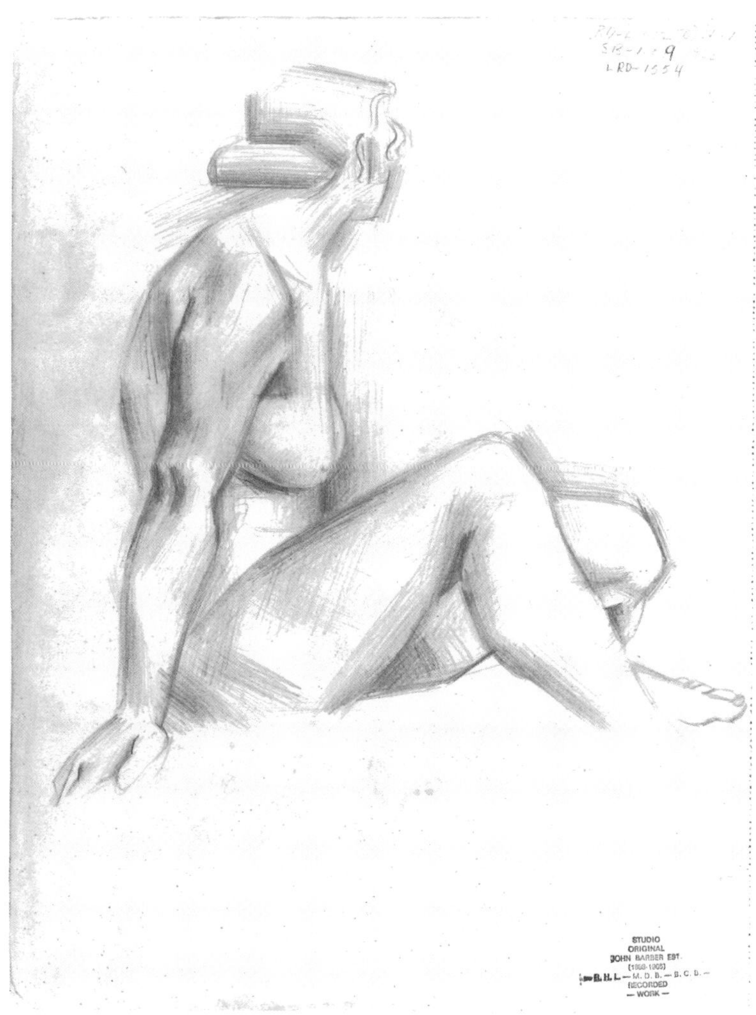

Fig. 27
John Barber
Study for "Five Bathers," ca. 1923
Graphite, 12 x 8 $^7/_8$
Collection of Dr. Margaret De Ronde Barber,
on loan to The John Barber Memorial Collection,
Bayly Art Museum of the University of Virginia

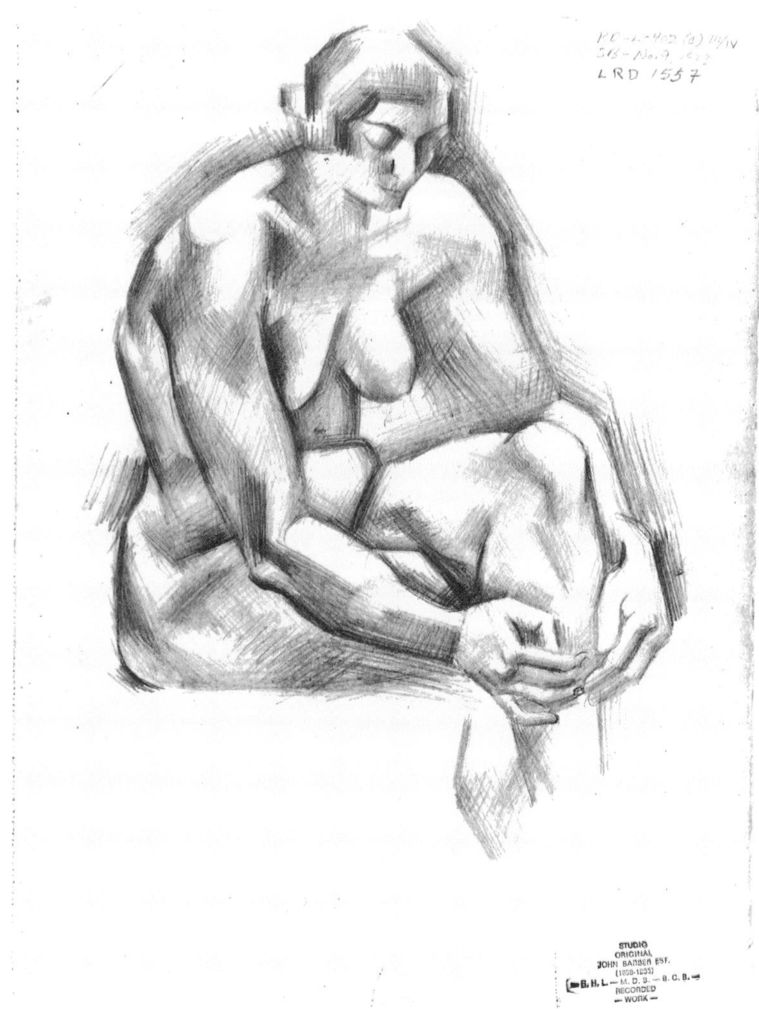

Fig. 28
John Barber
Figure Study, 1923
Graphite, 12 x 8 $^3/_4$
Collection of Dr. Margaret De Ronde Barber,
on loan to The John Barber Memorial Collection,
Bayly Art Museum of the University of Virginia

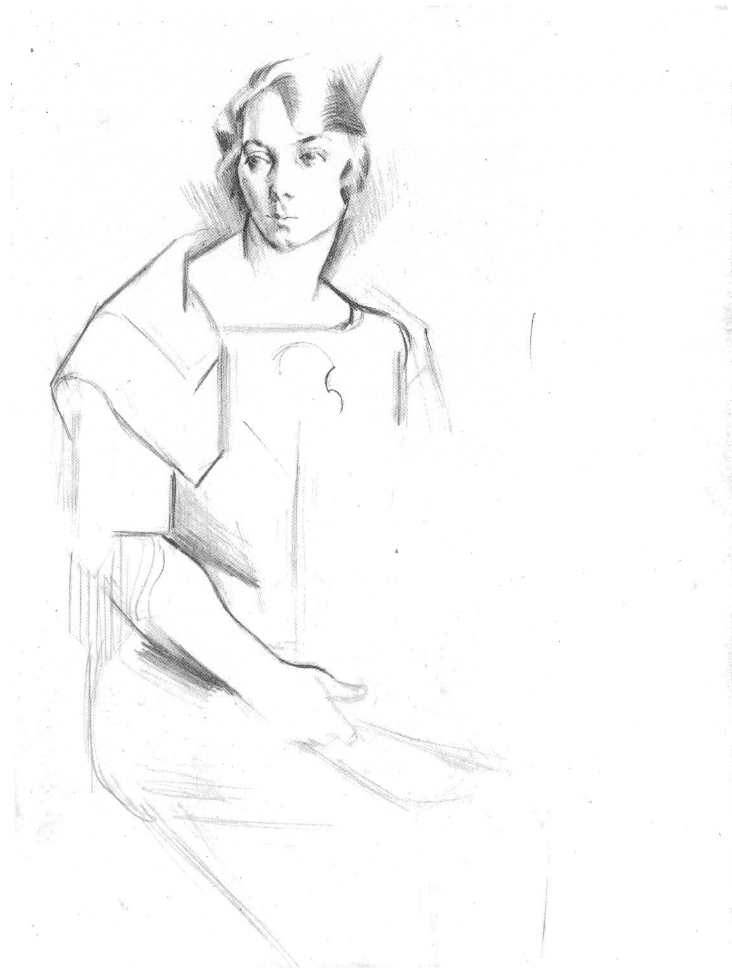

Fig. 29
John Barber
Portrait of a Young Woman, ca. 1923
Graphite, 12 x 8 7/8
Collection of Dr. Margaret De Ronde Barber,
on loan to The John Barber Memorial Collection,
Bayly Art Museum of the University of Virginia

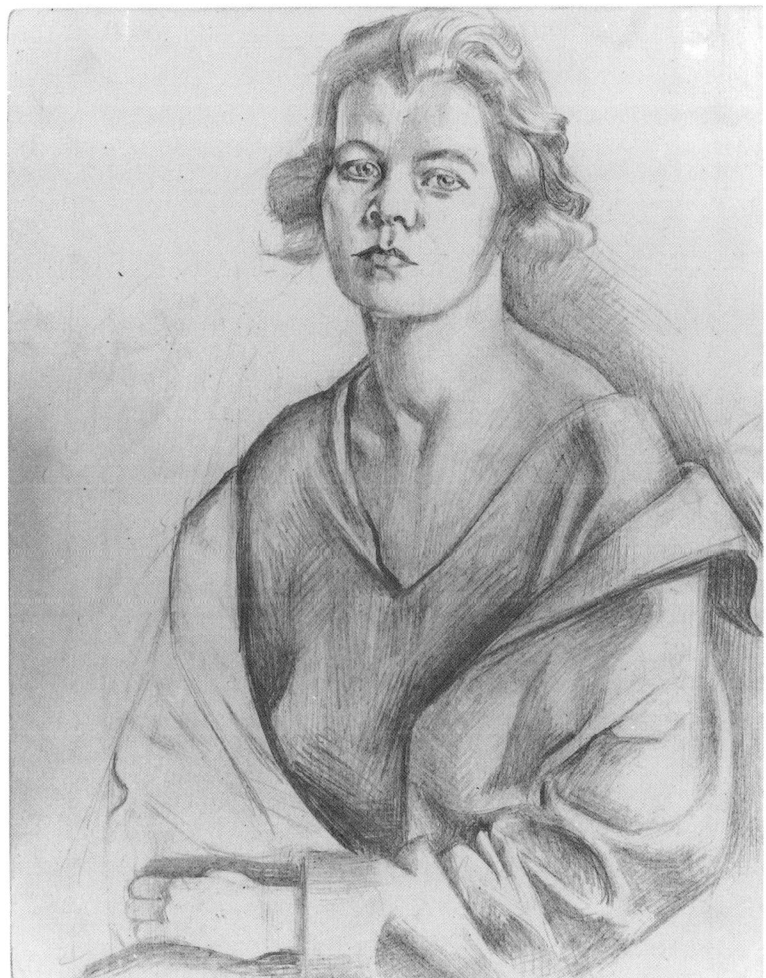

Fig. 30
John Barber
Portrait of a Young Woman, ca. 1923
Graphite, 9 1/1 x 7 1/8
Collection of Dr. Margaret De Ronde Barber,
on loan to The John Barber Memorial Collection,
Bayly Art Museum of the University of Virginia

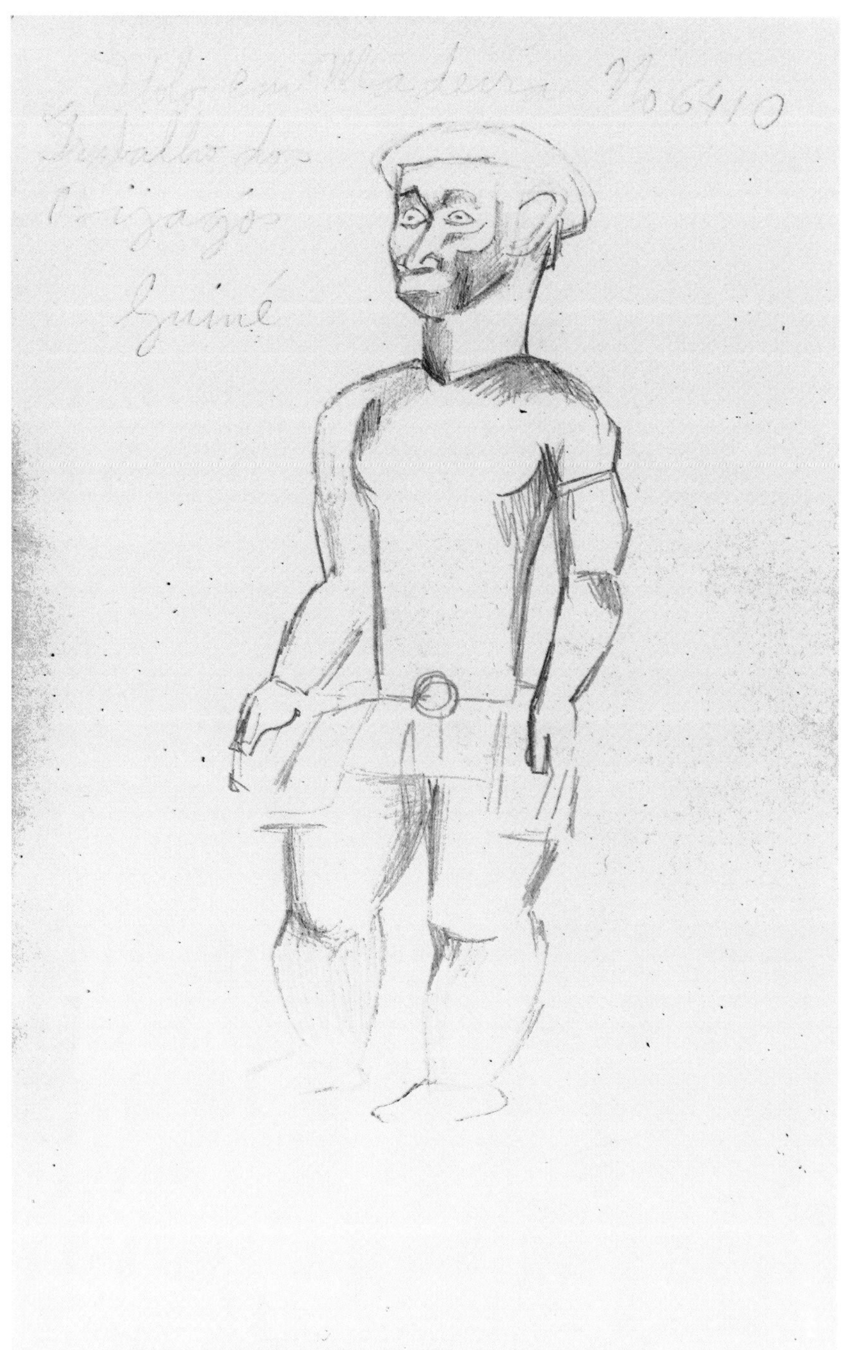

Fig. 31
John Barber
African Sculpture, ca. 1924
Graphite, 9 1/4 x 5 3/4
Collection of Dr. Margaret De Ronde Barber,
on loan to The John Barber Memorial Collection,
Bayly Art Museum of the University of Virginia

Postcards from John Barber
to his mother Betty and sister Rita

March 3, 1925

Mme. Betty Barber
Hotel d'Orsay
20 rue Alsace-Lorraine
Nice, France

Dear Ones,

Just reached Rome and had a good trip. The time passed rapidly and am not a bit tired. Lots of Kisses to you both.

John

Rome
March 5, 1925

Mlle. Rita Barber
Chez Hotel d'Orsay
20 rue Alsace-Lorraine
Nice, France

Dear Rita,

I am now resting up, sitting before a café facing the great St. Peter's square and sipping a good "*café espresso.*" It is 4 P.M. and saw wonderful paintings the whole day. This evening I am asked again to Mr. McKelvay's house. My trip is a very happy one. Lots of Kisses to both of you.

John

Rome
March 6, 1925

Mme. Betty Barber
Hotel d'Orsay
20 rue Alsace-Lorraine
Nice, France

Dear Ones,

Probably I shall leave Rome tomorrow at noontime and go to Assisi and Perugia. Last night I saw a wonderful performance of the Russian ballet with Mr. McKelvay and some friends. I certainly have an interesting time. Italy is not a bit more expensive than France, and for that reason perhaps I will stay 3 weeks; answer me yet to Florence because it will be about 4 days before I get there. Kisses to you both.

John

Assisi
March 7, 1925

Mme. Betty Barber
Hotel d'Orsay
20 rue Alsace-Lorraine
Nice, France

Dear Ones,

Just reached and will stay till tomorrow when I go to Siena and then Florence. Lots of Kisses.

John

Assisi
March 8, 1925

Mme. Betty Barber
c/o Hotel d'Orsay
20 rue Alsace-Lorraine
Nice, France

Dear Ones,

Am leaving this afternoon and will arrive in Arezzo in the evening will stay there half a day tomorrow and reach Florence in the evening. Will take my trip to Siena after I see Florence. I don't want to stay too long. I am quite homesick, although I am learning a lot in this trip. Kisses. The paintings by Giotto are marvelous. Kisses.

John

Arezzo
March 9, 1925

Mlle. Rita Barber
chez Hotel d'Orsay
20 rue Alsace-Lorraine
Nice, France

Dear Ones,

This is a place of indescribable beauty. Am leaving this afternoon for Siena with the auto-bus—a trip of 3 hours across the width of Italy. There is no railroad between these two places. This is the most profitable voyage I ever took. I have learned a lot, and shall be a much better artist for it. Also am taking good care of myself. I saw here the fresco paintings of Piero della Francesca. Will probably return in 8 days or so. From Siena I go to Florence and then Venice. Italy is not more expensive than France now. Kisses.

John

Siena
March 9, 1925

Mme. Betty Barber
chez Hotel d'Orsay
20 rue Alsace-Lorraine
Nice, France

I reached here this evening after a 3 ½ hour trip across the breadth of Italy—I can't say I didn't travel in Italy by auto as the rich do, but. . . . You can't imagine how beautiful Siena is—it's the only city that kept intact all its glory of medieval times. I shall try to be back in Nice in about 8 or 9 days the most. Kisses to both of you.

John

Siena
March 10, 1925

Mme. Betty Barber
chez Hotel d'Orsay
20 rue Alsace-Lorraine
Nice, France

Am leaving Siena at 4:25 P.M. and will reach Florence at 6:30 P.M. I am only traveling in daytime, late afternoons after the museums close. My watch stopped long ago but I wake up early because I leave the shutters open and every day at 8 A.M. I am already out on the street, washed, shaved and ready to see pictures. Constantine served me again in Rome and recognized me. Keep these postcards as souvenirs. Kisses.

John

Florence
March 10, 1925

Mme. Betty Barber
chez Hotel d'Orsay
20 rue Alsace-Lorraine
Nice, France

Reached Florence 6:30 P.M. Took a room at the same hotel called Rebecchino, and now am having dinner at the same 7.50 lire restaurant. Rooms at hotels cost me an average of 7.50 lire. The climate in Italy is wonderful—no rain at all, but a bit cold and dry. Love and kisses.

John

Florcncc
March 11, 1925

Mme. Betty Barber
chez Hotel d'Orsay
20 rue Alsace-Lorraine
Nice, France

I am at the American Express and read all your letters. Mrs. B. does not come back to Nice. You can still write me *two* letters to Venice Poste-Restante because I will not reach Venice before Saturday the 12th and will stay there 3 or 4 days. Am in a hurry to go to the Uffizi Gallery. Love and Kisses to you both.

John

Florence
March 12, 1925

Mme. Betty Barber
chez Hotel d'Orsay
20 rue Alsace-Lorraine
Nice, France

Dear Ones,

You can take that trip to Marseille for I will not be home before Saturday 21st of March for I am going from here Friday afternoon to Ravenna, then to Venice for 4 days, then Padua and Milan for one day each. So you see you must not deprive yourself of pleasure on my account. I am enjoying my trip immensely. Or else I would not have prolonged it. Kisses to you two.

John

Florence
March 12, 1925

Mme. Betty Barber
chez Hotel d'Orsay
20 rue Alsace-Lorraine
Nice, France

Met Mr. and Mrs. B in the Pitti Gallery—will have lunch with them tomorrow—they were very happy to see me. Will leave tomorrow with night train for Venice. The B's will arrive in Venice Monday. I will stay about 5 days in Venice. Do not go to Ravenna anymore—only Padua and Milan. Please save this postcard. Kisses.

John

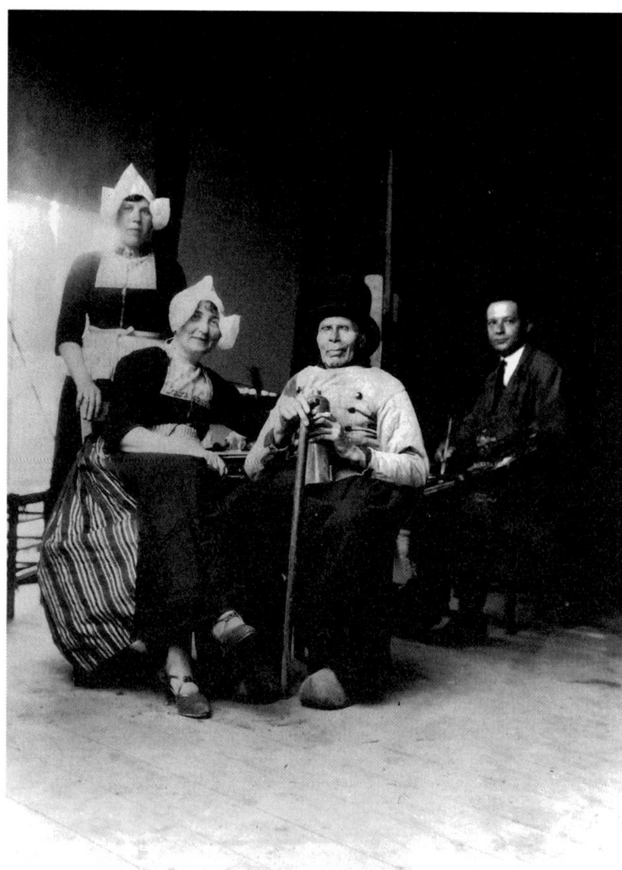

Fig. 32
John Barber and Models in Studio,
Holland, 1926

Venice
March 15, 1925

Mme. Betty Barber
Chez Mme. Delaye
94 rue Grignan
Marseille, France

I don't know if you are in Nice now or not, so I write anyway. The B's will arrive at 6 P.M. this evening and I will wait for them at the station. The weather is simply splendid—never any rain, always sunny, but quite cold. From Venice I will stop one day at Padua and one in Milan. Kisses to you both.

John

March 20, 1925

Mme. Betty Barber
chez Hotel d'Orsay
20 rue Alsace-Lorraine
Nice, France

Left Venice 7:40 this morning, saw some Giotto frescos in Padua and now I am writing in the train on the way to Vicenza where I stay till 3:48 this afternoon to see a painting by Giorgione. Will arrive in Milan at 8 this evening. Will stay there a day or two and then make a stop also in Genoa—it all depends how I feel about it. The train shakes terribly. It is 10:30 A.M.
    Kisses,

John

Milan
March 20, 1925

Mme. Betty Barber
c/o Hotel d'Orsay
20 rue Alsace-Lorraine
Nice, France

Dear Ones,

I reached Milan 8 P.M. It is an astonishingly beautiful city but terribly modern and up-to-date. Will probably leave tomorrow evening either for Genoa or for Turin or for Nice—just as I feel like. Am a bit homesick though.
    Kisses,

John

Postcards from John Barber to his family

Braunschweig
[Germany]
July 26, 1926

Mr. Frederick Barber
51 rue Rossini
Nice, France

My dear papa:

I stayed here overnight as the museum is very interesting, and will leave today at 2:32 arriving in Berlin 5:50. I like Germany very much.
    Love to all of you.

John

Volendam
[The Netherlands]
August 6, 1926

Mr. Frederick Barber
51 rue Rossini
Nice, France

My dears:

Your letter of the 2nd came and also the second one you sent to Kassel was forwarded to me.
    I am feeling fine and this afternoon I start again working on a composition of 5 figures with Mr. Hering in his studio.
    Think of staying here about another ten days or so before going to Paris.
    Love and Kisses to all three of you.

John

Volendam
[The Netherlands]
August 16, 1926

Mr. Frederick Barber
51 rue Rossini
Nice, France

My dears:

It's 6 P.M. am through with all my work, and tomorrow at 4:30 I leave Volendam and take the 17:42 express Amsterdam-Paris reaching Paris 6 something in the morning of Aug. 18.
    Am very glad to get that much nearer home and shall probably be in Nice very soon again.
    Love and Kisses to all three of you.

John

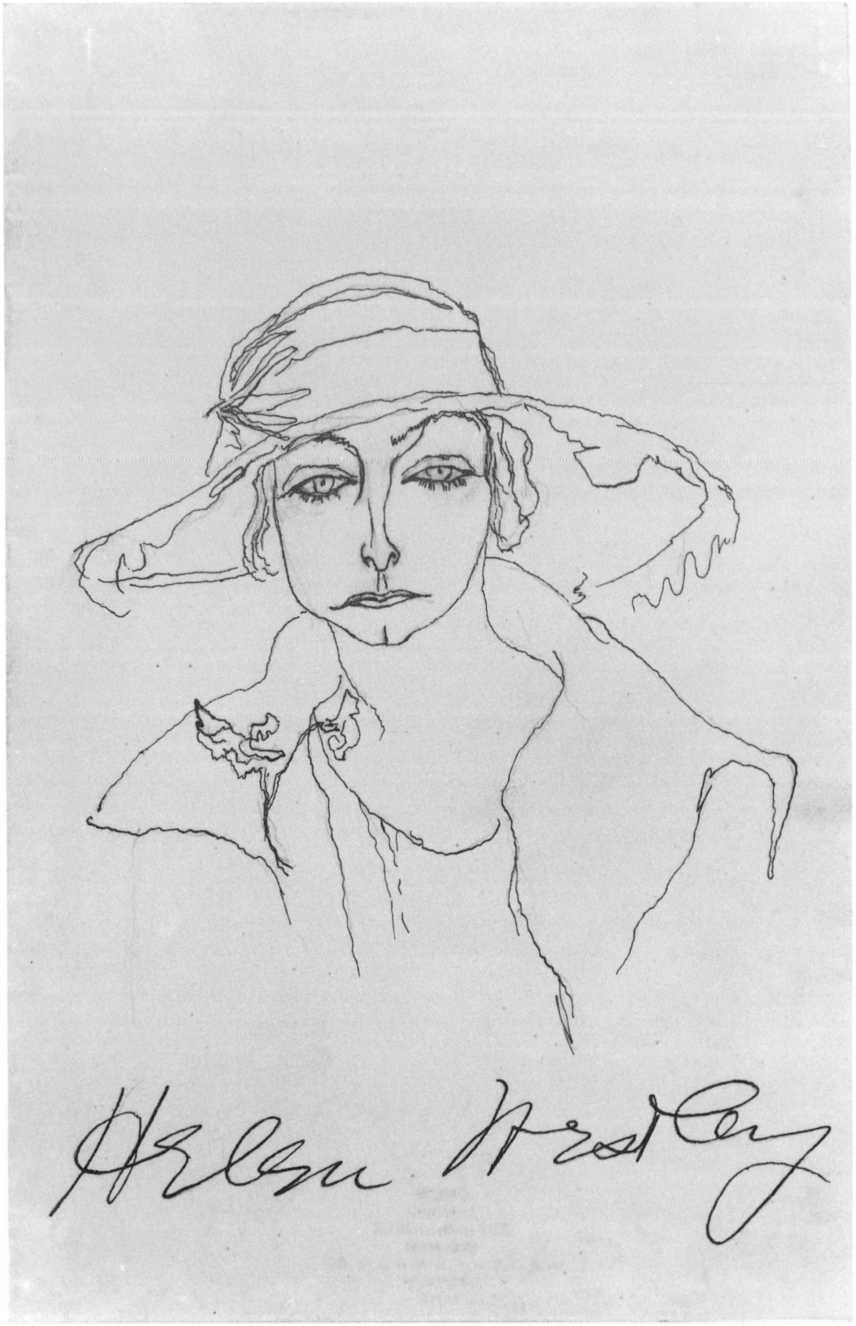

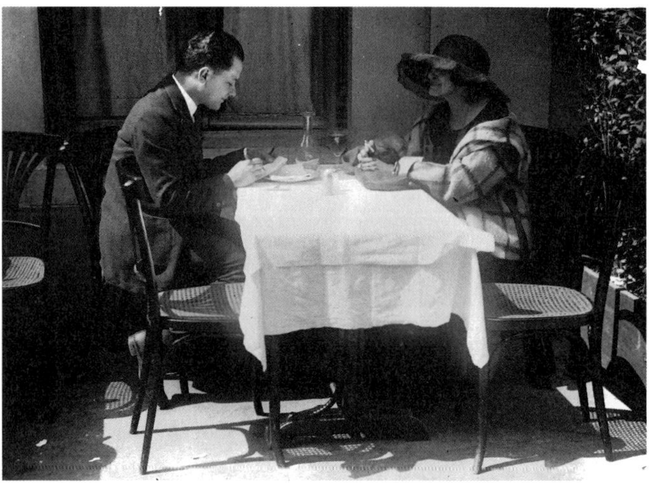

Fig. 34. *Above*,
John Barber and Helen Westley, Paris, 1926
Photograph: Henri Manuel

Fig. 33. *Left*,
John Barber
Helen Westley, 1924
Graphite and ink, 8 3/16 x 5 3/8
Collection of Dr. Margaret De Ronde Barber,
on loan to The John Barber Memorial Collection,
Bayly Art Museum of the University of Virginia

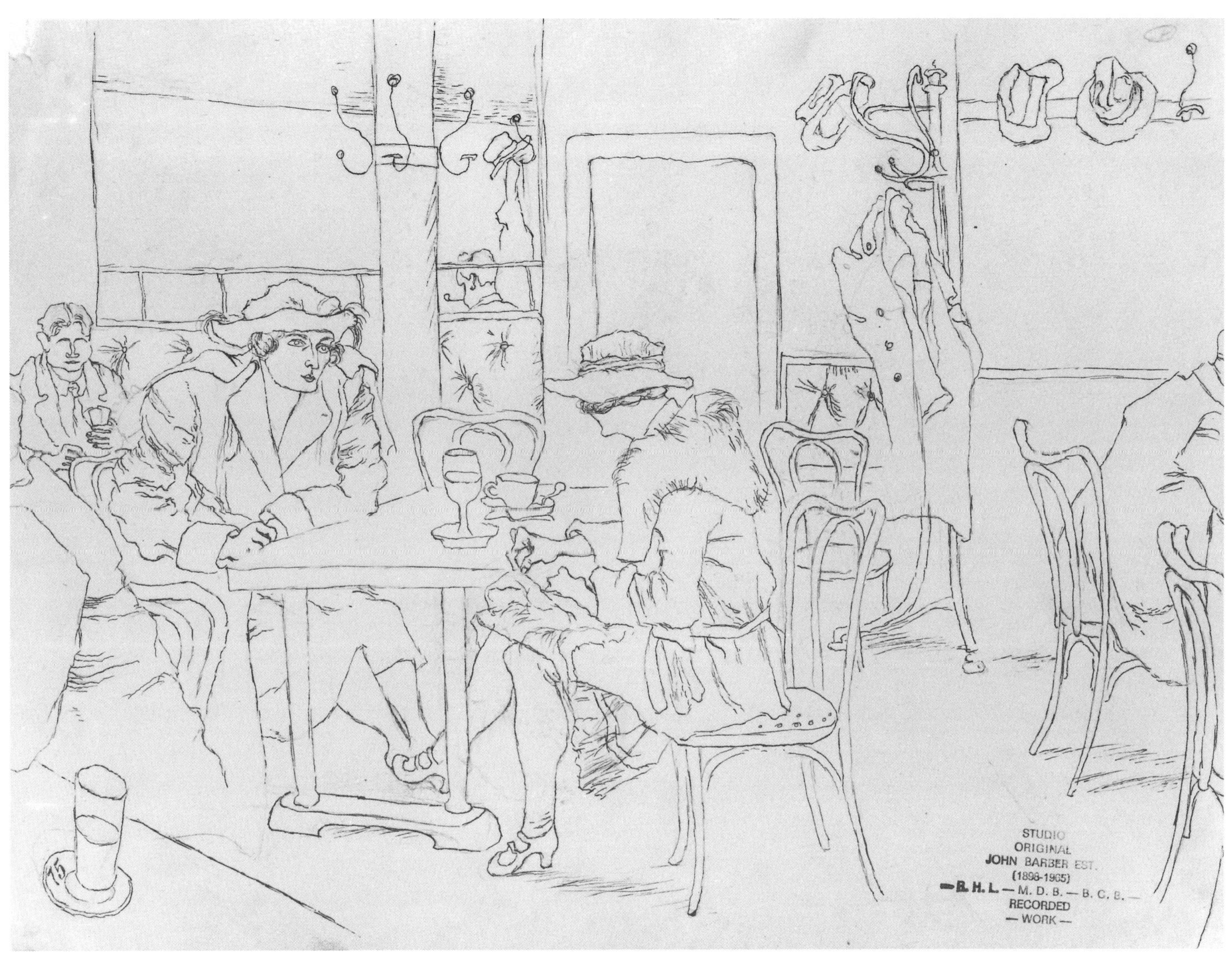

Fig. 35
John Barber
Café, Paris, ca. 1924
Graphite and ink, 7 1/8 x 9 1/4
Collection of Dr. Margaret De Ronde Barber,
on loan to The John Barber Memorial Collection,
Bayly Art Museum of the University of Virginia

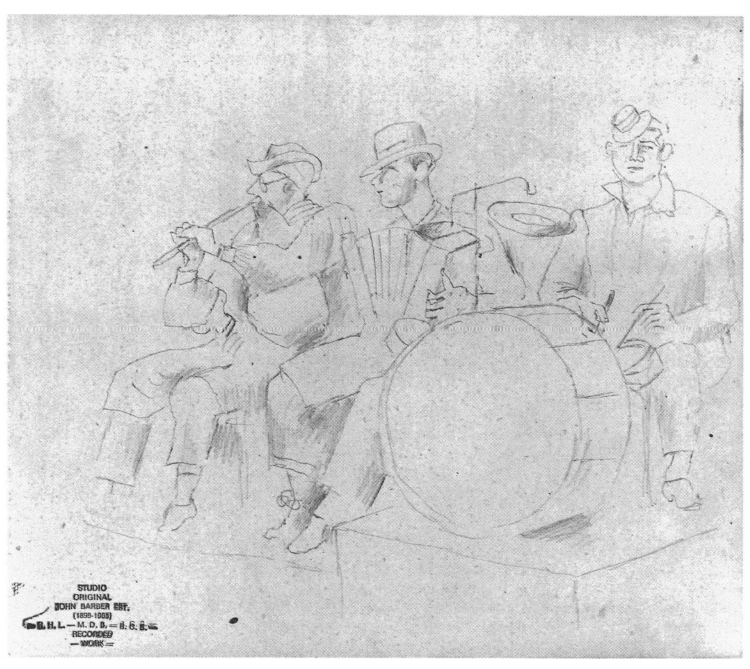

Fig. 36
John Barber
Jazz Musicians, Paris
Graphite, 7 $\frac{1}{2}$ x 8 $\frac{1}{2}$
Collection of Dr. Margaret De Ronde Barber,
on loan to The John Barber Memorial Collection,
Bayly Art Museum of the University of Virginia

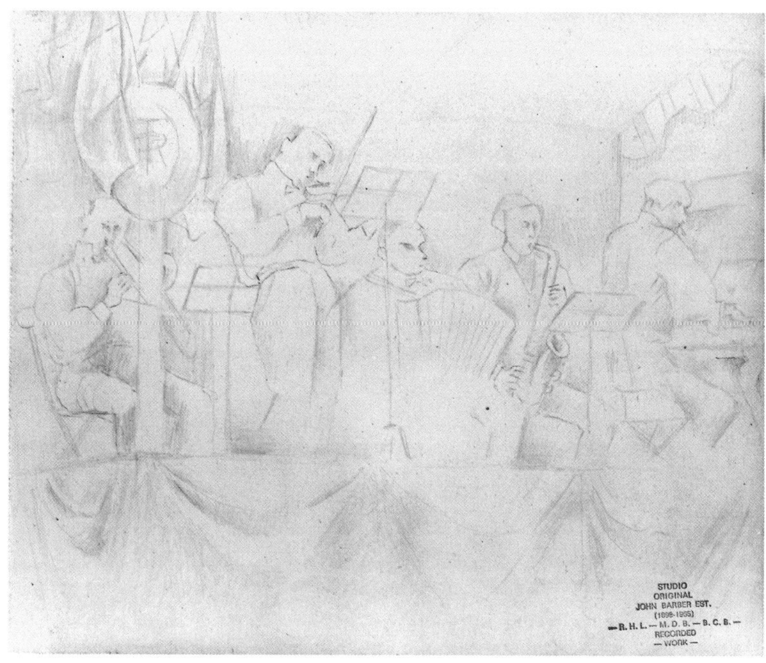

Fig. 37
John Barber
Jazz Musicians
Graphite, 7 $\frac{5}{8}$ x 8 $\frac{5}{8}$
Collection of Dr. Margaret De Ronde Barber,
on loan to The John Barber Memorial Collection,
Bayly Art Museum of the University of Virginia

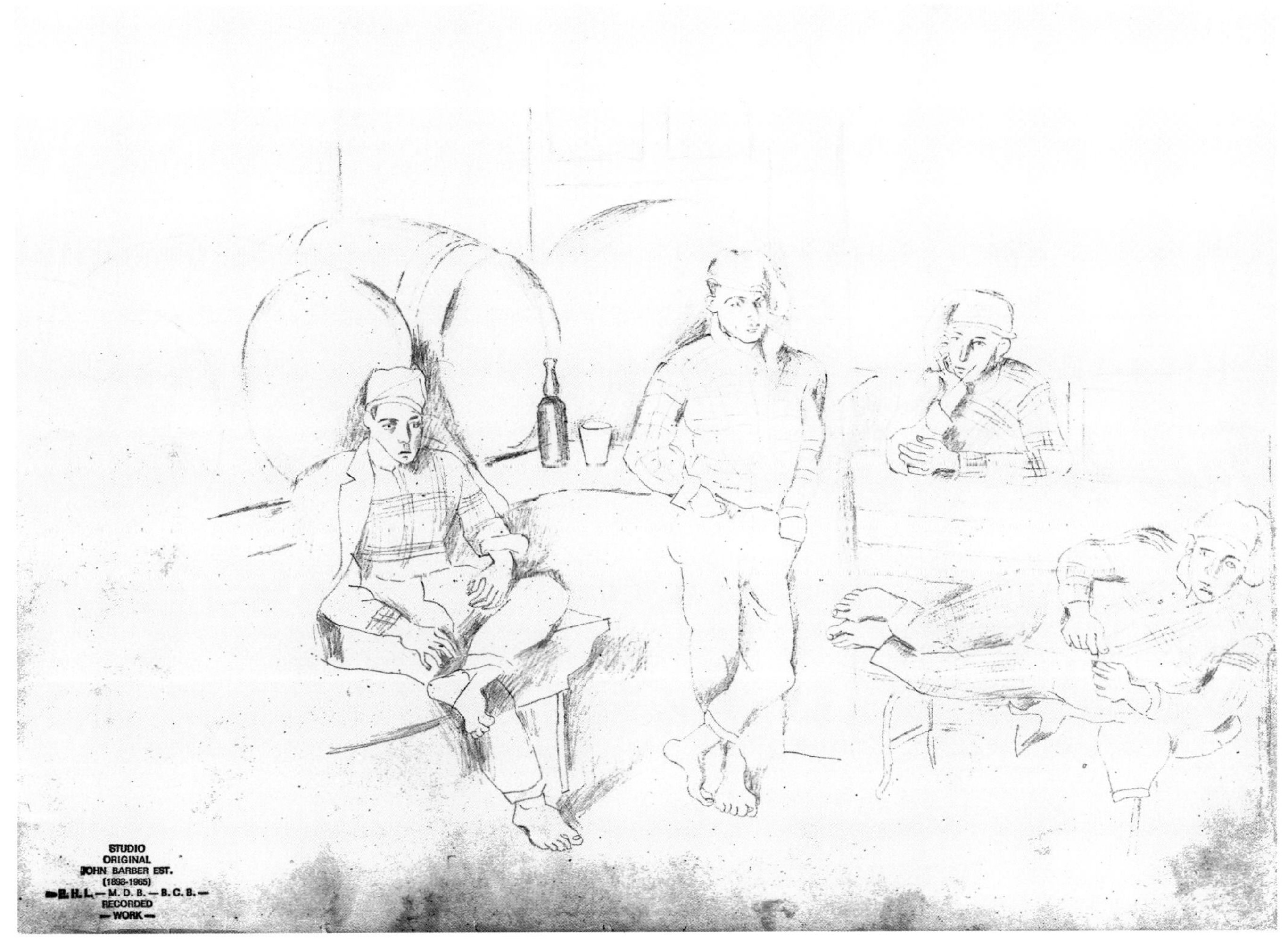

Fig. 38
John Barber
Tavern, Portugal, 1928
Graphite, 9 x 12 1/8
Collection of Dr. Margaret De Ronde Barber,
on loan to The John Barber Memorial Collection,
Bayly Art Museum of the University of Virginia

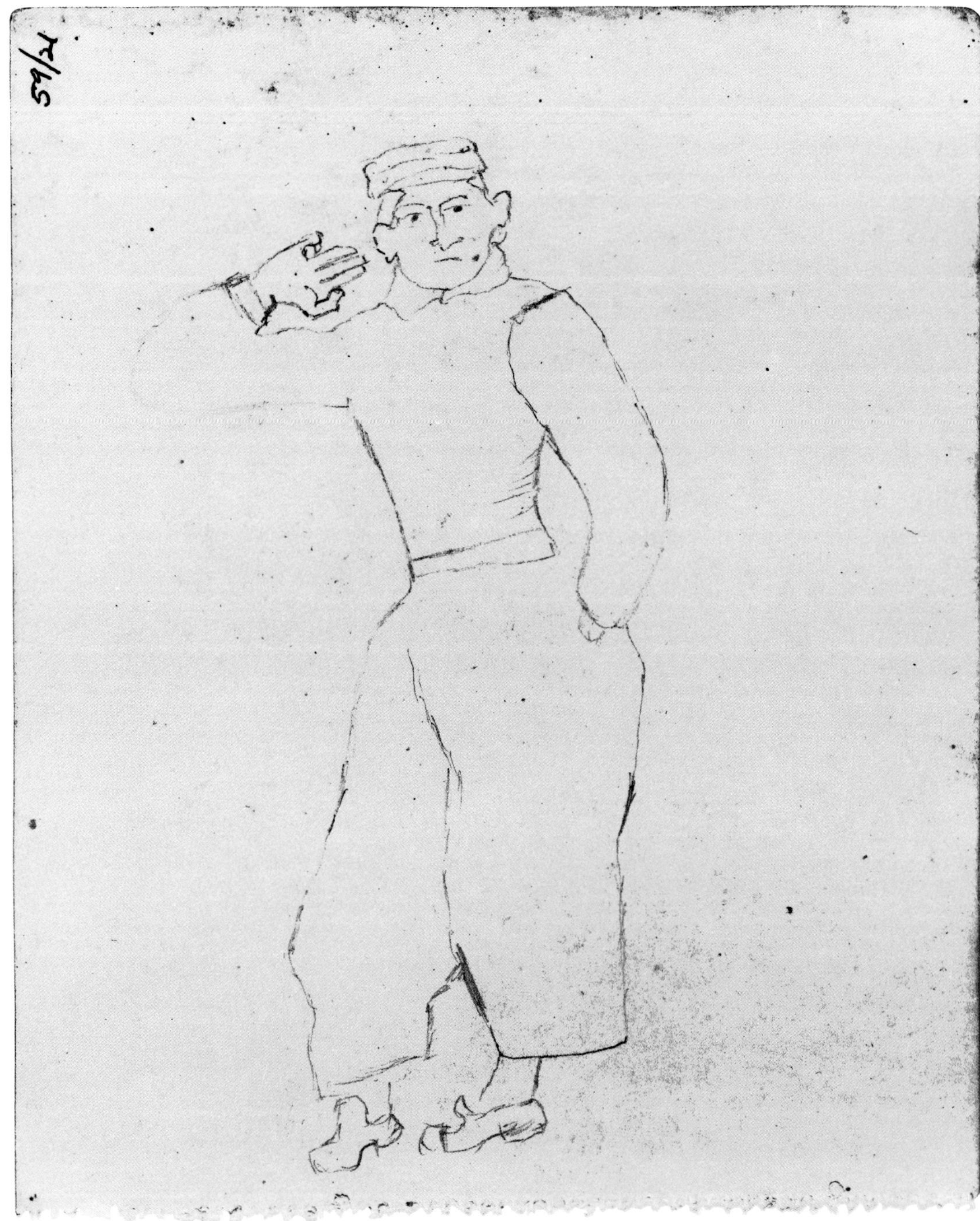

Fig. 39
John Barber
Young Man Standing
Graphite, 4 7/8 x 3 7/8
Collection of Dr. Margaret De Ronde Barber,
on loan to The John Barber Memorial Collection,
Bayly Art Museum of the University of Virginia

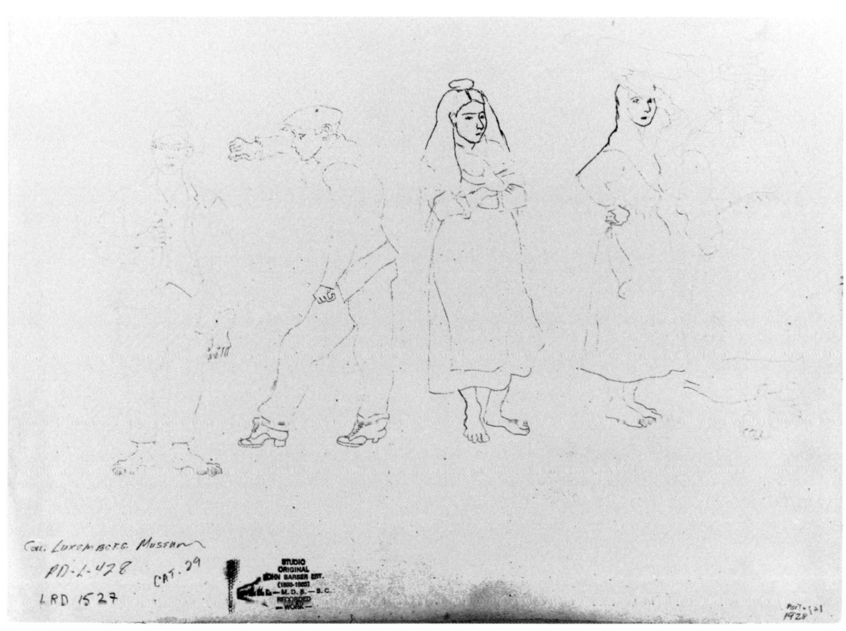

Fig. 40
John Barber
Five Figures, Portugal, 1928
Graphite and ink, 9 x 12
Collection of Dr. Margaret De Ronde Barber,
on loan to The John Barber Memorial Collection,
Bayly Art Museum of the University of Virginia

Fig. 41
John Barber
At the Fountain
Graphite, 8 x 10 1/4
Collection of Dr. Margaret De Ronde Barber,
on loan to The John Barber Memorial Collection,
Bayly Art Museum of the University of Virginia

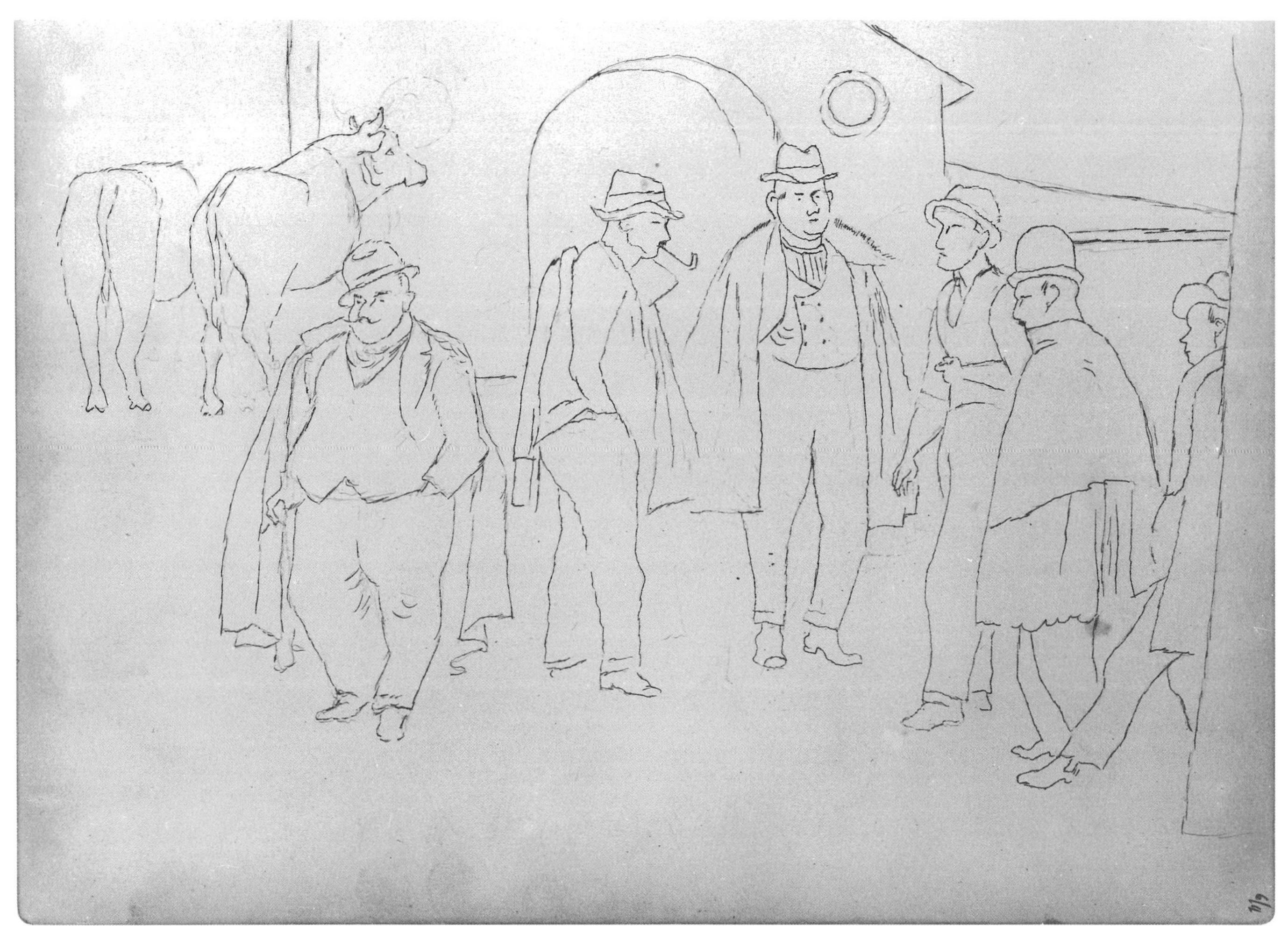

Fig. 42
John Barber
Six Men, Florence, 1930
Graphite and ink, 8 $\frac{7}{8}$ x 12 $\frac{1}{4}$
Collection of Dr. Margaret De Ronde Barber,
on loan to The John Barber Memorial Collection,
Bayly Art Museum of the University of Virginia

American Consular
Service
Marseille, France,
November 12, 1926

Mrs. Betty Barber
c/o The American Express Co.,
ROME (Italy)

Madam:

I am informed by your daughter, Mrs. Riviere
Burwick, that you have been notified of the death of
your husband, Mr. Frederick Barber, at Marseille on
November 6, 1926. There is enclosed a copy of an
official report of Mr. Barber's death which is being
sent to the Department of State at Washington.

It is my duty to call your attention to the provi-
sions of the Act of March 2, 1907, which states that if
a naturalized American citizen resides for more than
two years in his country of origin or for five years in
any other foreign country, the presumption of expa-
triation arises against him. This presumption may be
overcome in some instances by the presentation of
satisfactory evidence to the nearest consular office
proving that the prolonged foreign residence was due
to causes beyond the control of the person concerned.

I am, Madam, yours very respectfully,

Wesley Frost

American Consul General in charge.
Enclosure: report.
JCH/R

V. Jules Pascin

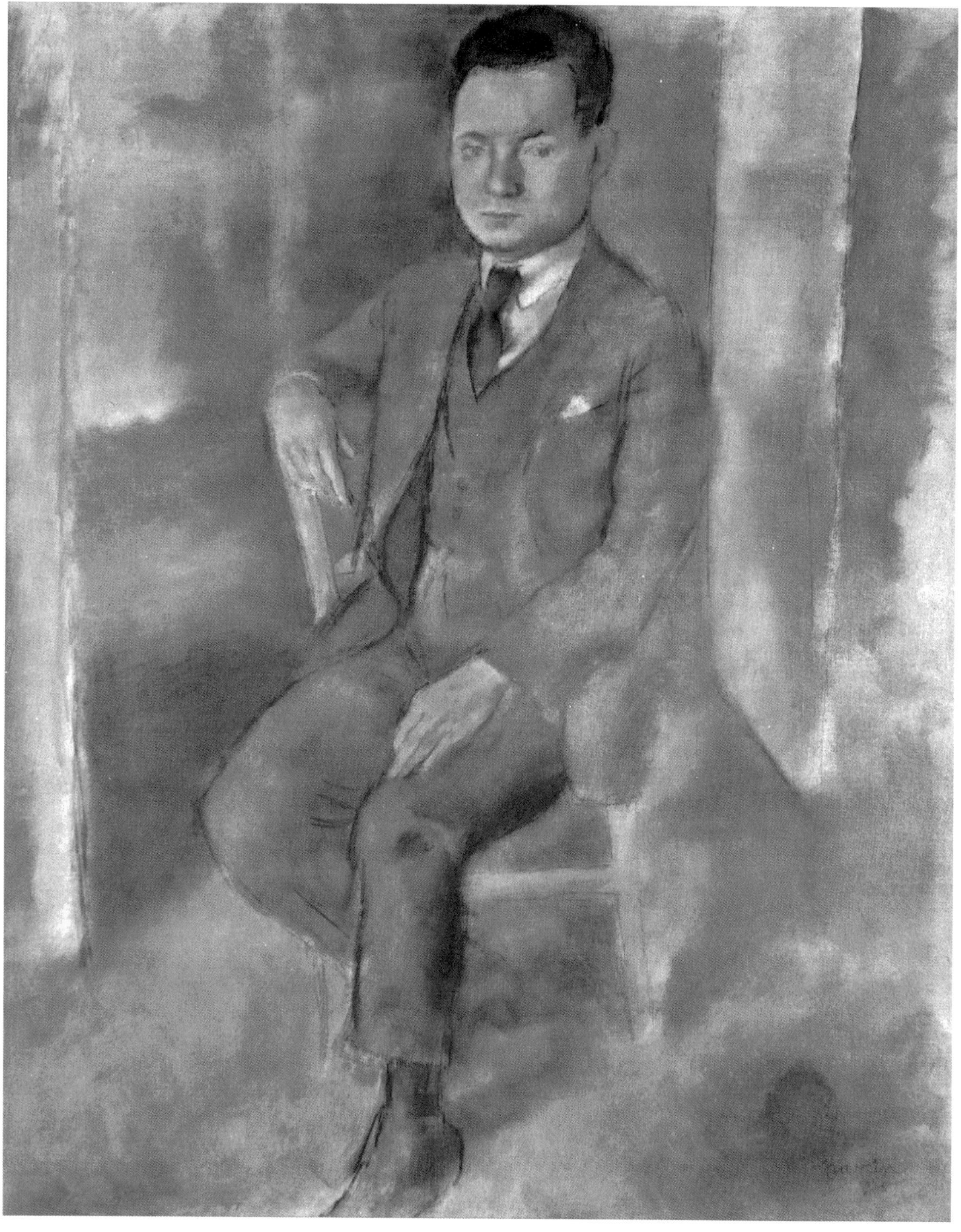

Fig. 43
Jules Pascin
John Barber, 1925
Oil on canvas, 39 ½ x 31 ¼
Bayly Art Museum of the University of Virginia
Gift of Dr. Margaret D. Barber, 1985.39

V. *Jules Pascin*

Autobiographical fragment

Jules Pascin also became a close friend, and although we both originated in the Balkans, we first met in New York. We had many bonds in common. First, I found he, too, had come to the United States of America for the same idealistic reasons I had; we were both inclined to look upon events and culture from a universal point of view. Perhaps, most important of all, we both saw and portrayed the comedy and drama of life around us. Pascin was a great gentleman, a man of enormous culture, and I owe many of my basic concepts of interpretation to his philosophy. Pascin was never a teacher of painting in the ordinary sense; in fact he frequently expressed his feeling that art cannot be taught. He never even talked art in gatherings, but it was his dedication to his work, his humor, his gentleness and generosity, his belief in the universality of human emotions expressed in art forms, that made him perhaps a greater contributor to a younger artist than all the academic and pedagogic approaches in existence. One of my most treasured possessions is a life-size, full-length portrait he did of me.

I also knew Pascin as a successful and esteemed artist in Paris where his work was even then in great demand. But I also saw him saddened when his adopted country, the land that had meant so much to him in his dreams, completely ignored him, and the art world of America apparently did not even "see" or understand his work. Although he finally gave up trying to exist as an artist in New York, and returned to Europe by force of circumstance, he did not become embittered, but simply accepted the point of view that this country was too young culturally to have established any real tradition of art of its own, and the fact that Americans had not yet learned to discover artists. It is perhaps ironical that each year, on the anniversary of Pascin's death, a representative from the American Embassy in Paris goes to the Montparnasse Cemetery and places flowers and a small American flag on his grave.

Paris
November 7, 1924

Impossible travailler aujourd' hui mais compte absolument vous deux demain 6 heure excuses et bonjour.

Pascin

May 1, 1925

Mr. John Barber
c/o Guaranty Trust Company
1 et 3 rue des Italiens
Paris

My dear John,

I hope you get this word in time. I am all crazy searching after my old passport. Lucy, who is away from Paris, must have put it aside in a bundle of old papers. At least I hope she didn't throw it away or leave it in a pocket of some old cloth I gave away. I hope to find it in the end or at least my second papers, but I have to go through several trunks containing thousands of papers, drawings, letters etc. Please don't trouble to come Saturday. I sure won't be ready. Can't you drop in Monday after 5. I hope the news will be better then. Excuse me! Compliments to Mrs. Barber.

Yours,
Pascin

May 26, 1925

My dear Barber,

I am back since a few days and would like to see you at the earliest date. To take an appointment for your portrait and also for another reason. I have been putting today some suits aside to have them sent to clean and in emptying the pockets I found in one I didn't wear since last summer the "lost" passport. I have been searching like crazy in all my trunks, old papers etc. but this old suit, lying round in my bedroom, never attracted my attention. Would you be so nice and phone to the lady at the embassy to keep my affidavit back? I found a letter to send some more information if possible, so I think they didn't yet send it away. And when can I see you to talk it over? I am in every day mornings till noon and from 3 to 6 in the afternoon. I could do the portrait this week but would prefer next beginning Thursday, Friday (if necessary Saturday).—

My best compliments to Mrs. Barber and to Rita,

Yours,
Pascin

Paris
May 11, 1927

My dear John,

We are going to the country Thursday.

Take the steamer *"direction Alfortville"* till the pont de Charenton. On the bridge is a stairway going down to the island "Saint-Maurice." You walk straight about 10 minutes or less and get to the "Grands Établissements Duchet" where you'll find us on the riverside or, if it is already quite after lunch, somewhat farther up on the lawns.

It looks like good weather and I think Mrs. Barber and you will like the country. Bring your sketchbook along.

Sincerely yours,
Pascin

New York
August 28, 1927

[John Barber
c/o Mr. Bell
55 East 86th Street
New York]

Dear John,

I was this afternoon reading at the library. I forgot the time and when I got up it was already 7 P.M. Too late to go home. I should be very sorry if you came to see me in vain. Excuse me, please. I don't know what I'll do Monday. This weather is awful. Will call at your home or phone.

Sincerely yours,
Pascin

New York
December 23, 1927

[Miss Rita Barber
c/o John Barber
340 West 88th Street
New York City]

Rita,

I am really terribly annoyed. I should come tomorrow, call on you, take you to the Harlem cabarets etc. Lots of things I would have so very much enjoyed, but *voilà:* I had the other day a telegram, asking me to a party *this Friday*. I went to see the people yesterday evening to explain I could not come, but they told me I *had* to come at any price as it was a party arranged for *me (ma chère!)* So I must go there after all.

The next day, Saturday, holly night, I must make some batiks and other things I promised as Christmas presents. If they are nice (I don't know if I still can do them) I will do after this, of course, some for you and Mama Barber also.

Now: On *Sunday* there is a very simple, but probably *very nice* party at Ganso's studio, 900 6th Avenue. I don't know exactly who will be there, but there will be certainly the best wine and best whiskey you'll get in N.Y. City.

So, please, Rita, excuse me and try to drop in on Sunday any time between 8 P.M. and 2 A.M. If you can stay in this town till the 28th I will take you to a very nice *bal masqué.*

Sincerely yours,
Pascin

Brooklyn, N.Y.
January 25, 1928

John Barber
340 West 88th St.

Will come today 7 to your place. Greetings.

Pascin

Paris
August 25, 1928

Dear John,

A person I have absolutely to see before I leave, called a while ago, but as I was again sleeping, Julie told him to come later. So I have to stay at home and won't be able to come today to see you.

But I will come *without fault Monday at 5 P.M.* Please don't arrange for me to stay for dinner, as I may leave the same night.

Sincerely yours,
Pascin

[Undated]

Dear John:

This trip starts really rather with complications: This damned man Coccoz (canvases) is not back yet. I asked at his place the concierge and other people. They have a funny way to smile, when I come. I am sure it is intention from his part. He expected me, as I had quite a nice debt with him, in delivering me canvases and other material for the trip, to give him a canvas in pay. He used to come every day up to the studio, but since I gave him a check for the debt he doesn't seem to care anymore. Last time, yesterday, when I came round and heard he was not yet back, it was too late to go to Montparnasse looking for canvases. I couldn't get anything decent up here. I showed the sample, they told me everywhere they couldn't understand who could sell this quality canvas at such price. I am very sorry to cause you more derangements but I can't do otherwise. I can't stay till tomorrow, as Lucy is very nervous and we are overrun by all kinds of people. Would you buy the canvases? If *possibly try to get same quality as the sample.* For me anyway take it even if price should be much higher. If not sure take two different canvases. There is Lamorelle and the shop, "l'ami des artistes," rue Vavin near you. There are also good canvases at Guichardaz rue du Dragon (near Square Sevre-Croix Rouge). Please buy also 3 pencils (Wolff-Crayon 3B) for me. Am joining cheque of *1000* francs. Awful sorry for the trouble I cause you. You'll get my telegram on Monday, as I leave only today and arrive very late at Cherbourg.

N.B. If by chance you should happen to pass near Brentano's Avenue de l'Opéra, would you buy me the *best* and *newest* guide to the U.S. (English or German publisher) Baedecker or imitation, provided *recent.* The *best* even if expensive. It will cost much more over there. But don't worry if you have no time. If you spend more, you have the difference in Cherbourg.

[Undated]

John,

Please come with mother without fault this Saturday, 14th to my Studio at about 8 P.M.

a bientôt !
Pascin

[Undated]
Saturday 18th
8:30 P.M.

On compte sans faute sur mama et John!

PASCIN, 1885–1930
An appreciation by John Barber

Troubadour of the pencil, brush, and colors, Pascin was a phenomenon in an era rapidly transforming itself. From the illusory glamour of the last days before World War I, the unhurried carriage elegance of belated Victorianism, there emerged an industrialism where the operatic "La Vie de Bohème" became an anachronism.

In spite of, or because of it, there is a universal nostalgia for those times, which chroniclers have enviously labeled "La Belle Époque."

As a surviving product of the beginning of the century, Pascin, though born in the Balkans, brought his talents to fruition in the sophisticated centers of Munich and Paris. A prodigal genius, his drawings in the satirical magazine *Simplicissimus* of Munich brought him rapid fame. He continued painting in Paris canvases reflecting the "Bon vivant" spirit of the early century that perhaps explain their present vogue, imbued as they are with a dream-like quality and charm not yet eradicated from our subconscious longings.

Painted in pastel-like, opalescent colors of delicate pinks and blues depicting almost virginal girls, demi-mondaines in semi-nudity of provocative aspect and disarming naive simplicity.

In spite of his assumed Bohemianism and ubiquitous bowler derby, Pascin was a man of great culture and extreme sensitivity. His generosity was proverbial. An outward gaiety and humor concealed the philosopher of profound and melancholy outlook. Like Baudelaire, he was conscious of "Les Fleurs du Mal"—the flowers of evil in his life and work. The exhaustion of his talents brought forth his complaint to me and a few friends: "I have said all I had to; what more do you want of me?" As André Salmon the French poet penned on his grave:

Pascin free spirit
Hero of dreams and desires
With his bloodied hands pushed the golden gate
Flesh and soul, Pascin dared to choose—
And master of life he ordered its end.

VI. Essays on Artists and Art

REMBRANDT

It seems so apropos to remember Rembrandt in these iconoclastic times when the very foundations of bourgeois or middle-class society are trembling under the impact of universal forces striving toward their destruction.

Our present day "direct action" totalitarians have only stolen the thunder of the after-war Freudian intellectuals. Pointing an accusing finger at our civilization, they, too, brand it as hypocritical, conventionally smug and economically unjust. It is exactly how one lone individual expressed it through his art and life just three centuries ago; were its consequences not so tragic to his private life, it would seem amazing to us now. Those who are struck by that mysterious thing called "genius" are of necessity innovators. Being a prophet means being a revolutionist. Any deviation from the beaten path scandalizes those who have settled into a comfortable complacency—man being naturally a lazy animal.

Genius is like a meteor—causing a commotion when falling amidst Dutch burghers. In that cold, calculating, practical community of merchants, respectable and unimaginative, a man with the poetical and oriental warmth of Rembrandt would be an anomaly.

At the early age of 36 he already created one of the world's masterpieces—*The Night Watch*—that in itself would be ample cause to put him in immediate open conflict with such fellow citizens. Instead of photographing in paint on this canvas each "customer" with equal importance, he dared to focus his "light" on the center of interest and to blend the rest into insignificance. He thus produced a great work of art but wounded the vanity of the lesser personages.

It was the first picture of its kind where chiaroscuro (light and shade) was thus handled. Leonardo da Vinci did it before him, but in a more dry, formal and academic manner. In that sense Rembrandt was two centuries ahead of the invention of photography. His are impressions in light and shade rather than the graphic and classically executed works of his predecessors. He was thus the first impressionist; the nineteenth-century French only continued its development.

He married for love and dared enjoy it—an unheard-of thing in a puritanical country. Depicting in paint his domestic felicity with his gentle and loving mate, he shows Saskia sitting on his knee, while, with hilarious expression, embracing his beloved and holding aloft a tall glass, he faces the spectator. Both are dressed in sumptuous cavalier costumes and seem to enjoy life to the fullest. Rembrandt considered existence to be a grand carnival and spent lavishly during the years of opulence. He meant to surround himself with the necessary background of one who had the "vision" of legendary oriental potentates.

When he painted the celebrated *Lesson of Anatomy* at the age of 26, his success was instantaneous though his vogue lasted only ten years. The death of Saskia in 1642 coincided with the catastrophic *Night Watch*. It seems strange that this Napoleon of the brush should also meet his Waterloo when "his Josephine" went out of his life.

Henceforth, his decline was rapid—mostly due to his proud, uncompromising nature. Rank and wealth meant nothing to him. It always means a lot in a middle-class mercantile republic. Holland was then a prosperous republic, similar to our own. The examples of Venice and Genoa and the Germanic Hansa cities prove that financial and maritime states find republics best suited to the advancement of their economic and class interests. Under such governments the homely virtues become entrenched in a prim respectability where there is no place for a pagan like Rembrandt.

Any restraints he might have felt because of his marriage to a patrician like Saskia van Uylenborch went overboard now. Forthwith he meant to do as he pleased—to the great consternation of his neighbors. This "great prince," born a miller's son, found his loves, as his familiars and subject matter, right among the lowly; he considered them the more humane elements of society. There was enough "magic" and a wealth of indulgence in his own nature to "see" in Hendricke Stoffels his new "fairy tale princess." She was a young, illiterate peasant girl who just entered his service to care for his orphan son Titus.

She posed for some of his greatest pictures. Her famous portrait now in the Louvre Museum is a triumph of Rembrandt's "lighting effects." It is unearthly in that it is not the result of anything external, but comes from within and shines forth in a mysterious glow.

His general approach, though realistic, depicted conceptions resulting from a mind rich in "fantasy."

He was Shakespearean in making us realize that all of man's endeavors culminate in that striving for immortality—a paradise. The creations of a true artist are always a manifestation of that universal longing—thus art is essentially romantic and pagan. For what is more pagan than the paradise promised by even the most austere religion; the average man looks forward to it as a future and a more joyous world, while an artist like Rembrandt tried to create and live in his own "fool's paradise." It inevitably led to bankruptcy. The remainder of Hendricke's days were devoted to shielding "her great man" from his creditors. Gone was the sumptuous background of his younger days, but being deprived of worldly goods only served to liberate his spirit and helped him to ascend that much more into the artist's heaven.

There was nothing Dutch about Rembrandt in the way Titian or Giotto were Italian, or El Greco Spanish in a mystical and Catholic sense. Rembrandt was universal. He would have been modern even today, in that henceforth his religious pictures could have been called a "proletarian interpretation of the Bible." In his famous *Pilgrims of Emmaus* he placed his characters in kinship with the masses, and within the comprehension of his matter-of-fact Nordic contemporaries.

He was one example of "man seeing clearer as his vision grows dim." The "Rembrandt browns" now gave way to a rainbow of color giving the full measure of that fire burning within him. He drew no longer, only blocking in broadest manner and kneading his forms into a unified whole. In his two last paintings, *The Family Group* and *The Prodigal Son*, we see the same broken color and vibrating tonalities Renoir used centuries later.

He was now alone and still experimenting—with himself as a model. To the last he poses, palette in hand and white bandanna on his head. His undaunted expression seems to defy destiny, for he still is Rembrandt.

Life he perceives as a dream—an accent of another world which renders real life cold and pale—thus strengthening his indifference to it—knows a better world.

Has proved light exists in itself independent of exterior form of coloring.

Art of showing invisible tone of picture may be regarded as a reflection of the artist's mood.

Phosphorescent art.

. . .

OF MICHELANGELO

Cry of suffering of human soul
Leaped to limits that cannot be surpassed.

. . .

Cry of suffering human soul. leaped
to height that cannot be surpassed.
Melancholy due to
pondering on tragedy ultimate destiny
Thundered like Jeremiah praised mightily,
like the Psalmists.

. . .

SAINT FRANCIS

. . . exuberant love and
enjoyment of nature.
Popes advocate Christianity wide
enough to embrace ideal pagan wisdom
and worldly pleasure. Classical is refuge larger
realities of life.
superman personality mystic.

. . .

Delight in life received great
impetus from S. Francis with his
exuberant love and enjoyment of nature.

Rome
1. Hard Light.
2. Atmosphere of Unreality and Artificiality of Rome as contrasted with joy of living and opulence of Venice.
3. Rome always had to import artists because it always imposed order and law by constraint, first of its legions then of its priests. Art, the zenith of order, cannot thrive under compulsion. Art is libertarian. The highest law.

Venetian Merchant Princes did not care to become Popes and Cardinals.

. . .

ALTAMIRA

1. Art–man's desire to perpetuate self comes from religious impulse
2. Harnessed to represent the story of Religion
3. Outcast–Age of Agnosticism (Doubt)– Transition.
4. and future for sake of Beauty above, when Man is content to live one life and live it to the full.

. . .

The reason for puritanism—one must not enjoy life here, lest it make people think this is the only heaven!—what else is there somewhere else?

All forms of human exultation cannot be explained, like Art, for instance.

. . .

ART AND FAITH

[Recto] *For 13 centuries* European art is religious. Artist has been man of faith. Now conviction gone.

Collective great periods of art exist only when faith is great.

In escaping Rome artists lost incentive. No artist since Rembrandt found spiritual reason for picturing to take place of naive Christian devotion.

Art henceforth serves man instead of God. Earth instead of hypothetical heaven.
[Verso] *3500 B.C.* Sumeria art of royalty.

Holland, freed of king and pope, democratizes art (not success for artist).

Revolt started 1567. Indep. 1579. War till 1609. *Hansa cities.*

Reformation removal from refreshment of spiritual sources.

Catholic art since Reformation also superficial and tasteless.

When (3rd estate) Bourgeoisie gains power, dullness the rule.

Geniuses henceforth outside natural development. Decay of faith is cause.

GENIUS NOT A PRODUCT OF ITS TIME

When the muses crown a human being with God-like attributes, certain leveling forces always seem to resent it. Ironically enough, destiny casts such a one amid unsuited surroundings.

We have seen how a joyous pagan like Rembrandt spent his life in the severe and prim atmosphere of his matter-of-fact Holland, and ended in worldly failure. Michel Angelo, on the other hand, though of a morose and melancholy nature—of utmost austerity—was destined to be idolized by the pleasure-loving Italy of the Renaissance.

With the advent of Angelo, the most glorious epoch in History reached the zenith of its development, and was therefore prepared to receive such a Titan and permit the development of such a fierce individualist.

The Renaissance not only signified the revival of the ancient world but a reaction to the Medieval expectation of joy in a future existence only.

GOYA, 1746–1828

Goya, the most Spanish of the painters of a great school and the last of the old masters, hailed from the rugged province of Aragon, that harsh land of shepherds who are considered so tough by the Spaniards that it's said: "When an Aragonian needs to drive a nail into a wall he bangs it in with his head—and he makes his bread out of a piece of granite ground into flour." Such was also the man and artist in his ways till the end of his life, as a rebellious refugee in France.

He started with a group of bullfighters in his youth, and on reaching Rome to study painting had an escapade with a nun of a nearby convent.

As a Court painter in Madrid, he became the favorite portraitist of the powerful Duchess of Alba. Rumor has it that it ended in a closer relationship. In a time of severe morality, he did a celebrated nude of the Duchess in defiance of the Church, which did not recognize that anything exists between the neck and shoes of a woman—except her dress.

His portraits of the Royal Family show all the wealth and decadence of an inbred lot. The French poet and critic Theophile Gautier considered Goya's large canvas in the Prado Museum of King Charles IV and his whole family as a burlesque on monarchy. Goya was, then, imbued with the enlightened spirit of the French Revolution, and an admirer of Bonaparte. After the fall of the great Corsican, the Holy Alliance

of Vienna placed Fernando VII on the throne of
Spain. This insane, bloody reactionary butchered all
the liberal elements, and Goya had to run for his life
across the Pyrenees. He spent the seven last years of
his life in Bordeaux.

In 1928, the year of the centenary of his death, his
remains were brought back in great pomp. His final
resting place is most fitting. In a valley behind the
Royal Palace, the little chapel devoted to St. Anthony
is embellished with Goya's rare and magnificent
frescoes. Under the cupola, Goya painted a balcony
scene showing the Saint preaching to the poor and the
beggars—while in contrast, on the pilasters of support, a galaxy of angels. In the spirit of the Goyesque
earthiness he painted those angels as beautiful, voluptuous females in silken, colorful finery. In his concep-
tion Paradise wasn't necessarily of the next world.

As an anticlimax Goya also left the world an
other testament. A profound and enlightened thinker,
he did a whole series of etchings of incisive satire so
characteristic of the Spanish soul—masterly compositions expressing the hypocrisy of the powerful, the
disastrous blight of war, and the bigotry that kept the
masses in darkness and misery.

VAN GOGH, 1853–1890

Such is the miracle of life, and its salvation, that ever
so often here and there a light bursts forth enriching
the patrimony of humanity. Those through whom
are channeled that divine fire—a burden heavy for a
mere mortal—often become either saints or sinners,
heroes or martyrs.

In that well-ordered land of the Netherlands, of
middle-class respectability and severe puritanical
Protestantism, a colorful pagan like Rembrandt once
made his appearance, and then it went to sleep again
for two centuries.

Van Gogh, another free soul, suddenly appeared.
A visionary of idealistic social conceptions of the
Gospels and a love of fellow men, he felt impelled to
uplift the lowly. Preaching as a lay missionary in the
coal fields of the Borrinage in Belgium, he shared
their hardships and the misery of poverty. Failing
very rapidly as was inevitable in those days, he decided to turn towards the embellishment of life by
other means. Feeling within himself the ability of
creating beauty through the arts, he became a
painter. That was the start of the apostolate of this
Christ-like individual, who even looked the part with
his short reddish beard and general appearance.

Living like a peasant in the south of France, he
painted with fury and violence, trying to put God's
sunshine into his canvases. By good fortune his
simple needs were provided by a loving brother in
Paris. Theo van Gogh, though employed by a prominent art gallery in Paris, could not interest anyone in
Vincent's paintings.

The intensity of such obsessive efforts and un-
ceasing perseverance in trying to obtain the almost
impossible in color and light finally broke his nervous
system.

While temporarily recovering in the sanatorium
of Dr. Gachet, he painted his portrait which became
one of the most celebrated of the modern school.

In the universal acclaim of his work, many feel he
could have reached greater heights had he lived
longer than 37 years—even though there is a parallel
in so many other giants who did not live longer.
Toulouse-Lautrec, Raphael, Mozart, Chopin, etc.
impel one to the conclusion that perhaps they have
all completely fulfilled their inspired missions too.

In the exaltation of intense creation they doubtlessly gave their whole—exhausting the divine source,
while other greats have spread it at a slower and
more even keel.

But van Gogh was one of those who kept at it in white heat until he realized, just as Pascin later on did, that he was finished. He therefore too put a stop to a life that would henceforth be meaningless to a spoiled darling of the Gods.

VAN GOGH, 1853–1890. ANVERS-SUR-OISE

Tried to save himself seven times. Religion, Love, and Art, torments of spirit.
Religious ecstasy like St. Francis.
Hallucination.
Art more singular than enduring.
Sold 4 pictures, one for 400 fr. $85,000.
Madness alone is entirely free from the commonplace.
Madly aflame at 27 paintings.

CUBISM

Proust, "Everything can be several things at the same time."

Modern psychological science, "We do not see each element as a whole singly—we see the whole first, then gradually identify elements composing it."

Art is in its infancy, full of unknown possibilities. What drama if objects talked to us as convincingly as to van Gogh.

Artists forerunners of what may become common lot—example Greece, Persia, China, Italy.

Beginning 20th century, Europeans, ashamed of secondary role and position of servitude imposed by limitation to sensory interpretation of nature, went to extreme of repudiating every contact with real world. In end found themselves painting sensations.

MODERNISM

Going back to elemental truth as a reaction against the decadent forms of a fatigued civilization.

. . .

One wonders if man's present-day preoccupation with the Heavens above, as demonstrated in projects of Lunar expeditions, is not based on another form of escapism. Too long has humanity's sojourn on earth coincided with the Hell below which in reality symbolizes something deeply felt about the imperfections of life on this earth. The greatest epic poet, Dante, chose his *Inferno* to illustrate man's travail as a means of evolving to a nobler destiny for the living.

. . .

GREEK ART

To such a degree did the Greeks excel in sculpture, in architecture, in poetry, in everything they touched, that the word 'Greek' has become the synonym for the word 'beautiful.' It is only they who are absolutely true, absolutely beautiful, because they saw, recognized, and rendered. You have seen them, those masters; they do not tantalize us with doubtful words; they say: "It is so!" The Romans imitated them; and they are still admirable. But for us, we are Gauls, we are Barbarians. And it is only by striving to approach the Greeks, it is only by proceeding as they did, that we can merit and attain the name of artists.

Art draws its vitality from gross earthy fare.

*VII. The 1930s: Documentary Photographs,
Drawings, and Watercolors*

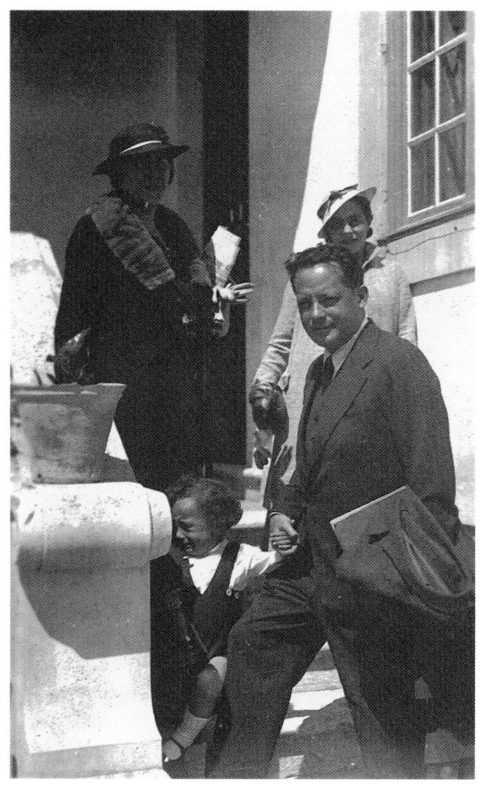

Fig. 44
John Barber and the Patrick O'Mengher
Family, Leiria, Portugal, 1932

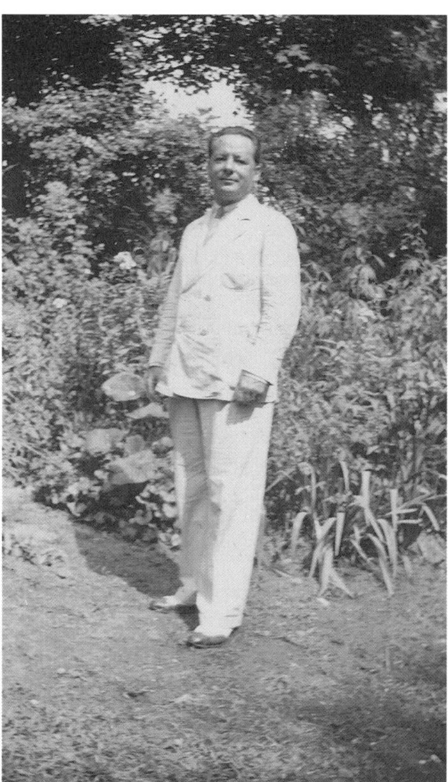

Fig. 45
John Barber, Larchmont, New York, 1938

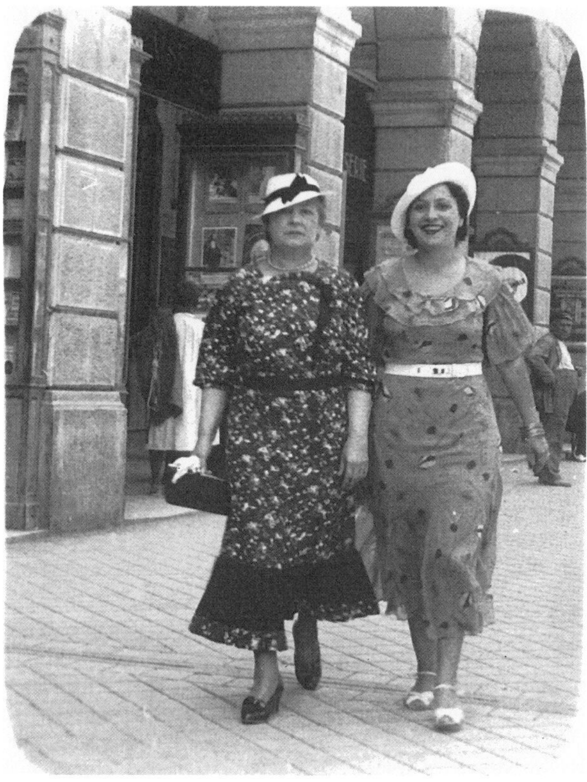

Fig. 46
Betty and Rita Barber, ca. 1939

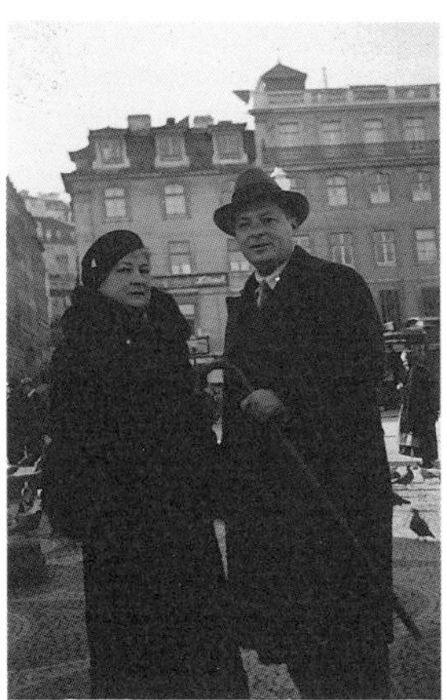

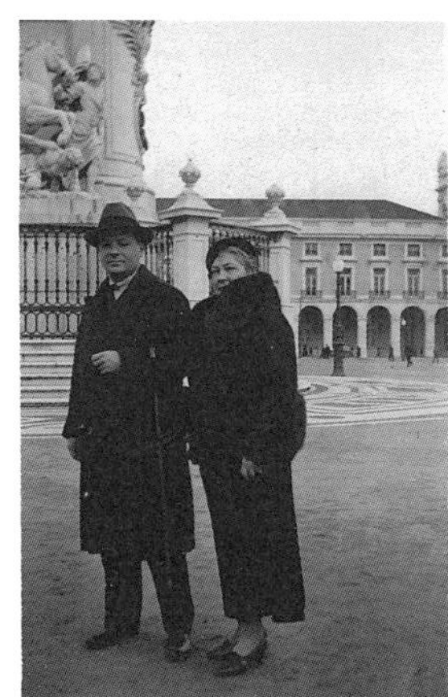

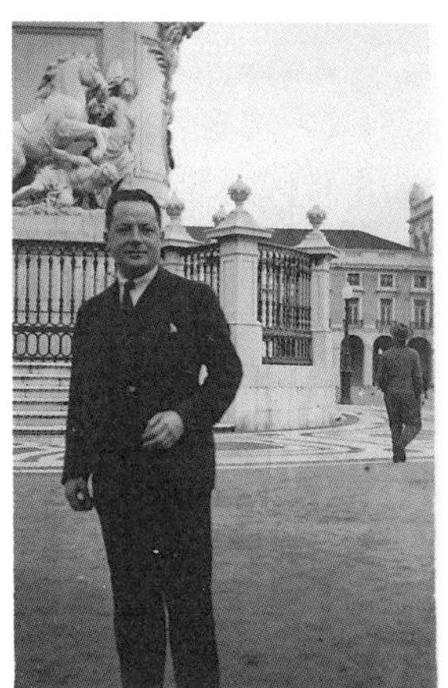

Fig. 47
John Barber and his mother,
Betty Barber, Lisbon,
Portugal, 1933

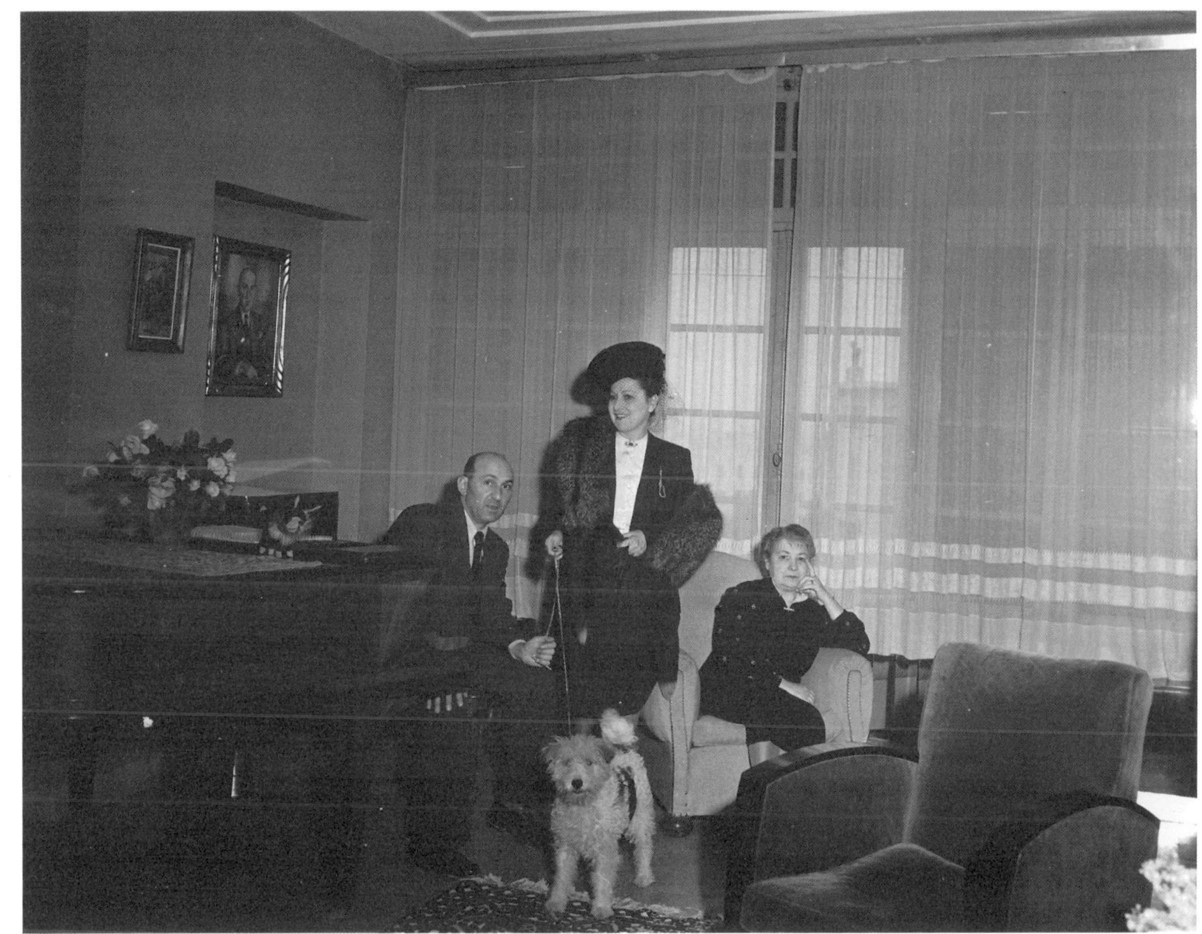

Fig. 48
Marcel Gozland, his wife Rita Barber,
and Betty Barber, Villa Gozland, Tunis, ca. 1939

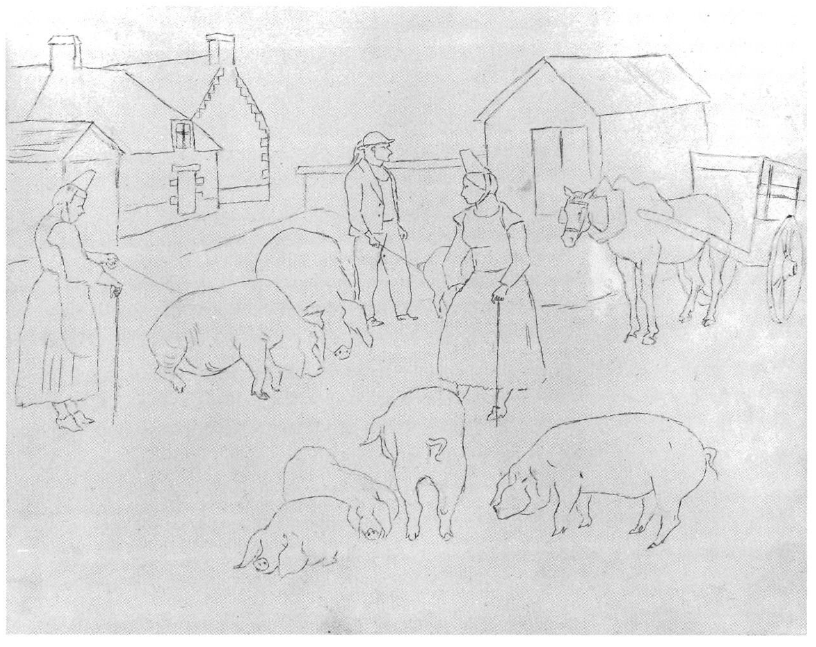

Fig. 49
John Barber
Barnyard, Holland, 1931
Graphite and ink, 12 x 14 $^{7}/_{8}$
Collection of Dr. Margaret De Ronde Barber,
on loan to The John Barber Memorial Collection,
Bayly Art Museum of the University of Virginia

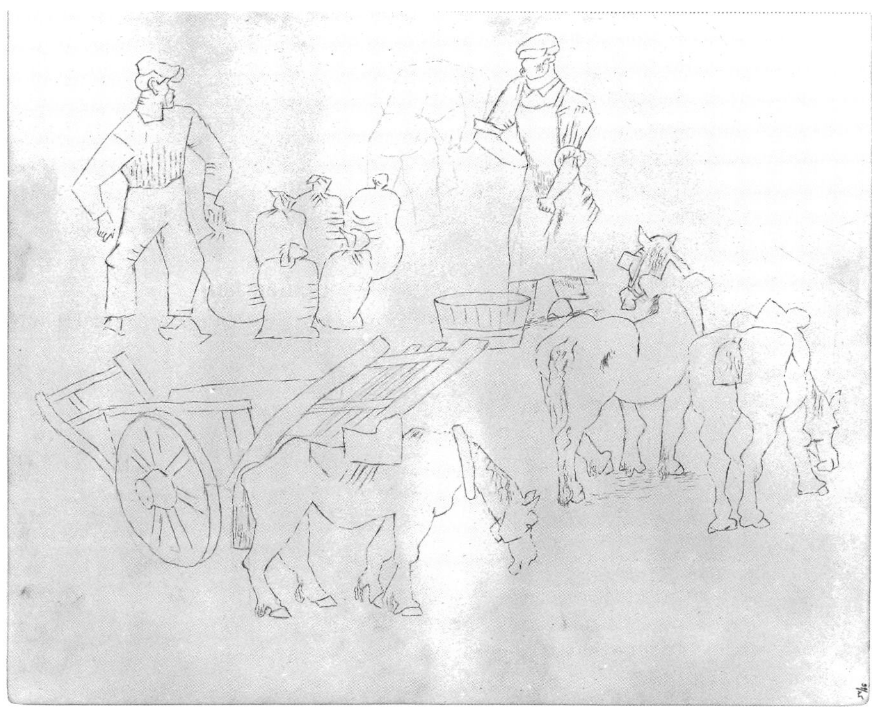

Fig. 50
John Barber
Men and Horses
Graphite and ink, 12 $^{1}/_{4}$ x 15
Collection of Dr. Margaret De Ronde Barber,
on loan to The John Barber Memorial Collection,
Bayly Art Museum of the University of Virginia

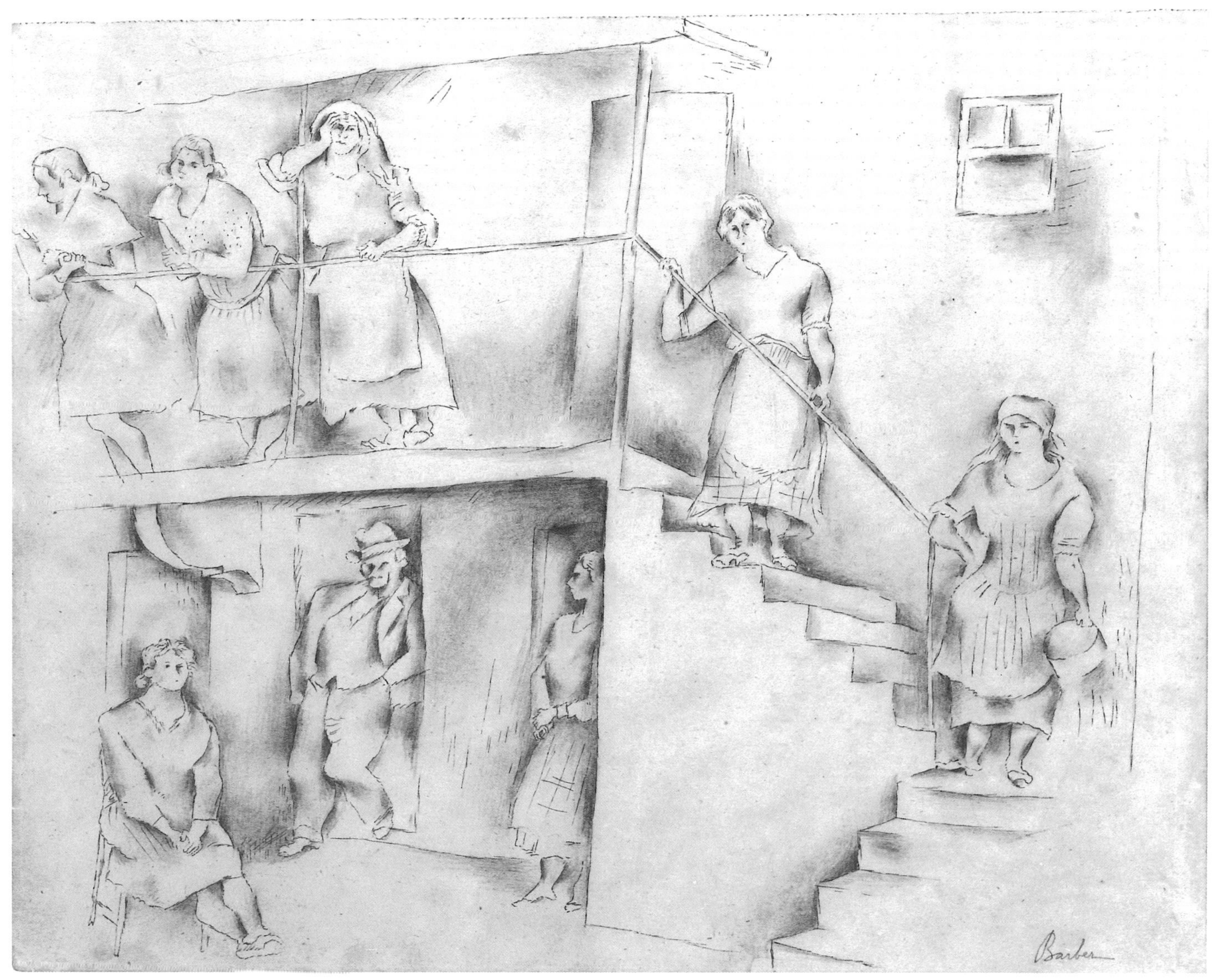

Fig. 51
John Barber
Figures on Porches and Steps
Graphite and ink, 12 x 15
Collection of Dr. Margaret De Ronde Barber,
on loan to The John Barber Memorial Collection,
Bayly Art Museum of the University of Virginia

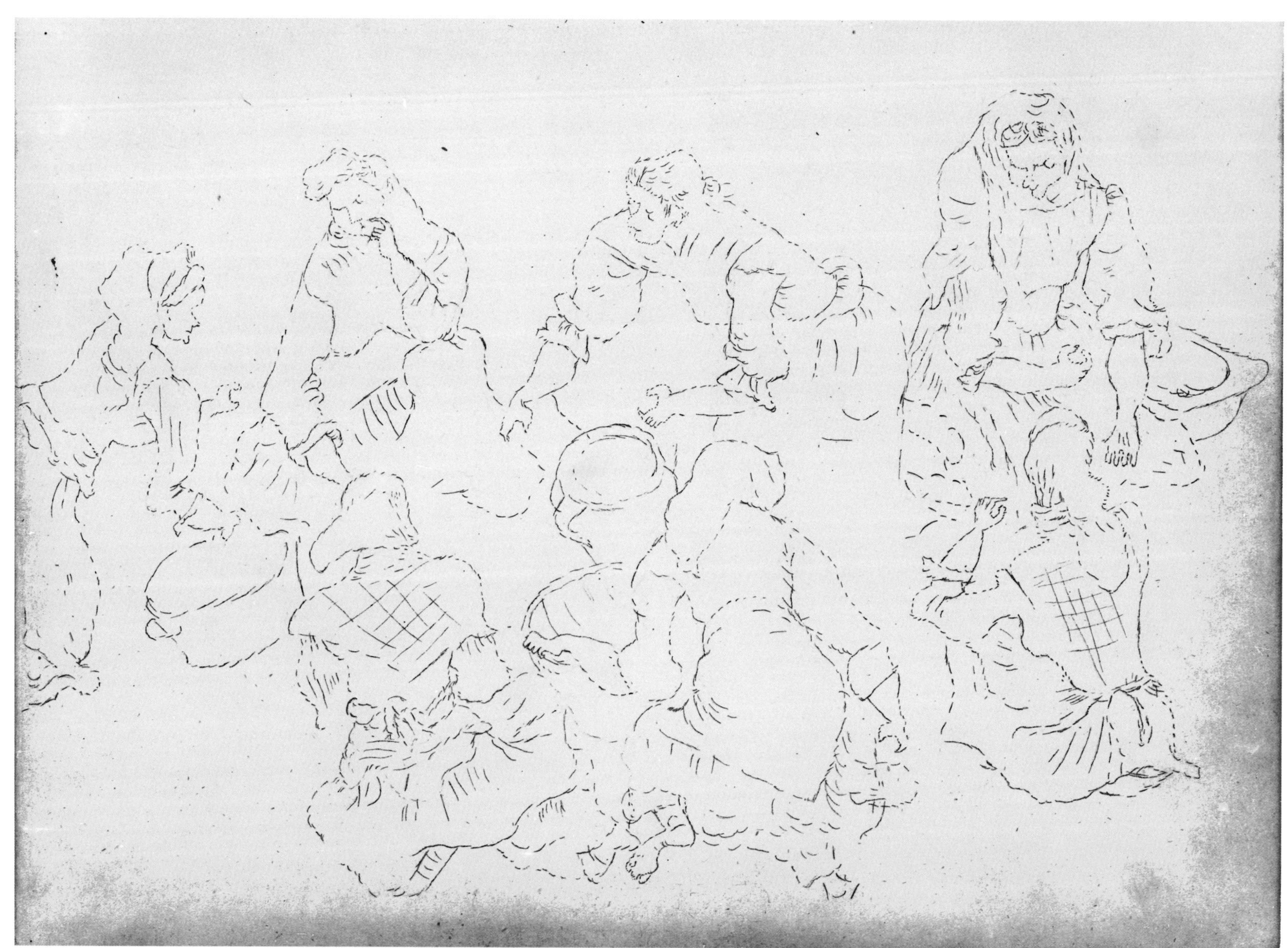

Fig. 52
John Barber
Seven Women, Portugal, 1936
Graphite and ink, 9 1/4 x 12 1/4
Collection of Dr. Margaret De Ronde Barber,
on loan to The John Barber Memorial Collection,
Bayly Art Museum of the University of Virginia

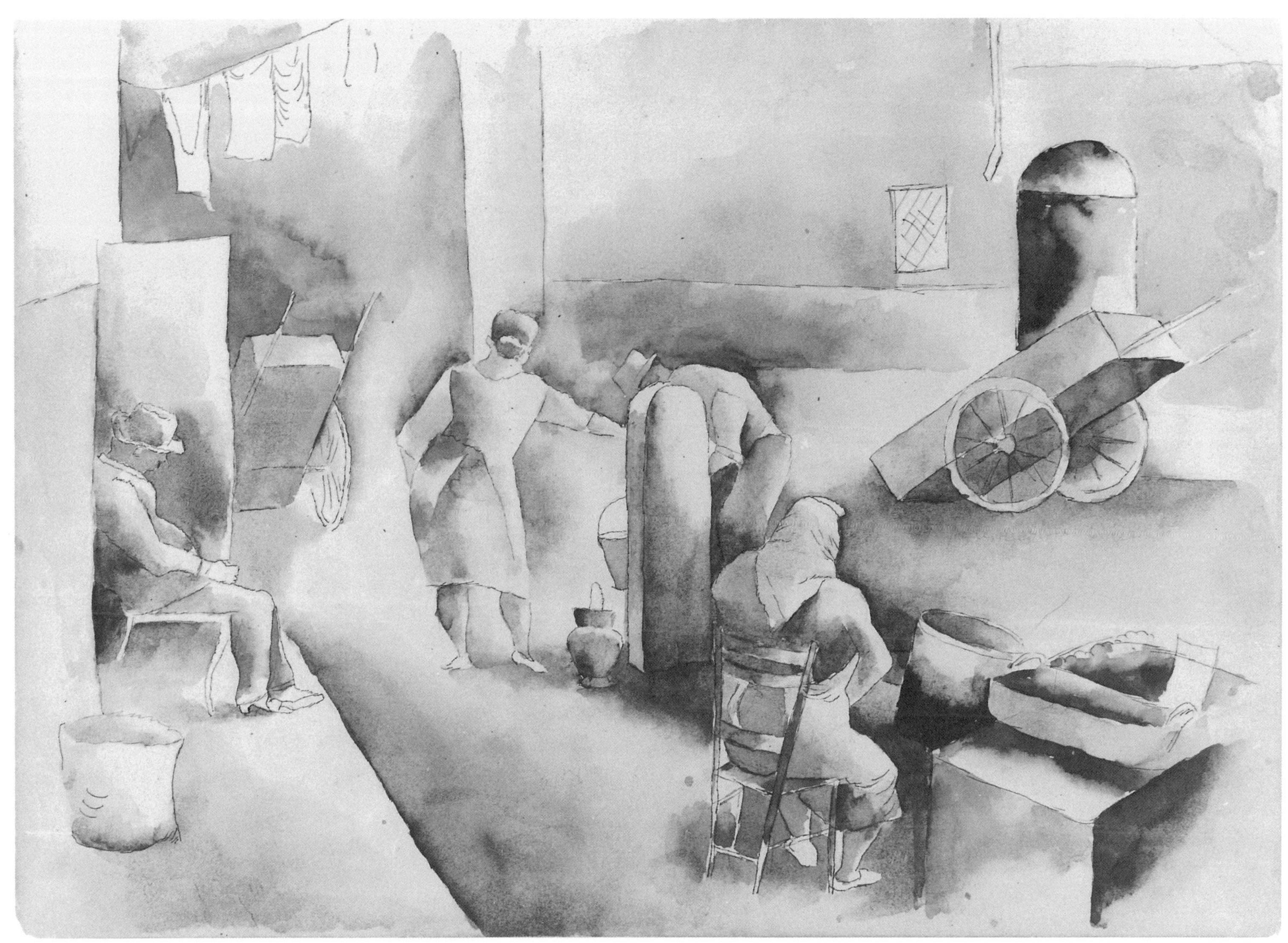

Fig. 53
John Barber
At the Fountain
Graphite, ink and watercolor, 9 x 12 ⅛
Collection of Dr. Margaret De Ronde Barber,
on loan to The John Barber Memorial Collection,
Bayly Art Museum of the University of Virginia

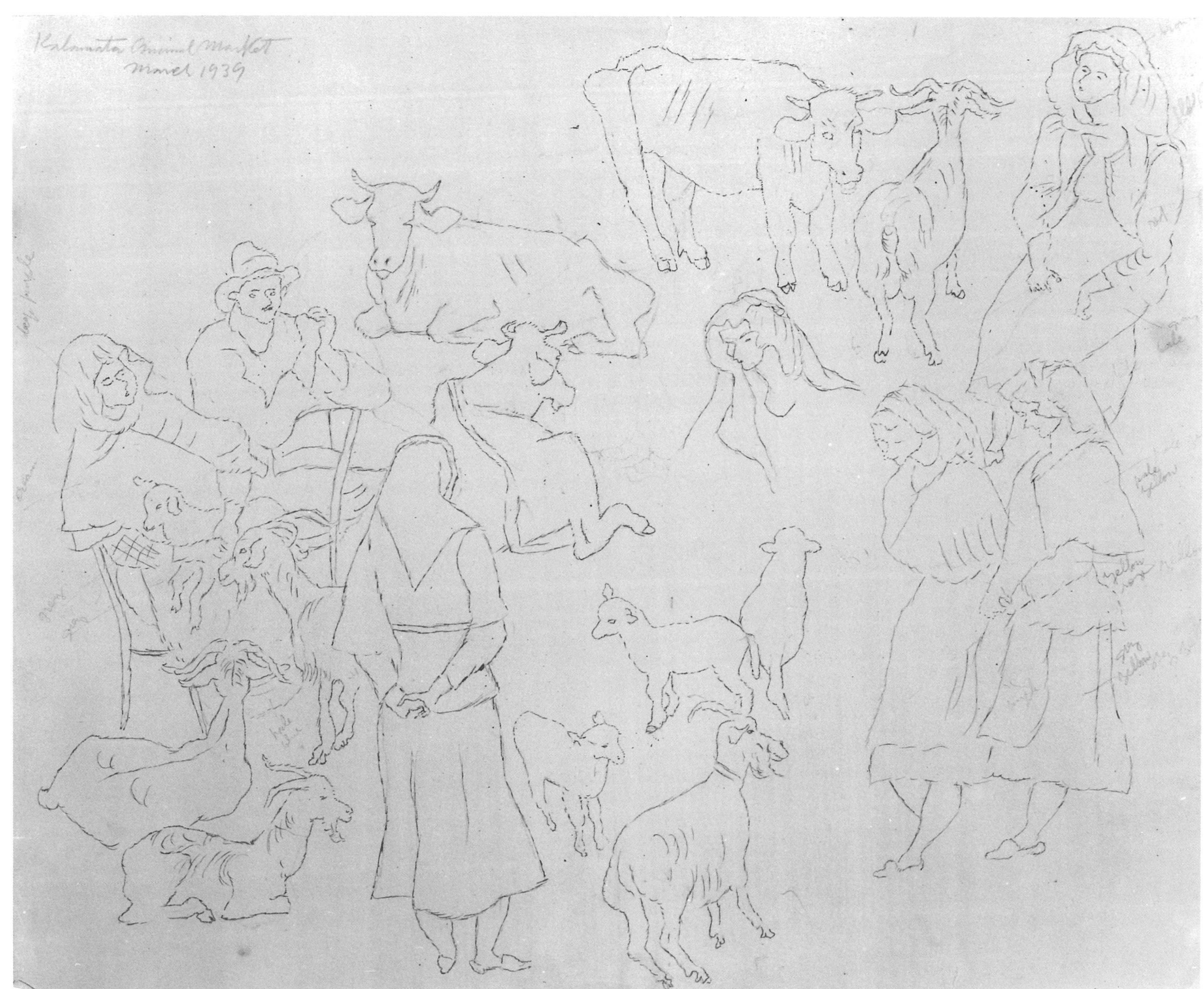

Fig. 54
John Barber
Kalamata Animal Market, March 1939
Graphite and ink, 11 ³/₄ x 14
Collection of Dr. Margaret De Ronde Barber,
on loan to The John Barber Memorial Collection,
Bayly Art Museum of the University of Virginia

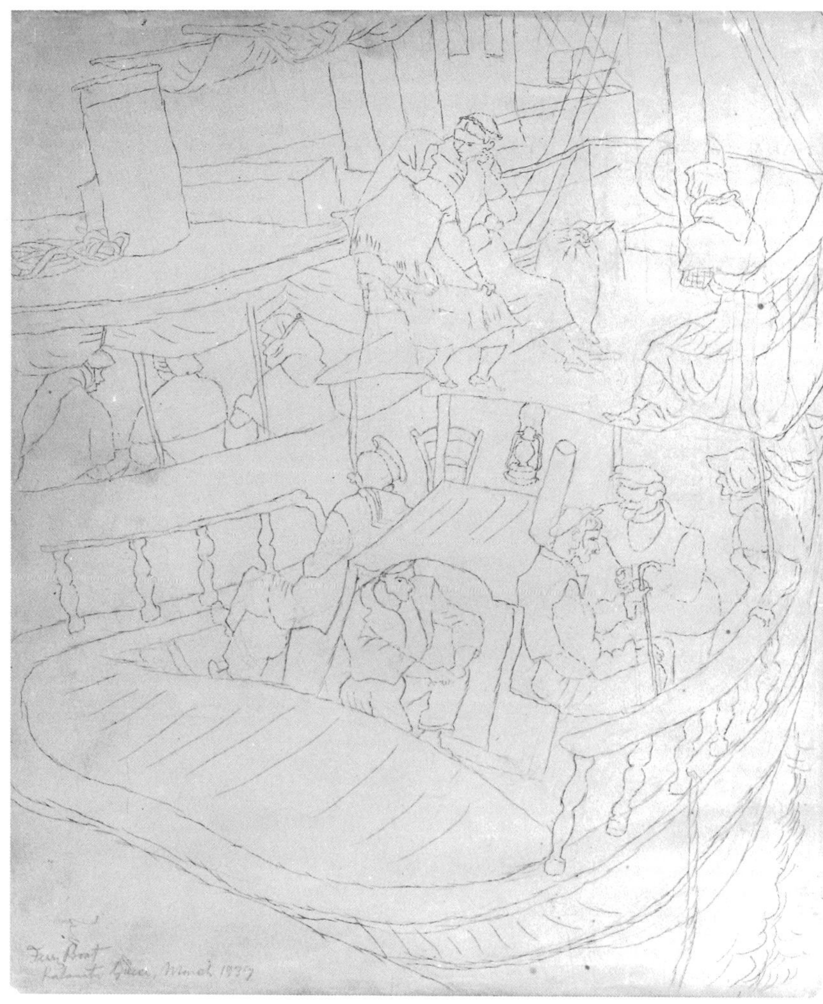

Fig. 55
John Barber
Ferry Boat, Kalamata, Greece, March 1939
Graphite and ink, 14 ³/₄ x 11
Collection of Dr. Margaret De Ronde Barber,
on loan to The John Barber Memorial Collection,
Bayly Art Museum of the University of Virginia

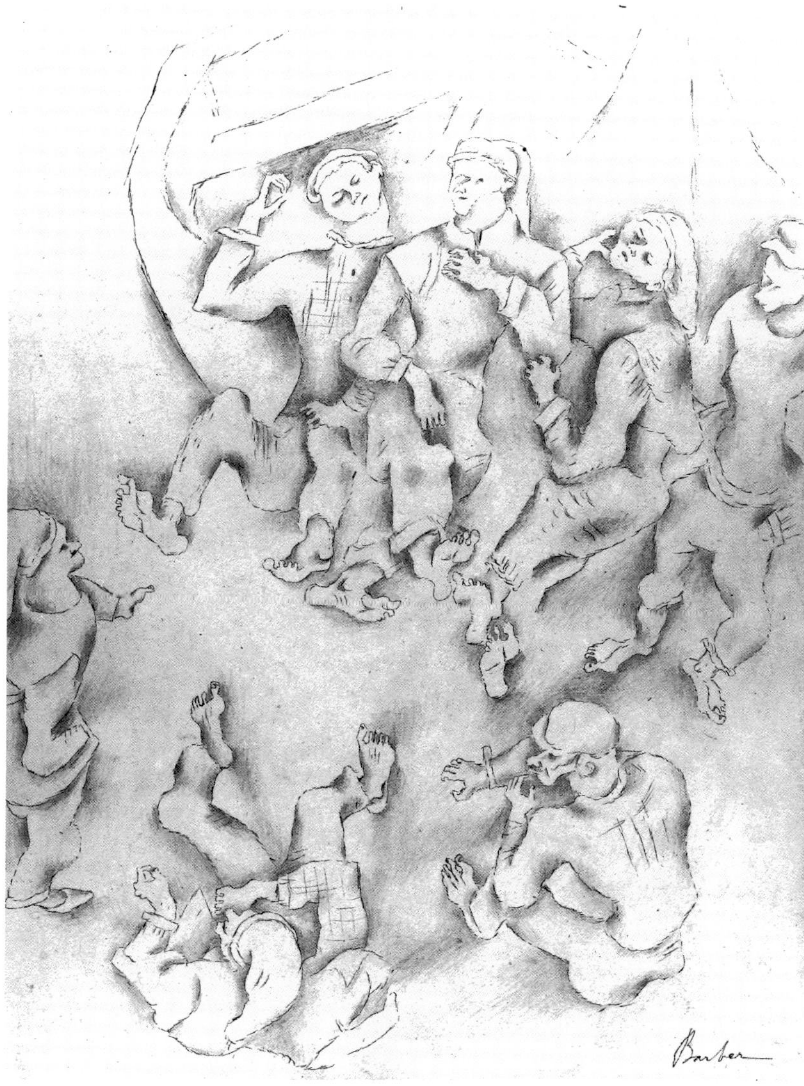

Fig. 56
John Barber
Barefoot Greek Sailors, March 1939
Graphite and ink, 11 ¹/₄ x 9
Collection of Dr. Margaret De Ronde Barber,
on loan to The John Barber Memorial Collection,
Bayly Art Museum of the University of Virginia

VIII. Travels, 1939, 1941

Travels, 1939, 1941

AN ARTIST'S ODYSSEY

Developed by Barber from the draft of a letter to a friend in America, written on stationary of the American Express Visitors Writing Room, Athens, March 2, 1939. The essay is here given in its entirety.

Standing on the promontory overlooking the Danube at Belgrade that early spring day of the fateful year 1939, seemed symbolic of the storm soon to break again over Europe. This was the spot where the first World War shells fired by the Austrians fell on the fortress on July 28, 1914. It is really an ancient Turkish citadel, built during the centuries when the Empire of the Sultans ruled over the greater part of southeastern Europe.

Journeying by way of Italy and slowly winding my way through the Balkan peninsula, I, an American artist, was en route towards ancient Greece, as though instinctively trying to gather as many of the fruits out of the fecundity of art and culture of ancient Hellas, while there was yet time. There always seems such pathos when one attempts to connect once again with the heritage of order and beauty derived from that classic land before the string is broken. The feeling that the whole civilization and social order based on the Hellenes is finally coming to an end haunts everyone.

Ironically enough, the nearer I get to the "Glory That Was Greece" the greater the dilapidation and chaos. Some invisible force is trying to point out the consequences when an era comes to an end and the centuries it takes to rebuild it. After two thousand years the Balkans, although located in the very heart of the past Greek and Roman civilizations and the Byzantine one that followed until 1453, are today the most primitive and lacking in all that bespeaks a developed society. Perhaps one of the main reasons for "dictatorships" in these lands is the belated attempt to bring them forcibly into line with the rest of Europe. In the meantime, this happy-go-lucky people suffers.

In my railway compartment on the way toward Greece sat a distinguished-looking old gentleman and his wife. He was the dean of the juristic body in a port on the Dalmatian coast. To a foreigner he dared to express in French that he is completely at sea nowadays as far as laws are concerned. The "Ukase" changing from day to day to suit the needs of the dictatorships is the law of the land.

As the train rolls southward through the whole length of old Serbia and Macedonia, I see sights incredible for Europe. Similar to the "kraals" of South Africa where the Kafirs are kept in seclusion when not slaving in the mines, tiny thatched-roof huts, huddled together within a straw enclosure, form a community. Surrounding it there is always a stagnant pool where a few ducks float, and some black pigs lie in the mud. The roads are only mud tracks. Peasants wearing conical-shaped hats of sheepskin drive around in vehicles reminiscent of those one sees in prints of old Russia.

In spite of the kindness and traditional hospitality of the Balkan peoples, the jitteriness of Europe is manifested by the same vexatious passport, visa, and monetary regulations at every frontier. One's cash is taken in hand and counted piecemeal. Everyone is suspected of being a spy, especially an artist with sketchbook under arm. In examining the sketchbook, they would turn every page upside down, for to them even an innocent enough looking drawing might actually conceal some secret war plan or map.

On reaching the Greek border, there is a comic opera interlude. A detachment of Hevzones (Greek highlanders in kilts) are posted the length of the station platform to salute the train and the newcomer into Greece.

On my way to Athens I stopped in Salonica—the port made famous by the First World War. The city of the Thessalonians of Biblical memory is still an example of Turkish misrule under the regime of the Sultans. In spite of a quarter of a century of Greek occupation, it retains an Asiatic aspect. Incredibly narrow, unpaved streets, small wooden houses crowded together at different angles, and some open spaces where stray goats promenade.

The landscape of Greece has not the sweet beauty of Italy. It is nature in all its ferocious grandeur—like the fantastic scenes in Gustave Doré's engravings of Dante's *Inferno*. The train winds on its single trackway by the ledge of dizzy precipices through tunnel after tunnel into Athens.

Strikingly characteristic of this capital is the complete absence of women in the streets and public places. Even in the great produce markets, it is the men who stroll around to do the marketing.

A modified harem system still prevails in family matters, together with other Moslem customs and habits Christians so readily acquire when their lands become provinces under the rule of the Crescent. The Greeks are so conscious of this fact and feel themselves so orientalized that when they speak of other lands on the Continent, they say: "In Europe things are so and so, etc."

The entire male population seems to be eating in restaurants—and at all hours. The *"pièce de résistance"* is mostly soup of all kinds. The kitchen and dining room are one. The cooking is done near the door on immense stoves where the copper kettles display the different soups. You point to the kind you like. The waiter fills a plate, rushes with it to the cashier's desk, and, taking a precious can, similar to those used by our railway men to grease axles, rapidly sprinkles some olive oil into the soup. To take the "curse" out of the grease, a piece of lemon is served. The tablecloths are always a mosaic of the foods consumed by previous guests—a sort of bill of fare giving an idea of the *"plats de jour."* No one ever dreams of changing them.

Turkish coffee is the ritual finishing off a meal—this not being a wine drinking country, though producing it for export. Everyone goes to the sidewalk cafe where they sip this ingredient while smoking the nargilsh, continuously twisting between their fingers the string of amber beads men of all ages seem to carry. This is just another oriental habit. The coffee is cooked in a container two inches high but having a handle two feet long. The Greek dexterously maneuvers it around some smoldering ashes, towering over the utensil, till it comes to a boil. You take two or three sips—that's all there is to it—the rest is sediment.

In Athens it is obligatory to have insomnia. Sweet nostalgic tunes, half sentimental, half voluptuous, float through the night till about 5 A.M. In the basements of taverns men, and only men, sit huddled together while a primitive orchestra is "at it." Every little while two or three of the guests get up to have some fun. They start wiggling their abdomens in a sort of "houtchy-koutchy" dance with arms flying over their heads in bacchanalian manner.

The Greeks love to be photographed in national costume—sort of *"banditti"* regalia, consisting of white, anatomically tight breeches, fluffy ballerina-like kilts, zouave vest, and fez tilted rakishly. On their feet, a one-piece, rawhide moccasin with a red pompon. A broad leather belt has a 17th-century revolver stuck into it; its cannon is so long the trigger is visible. They pose with one hand holding onto an enormous old rifle, the other holding the never-missing amber beads.

In the center of the city and almost never out of sight, the famous Parthenon stands majestically on the Acropolis Hill. The spotlights thrown on it at night give it an illusion of unreality—like a mirage in the skies—as it appears suspended in the darkness.

The Parthenon and the other architectural gems have become the shrine of Europe. With this achievement ancient Greece has proven that art is inseparable from life as it could be lived in an advanced civilization. It typified the soul of the race and the reason of its being. Through the centuries it proved a close human touch and was a sign that we change but little, if any. All other human endeavors become outmoded in time and sometimes even ludicrous, while a Venus de Milo will be marveled at forever. Art shows man's kinship to God because it is creation, and its mystery will ever baffle man's mind and fill him with wonderment.

While climbing the rugged paths leading to this famous plateau-like hill, I was struck by an astounding sight. On the slopes, and even in crevices under the splendid columns, are miserable huts artfully put together out of nondescript material—tin cans, tar paper, and stray pieces of wood. The inevitable

clothesline sways in the breeze. The ubiquitous goat—the cattle of Greece—jumps about from ledge to ledge, and a few half-naked children run around.

One wonders at the ever-present proximity of grandeur and decadence. Perhaps some jealous god tries to frustrate man's attempts at magnificence and thus prove his earthly limitations.

Modern Greece is not a happy land. It suffers the same maladjustment as does all of Europe. The "iron-handed dictatorship" amounts to actual martial law. The pressure this government exercises strangles business and industry; businessmen feel that the State seeks to take over everything. Our "New Deal" tactics seem mild in comparison. Banking has practically been nationalized, all financial institutions having been absorbed by the State-controlled Bank of Greece which has the sole right to foreign exchange transactions. The number and cipher on each dollar bill is carefully noted before you get Greek drachmas in exchange.

Here is a mild-mannered people. Their kindness and hospitality, though greater than that seen anywhere else in Europe, is not of the primitive peasant kind. Utmost elegance is shown in their attitude and consideration toward a *"xenos"* or foreigner, and the pride each one takes in expressing politeness bespeaks an ancient tradition. They are a Mediterranean people and not given to melancholy brooding like the Nordics; but one is conscious of the pressure under which they live—their readiness to respond to any violent attempt at change, anything to break the strain. In fact, an undercurrent exists which is similar to that perceived everywhere in Europe, bringing with it a readiness to march into battle as a form of escape.

An important factor resulting from my study of antiquity is a renewed confidence in Democracy—so on the defensive in these totalitarian days. Art has its inception in the soul of the people, the only form of expression truly representing it, and was brought to the pinnacle of its perfection during the great democratic era of ancient Hellas. Most people are deceived by the fact that the secular and ecclesiastical despots of the Renaissance patronized the arts; this was only a pretext used as a means for self-glorification and as a cloak to give tyranny a gentler appearance.

On leaving Greece by sea I embarked at Piraeus. It is thrilling to find the same famous horseshoe-shaped harbor one reads about in the school history books. As the ship slipped out of the port, it was amusing to see the name "Sex Appeal" painted on a little rowboat tied to an old Greek tramp steamer.

Though it is three months before the outbreak of the Second World War, the ships plying the Mediterranean are full of troops. The Italian steamer calling here comes from Rhodes, renowned by the exploits of the Crusaders. It is part of the Dodecanese group of islands lying off the Turkish coast of Asia Minor and annexed by Italy during the Tripolitanean War of 1911. The soldiers on board are men in their forties—reservists called back to the colors and now on their way to Italy on leave. They told me there are 20,000 men on this island ready to invade Turkey in case that country joins Germany's enemies. The officers are also from the reserve—men of distinction and intellect with no enthusiasm for organized massacre. Among them was the aesthetic-looking nephew of a cardinal, a young man very cosmopolitan in his sympathies and who no doubt will one day be at the helm of a future humane and confederated Europe.

When these officers found a stranger from America talking their language, all their Latin warmth and enthusiasm came to the fore, and, if anything, their attitude was one of compassion toward those on the other side of the barricade. In fact, I found that same lack of hatred for other nations in every country in Europe before this war broke out. Everywhere there was a fatalistic consciousness of the impending catastrophe.

The landing is at Brindisi at the extreme southern end of the Italian boot. In contrast to the newer totalitarian dictatorships in the Balkans, the Italian brand seems to have had its rough edges worn off by time. All border requirements are only formalities, and the officials readily facilitate matters.

To reach the French border from this port I was compelled to cross the whole length of Italy. To an American used to the ways of peace it comes as a shock to see to what extent the influence of years of war and war spirit has on a land of song and romance.

At every vantage point along the arteries of Italy, on wall and railroad stations, are painted in large letters bellicose quotations from Mussolini's speeches. As example: "For England the Mediterranean is a route—for us it is life itself," or, "Long live the Rome-Berlin Axis" and other exaltations of Il Duce and derision of democracy.

The people look grim and gray and ill-dressed. About the only thing left profitably to tax is food. Dire results are the consequences of such a measure on a poor population—but excessive armaments must be paid for. Hotel men whispered to me that people go without food for two or three days a week.

One feels that these descendants of Imperial Rome have by this time rid themselves of the primitive warrior spirit still pestering humanity at large. They are imaginative, musical, and love the good things of life. They abhor war, even though their high school boys are given rifle drills after school in the public parks of the cities.

During the Munich crisis of September 1938, when the rest of Europe mobilized, the anti-war feeling ran so high that Il Duce dared not do likewise—many tell you this now. The contention was that the women were ready to come out rebelliously into the streets to prevent their men from going away.

Whether it is the climate or a long tradition of art, music, and religion, the Italian people have not changed through eighteen years of a Prussianized state. If anything happens to this regime, they will shake it off with the theatrical elegance so characteristic of Italians.

An American cannot fail to notice, with an inner feeling of satisfaction, the prestige the United States enjoys among the masses in these parts of the world. Not only are they conscious of its humanitarianism, but what is more important, it is the only "power" not looked upon with suspicion as a "land grabber." However, it is well known that America is the ultimate deciding factor in any worldwide issue because of the weight of its wealth and power.

Of all my experiences on the Continent, there was none so delightful as reaching Paris in the very early summer. Gray most of the year, it is bathed in sunshine at this season, and the picturesque terrace cafes are filled by an elegant, cosmopolitan crowd. One has the impression that this is the only city where those who can afford it flock for temporary relaxation in this oppressive industrial era. The very atmosphere of a Parisian summer is impregnated with the spirit of romance and gives the illusion that the joys of life are within reach.

This is the normal Paris—but unfortunately these were not normal days. So far as the rest of the city was concerned, this was another side of the picture. In the sections where the bulk of the population lives, the impact of war's imminence was already felt. Small business was at a standstill. Many of the middle-class had rented little houses in the provinces as shelters in case death started to rain from the skies. To prevent an early exodus the Municipality had to post regulations ordering the public utility workers to remain at their posts. Every Thursday at noon there was a deafening roar of factory whistles and sirens lasting several minutes. This was the signal to be given in war-time at the approach of enemy planes. Every member of each family was in possession of a gas mask supplied by the fire department. In spite of the grim side, a stay in Paris is the crowning glory of any travel through Europe—especially before returning to America. For myself this interest was intensified by the professional adventure and thrill of painting the portraits of men of prominence. One was our Ambassador to France, William C. Bullitt.

Mr. Bullitt, a man of great personal magnetism and culture, enjoys, through his own making, a special status in France. His diplomatic abilities and statesmanship are highly appreciated by the government of France. He has often been accorded the unusual honor to a foreigner of fulfilling missions normally assigned to members of the Cabinet—such as unveiling memorials and speaking at patriotic occasions.

In his speeches, in perfect French, he knows how to interpret the true spirit of France and has thus won the hearts of the populace to an even greater extent than Edward VII when Prince of Wales during the Victorian era. Though not a Parisian boulevardier, as was the late monarch, Mr. Bullitt became beloved of the masses.

Here was a stranger, a man from the other side of the Atlantic, who felt with them and was aware of the coming tragedy. He was often front-page news in the Paris press in attempting to awaken the somnolent New World to the danger threatening all. Every man, woman, and child in France knows of "Monsieur Bouleet." Priests told their simple parishioners of this "Prince Charming" who is the *"Grand ami de la France"* in this hour of need. Never before has an American been so beloved and no foreigner so popular in this land, not usually given to adulation of anything *"étranger."*

Mr. Bullitt has an enormous capacity for work, sleeps little and dictates at all hours of the day and night to his faithful secretary, Carmel Offie, a sort of Good Man Friday, who never lets the "Boss" out of sight. Not being able to absent himself for long from his numberless tasks, he takes his weekends in the forest of Chantilly, thirty miles from Paris, where he has leased the Chateau of St. Firmin with two thousand acres of ground. The Institute of France, as the French Academy is called, is endowed with the ownership of this estate—probably the most beautiful in France. It is located close to the Chateau of Chantilly—the gorgeous Renaissance gem built by Francis I. The famous race track where the French Derby takes place is in immediate proximity. A brilliant garden party is given by Mr. Bullitt every year on occasion of this event. The elite of France is invited. The terrace of this chateau slopes toward an octagonal pool where the Prince de Condé held nautical Venetian fetes for King Louis XIV. Mr. Bullitt is a great host and loves to give informal dinner parties usually ending in a bridge game lasting till midnight.

I dislike bridge, and so did another of the guests at one of these dinners—a man who was four times Prime Minister of France. French statesmen enjoy being dilettantes. They dabble in literature and the fine arts and love to carry an air of cultivated Bohemianism. Nothing pleases them better than giving the impression that politics is not their main concern.

Frankness being a natural characteristic of the French, a tête-à-tête between statesman and artist, while appearing to watch the others playing cards, would be most cordial. The conversation naturally turned to the tense situation at that time and the chances of Russia signing up with the Allies—also, different intimates of his—personalities that played great roles in shaping Europe's fate during his long career.

While professing great friendship for the former Prime Minister, Socialist Léon Blum, he frankly expressed the opinion that were it not for the fact that M. Blum, while in office at the time of the Spanish War, allowed himself to be duped by the British with their pro-France and fake "non-intervention," the "betrayal of Munich" would not have taken place. He said: "France was compelled to sign when she discovered a 'Third Front' at the Pyrenees fortified by the Nazi and Italian interventionist armies." These were the days when France was breathlessly awaiting the outcome of the protracted negotiations with Russia—but strange was the attitude in allied countries.

A characteristic illustration of their point of view was displayed by an eminent editor while also posing for his portrait. It is not committing an indiscretion to reveal it now. Though desiring the much-needed help Russia could have given France, he hated the Soviets and, yet, with equal vehemence desired a rapprochement. This generally prevalent inconsistency both in England and France doubtless lost them that possibly invaluable support.

Getting in the sittings for the portrait of our Ambassador at such times was a stunt in itself. At best, it had to be squeezed in between times, mostly in the early morning hours, as Mr. Bullitt is an early riser. Although an enthusiastic model and intensely interested in the work, he was continually interrupted. Many a long-distance telephone call during these sittings came from Joseph P. Kennedy, who represents us at the Court of St. James. Mr. Bullitt, being a diplomat of great experience, is often consulted and as he expressed it: "I like to work with Joe," meaning our envoy in London.

During these sittings he gave vent to his bitterness and disillusion over the destruction of Republican Spain. He realized then that it made war inevitable. The Spanish episode, he felt, was a "curtain riser." It taught the dictators that they could strike with impunity as long as the Chamberlain crew of appeasers dominated the democracies. To such countries, weakened morally and militarily, they could deliver a mortal blow before the awakened conscience of Humanity could be rallied.

Being a true liberal and a patriotic American, Mr. Bullitt tried to give the alarm to a doubting world. It seems that one individual, no matter how highly placed, is always helpless to arouse those who will not believe.

With a heavy heart one realizes that all that civilization holds dear—the very patrimony belonging to the entire human race—is in great danger of going up in smoke and ashes. Poor indeed will humanity be if that comes to pass, even if "right" finally triumphs.

AN ARTIST'S MEXICO

Developed by Barber from the draft of an unaddressed letter dated Taxco, October 9, 1941. A short section of the essay is here omitted.

Though at present even a temporary expatriate is looked upon askance by well-meaning people, there is in most of us that latent desire for the stimulant of changed surroundings and the colorful backgrounds of older lands. For an artist it is obligatory in spite of chauvinistic ranting by certain art critics who, since the depression, probably use the xenophobian virus to protect the home market. It is so easy to forget that the world's heritage of beauty and art is a gift to the elect everywhere, prepared to partake of it and learn.

The doors of Europe being closed at present, one naturally remembers that exotic land—"South of the Border." At first the prospect does not seem alluring, when one recollects the sickly-sweet postcard effects and garish colors as depicted on so many canvases. Especially tiresome and monotonous is the stereotyped Mexican shown with the inevitable sombrero.

On crossing the border one is immediately aware of the falseness of those preconceived notions.

The panorama of native life unfolding itself is like a reanimation of frescoes by Giotto. The attire of the women, especially during devotionals, is reminiscent of the Italy of Fra Angelico. There is an austerity and monumentality in their appearance, plus a certain elegance lent by the beautiful folds of their *rebozos*. From a distance they look like porcelain figurines in pastel shades, or like "Tanagras" to those who observe the harmony of the color scheme.

Mexico is the most extraordinary country one could ever visit; it cannot even be judged by conventional standards—our outlook being so different and the ways of a *"mestizo"* race too baffling from our point of view. In a sense this is the real Spain—the Spain of the legend. Mexico is still strongly imbued with the seventeenth and eighteenth century atmosphere due to the unchanging Indian who is a traditionalist par excellence. The architectural style, especially that of the churches, combines Castilian severity of line with Neapolitan color. It is thrilling to step into village churches and see the multi-colored wooden images of saints in most ornate and crudely colored settings. The ensemble puts to shame the weirdest chromatic schemes of our Moderns. Religion is primordial here—but not as we understand it; it is an outlet for the overheated emotions of a race driven frantic by peppery foods plus pulque; the latter is a very potent cactus extraction—"white mule." At least once a week the Indian has to drink to the health of some important saint or archangel at the great church fiesta organized for the occasion. It starts at 6 A.M., when a barefoot brass band of peons marches into town full blast. In a circle in front of the still-deserted church square, they burst forth into a serenade for that particular saint. Without notes or leader, the latest or near-latest popular American songs like "The Beer Barrel Polka" or "Jingle Bells" are being played, continuing intermittently till midnight amidst the pealing of church bells and the noise of firecrackers. As the day advances improvised kitchens—a table, some earthen pots and pans, and a charcoal burner—do a rushing business of peppery concoctions, rolled into *tortillas* which are a great national institution—a half-raw, thin, flat, and round sort of pancake, five inches in diameter, made of white corn flour. It is used to sandwich in all kinds of strange things to eat.

The interior of the Mexican houses of God have nothing churchly about them in smell or appearance. In days of fiesta they look like a florist's and undertaker's establishment all in one. Though the women throw themselves on their knees and stretch out their arms full-length in sign of supplication, everyone has a marvelous time. It becomes a carnival with all that it implies to simple souls with uncontrolled emotions. Life would be drab without a touch of paganism in such lands. Intellectual religions can never mean anything in the tropics—it would perhaps be a misfortune, curtailing a necessary outlet of the kind such people require. To us, their mentality is a strange and closed book—the mysticism and magic of the Aztecs are still latent. They are quick to love and quicker on the trigger; the women use daggers in their quarrels of jealousy.

Courtship is still done in the comic-opera fashion of forgotten epochs. The *innamorato,* with his best friend as helper who zims-zims in accompaniment on his guitar, sings about amour, his hand on his heart. It is bad form for the *innamorata* to ever give a sign of acknowledgment by her appearance at the window even though all lights are on and the family is *d'accord.* All this is in complete oblivion to the rare passer-by in the darkened old Castilian-like street. Family life is still run on strictly patriarchal lines, and the respect for elders is Oriental. They do not kiss a lady's hand as Europeans do, but men and women will stop to kiss their old father's or uncle's hand anywhere in public.

The individual's weaknesses are taken for granted by these Indians, and lapses are considered human and natural—thus putting at ease the stranger who, once away from home, attempts to crash through the restraints of his previous environment. Being a primitive people they are very naturalistic. They accept as a matter of fact those conditions or situations repellent or shocking to what one might consider our more cultivated or perhaps more decadent sensibilities. Three or four smiling little girls would carry on their shoulders a little coffin through the town's square on the way to the cemetery, followed by a few musicians, playing anything but funereal music. Coffins seem to be also a toy of predilection in their love for the *lugubre*. Children eat little chocolate coffins on All-Saints Day, and all through the year real ones are painted in cobalt blue with silvered skulls and bones; it is a tradition inherited from the Aztecs. Lately Mexico City newspapers complained of the proximity to city hospitals of undertaking establishments with coffins piled high in view of all and of their salesmen approaching "accident cases" arriving at the hospital gates. One meets with this phase of existence everywhere in Mexico. Down the road a cavalier would be galloping while holding on to a coffin laid across the saddle; or a group of laborers finishing their noontime *frijoles*—a child's coffin placed on the doorstep would be waiting for one of the *señores.*

Traveling in Mexican trains is quite an experience for one who believes he can find here the equivalent of our democratic American day coaches. They run only one train a day on the twelve-hundred mile stretch from El Paso to Mexico City. It consists of one first-class coach and two for the common herd; out of the latter, half a car is partitioned off for a detachment of infantry in full war equipment. They are not there as a protection against the legendary bandits, who by now have become only a myth, but to keep order among the overcrowded passengers. The Mexican has the well-known Indian trait of running amuck and being really dangerous when under the influence of pulque—if he does not become numb and paralyzed. It takes two days and two nights to cover the distance. The overflow of peons sleep on and under the wooden benches in passage-ways amidst baggage and domestic animals. Like the stagecoach of old, the train makes long stops every few hours, and then the crew and the rest precipitate toward the *cantina* for eats. In-between, they buy *tortillas* and *enchiladas* at every station, brought to train windows by barefoot and pigtailed Indian women. Here again their naturalistic traits are mani-fest—in forever foraging. They do not understand our set hours for eating.

Physically they are a small race—one may call them a nation of five footers. The Aztec Indian-type predominates overwhelmingly, though certain peon tribes are so Mongolian in appearance that the men look like Korean priests with their mustache and the little "vertical" down the chin for a beard.

If the great conquistador, Fernando Cortez, could watch now a Mexican mob at a bullfight or proces-sion, he would realize the uselessness and vanity of conquest. They look and act and feel now just as in Montezuma's time. It is a miracle how they took to Spanish—a million of them speak only the Aztec language. . . .

They have even ceased calling themselves Latin-Americans or Hispano-Americans—now it is just Indolatins as if to prove their tendency toward revert-ing to type. The most outstanding trait of this Indian nation is extreme conservatism. This racial peculiar-ity has been disastrously overlooked by those who led them through continuous social turmoil since the fall of Porfirio Diaz more than thirty years ago. In spite of all reforms and anti-church legislation they con-tinue living and believing as their forebears did.

A group of present-day Mexican peons on horseback or women with papooses strapped to their shoulders look exactly as depicted in the popular prints of a hundred years ago.

For the artist, the lover of the picturesque, and for those who seek even a momentary relief from the colorlessness of a mechanized civilization, Mexico will remain for a long time, yet, an Eldorado.

IX. Love and Death, 1947–1948

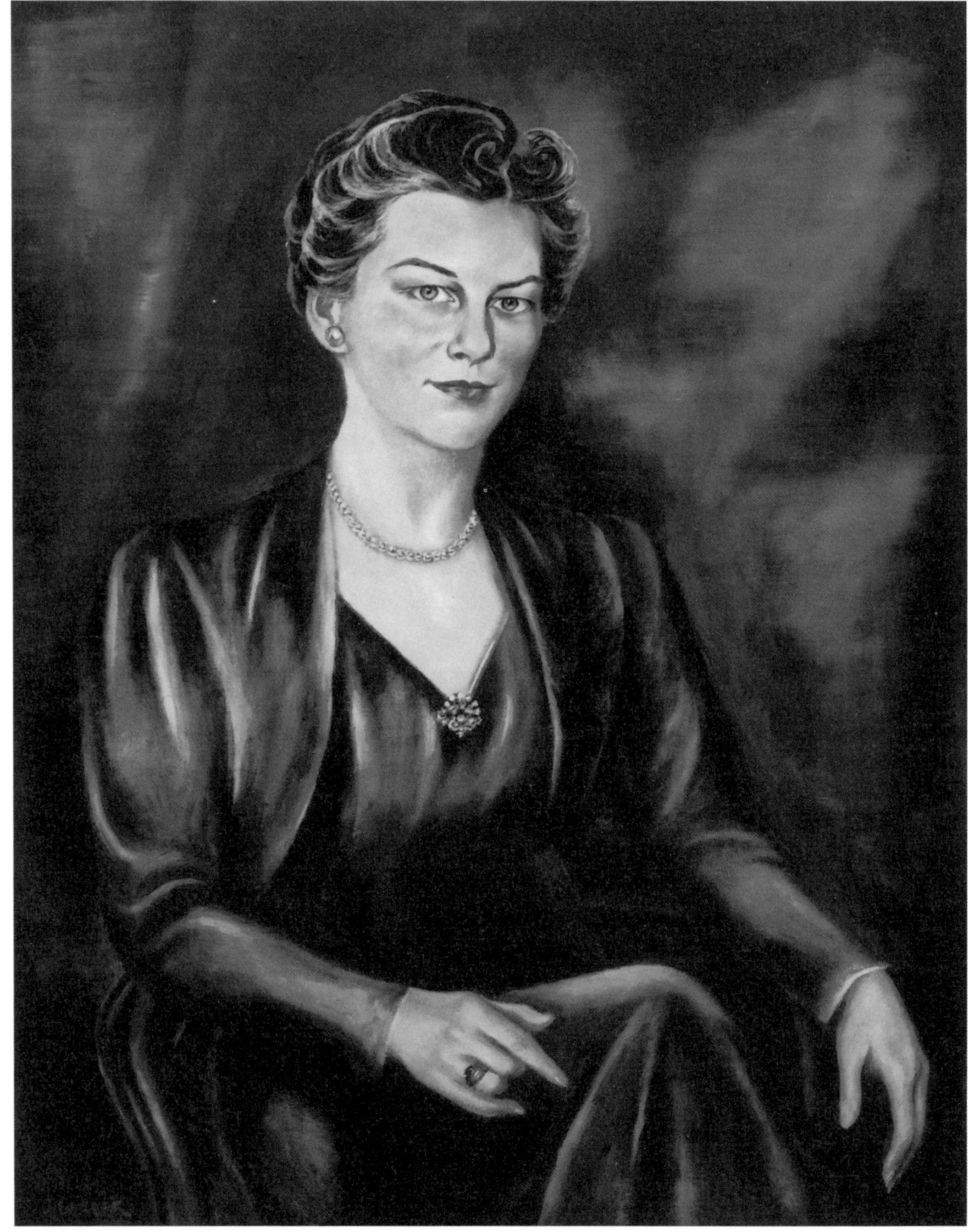

Fig. 57
John Barber
Portrait of Dr. Margaret De Ronde, 1947
Oil on canvas, 36 x 30
Collection of Dr. Margaret De Ronde Barber
Photograph: Michael I. Price

Love and Death, 1947–1948

The following extracts from the letters of John Barber to his future wife Dr. Margaret De Ronde represent perhaps twenty to thirty percent of the corpus. Preference has been given to passages in which Barber comments on his own experience and philosophy of art and life. Spelling, diction, and punctuation have been regularized only to the degree appropriate to the preparation of casual writing for publication.

Hotel Park Plaza
50 West 77th Street
New York

January 4, 1947

Dear Dr. De Ronde:

I somehow feel I should not hesitate to write to you on this matter since you seemed so interested while I painted Mrs. Herring's portrait.

This is not a business letter—I simply would just love to paint your portrait—and for many reasons besides the practical one that there must be an "oil" of so eminent a person in her profession, in whose great future I am firmly convinced.

Proposing this in such a manner entails on me the moral obligation of proving that the motive is most "disinterested" as the French use that word. I therefore offer to do it for the nominal sum of $250 which would just pay for my time and other expenses of coming to do it.

Also, since size of painting and proportional remuneration do not come into this, the painting could either be 25 x 30 (same as Mrs. Herring's) or 30 x 36. So if you decide on it, please don't hesitate to name the larger size as it would allow me more "largess" of background, etc.—provided that size would fit in with your ideas and space. The portrait could be painted in your lovely place during hours when you are at leisure, or weekends.

I send this with my warmest and sincerest sentiments,

John Barber

[New York]
January 21, 1947

Dear Margaret:

I am writing this little letter on an impulse—without having any particular message to convey except warm feelings and that mental well-being we get when our thoughts are directed to someone we like—and who brings harmoniousness.

By the way, did you notice that our good friend Mrs. "X" *did not notice* that your painting was larger—which confirms my theory of the amount of the sense of observation people possess.

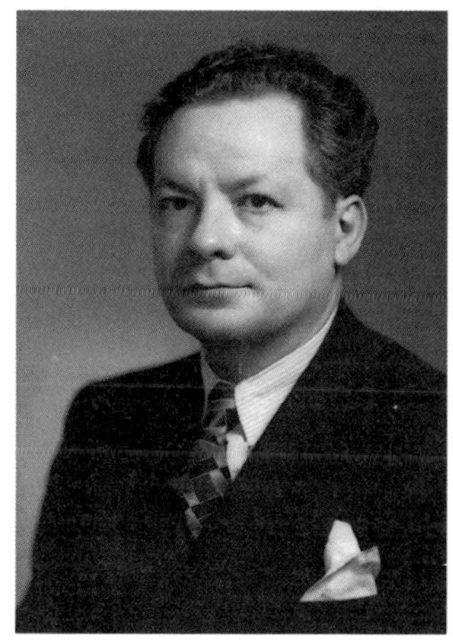

Fig. 58
John Barber as President of Harcum Junior College, Bryn Mawr, Pennsylvania, 1945
Photograph: Merin Studios

It was such a delightful Sunday in every way, that I look forward to the coming Sunday and feel thrilled when I think of the things I will add to the portrait to bring out even more what "I see."

With affection

[New York
January 1947]

. . . I left so abruptly the other evening—in order to leave at all. Everything was too wondrous and perfect and grandly harmonious in every sense. I think we should skip this weekend though, for, as I wrote you before, Sunday is my mother's birthday, and though we will not celebrate for obvious reasons—it would be delicate if I am at least there—more so because she does not demand it. It might also give you a chance to attend to matters you probably neglected on my account. Or perhaps you might make a start on the book that will surely add to your fame, even though you feel about such things exactly the way I do.

So let's count on seeing each other week after next Saturday Feb. 8th. Perhaps I might come in on an earlier train and go around the shops looking for a frame before they close at 1 P.M. and then get in touch with you. But will surely write to you again before then as you can well imagine. . . .

[New York
perhaps April 1947]

Your letter, just received, where you hint that I am "such a loon" for my indecisions and shifting of plans, is like a *coup de grâce.* I realize the sweetness back of your comments, but, nevertheless, I wonder if you do that purposely to get me out of my lair—like bait. If you did, you certainly succeeded, for I cannot hold it any longer! Don't you realize how harassed I am, darling? I am not a temperamental prima donna, not knowing her mind. But perhaps I should not expect that even one of the world's great psychiatrists like you, should be also one of the "oracles of Delphi" (who by the way were proven notorious fakers by history). I must not expect you to be a clairvoyant or seer or mind reader, must I? Every human has his limitations, thank God. Well, you deserve that I be as frank, open, and uninhibited as you are with me, though I assure you it's very hard and a heavy tax on my pride and vanity. I am really a very responsible person, and not temperamental; and that's why I deprive myself of so much, even though it might seem small and petty to you—like coming over whenever I wish (and that's often) or taking you to beautiful restaurants etc. etc. etc. I have to be a very careful engineer running on slippery rails with almost no fuel to draw on. I don't bewail my fate—far from it—it's of my own choice and volition, especially now at my age. If I didn't have yet the hope of painting for whatever years are in store for me, I would be ready to call it quits now—but I am tired of concealing things from you and being misunderstood; for you even made a little crack a few weeks ago about stinginess or avarice or something. It really did not hurt, because I realized you were innocent of the true situation. In truth, I cannot afford this hotel any longer and just have to go to Lansdowne. Creative artists have always suffered from a chronic disease, which probably is only a small pay exacted of them for their gift—opulence must evidently go to the less gifted as compensation. Of course, I am on the other hand delighted to go to Lansdowne for obvious reasons of our own, *n'est ce pas*?

Oh! I could say a lot more—but probably I have said too much as it is.

. . . Now again now, as to our plans. We would like to be out of this hotel by May 15th. There doesn't seem to be any place to move for the summer, so with my brother-in-law's weekly letter begging us to come to Tunis it's a temptation—I said temptation with tongue in cheek, and I'll give you a guess why? I know you know the answer! Life is not simple, is it? Yet I would not want to eliminate the sweet obstacle on my way to Tunis, would you? Of course if I go there I can just paint for years without any worries— and by this I mean the composition or genre pictures (which are my great love in Art). Two years ago in Mexico I did all the drawings for a series of paintings which when finished I'll give a one-man show with. I did not have the slightest opportunity to work on them yet because of college and portraits—but now with none in sight I am naturally tempted to do what I really want to do in life. You see, portraits are not art—(they are plumbing—to keep out the leaks, I suppose). But compositions are supposed to be Art. I am certainly taking you behind the curtains. . . .

Barber's brother-in-law was Marcel Gozland, second husband of Rita Barber.

[New York, May 1947]

It gives me such pleasure reading about all the "monkey business" going on around a female psychiatrist's life during a whole week. I certainly agree with your reflections about this life and the way to live it.

I have taken the second shot yesterday Sunday, and I feel *woozy* today—so don't expect an intelligent letter. I'll just confine myself to facts this time. It's a marvelous idea about May 22nd. It's just right, as it is on a Thursday when my week is always up at the hotel, so it would save us a lot of trouble, headaches etc. if we put the valises, easel (folding one only), and paintbox in the car—with my mother in the back seat and we two in the front—and drive over to Lansdowne on that date, and I am deeply grateful to you for thinking about it.

. . . as for the weekend of the 16th, why not let Hans see you then, as long as you are coming to New York on the 19th, and see me then. By that time I shall be through with my shots too, as I'll get the last one next Sunday the 11th. . . . You'll probably appreciate me that much more because of this lapse of time, as I am such a dreadfully vain and conceited person, don't you think so? and I must be so adored and adulated and pedestaled and worshiped! etc. It's worth waiting till the 22nd just for the fun and comfort of riding back together.

I really feel terrible today from the shot and will lie down as soon as I finish. . . .

[New York, 1947]

I deeply appreciate the beautiful letter describing the country in "poetry and prose." Does a psychiatrist have to be a poet too, besides other things like Juliet, for instance. I suppose it all goes together to complete the picture; for if one is endowed with the zest for life and living, the whole picture becomes colorful and voluptuous and very appetizing. Only few know the taste of nectar when they get it. . . .

I also must tell you that your free, frank, uninhibited manner of expressing your true feelings makes a tremendous hit with me. It's sensational, and perhaps the greatest test of a free individual—not shackled to all the dictates of conventions necessary for this half-witted humanity.

[New York
about August 1947]

. . . perhaps it would be better if henceforth (till we leave) you write to me at 37 Riverside Drive, Apt. 4B, where my mother is staying. I hesitated to have you write me there in the first place because there is a very sick lady there and I don't ever go there to disturb; but as I see my mother all the time she can give me your letters at once. I am staying here there and everywhere but haven't used any fountain as yet for my shaving. But we (my mother and myself) are busy together preparing for the voyage—and, by the way, you have to see to it that she gets her liver serum to take along to Tunis (probably a couple of bottles), and she could keep them in the ship's ice box. . . . Do you know that at last she admits she feels better! I wonder if it is so? or is it because a decision has been made to get her to Tunis—what do you think? Life is funny, isn't it—if it wouldn't be so tragic too, and full of sacrifices. You can imagine that several things are a great sacrifice for me to do at present. You know that, don't you?

You certainly ought to be proud of having a combination Casanova and Marco Polo. Twenty-five loves (mind, promiscuous ones at that) in that many lands. Also in one breath the hope my ship sinks, in the other the long life of 55—for I'll be glad to see that birthday, even though I am supposed to have left it far behind. For a Methuselah I am doing pretty well with my sex appeal. I am out-Goyaing Goya then, and there is hope I'll be like Goethe at 80. More power to us!

You might be able to write again to 37 Riverside, Apt. 4B, for I am beginning to be distrustful of the exact sailing. It might yet be delayed a day or so—for I just phoned the Company and they told me they are not certain yet as to the 11th, which is only day after tomorrow. So it is always with "cargo-passenger" ships where cargo counts, and passengers are just the luxury that takes the curse out of the word "freight.". . .

What an Odyssey or Hegira! After a mutiny of the crew at the last minute at Algiers, delaying the sailing for a day, we arrived at La Goulette—the dismal Arab village at the entrance to the Gulf of Tunis (half hour by car). It was dark and 7 P.M., but within 5 minutes the faithful Marcel [Gozland] appeared with his car, wouldn't let us dine on the ship, had us pass quickly the police formalities, locked our cabin with the baggage, and off we went to Tunis where friends and dinner were waiting. It will not be till tomorrow that the ship will sail into Tunis, and then we go and get our baggage.

What a trip! Two hurricanes of 4 days and nights each, two mutinies, one revolt of the crew, flinging the Customs men off the boat on the docks of Algiers, one serious accident necessitating an ambulance and leaving one man behind. One quarantine of 12 hours at Casablanca (suspicion of cholera). I saw things that added to my mental collection of events, denied to the average static person.

Tunis is very beautiful. The garden of the house has orange trees—they are almost ripe now. The view is very stupendous from the heights of Montfleury (flowery mountain) overlooking the bay of Tunis. The house is very big—enormous high ceiling rooms. We didn't sleep the whole night—each one, mama and myself lying awake full of sadness about Rita—for everything reminded us of her. I could hear her in the next room moving around while I tried to keep quiet. . . .

Rita Barber, wife of Marcel Gozland, died in New York, February 23, 1946.

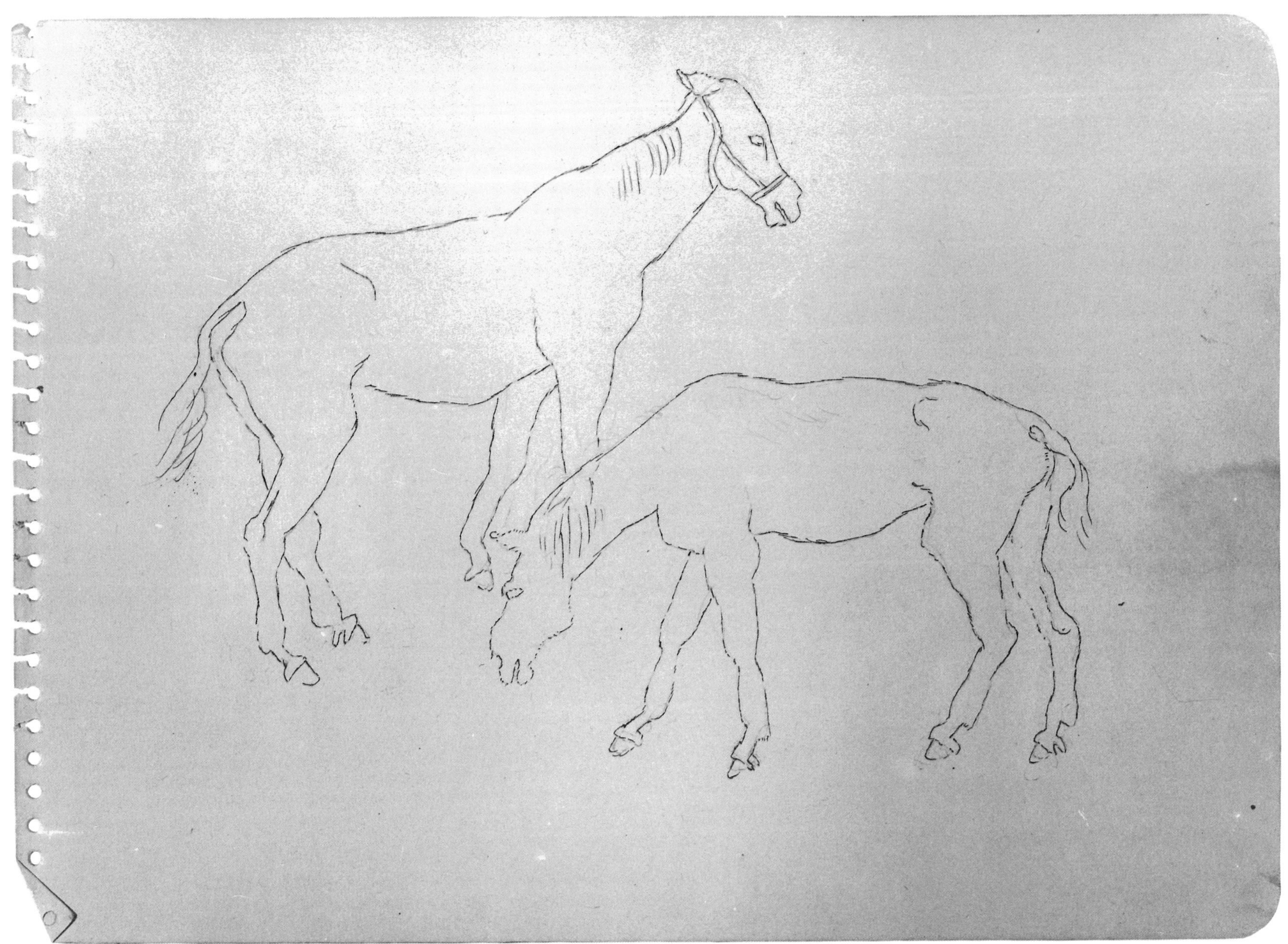

Fig. 59
John Barber
Horses, Tunis, 1947
Graphite and ink, 8 3/4 x 11 7/8
Collection of Dr. Margaret De Ronde Barber,
on loan to The John Barber Memorial Collection,
Bayly Art Museum of the University of Virginia

Fig. 60
John Barber
Tunis, 1947–48
Graphite and ink, 11 $^{5}/_{8}$ x 9 $^{1}/_{2}$
Collection of Dr Margaret De Ronde Barber,
on loan to The John Barber Memorial Collection,
Bayly Art Museum of the University of Virginia

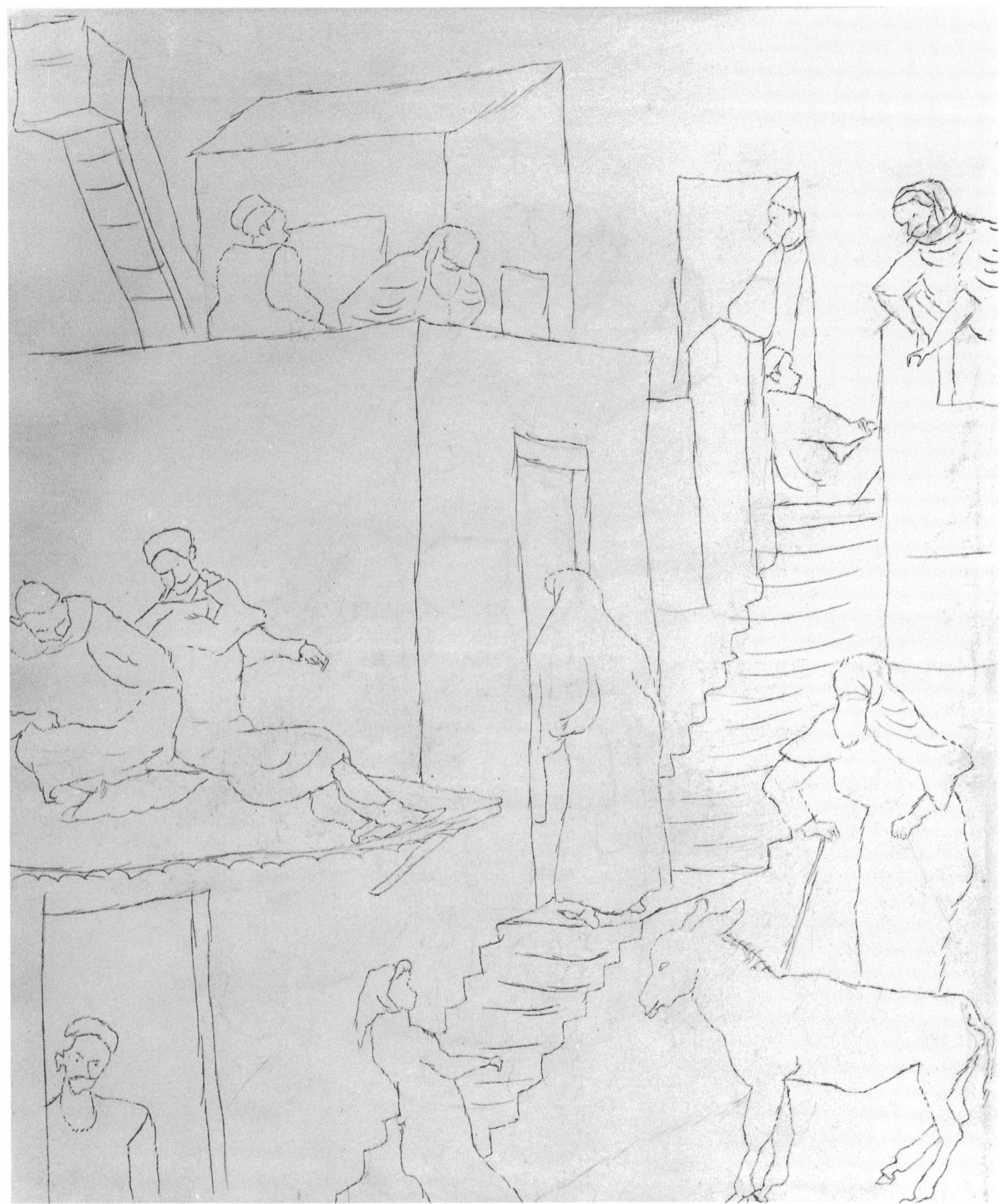

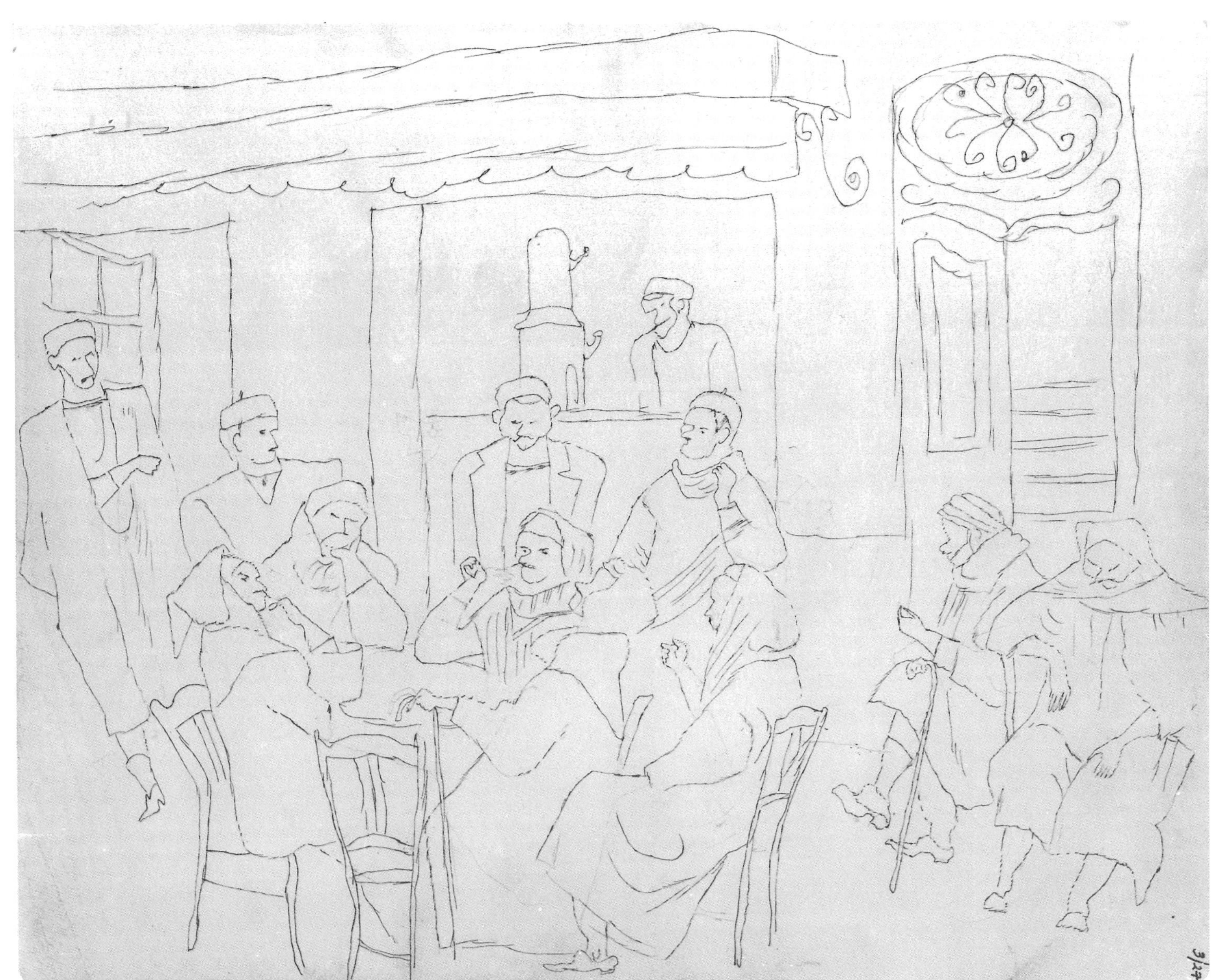

Fig. 61
John Barber
Café, Tunis, 1947–48
Graphite and ink, 9 x 12 $\frac{1}{8}$
Collection of Dr. Margaret De Ronde Barber,
on loan to The John Barber Memorial Collection,
Bayly Art Museum of the University of Virginia

[Tunis]
November 24, 1947

Your letters keep on arriving and injecting sweetness
into my veins. When I finish reading them I bubble
over with all kinds of fantastic answers to all the
things you say—but when it comes to actually writing
them, Basta! This is one of the queerest and most
unexplainable situations in my life, and I marvel how
it all happened—I don't understand it myself. Except
that I paint like a madman in order to have time pass
more rapidly—and also to prevent myself from thinking, planning, or being conscious. I feel caught in a
maelstrom of destiny—no matter which side I look at.
I don't know anything anymore! I adore your blind
faith and your rock-like steadfastness, but when you
write me about my happiness I have to answer you
that I am not aiming at such a thing. I am not aiming
at something that does not exist—(and this is written
without any sense of pessimism). All one can look for
in life is some monkey-business, some uninhibited
abandon to thrills—each in his own way, and according to his desires. One of the reasons I am pushed
toward such countries of "comic-opera," like Mexico
and Tunis, is to get away from the boredom of life
into such make-believe lands—it's for the fun and
monkey-business one sees all around. Happiness as
people understand it is for me just running away from
the grim practicality of life. I guess when I first
opened my eyes I thought it was in God's Heaven—
and ever since, I have steadily refused to see anything
else, and always ran away from the rest. I guess the
easel, instead of the zinc bar and spittoon, is my
refuge. . . .

[Tunis]
November 29, 1947

. . . No matter what happens, I must give you a lesson
in unprofessional psychology—once for all. People of
our quality live only in the realm of love and mag-
nanimous understanding, where such a petty thing as
jealousy does not exist. There are no degrees of
love—there is its absence, or its existence—and also,
above all, there are different kinds, and as far apart as
the poles. I love Giotto, Rembrandt, and El Greco.
One is a mother, one a wife, and one a concubine. . . .
The man who does not love and revere his mother,
does not love anyone. He might have a selfish and
temporary attachment to a female that satisfies him,
but his soul is dead; for love is all-embracing, and
spreads its benign and life-giving manifestations. You
are only a "professional intelligence"—but all things
professional bespeak of death and decay, whether
they are artists, philosophers, or doctors—only shoe
and boilermakers can be professional. In the arts—
which means the mind (and that's the only thing
divine), we are forever apprentices. The biggest fools
are professional philosophers and psychiatrists, as
you so well know—and academic professional artists
haven't the sense of canine quadrupeds. But your sin
is human and forgivable—only you have allowed
yourself to be dragged into temptation. Remember:
"And lead us not into temptation" etc.

Nothing in this world should disturb a "feeble
transitory mortal" if he had the sense of monkeys.
My ravings and rantings to you in letters are not
tragic or serious—it's only my way of getting closer to
you! and wanting to share emotions. Back of it all, I
know better! and am much calmer than I sound.

The cutest thing of all, is when you say: "My
patients are sane in comparison." I am just delighted
to hear that. I would suffer indeed if you considered
me a sane man. Look at them everywhere, coming

home from the offices at 6 P.M. All safe and sane and reasonably respectable religious husbands. I really begin to suspect that "the insane" enjoy it immensely. Think what they are getting away with—no "sane" man could. Yes, thinking about life the way I do, living the way I do, or don't at times, is not really sane—but would I change it? would I put myself in the harness of sanity and decency and reasonableness and responsibility? If I did, then I would really be loco, from my loco viewpoint. Should I feel compassion for you that Destiny threw or flung me into your path? Anyway you are not bored, and had some thrills—and that's a lot in this stupid life. If I wasn't loco I would really worry now—looking into a blank horizon and not even daring to make plans. Just idiotically dreaming for days, of fun and pleasure and thrills, that the future might unexpectedly bring again—somehow, some way. But now you know exactly how I take things, and I am ready even to face defeat. You say in your letter: "I'm just sorry that it is so, and I hope it doesn't defeat you." Darling, you ought to know that "defeat" is the only thing a human can expect, as every day is the march toward the defeat that is death. Victory is only in Paradise, and in the Paradise of the *"épanouissement de L'Amour,"* for which any price is worth paying if we only had the intelligence to realize it—and the luck to find it in this world. . . . You say in your letter that I have plans— no, I have only hopes and desires—the rest is up to the bountiful pagan gods to make possible their realization. I have always lived thus. How then do you think I have survived as an artist for all these decades? "Allah takes care," as the Arabs truly think—yes, of the fools and drunks and "tramp-artists." And I laugh at myself and the whole grand illusion that even psychiatrists take seriously. . . .

[Tunis]
December 25, 1947

I cannot let this day pass without writing to you, though I do it in my room, as the others have gone to sleep. It's eleven P.M. after a quiet day—but in the morning I took Nemo, my sister's Irish fox terrier, to the Kasbah, and sketched there for 3 hours. It was a day warm and sunny, like the end of April instead of December. The Arab kids played with the dog though I had his chain tied to a bottom hole of my coat. The Arabs must like my face, for they show me all kinds of courtesies when I sketch in the Arab city, though their religion is antagonistic to "graven images"—and the kids are wonderful and beg me to sketch them into the compositions. I usually draw horses, donkeys, camels, and Arab Fondouks, and then I draw the Arabs sitting before the Moorish coffee houses, and place them as though they are riding the animals—to the great amusement of the kids watching me—for as you know, I am one of the very rare artists who doesn't mind being watched while working.

We had, the three of us, our Christmas dinner of roast chicken and mashed potatoes and then drove on a "pious pilgrimage" in the afternoon. Fifty kilometers away in the wilderness is the Arab *gourbi* where Mama, Rita, and Marcel hid from the Nazi occupation of Tunis, as Marcel was one of the notables to be taken as a hostage by those beasts. They had to show me that place where they suffered in fear and trembling, with bombs falling. In a room half the size of your kitchen, Marcel and Rita slept and cooked, and mama had her rough couch in the corridor, if you can call it that—with the roof leaking. Anyway it gave mama a ride in the fresh air . . . .

[Tunis, December 1947]

What a wonderful anniversary of the beginning of
"Life, Electricity, and the Pursuit of Happiness"—
and so biologically perfect and within the great laws
of the Universe—whereby the female of the species
picks her mate. There is no more perfect criterion of
the right choice then the electrons aflame at the right
contact—it "turns on" the switch automatically. . . .

I am now working on my 14th painting. I feel
like the monk Fra Angelico in 15th-century Florence,
and I am also living in a cell; for that's what one
room and bed is, where on putting out the lights, the
cold loneliness is no just reward for the accumulated
warmth and sweetness seeking its rightful expression.

[Tunis]
December 30, 1947

. . . I just finished my 15th painting, but I am also
doing a lot of drawing from nature of subject matter
which I will paint sitting by your window one of
these days. I am gathering enough material for that,
and then when that's over we might take a flying trip
together for a few weeks, maybe to Haiti or Guate-
mala to gather further material for me to paint. Oh!
ho! I better stop before I go on and on with beautiful
dreams. . . .

[Tunis]
January 12, 1948

. . . The franc is now 300 for the dollar at black
market rates. Officially it's 119, but the Tunisian
papers carry on the front page, in a box, the daily
exchange rates of the Paris black (forbidden by law)
market—the white so-called official stock exchange,

or Bourse, is completely ignored. That's the kind of
times we live in at present. Everybody has dollars
here—all businessmen have them hoarded, at least by
the hundreds of dollars each—the big fish by the
thousands, etc. That's how governments are obeyed
when they take draconian measures to curb anything.
White bread is also forbidden, but little Arab boys
stop motorists on the road in front of the Bey of
Tunis' palace at Hammana Lif (15 Kilometers from
Tunis) and sell delicious French breads of white flour,
which others (adult Arabs) steal by the sack from
warehouses that are supposed to be bonded. One of
my chief amusements here in the evening is reading
and laughing at the daily accounts of stealing and
pilfering and most imaginative and immoral misde-
meanors. . . . It's unbelievable what comes into their
minds to do, or misdo. That's about the only thing I
like about Tunis, plus the fact that it's such abundant
comic-opera material for my composition. So besides
painting I am gathering enough material (drawings)
to work from for a long time when I return. But
when it comes to the philosophy of life these are the
only people who understand what life is about, and
isn't. They are the only happy people on this earth—
they enjoy everything to the utmost, and the simplest
things are a treat to them—because they have no
surplus of anything to fall back on. It takes a tremendous culture and strength of a higher type to equal
them in the above attributes. . . .

[Tunis]
January 21, 1948

. . . Darling, these two letters "corner me" insofar as
my conscience is concerned. I always want to be
honest with you, in fact I am, because "the graft life
has to offer" to the cheats is too contemptibly small
to "pay me" for being otherwise. I don't know

any more than you do just when I will return! For the first time in my life there seems to be a "low ceiling," and my flights of fancy, which at other times became a reality because I wanted it so, seem somehow balked by something I cannot yet explain. I don't have to reiterate here how much I do want to return to you. You know it! I told it to you in a hundred obvious and naively subtle ways in my previous letters—but the time has come for serious talk, since I feel like a burglar blackjacking Santa Claus as he is about to climb into the chimney bringing Johnnie to the adorable little blue-eyed child. The practical cold realities of life seem to stare me in the face, and I feel like a kid caught by the truant officer and torn away from his happy hunting ground. My happy hunting ground has been my careless self-confidence and unlimited faith in my fool's paradise. And just as Eve steps into it, difficulties beset Adam. Is that the law of life? Is happiness to be won the hard way? Are there hurdles purposely put there in order that, henceforth, we be grateful for the "great gift"? Are those hurdles only mirages? I hope this last might be the answer. Only please, I beg of you as a true love favor, please, please don't be upset or disappointed by my being in such a quandary. I am writing now as I would be talking to you sitting next to you on that couch. I will try to collect my thoughts together and concretize if I possibly can in my next letter. . . .

[Tunis]
January 25, 1948

. . . Every letter I write to you comes straight from the heart, and is also a record of thoughts, even passing thoughts. I am always really discussing things with you. Everything I ever say is neither an arbitrary ukase, for there is nothing despotic about me . . . nor is it something coming out of a cussed, stubborn nature. Whatever I say is always an invitation to your mind to collaborate and give me the benefit of your intelligence-—and thus together we can always cook up something better than separately.

What made me write you that abstract letter was the fact of you waiting for my imminent arrival, and it just broke my heart to think of disappointing you for the moment (not to speak of disappointing myself too). Yes, darling, everything I ever wanted to do I did—but there are limits to being God! don't you think so? I surely do want everything you do, and just as badly—but the practical sides of life are the real despots we must coddle and placate, till they soften and give us "the green light." There are things to be thought about and straightened out somehow; things that would have to be compatible with my pride and also sense of responsibility. In spite of my being a tramp and a fake bohemian, I am not a scatterbrained irresponsible fool—dashing into impossible situations, and then helplessly expecting others to straighten out things. I just adore you, and have the greatest confidence in the world in you and know that to you I can do no wrong . . . but just for that I must always see to it by my actions that you are justified in that glorious opinion you have of me. . . . I never had such unlimited tenderness for anybody before. The whole thing fits perfectly into the pattern of the great mystery. It is our "Passion Play" but a joyous one—giving us great happiness and the complete expression of our individuality with all the warm forces of life vibrating in harmony. . . .

[Tunis]
February 11, 1948

Here we are back from our jaunt to the Sahara desert and the oasis island of Djerba. It was quite an experience from so many points of view, and I have learned a lot. We were riding for hours and hours in the desert, when we suddenly came upon the oasis of Gabes—a forest of palm trees and torrents of springs running through ditches. It was symbolical of life. The whole mass of humanity are pebbles in the desert while here and there at very rare intervals the oasis of a great intelligence—but it's even worse than that— the whole mass from plebeians to generals and politicians are just two-legged hyenas and only here and there a man of art, culture, and wisdom—the three going together to form the "grand intelligence"— meaning God. The others make of this tiny planet a vale of woe and tears because of their abysmal stupidity. . . .

[Tunis]
March 1, 1948

. . . And now for some monkey-business: The Odyssey of the Abattoir. The place is about the distance from your place to Mr. Riley's—down the mountain where I have to be about 7:30 A.M. I wait at the gate for the arrival of the horses and pick the one that looks good. The first time I picked an English thoroughbred. A high stepper with neck like an ostrich. While waiting his turn to be weighed, I filled a page of my sketchbook with a composition of 4 horses, using him as model for all. He looked as if ready to gallop with a Cossack standing up on his saddle, sword between his teeth. Then he was led by a young Arab to the slaughtering pen, facing an open stable where they are given half an hour's relaxation—and what relaxation! It reminded me of the *"Jardins d'Amour"* of feudal times, where ladies and gentlemen of the courts of Provence of the 14th century used to "relax" to the accompaniment of the troubadours. The stallions innocently parade around their tempting appendix to excite the equine ladies, and the attack begins and ends with the swiftness of lightning—to the great amusement and delight of the Arab butcher helpers. All I can say is that horses are "lousy lovers," and I pity the poor mares. It's all over before she can get her breath! How ironical to have such an *"Antichambre de l'Amour et de la Mort."* Then the horse is taken and tied to the wall, and an Arab butcher jabs a long knife into his chest. Like a fire hydrant a cascade of blood spurts. . . .

So, darling, stop taking seriously my calling science a fake. Everything is, and everything isn't. Depending on mood. As I wrote you once before, I would not have you be anything else than a doctor, for it is traditional, the bond between doctors and painters. The doctor spills it—the artist paints with his blood. There is the famous portrait of Dr. Gachet, the great friend of van Gogh. The lesson of anatomy where Dr. Tulp of Amsterdam posed for Rembrandt. There are the portraits of the doctor friend of the famous Philadelphian Thomas Eakins. And the way most people say "Some of my best friends are Jews" (especially those that hate them), so I can say: "Most of my best friends the world over are doctors." So . . . stop grumbling about my iconoclasm. It applies to everything human, including myself, that's why I never take myself or my art seriously. I would be a successful artist if I did—but thank God you wrote me you don't want me to be a successful artist, so that made me happy, for no one is more conscious than I of *"Sic Transit Gloria Mundi."* . . .

[Tunis]
March 2, 1948

This is mama's birthday, and what more fitting day to give you the treat of something definite as to our plans and what I have up my sleeve. It's only two weeks since I was despairing about mama, but even such a short time can make a lot of difference. The latest opinion of the doctors is that mama will survive this ordeal, and I can therefore look forward to happier days to come and make some plans. So here it is. We will leave end of April—the 24th is a sailing for Marseille and then the 12-hour train to Paris. And now here comes the proposed project which, of course, includes you in a *big way*. You will come to Europe and sail back with us! but a bit later. You will fly to Copenhagen by July 14th (remember last year in Maine—the same day). Spend with us a month or 3 weeks in Denmark, then 10 days to 2 weeks in Paris, and sail from Cherbourg or Le Havre either on the S. S. America or S. S. Washington the beginning of September. And here is how this happened. I figured it all out that by April 24 she will be strong enough (and the doctors assured me and approve of the plan). . . . The doctors and all of us thought it would not be wise to arrive in America in June (for it couldn't be before) when the great heat and humidity starts for months—very pernicious for an anemic person. We chose Denmark for the following reasons: Climate cool and invigorating. The only country in Europe with meats and dairy products and pasteurized milk in abundance—and cheap when you have dollars. For the three of us it won't cost as much as for one in the States (in the mountains or other resorts). That will settle your vacation problem in a grand way. Will be your opportunity to be in Europe—and most fitting of all to see Paris for the first time with me. Also Copenhagen is the Paris of the North—a lively city of cafés and good food and

Danish pastries and Smörgåsbord and the finest beer in the world. And that's one country in Europe I have never seen—so it will be a novelty to me too. So when we reach Paris by May 1st, we will stay with friends for a few days, or maybe 2 weeks, make our reservations on the U. S. Lines for 3 tickets, for by the end of August all schoolteachers and tourists have already sailed back, so in early September we will not be crowded. In Denmark we will eat good steaks, drink good dark beer, sit before cafés and enjoy life in every way with you for those few weeks you will be with us—and then how wonderful it will be to sail back together even if on arrival your car isn't there at the pier. . . .

[Tunis]
March 10, 1948

Another letter of March 3rd arrived—all of them stressing that I be practical, use sense, etc. Day before yesterday I answered at once to the impact of the two letters though my heart was bleeding and still is, though mama seems better—she walks and she eats with appetite for the first time in her life—and yesterday afternoon while sitting in the garden back of the house, I dashed off a little portrait sketch in oils of her, as she has a nice pink coloration on her face in contrast to the way she looked before [Pl. 20]. Her morale is good and she keeps assuring me she will get well. . . . She is far from being an invalid. Even cooks some of her fine dishes, like the Arab coos-coos, and sews. So maybe I exaggerated her condition to you. But all this is not the reason for writing this letter, rather it is to answer a few personal things concerning you and me, maybe misunderstandings which are bound to be between two complex individuals till time teaches them to know more about each other.

In the first place, there is an undercurrent of rancor on your part, or seems to be, about me not thinking you have any sense or my not having confidence in you as a doctor or for other opinions. Darling, you should know once for all that I always loved you the more for not having any sense or for being an "ignorant psychiatrist," as I used to call you to your face to your apparent delight. Everybody has sense and is practical, but I never met anyone as intelligent as you. Intelligence is divine and abstract and spiritual—sense is earthy and commonplace and half-witted compared to the true values that aren't petty and immediate. "X" and "Y" have sense and are practical—that's why "Y" drinks herself to insanity to escape the grimness of being sensible and practical. I wouldn't even speak of "X"'s attempts to escape from the slavery of knowing how and facing facts. Sense is for the "battle of existence" but who wants to exist? Do you think I had any sense or practicality to give my life to a calling that is not useful, cannot be worn, eaten, etc.? So don't ever expect me to try to have those qualities. Yes, I probably could dragoon myself into it but I would cease to be me. I have somehow managed to drag through life in a "monkey-business" fashion and get fun and wealth (of my own invisible kind, of course) out of life and probably will continue so in spite even of myself.

As for confidence. How can I have confidence in anything living and fallible like a human being. I might as well have confidence in a volcano—and it all works on the same principle. Do you think I have any confidence in myself?—perish the thought. Everything a human being does is a mistake—when the result is successful, it's only accidental, because of propitious circumstances—and the wisest strategy of life can go askew for the adversity of events befalling it. And above all, darling, nothing in a human's short life is important—so don't please attach any importance to what I say regarding faults in you, or appar-

ent disrespect for you or your abilities or opinions. The very fact I write you such a letter (which I never did before to anyone) is enough compliment of the highest order. I know that no one is so scared of the law and of courts as a lawyer. No one so scared of sickness and the reaper of Father Time as a doctor. Actors all suffer from stage fright. Even preachers, though in cahoots with Satan, deal in fear and superstition. So I idiotically and senselessly refuse to bury mama as yet. I don't say that you don't know what you are talking about—I'd rather be the one idiot like Clemenceau (who was by the way a doctor too), who at the age of 30 was sentenced to death by the doctors for his defective heart—then lived to 86.

Right now mama is sitting across the table sewing a woolen black dress for herself—she hasn't the slightest notion of what is going on between you and me. Also don't ask me to be practical. That's the reason the life of most people is so grim. I am not interested except in the experiment of seeing how one can pass through life without that dreadful quality. Half a century ago Oscar Wilde said: "Women are so damned practical—therefore so dangerous to man." That's what's wrong with this colorless world. Don't you know Art, Music, Drama are the escape from the practical, sane, sensible in everyday life. Many a very gifted man was extinguished by a practical wife.

So now I make no more plans. My reservations for Marseille for April 24th stand. We will see what happens between now and then and will act accordingly. I have faith, blindly and fanatically, against all the hurricanes of life; and that's all a person like me, who is only "heart and sentiment," can do if he wants to live. Otherwise I'd just crumble to pieces. I have all I can do to keep my heart from bleeding in the great grief I undergo, and then, little by little, I just have to dope myself with wishful thinking in order not to collapse, and remain alive yet.

[Tunis]
March 18, 1948

Your two better letters of March 11 and 13 have arrived. I did not write to you for exactly a week after I answered your March of the Barbarians letter. My heart makes me answer these immediately and mail them at once, for I would like you to have a little more reassurance and a little more peace and tranquillity about me. Probably my doing this is a true barometer of my feelings, even though I asked you to fling me "off the pedestal" entirely. Of course you are not compelled to do it, and if you still leave me there, I'll probably, like an "incorrigible male," smile and stretch and swell out my "priza da fighta" chest once more. Of course your letters are full of common sense, but that, alas, does not seem to be the thing that rules the world or human beings. There are intangible, incomprehensible little things that really do it, and we all are toys in the hands of those mysterious forces. So why try to be intelligent—it's a sheer waste of time and good grey matter. The only thing we helpless, buffeted, harassed mortals can do is just use a little good will, a *great deal of love*, and patience, and things somehow straighten out by themselves. For there is also a law of harmony and order that puts things straight just when they seem most chaotic. . . .

[Tunis]
March 23, 1948

. . . How wonderful! your letters keep on coming— and each with better and more encouraging news . . . So be it then, as it seems to be the wish of all the pagan gods we have adopted. After reading once your letter of March 18th, I reread it completely with every word of it to mama, just as you asked, and she was *"d'accord"* immediately and so am I—for it

makes "sense in a loco sort of manner," so that should be reason enough to accept the project. I think it goes with an uncommercial artistic temperament such as you have, and for me to feel that henceforth you will not be harassed by all *the practical* sides of business (as such your place in Philadelphia certainly has to be) is enough to make me happy for your sake, and for me to be able *to paint* with a completely clear conscience. *Compris*? You know exactly what I mean! I'll feel then as if some resurrected Lorenzo the Magnificent is subsidizing a beautiful life of Arts and Sciences.

I am still awed and deeply impressed by your anointing me so royally and conferring on me supreme power. Well, darling, all I can say is that there is nothing megalomaniacal about me, so you are perfectly safe. My head will not be turned. I am not an upstart like all the European dictators. I am a very humble person trying to wrest a bit of the divine fluid from the Muses—so will use all power in trying to make you as happy as it will be in my power to do. Therefore this crowned head will not lie uneasy, because its conscience will be clear, and its soul unselfish. . . .

[Tunis]
April 16, 1948

. . . I sympathize with you in your impatience—but, darling, think of me when it comes to being patient. I will be a long time in Kingdom-come by the time I come into my own insofar as recognition as an artist in this world is concerned—and I don't give a damn, provided I enjoy and am able to paint. So I am an old horse in the game of patience.

[Tunis]
April 23, 1948

. . . This is the last letter from Tunis. At last we are ready and packed and very glad to go tomorrow morning at 10 A.M. when the ship pulls away from the African shores. . . .

Paris
April 24, 1948

Today is Liberation Day, commemorating chasing out the Boche in '44. As I am right by the Arc de Triomphe, I see all the "monkey-business." Everything has to take place at the feet of the "Unknown Soldier." It's become a fetish, a cult, and a national obsession and sanctuary. Jehovah has been abolished. The Holy Sepulcher is now under that Arc, with the perpetual flame burning, and two gendarmes with their funny capes walking back and forth, always. Day and night yokels from all over the world come and gape at the flame. Humanity just must worship dead bones; and it all started with Christianity. The Catholic church perpetually pokes into graves for relics. The ancient Etruscans had more sense—they at least worshipped the "living Bone" (salami promptness) of their phallic religion, full of fun and humor. I cannot help this pornographic pun. . . . I think everything national is caricatural and ridiculous—that's why loco people cannot "belong." I laugh in every and at every country in spite of myself, even though I feel perfectly at home only in Paris, and will always have to come here all my life like a whale coming up for a breath of air. . . .

Paris
April 28, 1948

. . . My Romanian doctor, a childhood friend, saw mama at once, and he too recommended Denmark even for the reason of food. Privation here is incredible—butcher shops closed 4 days a week, milk nonexistent, bread like melted terra cotta. France is in Hell. Paris is gloriously beautiful. My friend André Daudé, with whom we are staying, took me around in his car for a bit of sightseeing last night, and I was thrilled at the beauty of the city after 9 years' (1939) absence. Paris holds on forever, but it's no place to live in now—especially with a sick mother. . . .

Copenhagen
May 10, 1948

. . . To make a long story short the two great professors we consulted have decided to have mama treated in the hospital where I take her Wednesday at 2 P.M. —they think she will have to be there about 3 weeks. Also I must tell you at once they decided it is not pernicious anemia, and they assured me they will save her. . . . But she cannot walk except with difficulty, so it was time to do something drastic . . . .

The Danes are a serious, decent, honest, and gentle people—easygoing and extremely courteous to foreigners. They did already countless courtesies to us in the short time we are here. I shall not annoy myself while mama is in the hospital, as there are marvelous museums for me to see, and the city is so picturesque that I'll be busy sketching at the canals of its port, with sailing and fisher vessels and folk, and medieval houses. Mama is glad to go to the hospital, as she is tired of all this useless torture. That transfusion of 250 grams of blood in Paris last Monday nearly killed her. . . .

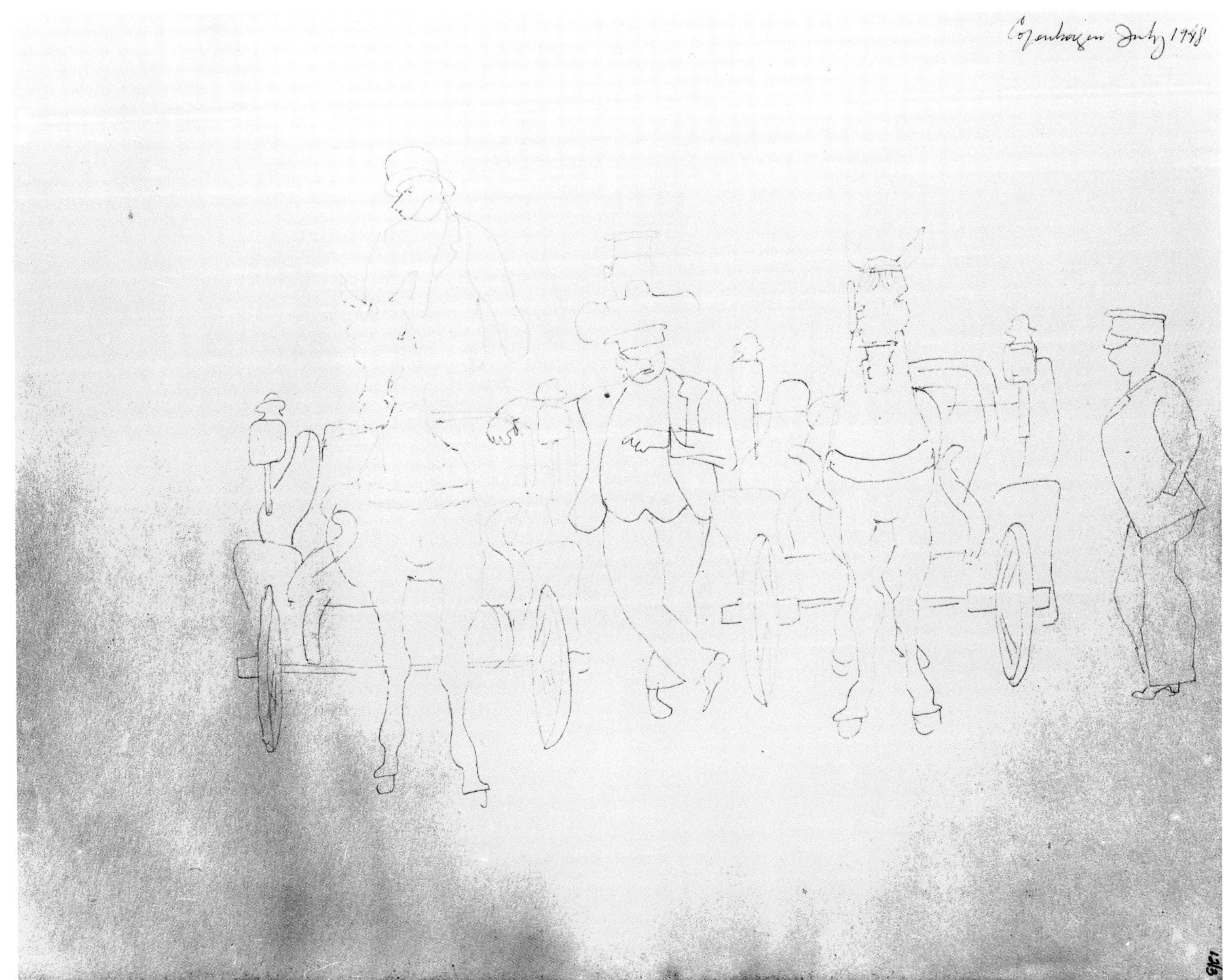

Fig. 62
John Barber
Carriages, Copenhagen, July 1948
Graphite, 9 3/8 x 11 1/2
Collection of Dr. Margaret De Ronde Barber,
on loan to The John Barber Memorial Collection,
Bayly Art Museum of the University of Virginia

Copenhagen
May 13, 1948

. . . It seems I am writing you every day, but I want to contribute to your morale too while at that convention in Washington. I just came back from the hospital. It's 6 P. M. Well, the situation is this: Mama just has enough blood to be able to live while lying in bed! The professor, who is also the head of that great hospital, told her so this morning in front of 6 young doctors and 4 nurses, and one who took notes of what he spoke to his disciples. . . . She has a big private room, and he told her she will have to be there a long time. Of course, he told her she will recover. Her hands are bloodless almost. She wants so badly to live now that it's pathetic, and wants to be able to return to America. Her trip to Tunis has cured her of her apathy and grief, but I fear it's a bit late!!! . . . It's terrible, isn't it! I had a hard time restraining my tears in the hospital, and did a good job of it—*woe is mine*! This is a hell of a way to contribute to your morale.

The hospital is beautiful, with a little park in front of it—but just behind, and bang against the wall starts the graveyard, believe it or not. That's Danish with a vengeance—it made me smile in bitter irony. "There is something rotten in the grimness of the land of Denmark" (shades of Shakespeare). But, darling, it was a Godsend that we came here, and even mama says so now. We couldn't have had this, neither in Tunis, nor New York or Paris. Such cleanliness, such marvelously willing nurses. Such excellent attention from the doctors, and that professor who is a god here takes special interest in mama's case and not from a lucrative point of view either. Compared to American standards it's even finer—both in the room, food, treatment, etc., in fact incomparably superior. . . .

Now, darling, again I must say it's now a matter of watchful waiting, and I doubt if it would be worth your spending a little fortune just for a short few weeks here, especially now when mama's life hangs by a thread, and I couldn't dream of leaving her to go to Paris for a couple of weeks—you know exactly what I mean! So now, if only miracles exist I will come with mama to America—more than that, it's in the hands of *Destiny*. . . .

Copenhagen
May 27, 1948

. . . Yesterday mama seemed on the way out—she was pale like a cadaver and at the end of her strength. After the transfusion she was rosy like a baby, and even her lips were red instead of blue—but I fear your original diagnostic was right and now only wonder *"how long"*? Fortunately, she does not suffer, has no pains whatsoever—but yesterday her weakness was a form of suffering to her—and the worst of it all is I fear she knows the truth. Some of the things she tells me make me feel she knows and is trying to fool me into peace of mind for the time being. But, darling, I am daily fortifying myself for what is to come, and I'll face it bravely if I have to, for I still stupidly hang on to a thread, like all idiotic mortals—being one of them myself. I believe they start to feel that the white is eating the red blood—which means leukemia, *n'est ce pas*? and that's mortally dangerous and hopeless. It is 6 P.M., and I will now stretch out on my bed and get back my strength as I always do—then eat something and read myself to sleep. Have a nice tiny room at a hotel at a very reasonable rate at least. It's very clean, and has hot running water all the time which is a wonder in Europe now. . . .

129

Copenhagen
May 31, 1948

. . . And so the month of May is slipping away too, as so many things in life do, and it now looks as though mama too will soon slip away from me forever. I *don't even want* to fool myself any longer. Yesterday, Sunday, I spent it all at the hospital; and what is worse, mama too realizes it, that she is lost. Yesterday she cried for the first time since in the hospital, says mama: "John I am very sick." Meaning (as I know her) John I am dying. She has no more strength to walk the six feet from her bed to the washstand in her room, and she is no fool and knows she is weaker every day. She is very sad at the thought of *leaving* me. The nurses tell me that. She is a marvelous patient, and the nurses love her. The head nurse herself helps her eat—cuts her food, etc. for her. I never saw such humane, loving care as she gets here. You will never see mama, I fear. Fortunately such things as where one is buried or how mean nothing to me. Yes, I have to think of that already, Alas!!! I am drawing my own conclusions from the way she looks or feels. The big transfusion she got only 4 days ago seems to have evaporated as far as her coloring is concerned. She is just yellow and bloodless-looking, or a sweet face without a wrinkle—almost like the mask of a Chinese doll.

No, darling, it would be useless for you to come here now, and a pitiful waste of energy and everything else. The only way you can help me is by keeping up your courage and patience and morale right there until I return. . . .

Copenhagen
June 4, 1948

. . . I didn't think necessary to bother with the detail that Dr. Faber is almost 90 and retired. . . . He received us very graciously in his palatial home and phoned his disciple, a Professor Gram, about 60 years of age, who fortunately is also the head of the hospital which is a Government institution here, as they have a socialist government. Well, to make a long story short, Dr. Gram made a marvelous impression on mama; and, as he is a man of great culture and a linguist, we became friends. At present he poses for me at the hospital from 10:30 to 11:30 in the morning, and I am doing a fine portrait of him. He wanted to pose in white (surgeon's jacket), but I refused and told him butchers and ice cream peddlers look that way too. Of course the portrait took care of his high professional fees, and he thinks he has the best of the bargain—so much the better! . . .

Fortunately too, I am kept from too much melancholia by some Danish professors who took me up. Last Sunday evening I attended a dinner party of ten professors who toasted: "The illustrious foreign visitor," *me*, if you please, and don't you dare laugh, baby!!! But mama has a very short time to live, alas! So it's all under a cloud of repressed tears choking me at times. You will never see mama again—and she was a real, real friend to you. Her voice is weak too. It's leukemia killing her—she has fever too now. . . .

Darling, I don't feel stranger in this country than anywhere else. I am at home in every land and a foreigner everywhere. I was born that way—that's why I left my native country in the first place. I didn't belong there, and neither do I everywhere else. I have no fear of getting or not getting along—I somehow always manage by hook, but without any crook about it. I don't fear life—I only fear death— and not for myself, but for the very, very few I love in this world, and there are only two left now and one is going fast—but the other must wait patiently in Philadelphia. I want to bear this cross myself right here, and I want to spare you—spare you for future use—but happy use, and not the kind I am undergoing at present. I hate awakening in the morning these days, and that's a dreadful feeling—but it's all "a dare" to me, and I have to test my strength and carry it through alone. You see I don't resent being called a tramp by "Z"—perhaps that's my true profession—at least I love life to that extent, of having perpetual curiosity and enthusiasm enough always to seek the elusive "pot of gold" but will be happy to do some research work with you in that field—our own.

[Copenhagen]
June 11, 1948

. . . This month at the hospital (for mama got into the hospital May 12th) was a tremendous lesson and experience to me, and I am still learning every day there. It has changed my outlook on life and death— with "death preferred" to use "Wall Street verbiage." I think we are selfish beasts to torture people into life and away from the relief of the grand nirvana. Life isn't worth it—the price is a usurer's fee. If I ever get to that point I'll be sure to have a quadruple dose of sleeping tablets, and Morpheus can have me forever then. Poor mama, her weakness has become a great weight—she has also lack of breath at times. I am getting prepared with all my mind and strength and philosophy to face the inevitable. The matter-of-fact Danes not only have a cemetery and crematorium smack against the back wall of the hospital, but an enterprising Dane has a shop with a white painted casket in the window facing the hospital. . . .

[Copenhagen]
At the Hospital
June 20, 1948, 6 P.M.

This is the saddest Sunday in my whole life. Mama is in a coma now. It came all of a sudden day before yesterday, and I have been living at the hospital ever since. They have put a room at my disposition where I sleep—just a few doors away from mama's room. But I am at mama's bedside from 7 in the morning till almost midnight. Since this morning, she does not give any sign of recognizing me—but she does not talk since the last 48 hours—and that is a great agony to me. Yes! I have shed buckets of tears by myself lately—but before the Danes I put up a front. They are simply marvelous to me, and treat me royally. Such service, and such consideration I never experienced. They bring me the best of food, and all that with the compliments of the hospital. I think the portrait of the great Professor has something to do with all that. Friday he took it away proudly to the framers. So here is where it all came to, just as you prophesied. The doctors tell me against anemia they are helpless, and that it's only a relief and release for mama. They gave her morphine injections for two days, but stopped it today, as they don't feel it's necessary. Her temperature is very high: 39.6 centigrade. But her pulse is 88. Her heart and lungs are very strong they say, and that's the only reason she still lives. I feed her milk during the day whenever possible through a funnelled cup, and the nurses marvel how well I manage to do it. They keep her immaculate, and attend to her several times a day. You cannot imagine how grateful I am to these people. They feel strongly for me, being in this predicament in a strange country, and they said they will help me with everything when it comes to it—and that may be any hour now. I am writing right by mama's bed, as she breathes hard, and I assure you I am steeling myself to go through this great ordeal—even writing this letter right there is part of my attempt to be strong and face it. I am glad though that you are not here—for I don't want ever to connect you with my mental picture of this horrible period in my life. I want to be able to come back and find in you "the picture of life" to bring forgetfulness of images of suffering and death. And I suppose it will take quite a while to go through with all that I will have to attend to—so you better prepare, darling, to go to Hot Springs or Northampton and just leave it to me to come back as soon as it's humanly or decently possible to do so. Anyway you should give me the addresses of the places you go to, so I can write you there without any break in the continuity between us.

Mama just passed away. It is 4:45 Monday morning. I am calm.

[Copenhagen]
June 22, 1948

I am writing this letter just for your sake, as you can understand—so that I can put your mind at peace about having any misgivings about my suffering the last 24 hours. Yes, I do suffer a lot and there is a lump in my throat, but I can take it as I can take everything in life. I am putting up a strong fight against myself and my emotions, and I am winning the battle. I just came back from the hospital. They are doing everything for me there, and a doctor is doing the embalming too. The head nurse, who is an aristocratic, elderly lady, is arranging everything. She has become a friend, and she used to feed mama like a baby. She speaks English quite well too, so she used to keep mama company for hours. I feel rather tired, and you can picture me lying on my back for hours in my hotel room just dreaming and resting up and

gradually getting back to myself. I had the disciplinary presence of mind to write that postscript to my letter just about 15 minutes after mama breathed her last at 4:45 A.M. Monday, so you see I am not such a weak sister after all, and the Danes did not see the slightest outward trace of my emotions. I am getting more and more reconciled to the inevitable, and, imaginative as I am, I am glad you are not in the picture so I don't have to connect you with it forever—I'd rather connect the head nurse—lovely old lady as she is—but she will soon be out of my consciousness or daily life—so I want to come and find in you something fresh and unconnected with this. Perhaps it's even better that the whole thing did not continue in America with you inevitably being involved in such sad business. You did more than your best over there. Of course, I didn't really want to believe the truth. I hate the truth anyway, and, for the rest of my days, I want to live in the world of make-believe which is the only one one has fun in. That's all there is to life, and such experience as I am passing through affirms it that much stronger. Anyway, even in such times I think of you with great love.

. . .

[Copenhagen]
June 25, 1948

Again, I am writing to you in order not to keep you in suspense and to avoid as much as possible your worrying about me. Death has somehow calmed me. I bow to the inevitable with Oriental fatalism. There is something so real about death, that it brings you to a realization of realities, and brings some sense in our senseless love and emotional imbalance about something that cannot be helped. I just got a beautiful letter this morning from the Professor Gram telling me how much greater and more finished my art is

than his. The portrait has created a sensation, and the
hospital people beg him to let it for the hospital—but
his wife likes it too much . . . .

There is really a great meaning that you came into
my life just when mama was starting to go out of it.
It's the law of order and balance, so I suppose I'll
have to transfer completely to you all the tenderness
and affection for mama—for now it seems to me like
a "blending" (if you know what I mean) rather than a
tearing away. So if I can reason like this, there is still
hope for me in seeing my way through this maze. I
admit my pain is very great indeed, for I have really
lost a beloved child, rather than a mother—for that's
what she really was to me for years now, especially
since her illness developed and progressed. So now
the best way for you to help me is to be calm and
confident in me, and *just know* I'll be all right—I'll do
the right things, and I'll return as soon as humanly
and decently possible. Thank God I, also, am not
obsessed with the fetishism of death and the worship
of dead bodies. . . .

Copenhagen
June 30, 1948

And so ends "June"—the fateful month of a decisive
year. I felt it was going to be decisive, but not to that
extent, and all I can do about it is just reflect on the
fact that I wasn't so wrong when I decided long ago
that everything was a fake. And the biggest faker of
all is that imaginary Santa Claus in a Prince Albert,
called God by most fools. Yes, darling, we are only
rabbits pulled out of the hat by that gentleman magi-
cian, and as quickly disappear. I was there to see Rita
and Mama in the moment of passing into eternity,
and I assure you life is a farce. There is no such thing
as life. It's only an illusion. Even there God is impo-
tent—he does not give life—he only shows us a mi-

rage which we believe is it. The worst part of it all is
that it lasts more than a flash—just long enough for
us to imagine we are something. How pitiful. We
imagine we are rich, or poor, powerful or weak,
talented, intelligent, and all that humbug. We are
nothing! We are just a fractional manifestation, like
lightning for instance—no more, and don't last
comparatively much longer either. Of course, human enough, you will ask: "What are you going to
do about it?" Well, all I can do is give a modern
version of Omar Khayam as a solution. "Jewish
black bread with seeds on the loaf. A two-inch steak
(bloody). A bottle of red wine. And thou in bed—
with me!" Not forgetting, for good measure, some
salami promptness. That's all we can rescue out of
the catastrophe called life. There is nothing else.

And so the days pass, and I am attending to
things here—all kinds of formalities—all kinds of
stupidities that organized humanity in its pompous
respectability pries into open wounds. Perhaps it's a
good thing I have to be occupied that way—anything
to take my mind away from reality, even though it is
to liquidate terrible reality, and then try to forget
about it. At least I will not pester you with writing
you all about these details. It's enough that I have to
attend to them. It's punishment enough, without
shifting it over to you. When I return, I hope I can
put up a serene front anyway, and start enjoying
with you the above prescription.

[Copenhagen]
July 8, 1948

. . . And so time passes while waiting for the time to
be through here and on my way back alone to the
States. It's all so unbelievable as yet, and life never
seemed to me more unreal than at present. I am in a
never-never land of make-believe, and everything

seems so naive, including even the acts of drawing and painting. Of course I realize that we are made in a way that the so-called reality of life comes back to the fore sooner than we realize—but at present it is still too early for those forces to have any power in reasserting themselves. . . .

[Copenhagen]
July 20, 1948

. . . What matters what I consider a fake? Most people, most social systems, most conventions, etc., etc., etc., are fakes to camouflage this great jungle, and I say it without any tragic implications. I laugh at it all, including myself, who is also caught in it, because I am still only a human being. At times I only revolt because we are not really the "lords of the universe" but powerless and weak and temporary. We ought to have been gods or else not given the intelligence to crave to be that. And, darling, those lines sum up the whole feeble philosophy which we think is such a marvelous patrimony given by the great(?) minds. So please be a happy darling and know that soon (means very soon) I'll be back and laugh with you again. I am going to Sweden for the first time, also as an attempt at propping up my morale by a change that will take my mind away from death. . . .

Stockholm
July 27, 1948

. . . I arrived at 10 P.M. (2 hours late) last night and at 11 was in bed after having taken a good hot bath and washed socks and underwear. Up at 7 this morning all excited to see this beautiful city—incredibly so! And my greatest reward for coming was the tremendous surprise that the Vienna Museum's Imperial Art

Collection is here till August 15th. I nearly jumped with delight. One of my great heartbreaks was not having seen it since early youth. Just missed seeing it before World War II outbreak, and here is one heartbreak cured. It is one of the grandest surprises in my life, and I would have gone much farther than Stockholm to see it. What a piece of good luck it's on a loan tour here.

I am at the Skandia Hotel—one of the finest in town (what a fake tramp I am!), but I manage it very cheaply the way I learned to get "the right kind" of exchange on dollars. It's an art in itself, of which most tourists are woefully ignorant. . . .

No I don't fear heat or cold or anything—that's not the reason—in fact I have no reason for anything and that's the greatest truth about me. . . .

Stockholm
July 29, 1948

Stockholm is not a city—it is a fairyland and the most beautiful capital I ever saw—and so full of gaiety, as no other place in Europe. Everywhere magnificent outdoor restaurants with orchestras playing and, above, long balconies full of diners listening to Viennese waltzes. All illuminated and boats plying on the rivers and canals of this Venice of the North. The Royal Grand Hotel is full of moneyed Americans talking business and selling each other a "bill of goods," as I cannot help overhearing. And inviting their apoplectic white-haired prospective customers to come look over the plant and see the new innovations. The Swedes eat, drink, and—four-letter it! The Svenska blond flickas flicker all around one most invitingly—but I have discovered I am just as much a fake philanderer as a tramp and have inherited too much straight-lacedness from my mother and the abstemious ancestors. . . .

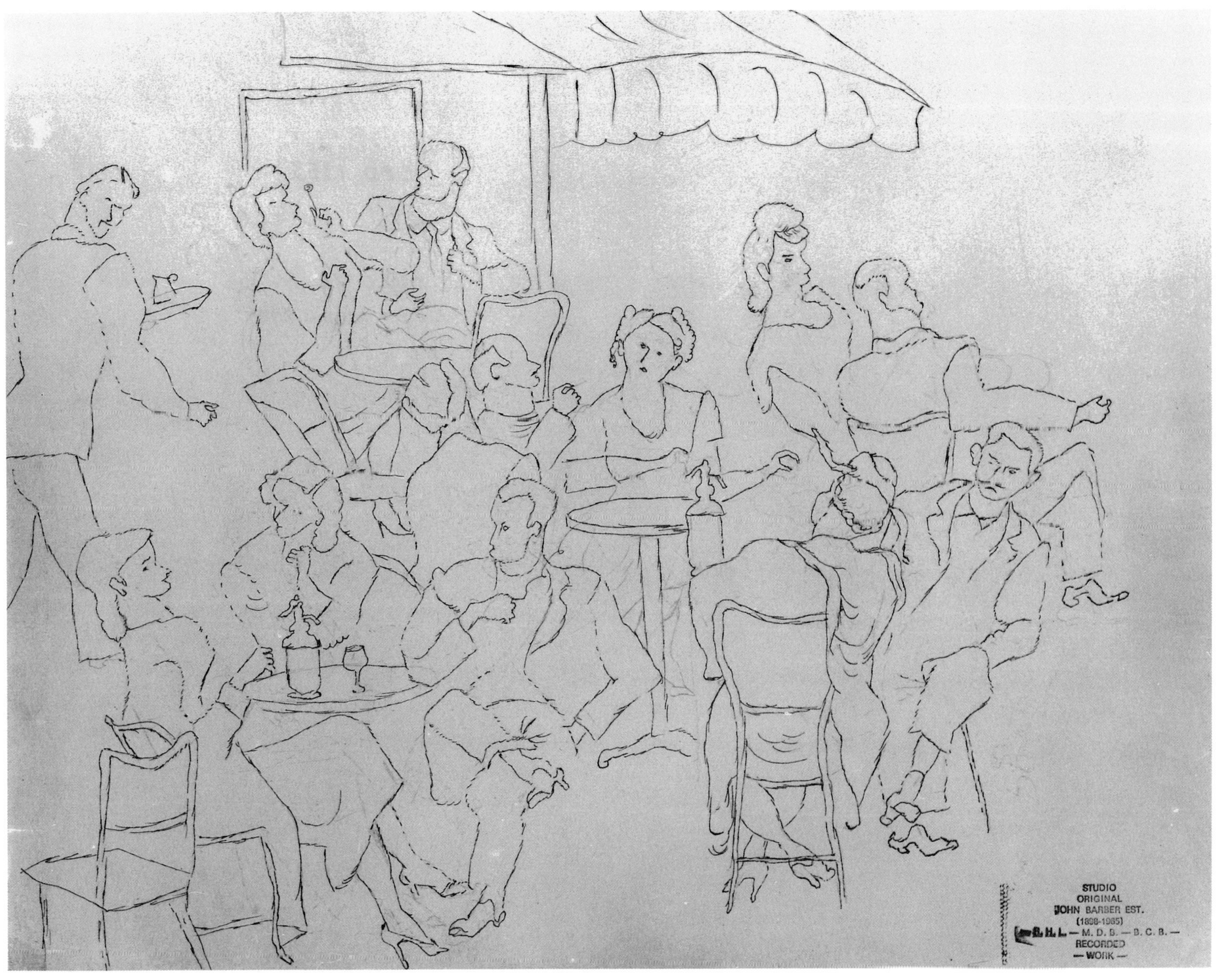

Fig. 63
John Barber
Copenhagen, 1948
Graphite and ink, 9 1/2 x 11 5/8
Collection of Dr. Margaret De Ronde Barber,
on loan to The John Barber Memorial Collection,
Bayly Art Museum of the University of Virginia

135

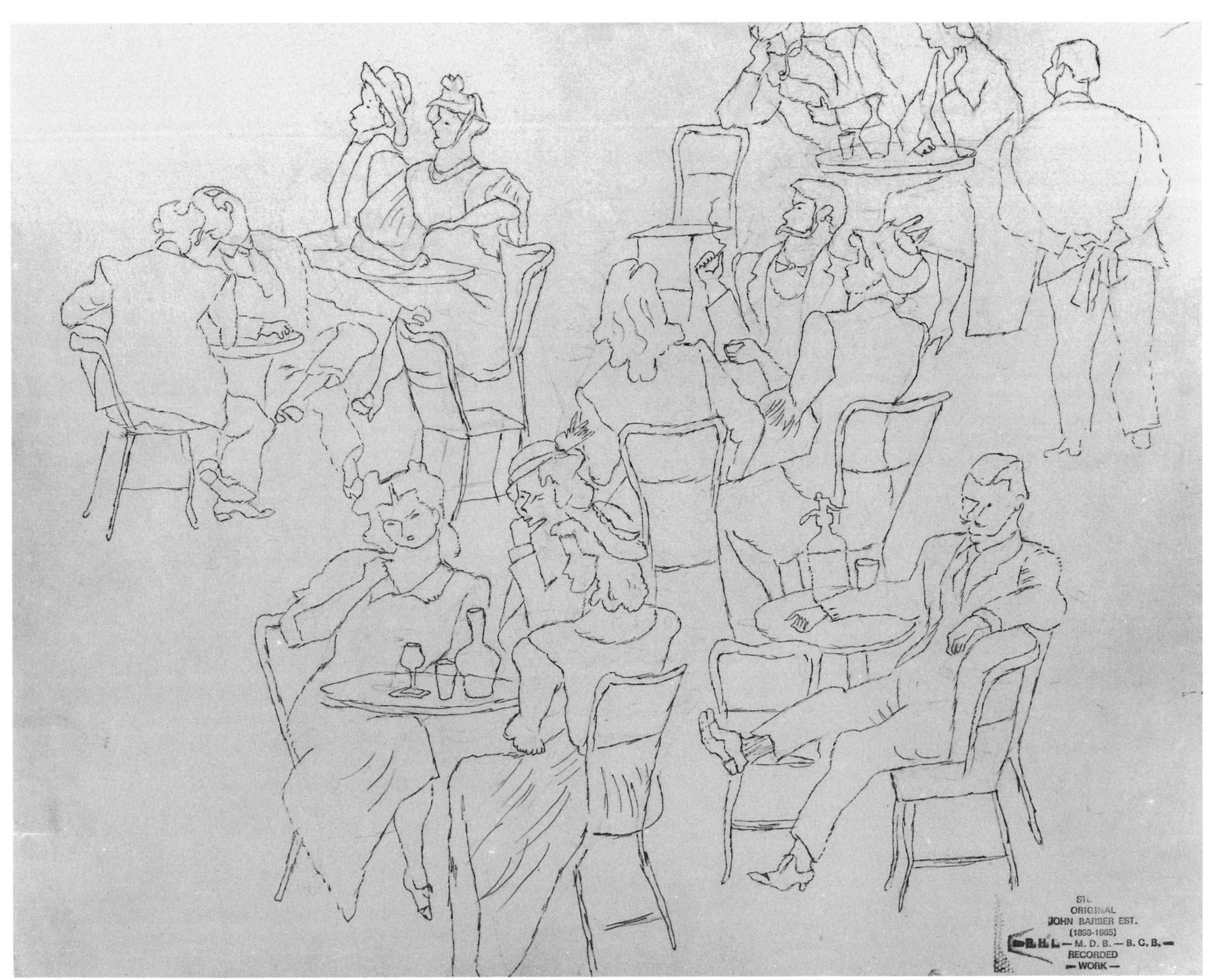

Fig. 64
John Barber
Café, Copenhagen, 1948
Graphite and ink, 9 $\frac{1}{2}$ x 11 $\frac{5}{8}$
Collection of Dr. Margaret De Ronde Barber,
on loan to The John Barber Memorial Collection,
Bayly Art Museum of the University of Virginia

I am writing this sitting on a bench facing a beautiful lake in front of the Nordic Museum, waiting for it to open at 12 o'clock. I am getting Culture galore here and filling up the Northern vacuum in my life's quest for savantry—(never heard of this last word before, and just coined it).

At the Imperial Vienna Museum Art Collection, I found Vermeer's self portrait, painted as he sits with his back to the viewer in his studio while painting his stupid-looking Dutch wife, with a bunch of leaves on her head. Vermeer was so puny and homely that he thus avoided showing his face. This painting is from the Czernin Collection in Vienna. I never saw it before, and from reproductions I just longed to see it. It's an extra treat.

The museum is just jammed with visitors from all over the world to see the show, and I'll be there every day. The Rembrandt is ever beyond my expectations. It's in his last period and the most free, colorful, and impressionistic. It's worth the trip itself, and it's a source of knowledge in how to lay on colors like precious stones. . . .

Stockholm
July 31, 1948

. . . The clock just struck 10:30 P.M., and I am back in my room after Haroun Al Rachiding it, to see how the Swedes live on Saturday night. They do, and they know how. All the waterfront of the innumerable canals is illuminated, and open-air restaurants and orchestras right by the edge of the quays make a feirie sight. Boats fly back and forth full of people being taken to and from such places, for just a few cents. They don't sit on the porches or the back gardens being eaten up by mosquitos in the darkness—drinking whiskey, as poor, unimaginative Americans do in summer. Life means something to these people, and they enjoy it as I never saw a nation do anywhere

before—and in an elegant fashion too, and for very little money. I have spent my evenings sitting on balconies of outdoor restaurants and sketching the people and the musicians. At least it's a comeback for me to be interested once more in drawing for paintings. I guess America is a good place to live clean and comfortable and enjoy steak and roasts (2 inch slices) and Jewish black bread and wine (there is no wine here, alas!—neither in Denmark). But never will we spend a vacation there—it's too grim! To Europe we shall go for a month or six weeks, and that's why all these well-to-do Americans are here— and Stockholm is full of them, the foxes, and they live royally for very little money, in comparison to the next to nothing one gets for the dollar in the States. This is going to be part of the education or culture I am going to give you in the future, and you will enjoy it all as no one ever did. Believe me, I feel sad when I think (and I do so every day) what a corking time we could have had here. As it is, I have to do everything very sparingly and economically—and just content myself with getting the cultural and artistic part and leaving pleasure for some future time.

I also sort of renewed my Parisian youth this morning by paying a visit to the *Vecko Journalen*— the great Swedish magazine. I used to be artist-correspondent for them years ago, and did "Paris life." It was a treat to me to look over the files and see my drawings, also in one number a whole page devoted to me, if you please—and with a photo à la Hollywood. I started to laugh when I saw myself so Greek godified, as I looked in those far-off days. In comparison I now look like an oversized Tom Cat— but I prefer it—there is more force to it. There is something feeble about "pretty youth." And so ends my Scandinavian episode. I am leaving tomorrow, Sunday evening, to reach Copenhagen Monday morning. Swedish trains are comfortable, so I can recline and rest in my seat very well. . . .

Copenhagen
August 4, 1948

. . . This is the last letter from Denmark, as I am leaving tomorrow morning for Paris. . . .

You know my strong opinions on the sacred rights of the individual to be a law within himself—with no one having any ethical right to stand in judgement. So, irrespective of personal feelings, I would be the first to give blessings if you obeyed the laws of preference and natural selection—no matter with whom. . . .

Remember, every individual is a world within himself, and all begins and ends with him, and all experiences are unique even if the whole world goes through the same thing. Such are we imperfect fool mortals! . . .

[Paris]
August 18, 1948

. . . I must tell you at once that my Paris spree consists mostly of drawing and museums. I did 2 beautiful Paris café compositions so far. The sidewalks of each side of the Champs Élysées are wider than the whole of Market Street in Philadelphia—so beside a tree and the back of a car, I sketch the great mass of people sitting before the enormous cafés—without being seen by them, and I have fun. An occasional gendarme is amused by my distortions in the drawings—that's all. I usually sketch between 4:30 and 7:30—that's the great aperitif hour, as no one eats here before 8 or 9 P.M.—it's delightful. This is the only city in the world—the rest are agglomerations—some charming and some ugly—but villages in comparison. I almost envy you for never having been in Paris because of the overwhelming thrill you will have when you see it with me some day. . . .

[France, in the country]
August 23, 1948

. . . Tomorrow morning we return to Paris, and I am glad of it, for I want to go to the Louvre Museum etc., and see further about the chances of getting passage. . . .

Have been doing a lot of drawing here every day. Otherwise, I couldn't stand it in this isolation among peasants. I really don't like rurals and plebeians—they ought to be abolished. I don't like primitive life and lack of bathtubs. Am dying to take a hot bath in Paris as soon as I get there. I cannot draw or paint otherwise. . . . But above all else, I itch to paint again my own "Genre pictures." While waiting for my passage, I'll see the museums and draw out-of-doors the life of the Parisians for paintings to be done in Overbrook or is it Merion, Pa. I'll reverse what old Sinclair Lewis used to do—write in the south of France the American Babbitt stories from his notes in the States. Perspective is a great purifier and eliminator of unartistic and unnecessary details.

Please don't take tragically any sort of ravings of mine—they are momentary expressions of my daily reactions to life and living—that's all—but, as for me, I always am the same as you know me. I don't change like a flighty superficial being. I don't butterfly around. My appreciation and love of you are greater than ever.

The great and terrible experience of this past year has been a proof of how deep and real it all is between us. Such things are divine, and I can even say preordained—without meaning it in a religious sense. There is a great law of harmony which serves as a magnet in life as well as in art—and that is strongly at work with us two.

Paris
August 26, 1948

Red Letter Day!

Just got booked for October 5th on the "Marine Falcon" (U. S. Lines) reaching New York the morning of the 15th—so we will celebrate our birthdays in one.

I just ran over to the Post Office the minute I got it and almost sent you a cable—but didn't want to scare you with one, so will leave it that way. You were right that I would find a way. It was by the favor of a man at the offices of the U. S. Lines, whom I used to meet at cocktail parties in Paris before the war. He recognized me and ran back and forth from one office to another of the building and squeezed me into a place on that ship. This morning the situation looked desperate at the American Express. The earliest they could book me was for November 19th—more than six weeks later than October 5th. Anyway, October is my lucky month, so I am as pleased as could be. I feel like throwing my cap over the windmills. I feel like my last 3 years of misfortune have come to an end—the spell is broken!. . .

[Paris]
August 31, 1948, 2 A.M.

. . . Am all alone in the house. The Daudés are at the farm tonight. I couldn't sleep, thinking of your two letters of August 23 and 25, though I answered you this afternoon. Darling, you still don't understand me at all in many ways. The things I write are pure fantasy—like the St. Peter's doors. It's all monkey-business, and it's part of my way of life to connect something silly and foolish as an excuse for doing something sublime. Italy is divine to me in all its meaning of art and the creative spirit, but I love to connect spaghetti and church stupidities as a foil to keep me on earth, and not in the skies. Everything is monkey-business, even painting Mexicans on horseback or Arabs on camels. It's to me the external human idiocies that amuse me and are a safety valve of humor, to keep me from floating away with the Muses. Some day you will understand and not take tragically the fact that I play marbles to keep me from losing my mind, thinking and looking towards the infinite. That's why I speak of the walled and bricked door when I mean Giotto and Dante instead.

. . .

And, darling, do you realize that I saw mama turn into marble whiteness and coldness when she was so warm and alive and young and intelligent. Something happened to me then that will color my life! In only a few years that will happen to me too. So this has suddenly torn me from everything that makes one "earth-bound" except love. But even then, I must feel that I have nothing to explain to any other mortal! All my actions, attitudes, doings must be looked upon unquestioningly and with benevolent understanding. In fact, one must not even attempt to understand them. Who understands anything? That's exactly how I feel that you also have a right to act and be towards me, and we shall love each other that much more because of the enchantment of mystery and the unobvious—and freedom! If I suddenly decide to get up at 2 A.M. and go shooting ducks, or like this minute, take a shot at you across the ocean, I'll do it. . . .

[Paris]
September 11, 1948

For haven't I learned long ago—around the age of 18—that the symposium of the aim of life as conceived by all the Greek philosophers is as follows: "Pursuit of pleasure and avoidance of pain." Yes, we have exactly the same ideas of ownership or property or anything, and we both know that the only reality and truth is the abstraction called "Love" and romance and all joyousness and delight and everything that goes to make a little heaven out of everyday life—and which so few people are aware of or even capable of. . . .

Am going to the Louvre this afternoon—but, you know, something has happened to me. I look at the same paintings I used to years ago, but today all mystery has evaporated—every stroke of the brush is just matter-of-fact, as though I did it, and I am beginning to wonder why the world calls them masterpieces. Am very impatient to see myself on the boat leaving Europe behind. Somehow I have an intuition of great perfection in our life in the years to come, and very deep satisfactions. . . .

[Paris]
September 14, 1948

. . . Well, darling, this has been one of the greatest periods of study for me. I can say "I swallowed the Louvre"—but I fear I am doing with it the same thing—the same thing that happens to food, alas! Beginning with the Italian primitives—they seem to me crude and barbaric compared to the Persian miniatures and Chinese scroll paintings. Then when it comes to the "Old Masters," I have the feeling that they are as much a fake as all other so-called cultural manifestations of the Western World. Compared to the great Orientals, they were imitative craftsmen. The Old Masters are the fake pompous attempt of the White Man to intimidate the world with his phony greatness—and on such a colossal scale. It's all sign painting—advertising a material civilization with the hypocritical facade (screen) of its religion— the religion of love? The whole thing seems so transparent to me. To give but one example. There is in the Louvre a portrait by Goya of Don Alveiro de Perez Castro, president of the Council of Castile (not of Castile soap). Twenty and twenty-five years ago I used to be literally on my knees before that picture— considering it a miracle. Today it lies before my eyes as a dissected piece of work, no more complicated than a piece of window-glass, and I wonder how I could have been so hypnotized before. I suppose all this could be considered heretical sacrilege—but you are the only one to whom I dare, or rather care to breathe my suspicions. As for the museums of modern art—I think the brass cuspidor/spittoons of an old fashioned saloon are more artistic or useful. Maybe I have lived too long, darling—or perhaps I have to build a little universe of my own. Not an ivory tower, but a place to laugh at the whole business, and eat good Jewish coal-black bread with Greek olives, Italian spaghetti, German frankfurters, Russian borscht, Romanian eggplant, caviar, Bulgarian yoghurt (shades of Metchnikoff), French wines, Swedish smörgåsbord, German sauerkraut, Austrian pretzels, Danish pastry, Dutch cheese, Portuguese caldeirada, and Spanish sardines. That's all the culture Europe has—the rest is a colossal hoax that the bastardized, inartistic, and bellicose White Man has intimidated the rest of the world with. And this rounds up a year in the old world!!! So when you come here with me, there will be plenty to laugh at and about. At least the veil of the Muses has been torn off my earnest brow. There are no gods on earth—there have never been any—perhaps Father Divine.

[Paris]
September 27, 1948

. . . And this is the last week in Paris, and I am quite impatient to see myself on the 8:25 A.M. train on Friday morning October 1st for Le Havre. Will lunch on the S. S. Washington as departure is at noon. My cabin is a 10-men affair (no horses). Remember the 40 men and 8 horses of World War I memory. But my friend of the U. S. Lines, who is a great friend of the purser of the Washington, hopes to put me in a cabin by myself, if possible (as is due a *grande signor* like me!). But it's an outside cabin, B deck, cabin 35 (upper berth, thank God! number 10). So now you know, and my berth is right by the porthole—and I love air, and hate/loathe the odor of men. . . .

I never read, write, or draw on board ship if I can avoid it. I just enjoy the vast expanse and dream about it and of the stories it tells me of the great infinite. If there is moonlight, I enjoy the spectacle and hate to go to sleep. . . .

[Paris]
September 30, 1948

. . . And I am certain you would like a few words from me this last day before sailing tomorrow. The last couple of weeks Paris has been in all its autumn glory. No one remembers such a beautiful epoch at this time of the year here. I have been hiking a lot, especially six days ago when a 24-hour subway strike paralyzed the city. Have been taking it all in, in a sort-of farewell draught of the beauty and atmosphere and spirit—and still I am somehow very glad to go away. Not the slightest regret. It seems all part of the perfect rhythm of my life, and within the logic and perfection of things. My heart which usually is in perfect tune with my intuitive feelings is very light,

and for the first time in years I am looking forward to a good taste of happiness—and I know it's coming! How different I felt last September. I should have known! My heart was very heavy, and there was melancholy music in my consciousness. I am beginning to take everything that has happened this past year in a spirit of Spartan resignation and consider it all as part of the unexplainable in life which should not be questioned.

Last night my friends gave a jolly dinner party in honor of my departure, and we drank champagne—and I drank it to you only. Will mail this tomorrow morning at the post office of the Gare St. Lazare where the train for Le Havre pulls out at 8:24 A.M.

[Paris]
October 1, 1948, 6 A.M.

Am up and ready and the day promises to be beautiful, as there is a pink streak in the sky. It's light enough for me to see the Parisian street sweepers cleaning the square below amidst the circle of trees. There is still the red light on the Eiffel Tower though. I am writing this standing by the window looking at the poetry of daybreak. The news-vendor has started his sing-song in front of the subway station. It's Paris awakening, and it's enchanting, as 5 boulevards lined with trees ramify out of this round plaza of Place des Ternes. The pink streak has become quite red behind the barbaric cupola of the Russian Cathedral on the left—it's going to be a gorgeous day again. And now will wake up André, who insists on wanting to go to the station with me. I think he likes to see the monkey-business of departing Americans. It's getting quite light very rapidly, and so, my darling, I will say *au revoir*—I embrace you with all my love and tenderness. . . .

*X. At Home in Merion, Reminiscences by
Margaret De Ronde Barber*

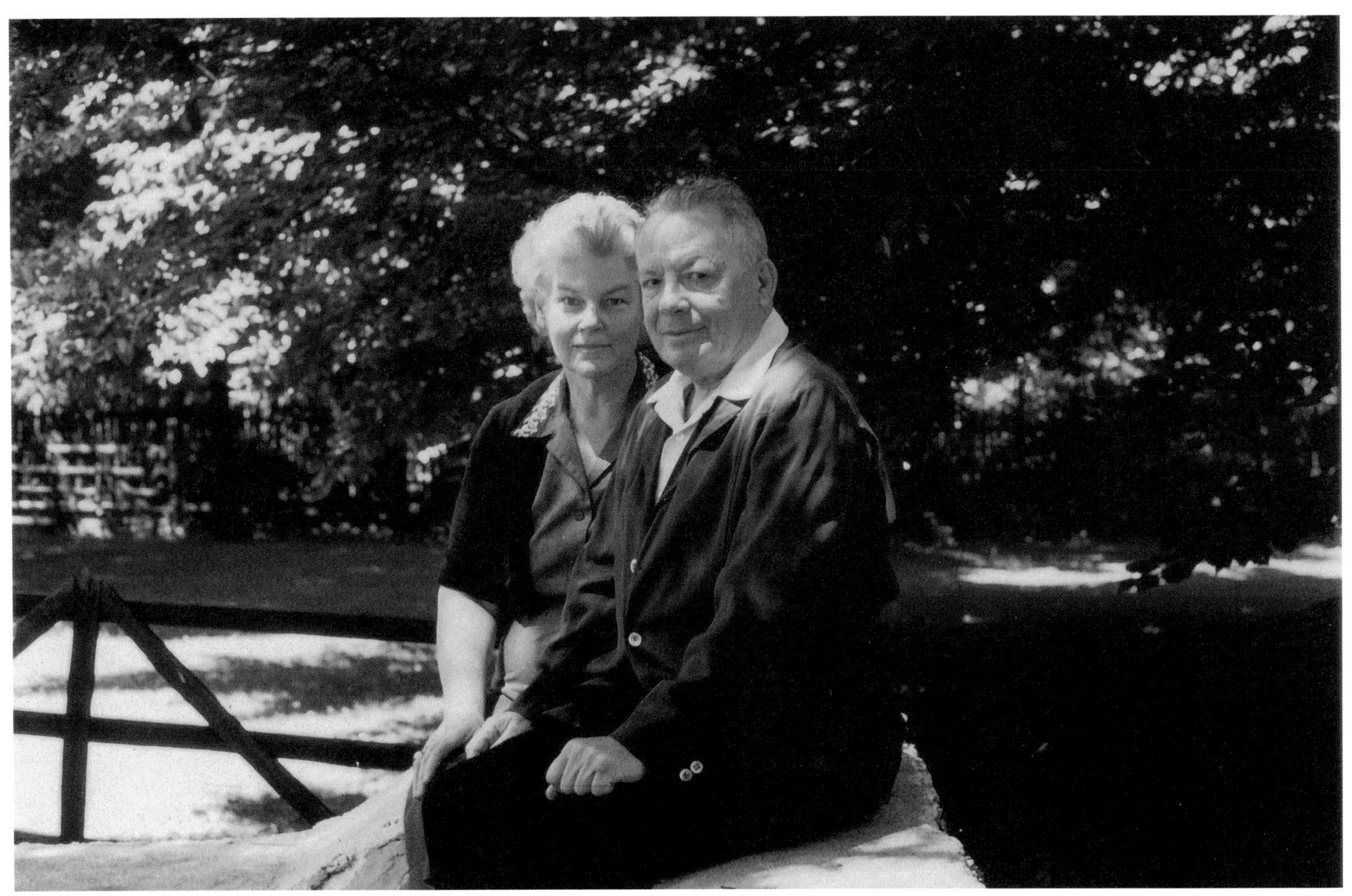

Fig. 65
John and Margaret Barber, Merion, Pennsylvania, 1962

REMINISCENCES
by Margaret De Ronde Barber

*Dr. Margaret Barber's "Reminiscences" were written
from time to time, as memory or occasion prompted,
in the years following the death of her husband.
The following selections are samplings that reflect
the artist's later years and the methods and aims of
his work.*

Looking over the inventory from the gallery, my eye
was caught by the title of one of the paintings—*Gin
and Tonic*. I doubt very much that John ever used
the term or that he even knew what it was. John
never drank any alcoholic beverage except wine with
dinner. We never had "hard" liquor in our home but
always served wine with the meal. It seemed to us
that our friends, who usually drank in their own
homes or elsewhere, did not seem to mind our habit
of not serving cocktails. John's attitude was that our
friends came to see us; and if they gave up coming
because we did not provide cocktails, they were not
worth bothering about. I can't think of anyone who
stopped coming. John had no moralistic attitude
about drinking. At cocktail parties, he would always
see to it that I or whoever else was with us was properly supplied; he just didn't like the stuff. And neither
did he smoke. I smoked, and I do not remember his
ever voicing any objection. I know there were times

in Mexico when he made a trip to the local store to
get me a pack of cigarettes.

John had such an enormous amount of knowledge that he came to be known among my psychiatric
friends as a walking encyclopedia. His memory and
ability to recall dates in history were completely
phenomenal. It became a sort of game at dinner
parties. Someone would mention a date such as the
beginning of the Russo-Japanese war, the building of
the first railroad, or the creation of the Spanish
Chapel in Florence. John always knew exactly. If he
did not, he was the first one to make it known and
never made any pretense of knowing something
unless he really had his facts not only in order but in
focus. But his own telephone number—never. The
idea seemed to be that it was much more efficient to
keep his little book of meaningless numbers than to
clutter up his mind with this mechanical sort of information. And in the same realm of "useless information" was how to screw a lightbulb into an overhead
socket. I always stood by and gave instructions. But
even this was part of the game, and it was always fun.
He could and did laugh at himself. He knew it was
ridiculous not to be able to do it without direction.
We usually ended up making such an occasion an
excuse for celebrating by going to a movie or perhaps
a Greek restaurant.

John's curiosity was enormous. He read extensively and included in his collection of books and

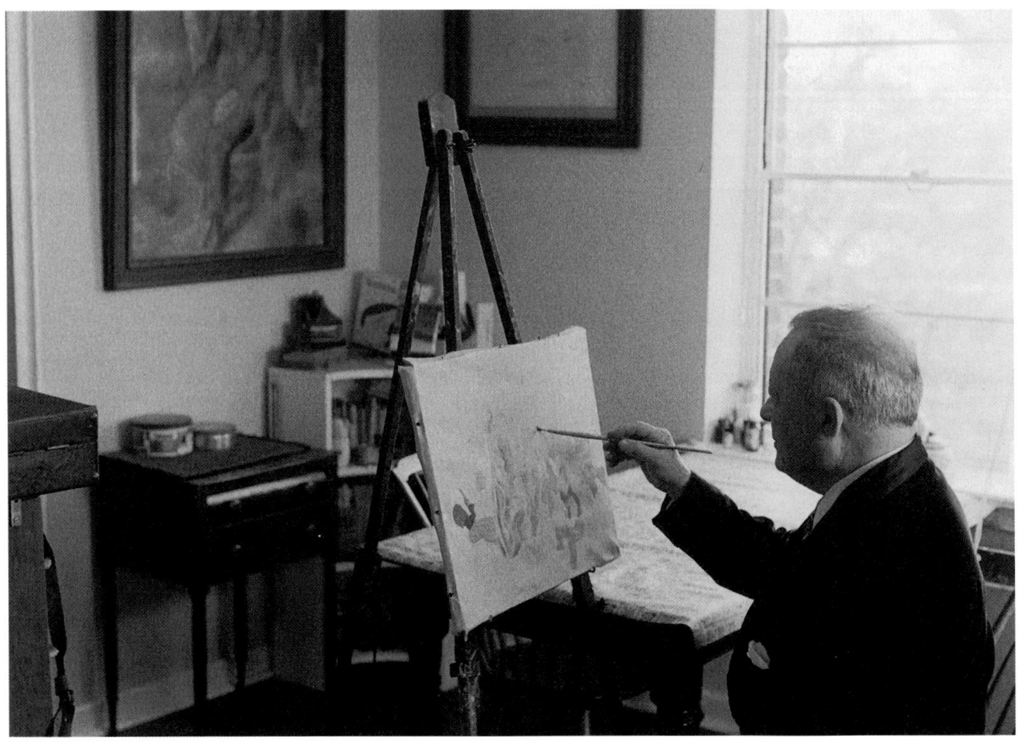

periodicals an amazing variety of subjects and philosophies. He knew the history and development of many of the religions of the world. At a party at Fred Taubes' studio, as we entered, John was immediately aware of a new portrait hanging on the wall. It was as if the motion involved in entering the room continued, and he went directly to the painting and began talking about the meaning of the various symbolic colors of the robe of the rabbi depicted. Fred listened in awe and finally said, "It was my grandfather who was the rabbi; how do you know all that, and I don't?" On another occasion, we were having dinner with Walter Damrosch's nephew, Father Frank Damrosch. They began talking at table about the symbols of the vestments worn by the Episcopal priests. Almost as soon as dinner was over Frank and John walked the several blocks to the church where Frank got out all the robes and trappings of the ministry. They talked at length of all the significance and meanings attached to these.

• • •

Driving through Mexico, we frequently were in unexpected places. John seemed always to know exactly where to go and what was to be expected of interest. We first sought out the museum or cathedral or the public building that had murals on its walls. But also we never missed a church. There might just happen to be something of unusual interest or artistic worth. At one point I drew the line. I had had enough of incense and plaster images. So at the next small church in an isolated village when John said he wanted to see what was inside, I stayed in the car. In a very few minutes he came out to tell me that I must come in as there was a real "accident case" in there that I must not miss. It was just inside the entrance— a life-sized wooden figure of Christ enclosed in a glass coffin. The Christ was battered and bruised and bleeding as if he had been put through a meat grinder.

Fig. 66. *Above,*
John Barber in his studio,
Merion, Pennsylvania, 1955

Fig. 67. *Left,*
John Barber, at an exhibition of his paintings,
Philadelphia, Pennsylvania, 1963

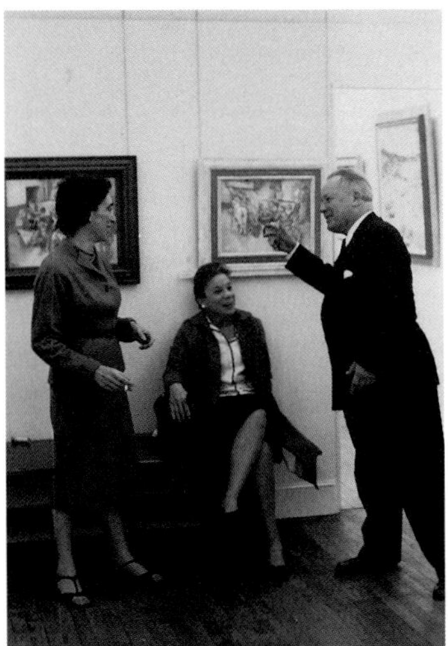

Again in Mexico. We were en route from
Mexico City to Taxco. There was a market going on
in Chalula, and that was a signal to stop for a few
sketches. There were women and children and men
and donkeys and the typical colors of Mexico. After
walking around a bit, John picked a woman holding
a child on her lap for the first figure on a new page of
his sketchbook. Then others were added as they
seemed to fit the emerging composition. A donkey
nearby was promising, but John wanted him facing in
the opposite direction. He went and tried to turn him
around. At first he was successful, but the minute he
stepped back to start drawing him, back he went. So
again the same procedure and the same result. By
this time the Mexicans who were watching were
intrigued and came to help. With half a dozen men
hauling and pushing and holding the stubborn donkey, he was incorporated in the drawing. I was
amused at all the activity but particularly by the fact
that John was drawing a woman who was occupied
in picking lice from her child's head. Later when I
asked if he knew what she was doing, he had no idea
and went into gales of laughter when I told him. His
interest in this woman, as in all of his figures, was in
the stance of the figure, the composition of mother
and child together, the rhythm, the movement, the
colors, the light, and always the problem of integrat-
ing the elements in a complete composition. As for
any social significance, I doubt very much that he
thought of the Mexican donkey as a downtrodden
beast of burden that needed to be liberated. I think
he rather saw him as an amusing touch to be included
to produce a bit of local color and also to depict the
reality of life in Mexico.

During one period we went quite frequently to a
particular area of Fairmount Park in Philadelphia
where the majority of the people were blacks. It was
a large picnic facility. John was fascinated by the
people and their way of life in the open. The dress

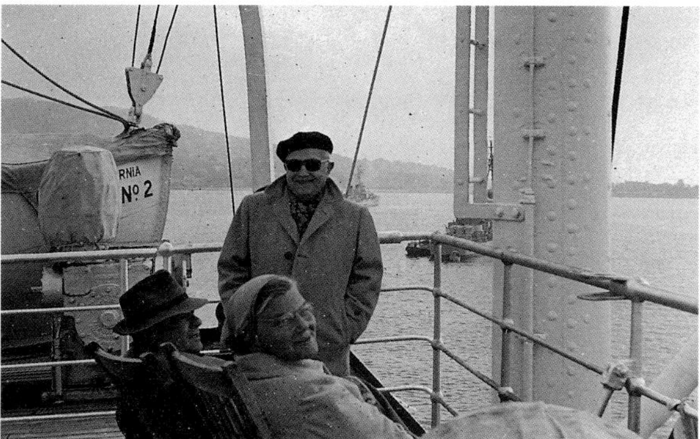

Fig. 68. *Left*,
John (standing) and Margaret
D. Barber, on shipboard, 1954

Fig. 69. *Below*,
John Barber on the Acropolis,
Athens, 1955

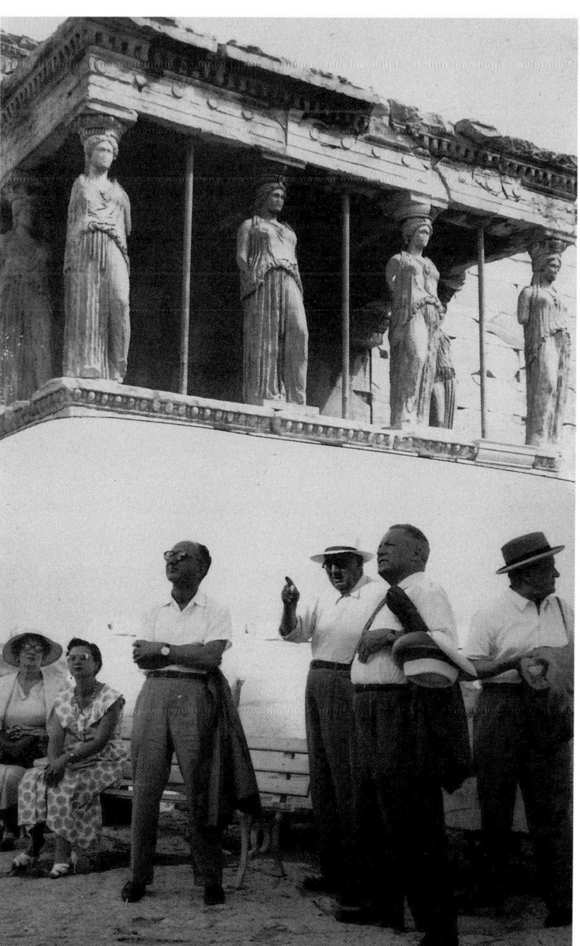

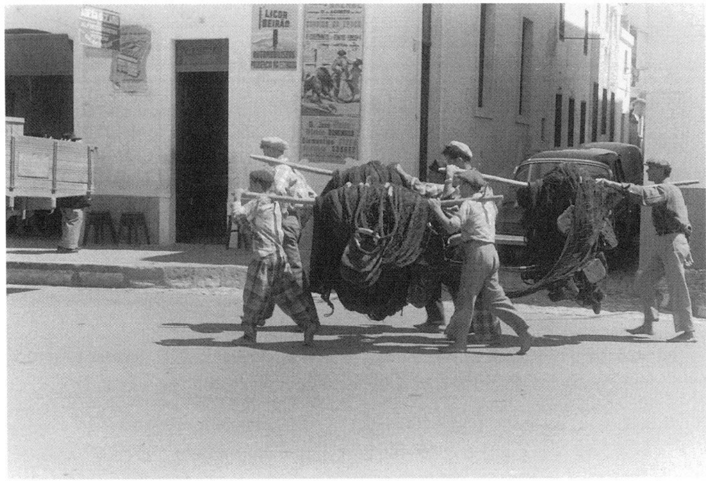

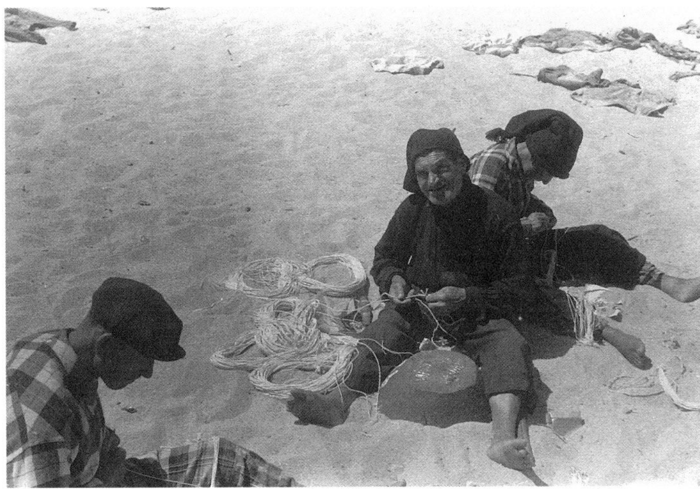

Figs. 70 and 71. Portugal, 1958

was somewhat different from that of people in downtown Philadelphia. The attitudes of sitting and standing, the expressions of emotions, the games they played all became part of a drawing. Even here, John did not depict these people as black—but simply and directly as human beings doing things in a different way and interesting to the eye of the artist. Again there was no thought of eulogizing or condemning a group of human beings. They simply served as a medium for John to express his love of form and action and movement and color when he translated to canvas the drawing in which he caught the basic elements of life.

John had friends in all walks of life. He enjoyed different people for different reasons. He was a master host and had a great capacity for making guests feel at ease and free to express themselves. The stored wealth of his travelling, his associations with the various peoples of the world, his extensive reading, his familiarity with many languages, his passionate love of great art, his goodness and interest in human beings made him a great conversationalist. There was never a dull moment during our evenings of entertaining at home. One person did not monopolize the conversation, but there was a never-ending flow of interest to all. His sense of humor also contributed, but I never heard him tell an off-color joke, nor did he ever use four-letter words. With such a vast vocabulary, he didn't need to. He did borrow from other languages and would often laugh at himself when he realized the eccentric sound of the phrase used.

Architecture was always of great fascination and an integral part of many of his own works. The principles of architecture he understood and used continually. Frequently he would take time to explain to me the reasons a painting was considered great. He made reference to the structure of the composition and the elements of balance and the force of gravity. In his own work, he would show me what he was trying to accomplish in the way of getting the composition to hold together, "like a well-built structure."

He identified with the great men of art, but was also constantly looking for a contemporary of great talent. He knew with one glance if there was enough to warrant further investigation. But never did I hear John discourage a struggling artist. He labored at times to find something positive to say, but by the same token he never said anything negative. When he found something really worthwhile, he was quick to express himself.

John had a habit of looking only at what he considered the best and finest the world had to offer. The usual procedure on visiting a museum—whether the Louvre, the Pitti Palace, the Prado, or any of the other great museums of the world—was to go rapidly through room after room, directly to the one room where he would study one painting for a long time. Then we would proceed to another room, perhaps the El Greco collection in Washington, and spend the rest of the day there.

Among the most exciting moments with John were when he walked into a museum. Somehow he grew taller and tossed his head with the pride of belonging. That was his world, and he was at home. By the same token, I never saw him look more deflated and lonely than when we went on rare occasions to a display of so-called American Abstraction. John Sloan's remark was so apt when they were at one time talking about the obsession of the art world with the then-popular art forms. He said that he wasn't really disturbed by it, as it had nothing to do with art.

John eventually developed a philosophical faith in his own work. He just about gave up even trying for acceptance and settled down to working on his own theories and the problems of color, form, action,

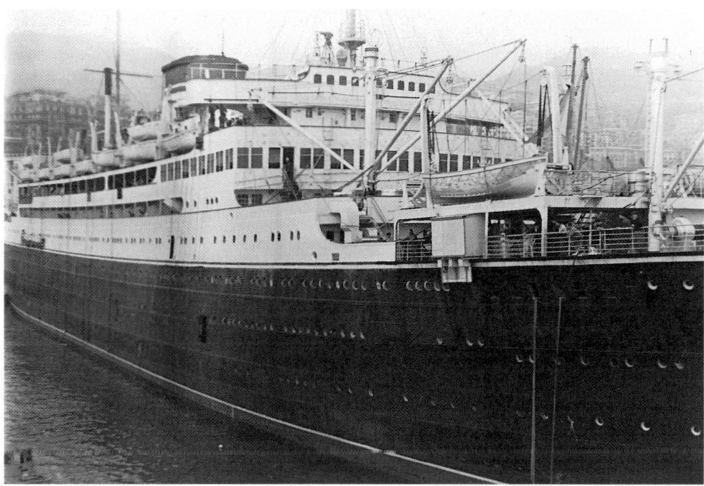

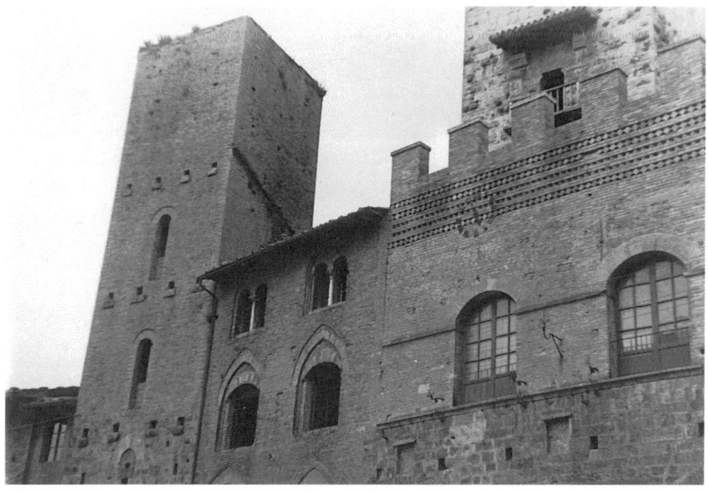

Fig. 72. *Top*, Genoa, 1953

Fig. 73. *Below*, San Gimignano, 1953

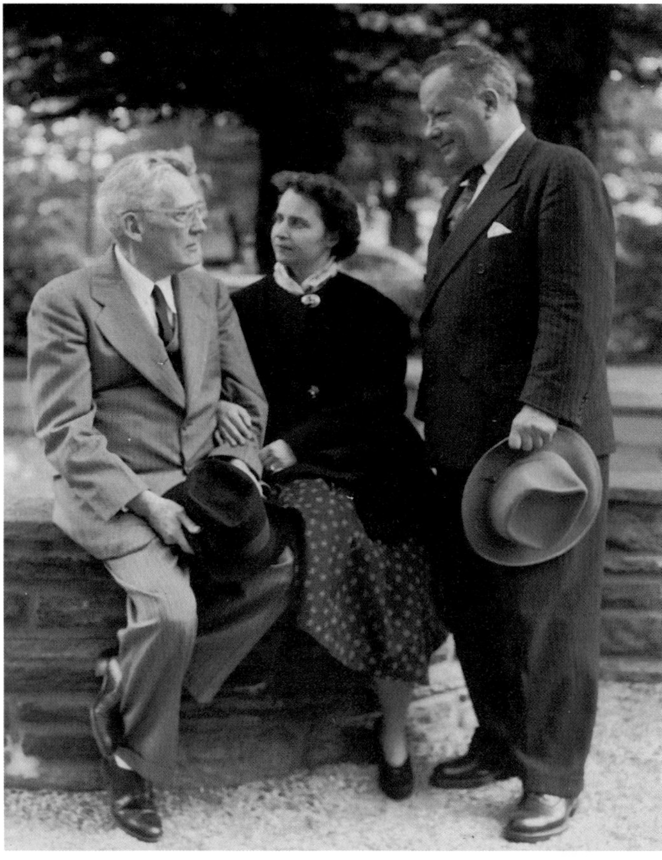

Fig. 74
John Barber (right) with Mr. and Mrs. John Sloan
Merion, Pennsylvania, 1951
Photograph by Dr. Margaret D. Barber

composition, balance, and power. He was obsessed with the desire to produce great paintings. The figures were for the purpose of portraying ideas. They were the vehicles for his drive to create. There was no thought of eulogizing the "working classes." John was interested in action and life. The worker was doing something and was available. A horse show was an excellent source of material, and I am sure he did not know or care who was riding the horses. At a café in Milan where the society of the city congregated, John again sketched very happily. On ship board he sketched a group of nuns who were wearing an unusual type of headgear and made an interesting group. He also did the people in the first-class lounge listening to a concert and the deck-hands painting the superstructure. I can think of only one painting that has anything like real social significance. That is of a Mexican prison. The windows are barred, and beggars in the street are asking alms of the men behind the bars. Even here I really do not think John was interested in reform or the plight of the prisoners. It was the comedy of the situation that struck his fancy.

• • •

At an early stage of his career, John was told that the best way to lose a painting was to give it away. And in the tradition of all great artists, he could not create for money. The compositions that he constantly worked upon or dreamed about were neither commodities nor a way of making a living, but a consuming way of life. He was so dedicated to his work that he was willing to make many sacrifices in order to accomplish what he believed in. He lived simply and had no desire for material things. The pride of ownership was as foreign to his way of thinking and feeling as could be imagined. His basic philosophy was that that man is happiest who owns least. For example, I got rid of an ocean-front lot where I had planned to have a cottage some fine day, when John announced that he did not want to be a janitor.

From that day we always lived as he wanted to. Our rented apartment suited his needs. He had a separate room for a studio, the light was good, the grounds were beautiful, the railroad station of the main line was practically at the door, and there he felt as if he were living in a suburb of New York. New York he considered to be the center of the world of the arts in this country.

He told me many stories of his life in Europe. A room in a walk-up, side-street hotel, a nearby market, a hot plate on the table. There he might stay for a winter or a couple of months until he got the essence of the place recorded in his typical rapid drawings. One such place I saw in Florence. It was 1950, and Italy had not yet recovered from the war. There was no new building and very little reconstruction. Hotel rooms were at a premium, and we were having difficulty finding a place to stay. Finally John announced that he had a friend, a hotel man who might help us. There we landed, were greeted effusively and given a small but adequate room for one night. That turned out to be one of the hotels where John and his mother had spent a winter some time before and subsisted by the use of a hot plate for cooking and the ready availability of Italian food shops. There was never any note of heroism or of a plea for sympathy but always a sense of the ridiculous ways in which human beings can and do exist.

He liked and appreciated good food; but if circumstances dictated that only the simplest was available at the moment, he was entirely willing to accept it. As a matter of fact one of his sayings was, "I like simple direct food." This was meant to imply his active dislike of chopped up, mashed up, mixed up concoctions. It was through John that I came to distrust most foods labeled "gourmet." Part of his approach to food was quite naturally visual. He wanted it to look right and thoroughly enjoyed having dinner parties where the food was properly presented. He liked the fact that I could prepare and serve the kind of meal that appealed to aesthetic as well as gustatory senses. And he always showed his pleasure at these simple attainments. It was all part of our way of life that was so happy.

Another aspect of our almost strange compatibility was our mutual feeling about details. One of his precepts was that it is the aim of art to eliminate detail. And this he did in such a wonderful way. An example is the almost complete elimination of features in the faces of the figures in his compositions, yet everyone has a definite personality. But behind this deliberate exclusion of detail there was the most meticulous adherence to principles of architecture, physics, anatomy, and even music.

He never stopped learning. He read extensively, his interests were wide, and he had a prodigious memory. His knowledge of geography was as extensive as that of history. He first became interested in drawing as a very small child in a geography class in school. He began drawing maps and was fascinated by the relationships of land masses. This interest was strengthened by the fact that his father traveled a great deal. His father was born in England; his mother in Romania. The servants in the home were Hungarian. French was the common language of social intercourse. His father wrote German poetry, his sister spoke Greek. John did not talk until he was five years old. The family was becoming worried about his mental capacities, when one fine day he announced to the maid (in Hungarian) that he wanted a glass of milk and a piece of black bread. It seems that he had a grand conglomeration of languages in his head, and it took some time to get them sorted out. It was some time later that he added Spanish, Italian, and Portuguese. It is probably true that he spoke no language without an accent. He never forgot any of them. I was with him when our boat stopped in Lisbon. His old friend Dario met us

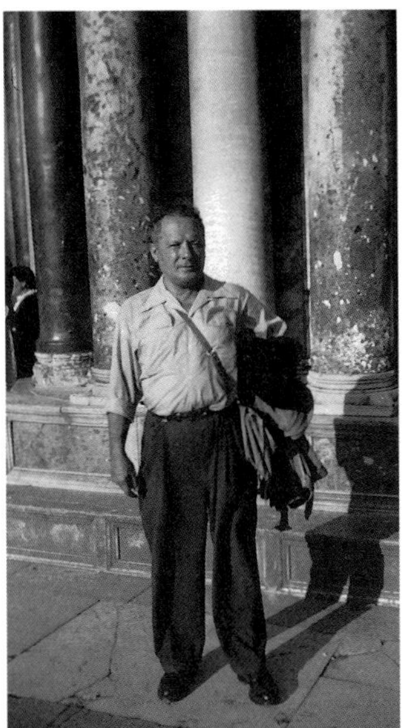

Fig. 75
John Barber, Venice, 1950

and took us to his home for a gala dinner. John had not been in Portugal for seventeen years, but that night he carried on a fluent conversation in Portuguese with his old friends. Occasionally he saw some of his Romanian friends in New York and again spoke fluently in their language. This background of multiple languages contributed a great deal to his wealth of expression in English.

· · ·

He was never perturbed by people watching him sketch, as long as they did not interfere. Actually, he drew with a very hard pencil with a very sharp point, so there was not much for the casual observer to see. He found out early that the less attention he paid to people gaping at him, the quicker they became discouraged and would move on. There was a comedy of errors when John was in Crete and as always drawing the local color and attitudes and feelings. He was noticed by the police standing near the docks day after day always "writing" in his book. Finally, he was called to the local police headquarters where the official in charge asked to see his book. He examined it very carefully, turning it sideways and upside down, looking for clues as to its meaning. It turned out that they suspected John of being a spy and that his sketches were disguised maps or coded bits of information. The whole incident ended, when they finally understood each other, in a great deal of merriment. When John left the island, it was the police that gave him a farewell feast at the station. He was taken completely unawares, and when he was summoned to the station he thought that someone else had become suspicious of him. So the whole incident ended happily, even to his being given a present of a huge basket of fruit and flowers as he boarded the ship for his return to the mainland.

There was an amusing incident at one of the elite clubs of Philadelphia where we had been invited to hear a well-known man speak on the current prob-

lems of the Near East. At one point John suddenly stood up and announced that the land area of Israel was some 100 square miles less than the speaker had stated, and as usual he was right, for he and the speaker got together after the meeting and discussed the matter. There was a corollary bit of amusement associated with this incident. When John made his statement of disagreement (no one ever disagreed with this particular speaker), a woman sitting next to me leaned over and said, "Is that man a Communist?" And my most brilliant reply was, "No, he is my husband."

There was never a dull moment living with John. I have no memory of him staring into space as I have seen so many people do. He was reading, sketching, listening, observing, talking, making plans for a new composition, testing color combinations, writing letters, planning a trip, indulging his hobby of making Romanian eggplant, or telling me how to make a favorite dish—mamaliga, stuffed red peppers, Greek grape leaves, Tunisian cous-cous, or Italian grilled sardines. It was all fun. He used to say that cooking was my occupational therapy after spending a usual day struggling with the complications of my patients. Running the house, entertaining, cooking never seemed to me anything but an interest and a joy. It was part of our total lives together, and we always seemed to be in high gear.

· · ·

Every mental picture I have of John depicts him as one of the most secure people I have ever known. His cultural background and his intellectual interests only added to his sense of independence and freedom from the ordinary dictates of society. In the course of everyday living, these qualities were seen in his complete abandon of convention when the situation permitted and his complete acceptance of the same dictates should circumstances be changed. As an example, the matter of clothes. A suit had to be tailor-made, and the material was chosen with the greatest care. He enjoyed being well-dressed and took pride in his appearance. But for traveling we were both of the same school and for the most part accepted the slogan "when among strangers, it doesn't matter what you wear, and when among friends it also doesn't matter." The most comfortable, the lightest weight, and the most useful were the bases of our travelling wardrobes. This was one more contribution to the so-important sense of freedom. There was usually no need to wait in line for a porter, for all we had could easily be carried between us. Once in a hotel room we could be established in about fifteen minutes. We often laughed about all the trouble we had avoided. A typical experience was arriving in Venice—and nothing is more beautiful than arriving in Venice by train. The walk through the station is short, and the sudden impact of the Venetian scene is overwhelming as it flashes into focus as we emerge on the plaza between the station and the Grand Canal. The light, color, excitement, noises, movement, sky, water, people, bridges, walks, buildings—this is Venice! After a few brief moments of drinking in as much as possible, we walked perhaps two blocks to the hotel which was to become a familiar landmark. We got the room of our choice, a corner room facing the canal, away from the street and its all-night noises. In just half an hour we had showered, unpacked, made ourselves "at home," and were out on the street walking toward the busy market area. The aroma of roasting coffee, the ridiculously and artistically displayed edibles in the windows of the restaurants, the crowds and crowds of people, the chattering, the selling and bargaining, the laughter, the good nature, sometimes shouting and scolding, and everywhere children playing—all this followed us until we reached an outdoor restaurant in a beautiful garden beside the canal. And so we had our first meal together in Venice. I felt a peculiar sense of having

always been a part of it, and I think if urged I would have settled for staying a long, long time. Shopping in Venice was probably unique. After walking from one end of the city to the other and all the cross-walks in between, one fine day we spied a "5 & 10." It was large and in general very much like the American store of similar stature. Anyway we had fun just poking around to see what they had to offer and ended by buying something like toothpaste and what was analogous to Ivory soap. Our next and only purchase was an espresso machine. In Venice, on a back street there is a shop that deals in espresso machines only. They are of every type, size, and shape imaginable. So we came off with one and not only carried it with us the whole rest of the trip, but used it daily for the next ten years.

. . .

Recently in a television episode on World War I, there was an account of the sinking of the Lusitania. There was a full screen blow-up of a page of the *New York Times* heralding the sailing of the ship the next day. In the contiguous column was a notice by the German government stating that, in essence, the ship would be subject to attack. John and his father were in this country at the time and had passage to sail on that trip. John read that notice and, as was so characteristic of him, interpreted it correctly. He told his father that they should cancel their tickets, which they did just 24 hours before the ship left New York on its fatal trip.

As a child, John was very proud of being able (according to his own evaluation) to speak English and would show off in school by reciting in English the names of all the states of the U. S. A. He then added the principal rivers and capitals of the states. This recitation remained one of his parlor tricks throughout his life. He would do the recitation as he had done it originally with all the odd bits of pronunciation. Portuguese came later when he went there as a young man. By that time he had already found that, for him, there was so much in common among the various languages, particularly the Latin-root languages, that he considered learning a new one only a matter of a little listening and a bit of practice. Portuguese was apparently no problem. One of his more fascinating stories was how he learned Italian. It seems that he made up his mind to go to Italy. With his usual direct way of doing things, he bought a ticket and an Italian dictionary. The trip from Paris to Marseille was in the nature of eighteen hours. The entire time was spent in devouring the dictionary, and, according to John's succinct way of expressing himself, he simply got off the train speaking Italian. When I first heard the story, I wondered a bit. But many years later I went to Istanbul with John. It was one of the few places we visited he had never been before. And there I witnessed that, even without a dictionary but by observing and listening, he was picking up words and phrases of modern Turkish.

· · ·

Very often over the years people have remarked when seeing John's work, "He must have been a very religious man." Similar remarks have been made by sophisticated as well as uneducated or even somewhat primitive people. Perhaps the most interesting have been made by the uneducated, at least as far as formal education is concerned. By far the most discerning and pertinent remarks have been made by those with no exposure to the art world of today. This group also includes children.

As John had so well digested the history of the world, the history of religion was automatically included. Perhaps his earliest lesson in religion came from his father. He was quite young. It was a Sunday morning when he and his father were out walking in the center of the city of Galati. As they passed the Greek Orthodox Cathedral, the sounds of music—choir and organ—could be heard. With his

usual if still-young curiosity, John asked what goes on in such a place. His father stopped short, took him by the hand and answered, "John, the greatest stupidities in the world," and they proceeded on their way. That was enough to make him want to know more. As he began moving around the world, studying the art and culture wherever he went, religion became an integral part of the art world. Since the greatest works of art are in some way related to religion, there was an automatic interest engendered.

We went to Ravenna for the sole purpose of seeing certain frescoes in a church. He could not find the church he remembered so well. It was most unusual for him to forget a location, especially one connected with art. We were referred from one church to another, all to no avail. Finally we met an old priest who told us very vividly of the sack and utter destruction of the church we were seeking. One more of the utterly senseless results of the German scourge of Italy. John wept and we left the city.

Going into the Cathedral of St. Francis in Assisi was an experience never to be forgotten. John kept up an uninterrupted discourse on the history of the structure. As we went from one level to another, he pointed out the meaning of everything we could see. The balance of the structure, the beauty of the arches, the grace of the whole in its complete form, all formed part of the ultimate enjoyment of the frescoes of the lower level. Not only were we looking at the paintings but there was a service going on at the same time, and the priests came and went paying no more attention to us than we to them. The organ was playing beautiful music. All of this was a background against which John could enjoy and absorb and love the paintings. But even here he knew perfectly well the meaning of the Mass and never did anything to interfere in any way.

In another church half a world away, in the Cathedral in Guadalajara in Mexico, we were sitting quietly in a pew while a service was going on. A priest, who had apparently noticed John working with his sketchbook, came and sat down beside us. He asked to see what John was doing. John made a small contribution, was given his blessing and told: "Write as much as you want." It was in that particular church that John made a drawing which included a statue of the Virgin wearing a crown. The crown was at a slightly rakish angle which might just be lost on many observers.

When travelling, we frequently met priests, ministers, rabbis, and nuns. By and large they always seemed to be the most intelligent of the group no matter where we were. I remember an orthodox rabbi on the old *George Washington* who became a character to talk to. He was "so kosher" that he did not trust the U. S. Lines' assurance that they had a kosher kitchen set up on board. He carried his own food in packages for the entire crossing. Another was an Italian priest on the ship with us from Venice to Istanbul. He was primarily a musician and had been the organist at the Church of St. Francis in Assisi. He and John had long conversations throughout the four-day trip. They exchanged ideas and discussed many subjects. By the time we reached Istanbul, John was invited to have lunch in the monastery where the priest lived. At that time he was head of the only Catholic church in the city. We often wondered what happened to him in the great upheaval of church and state that happened in Turkey soon after. We never heard from him again. An Australian priest was another of our shipboard acquaintances. Some time later he came to Philadelphia. We entertained him for dinner and showed him the city. I remember most vividly his comment as we drove along the Schuylkill through Fairmount Park, that nowhere was there a single person to be seen. It was a beautiful day, the park was in full bloom, and not a soul in sight anywhere. His remark reflected the contrast between a certain way of life in this country and the rest of the world. This is a lonely country. Often the foreigner is disturbed by, even if not altogether aware of the real meaning of no one in the park.

In Mexico as we drove through the villages, we never missed a church. Always looking for something of beauty or interest, John never failed to make an extra sojourn to a shrine, church, wedding, or funeral. And it was all worthwhile and is all in his paintings. We went into the secret convent in Mexico City and crawled through the secret entrance. We watched and listened to the Catholic service through the same bars that the hidden nuns peered through in silence and secrecy. There was also a room for flagellations. The robes and whips and leather straps were hanging on the wall. And John told me the whole story of the convent.

. . .

John's first trip to Mexico came about unexpectedly and unplanned. He was living in New York alone in 1941. He became restless and rather depressed. So the idea of seeing this country appeared to be the only solution to his feelings. Had it not been for the war in Europe, he probably would have gone there, but as second choice he arranged for a bus trip to California. He found little of sustaining interest there and started East. The route took him to a border town. Again, and so typically, he used the short stop to walk across the line into Mexico. He did this with little enthusiasm, as he had always shunned Mexico because of the examples he had seen of its art and the garish coloring in everything he had seen. But on seeing for himself, he immediately fell in love with the life, the grace of movement of the people, the rhythm of life, and perhaps above all the coloring. He considered the Mexican color of life in all forms beautiful and completely compatible with his way of looking at the world. The muted colors of the peasants' clothing, the faded walls of buildings, the subdued forms that pervaded all struck a sympathetic note in his thinking and feeling. He left the bus tour, went to Taxco, where he rented a house on a hillside, and stayed for several months. In fact, he left on December 7, 1941. It was on that fateful morning that he became aware of strains of the "Star Spangled Banner" coming from the radios of the neighbors on the hill above him. He knew immediately that something unusual was happening. As he had not been in touch with the news of the world for some time, he suspected the meaning of this radio announcement. He also knew that a naturalized citizen outside the country when war is declared must return immediately. And thus the sojourn in Mexico was ended. But the drawings in the sketchbooks were the basis for many paintings over a period of years.

Every painting of his mature life was done directly from a pen-and-ink drawing. And the drawing was done "on location," as it were. Every figure was done from life, and the whole was a complete composition. It was said many times by people who understood his work that perhaps his greatest genius was in composition. The drawings took many days of work. There were usually several in the making at one time. A figure would be added here or there, a background of special interest might flash into view. On the last trip to Italy, in the summer of 1965, we were in Genoa for a few days before sailing. It was raining, and the day was dreary. John asked that I stay in the hotel while he ran down to the market. He wanted something special for the background of a drawing, and he knew exactly what he wanted and exactly where it was.

• • •

John learned from all the art he saw. Nothing seemed too small, too insignificant for his attention and investigation. The same inquisitive vein led him to explore the new forms and techniques that were appearing in the world of art. But after pursuing the

new techniques, methods, and media, nowhere did he find any semblance of "fine" art in the mechanical construction of simple geometric forms done in direct colors and even less in the unplanned productions of abstract expressionism. John always used the classical meaning of the word "modern" in relation to art. And that meant anything beyond ancient or in contrast to ancient or classical. To be able to abstract the human qualities of a personality and record them on canvas is genius. To draw lines forming nothing or drip paint in confusion is simply a confession of utter failure. Fortunately, John knew so well the values he believed in that he was never tempted to adopt the prevalent popular forms of expression.

The universality of John's art is obvious in his portrayal of people. A man working or a woman carrying a baby was of any nation or race. The only definition of locale is in the trappings of the background or in local customs such as Mexicans eating in the market place. A Dutch child might be equipped with wooden shoes in one painting, but in a portrait the same child could become again a universal child.

• • •

A scheduled life? Never. The quick reaction and spur-of-the-moment decision, the bits and pieces of living. Schedules? One cold and snowy night a few days before Christmas, I came home from my day in the office to be greeted with a wonderful excitement and air of anticipation. John had just read that the lights were to be turned on that evening in the town of Bethlehem. He was impressed by the description and thought we should go see the display. So off we went on an adventure. The snow, the ice, the cold wind all became a confluent sort of background for our spree, and there was not the slightest hesitation about the pros and cons of going. That, too, was very typical. John had a wonderful idea about something a bit out of the ordinary, and I accepted it wholeheartedly without the remotest idea of being negative about it. And, of course, it was one of the many little episodes that made life so wonderful. There is one more addendum to this little episode. We got back from our toot about 11 P.M. and then had dinner.

Another fine day I came home to an aura of excitement and was promptly told that we were going to Holland the next week. John had read of the opening of the Rembrandt 350th anniversary, and it was immediately obvious that we would go. We went on a Dutch ship which landed in Rotterdam. That was my first view of the devastation of war. There was not a single building standing in the whole city. We walked through rubble and somehow managed to get to the station and got a train for Amsterdam. There the city was straining at its seams. There was literally no hotel room available. But John always had a friend no matter where we found ourselves. This man had a small hotel on a side street. He told us of the impossible situation, tried some of his colleagues to no avail. Finally he gave us an address. He also promised that the following day he could accommodate us in his establishment. So off we went to one of the more exciting nights I ever spent. We were a bit taken aback at the general aspect of the place but under the circumstances decided not to be too critical, and in we went. Only after we were well established did we get the message loud and clear that this was one of Amsterdam's best brothels. We laughed half the night and had a great time being privy to the ways of "the other half." We did move the next day and spent a week on one of the islands just outside of the city.

There was another time of great adventure in Italy. That year John had decided to take in some of the small towns north of Florence. He knew the history of the region and of the towns. After a few days in Florence, we set out for Mantua. For some reason we did not find it very interesting or perhaps not as colorful as most of the other places we had stayed. So we proceeded to Parma, where bad weather contributed to our feeling not completely comfortable. We did manage to see most of the town, and seeing the old buildings, the background structures of the history of some of the powerful families of the past, was like being in a fairy land, but somehow a real fairy land. The following day we took off for the third town of the tour that we had outlined. Cremona was a delightful spot. We found a very fine little hotel, the weather was a cool bright early fall day, and a festival of cheeses was going on just outside our window.

But enough of following a schedule! Next morning I woke before the sun was really up to find myself alone in the room. Within a very short time John came steaming in, saying as he opened the door, "Can you get ready in fifteen minutes?" He had been to the local station and found that there was a train leaving in half an hour for a town I had never heard of, where we could catch the only train of the day for Chioggia, of which I had heard but vaguely. So, into the bag our meager belongings and onto ourselves our traveling clothes. We made the train and even managed a cup of café en route. Finally we got to the new and strange town and found the connecting train waiting. That one was a cross between a streetcar of my youth and an old-fashioned local train. We chugged along, stopping every few miles at all the local stations. Finally, we seemed to be heading out to the hinterlands with no visible signs of habitation and were the last two passengers. This called for at least a half hour of fraternizing with the lone conductor. He recommended an *albergo* just across from the station. As we got off the train the local bus pulled in looking for passengers. We did not take it, as we wished to investigate the recommended place. But we decided not to stay, as it was on the very outskirts of the town, and John's inviolate rule was to stay in the center of any town. Having made the decision, we went to the usual café beside the station and waited for the next bus. After some time had passed and no bus, we asked about its schedule. It had a schedule based on the arrival of the trains, and there were two per day. This added up to the fact that there would be no more bus transportation until the next morning. And so we walked and laughed and stopped and talked. As we got just within the town, John suddenly put down the suitcase, dashed out in the street where he hailed a garbage truck. His later explanation was that garbage collectors always know the best hotels, and since we knew nothing of the town he thought he should get some good information. We took the man's advice and had a delightful and almost perfect ten days. The hotel was the best in town, very comfortable and delightful even to its location right on the edge of the southern tip of the Venetian lagoon and facing the town square. Not only is Chioggia everything the books had recorded but beautiful boats, beautiful fishermen, and beautiful people. John worked all the time. On the piers, in the boats, in the square, on the beach, we made friends everywhere. We ate at the fishing pier. The owner and chief cook and waiter all in one became a friend and invited us to come any time and he would make us a meal from the boat that was being unloaded. One day we asked for something special, I think it was fresh sardines. He asked us to wait as the boat had just come around the bend, and it would take him only minutes to get them. We waited and had a great meal with great company.

· · ·

John referred to himself as probably the only true abstractionist of his era. The things that he saw constantly being promoted as art he regarded as expressions of the decadence of the age. The best summary was probably expressed in his simple statement that the so-called abstract art of the 20th century was the logical expression of the decadence the Western world had achieved. His very succinct version was, "A world that could produce a Buchenwald, is the same world that has produced so-called abstract art."

In his own work, he constantly sought the elements of what he believed to be true abstraction in the field of art. He talked a great deal about abstraction, and his main goal was to get at the heart of a composition by bringing into play as much abstraction as possible. By this he meant seeing the whole without the inclusion of detail. This pertained to all the elements at his command, and he incorporated into his compositions the feeling and emotion of unusual proportions. But he did not ignore the basic elements of composition that have been used by all art from the beginning of Man's time on earth. There was always a mathematical and very fundamental concept. It was so well imbued in his thinking that never was it obviously portrayed by resorting to the kind of productions that some of the accepted abstractionists were producing with lines and angles and splashes of color and dots and dashes and all the rest. John knew the principles of architecture and music as well as anatomy and the physics of light and balance. He delighted in pointing out in a finished work the musical cadences. It was with great joy that he would look at a work and say very frankly that he was looking at it objectively. But there it was, full of rhythm and perfectly balanced. It had all come about without the kind of planning that would go into a scientific project—more like the dreaming that a great mathematician might indulge in before formulating a new concept. Again he would look back at a day's work and with glee point out some element, such as architectural balance, and remark that he really had not planned it that way, but it always came out with the true and real elements of composition there and intact. And so he abstracted.

John painted life. This in itself is an abstraction and he dealt with it as one of his main problems as a painter. Not only are his compositions complete but the individuals in them are all real people. Each and every figure was drawn from life, and they were never posed. But each has its place in the whole, so that the end result is always a complete composition. There are almost no facial features portrayed in the figures. The essence of Man was caught and transmitted to his work.

There are many incidents that would demonstrate this particular aspect of his paintings. It took several trips to the Amish market outside of Philadelphia to get a complete drawing. Each time, of course, the people were different and the scenes were not quite as they had been a month previously. But each time a new figure would be added, or the position of another might be changed. On one occasion an Amish man came to look at the drawing and with great glee pointed to the back aspect of a figure and called him by name, saying over several times, that's him, that's him.

And then there were color and light to be played with. He liked to play with perspective and frequently spoke of using tones of color to indicate perspective rather than the more academic approaches to the problem. Color harmony was also very important to him and always he worked and reworked his palette not only to balance the spectrum of his composition but also to create a balanced whole in the finished work. He felt no need to paint a woman with one bright yellow breast and the other bright purple. But should he need a spot of yellow to complete his color balance, he would incorporate it into the composition, in a logical, beautiful, and soul-satisfying way.

· · ·

It was during his very early years that John became fascinated by the world outside of his own little world of childhood and family life. It was his maternal grandfather who first introduced him to drawing. They would walk hand in hand to the riverfront where his grandfather would point out the grace of ships, and then, most exciting, would be the appearance of a horse-drawn cart. And therein was the birth of John's lifelong fascination with horses. He always maintained that the horse was the most beautiful animal and spent many many hours studying and drawing horses. Very early in his school a teacher evidently recognized his unusual ability to draw and did a great deal to encourage him. This was to develop into his already burning curiosity about the outside world. He studied the maps of the world and became known in his school as the one who always knew where places were. By the time he was six years old, the Russo-Japanese war was in full swing. For some reason he became engrossed with the whole thing. He recalled that he would hurry home from school to read the newspapers about the war. He would spread the papers out on the floor and lie on his belly by the hour, reading every possible detail available. It became a family stunt or at least part of the family life of the times, that John would be called to the living room, after there had been a dinner for his father's business friends, to explain the progress of the war. He loved doing this and developed a prodigious memory for names. He never forgot the names of all the Russian and Japanese captains and generals involved. The era was the beginning of his abiding feeling that the whole world and all peoples are one, and it was his mission to interpret his feelings and beliefs with his fast-developing talent to put on paper a line or a finished figure that had meaning and feeling. The universality of John's interests and exposure to life, from the earliest time of his life, is reflected in his paintings and drawings.

XI. Late Drawings

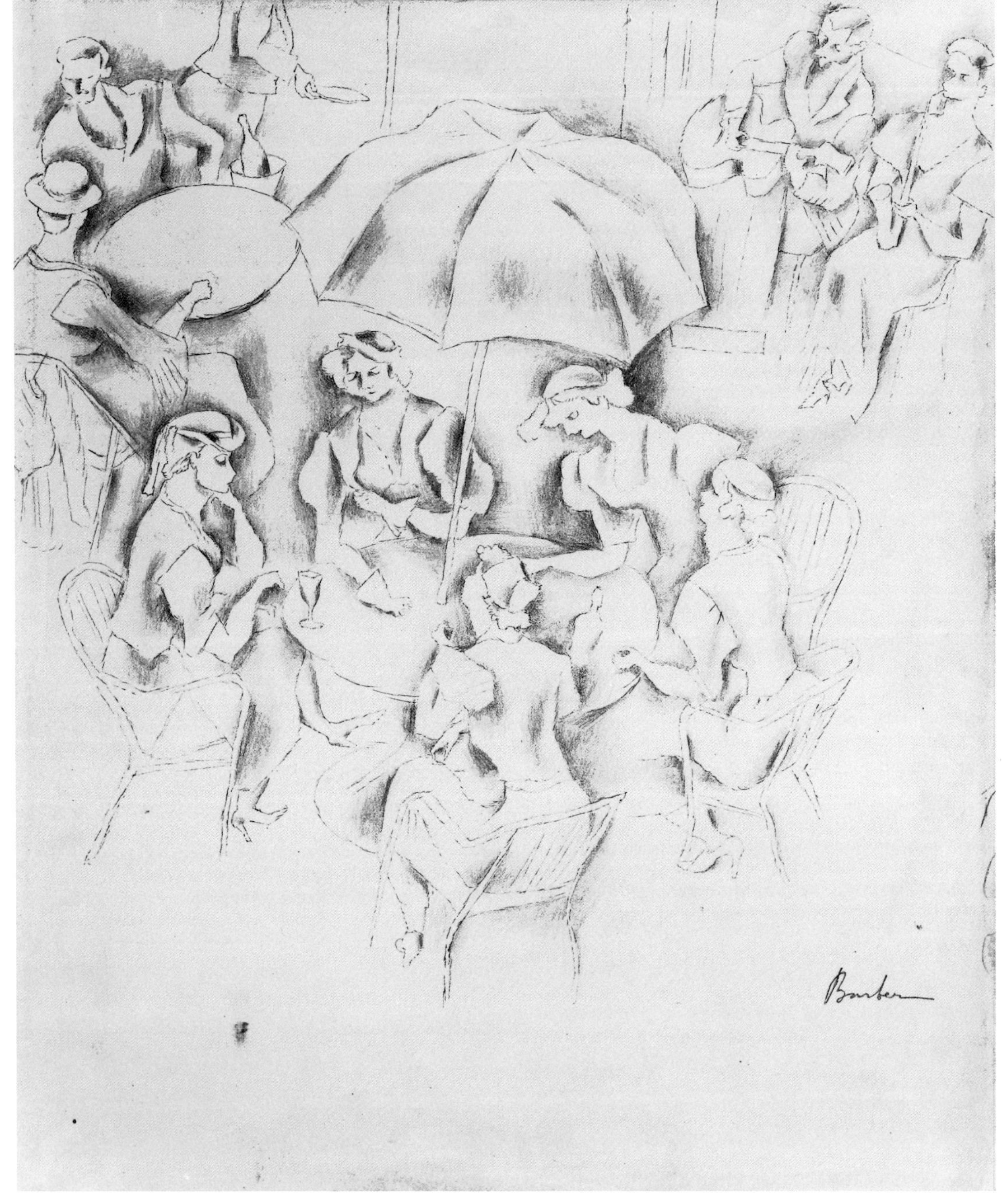

Fig. 76
John Barber
Café Umbrella
Graphite, 15 x 12 ¼
Collection of Dr. Margaret De Ronde Barber,
on loan to The John Barber Memorial Collection,
Bayly Art Museum of the University of Virginia

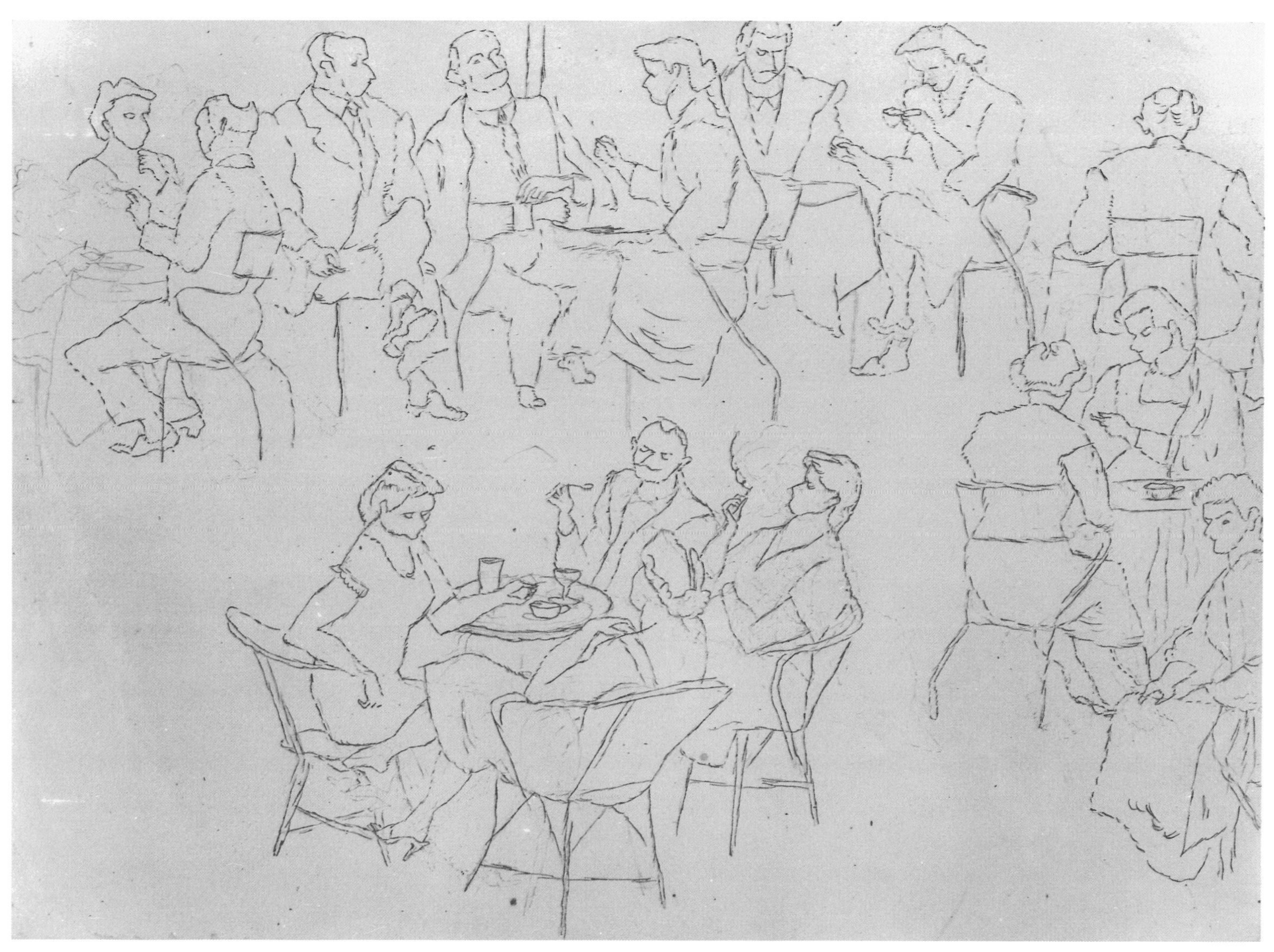

Fig. 77
John Barber
Café, Italy, 1955
Graphite and ink, 9 x 12 1/8
Collection of Dr. Margaret De Ronde Barber,
on loan to The John Barber Memorial Collection,
Bayly Art Museum of the University of Virginia

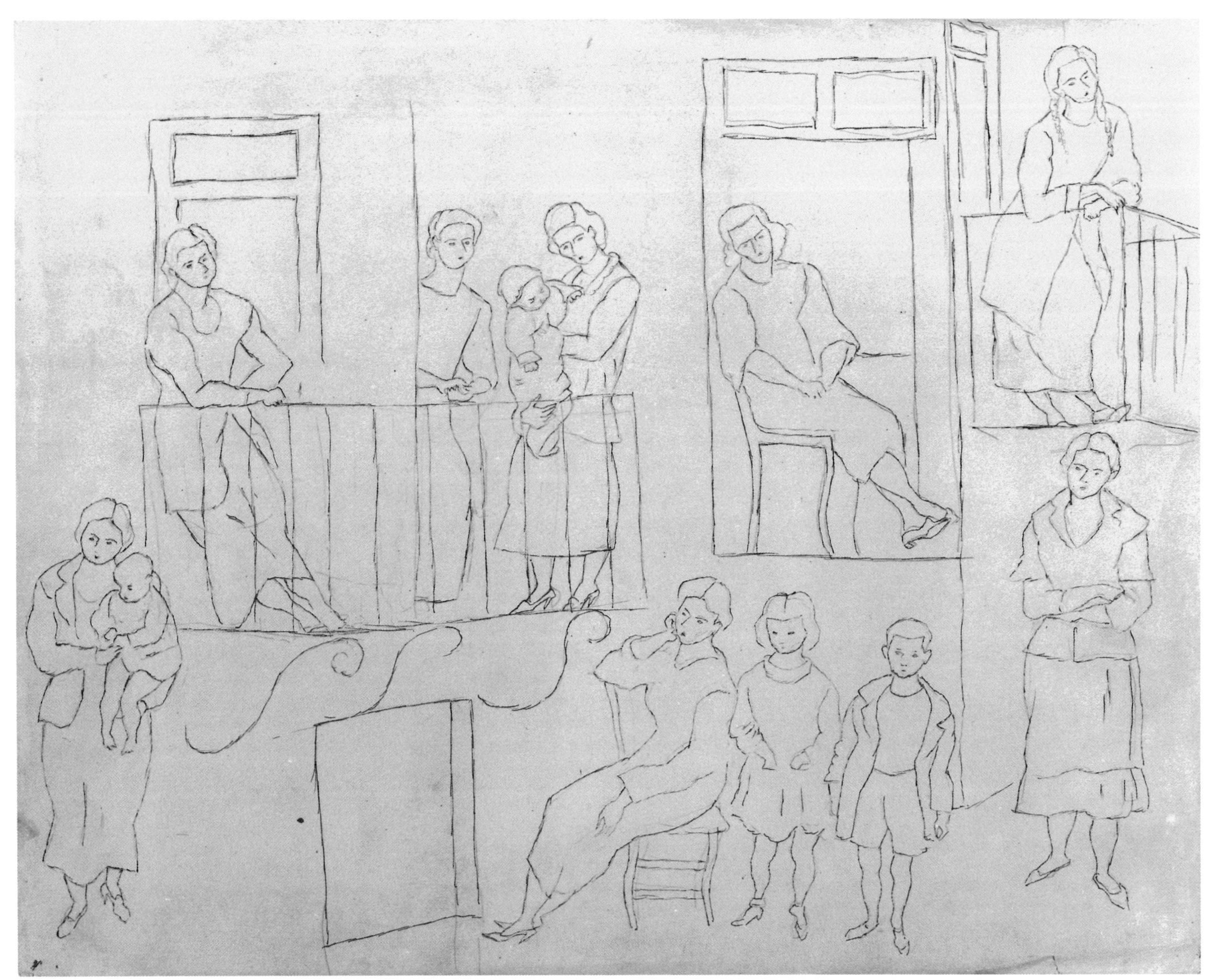

Fig. 78
John Barber
Women, Children, Infants
Graphite and ink, 12 1/8 x 14 3/4
Collection of Dr. Margaret De Ronde Barber,
on loan to The John Barber Memorial Collection,
Bayly Art Museum of the University of Virginia

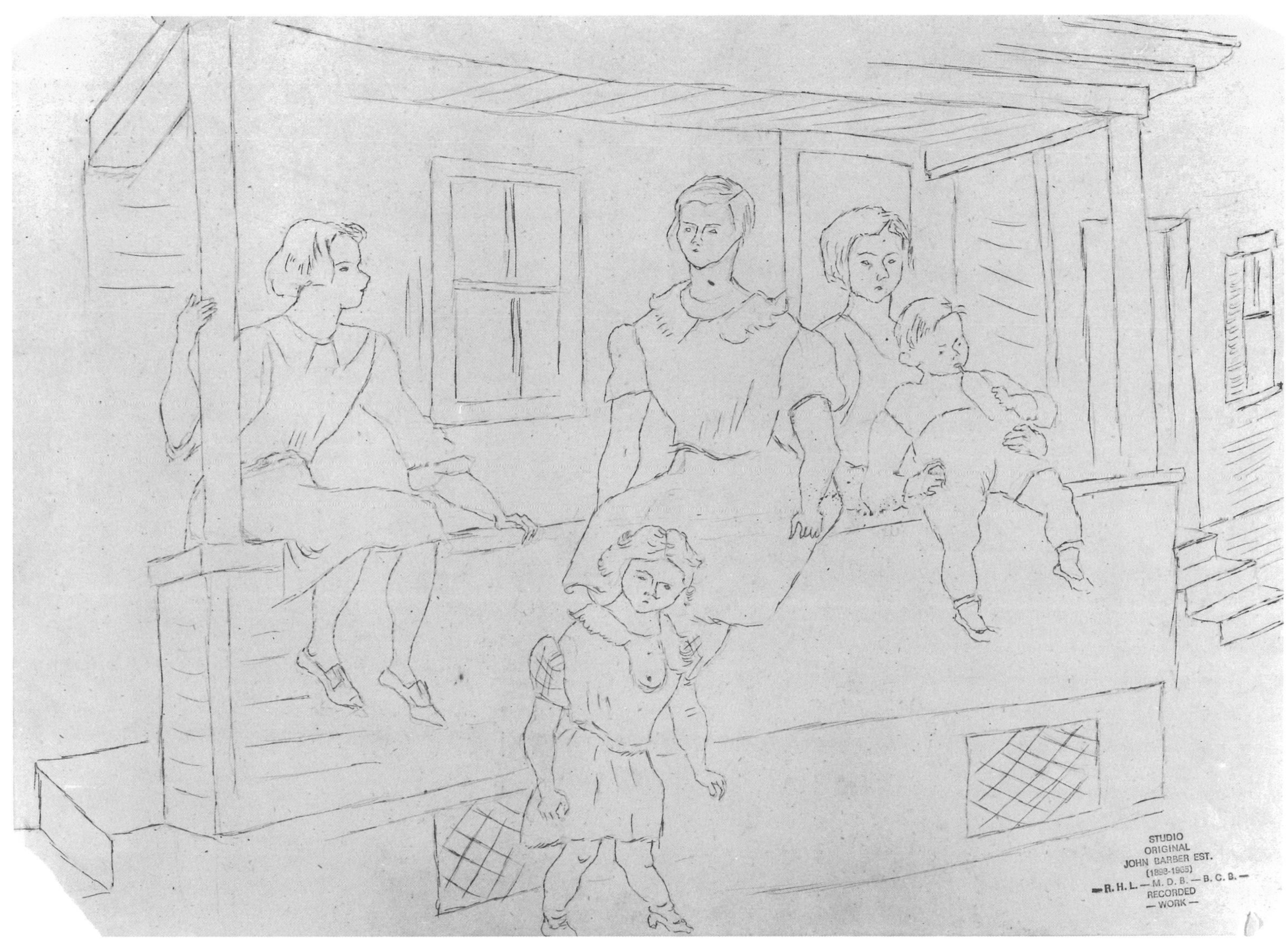

Fig. 79
John Barber
Children on the Porch
Graphite and ink, 9 x 12 ¹/₄
Collection of Dr. Margaret De Ronde Barber,
on loan to The John Barber Memorial Collection,
Bayly Art Museum of the University of Virginia

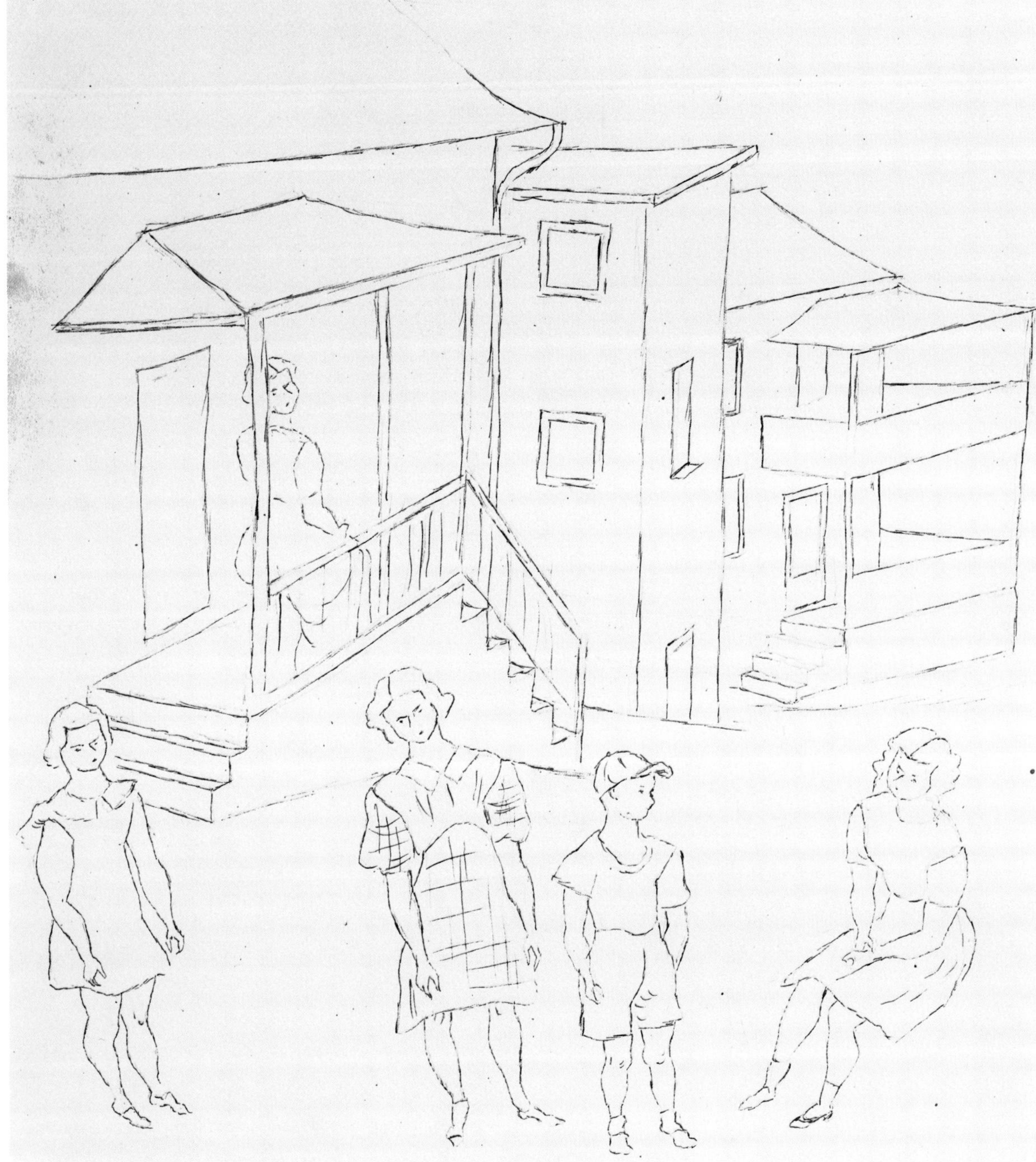

Fig. 80
John Barber
Children in Front of Houses
Graphite and ink, 13 1/4 x 11 5/8
Collection of Dr. Margaret De Ronde Barber,
on loan to The John Barber Memorial Collection,
Bayly Art Museum of the University of Virginia

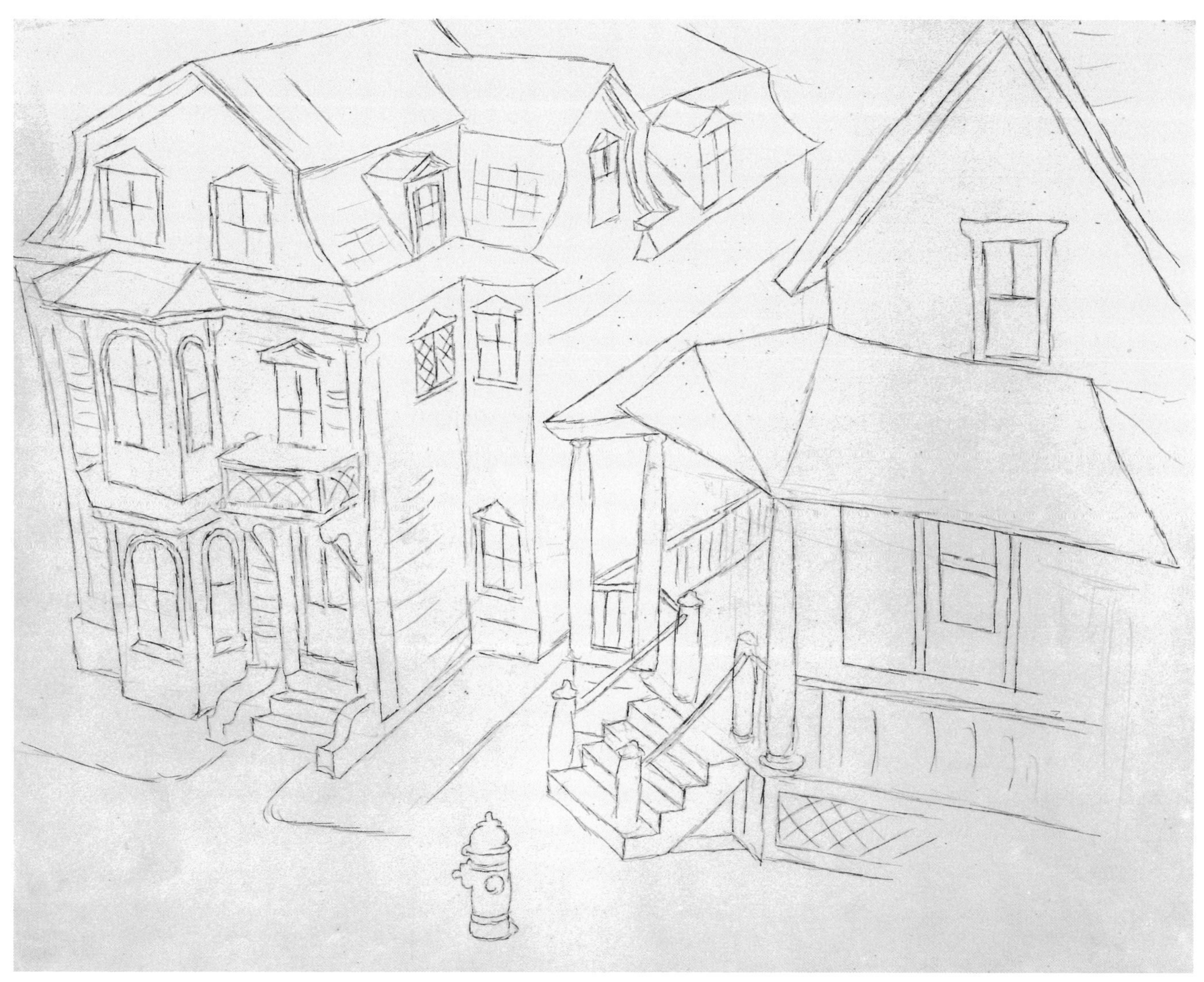

Fig. 81
John Barber
Houses
Graphite and ink, 12 $\frac{1}{8}$ x 14 $\frac{7}{8}$
Collection of Dr. Margaret De Ronde Barber,
on loan to The John Barber Memorial Collection,
Bayly Art Museum of the University of Virginia

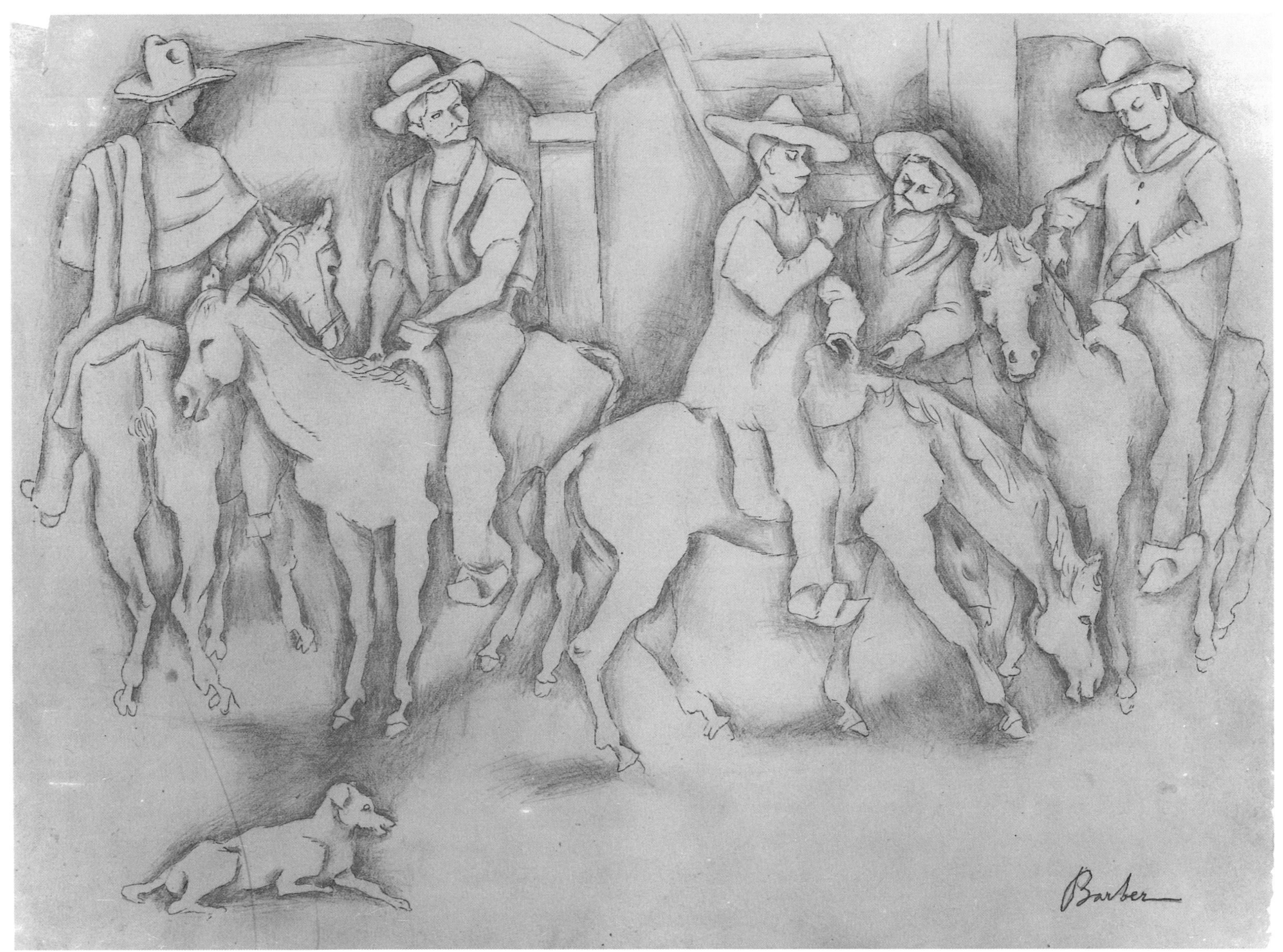

Fig. 82
John Barber
Horsemen, Mexico
Graphite and ink, 9 ¼ x 12 ⅛
Collection of Dr. Margaret De Ronde Barber,
on loan to The John Barber Memorial Collection,
Bayly Art Museum of the University of Virginia

Fig. 83
John Barber
Worshipers, Mexico
Graphite and ink, 11 ¼ x 8 ¾
Collection of Dr. Margaret De Ronde Barber,
on loan to The John Barber Memorial Collection,
Bayly Art Museum of the University of Virginia

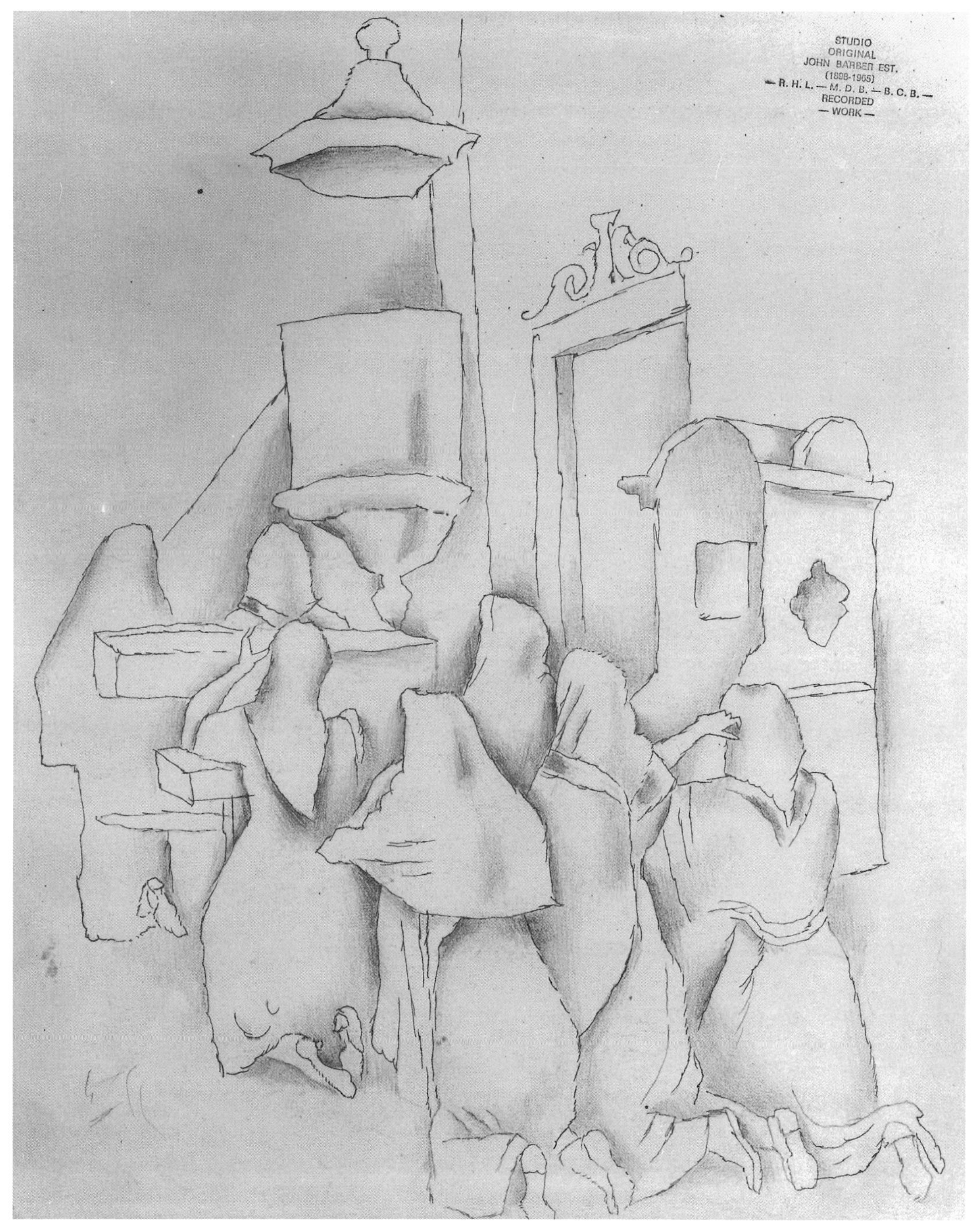

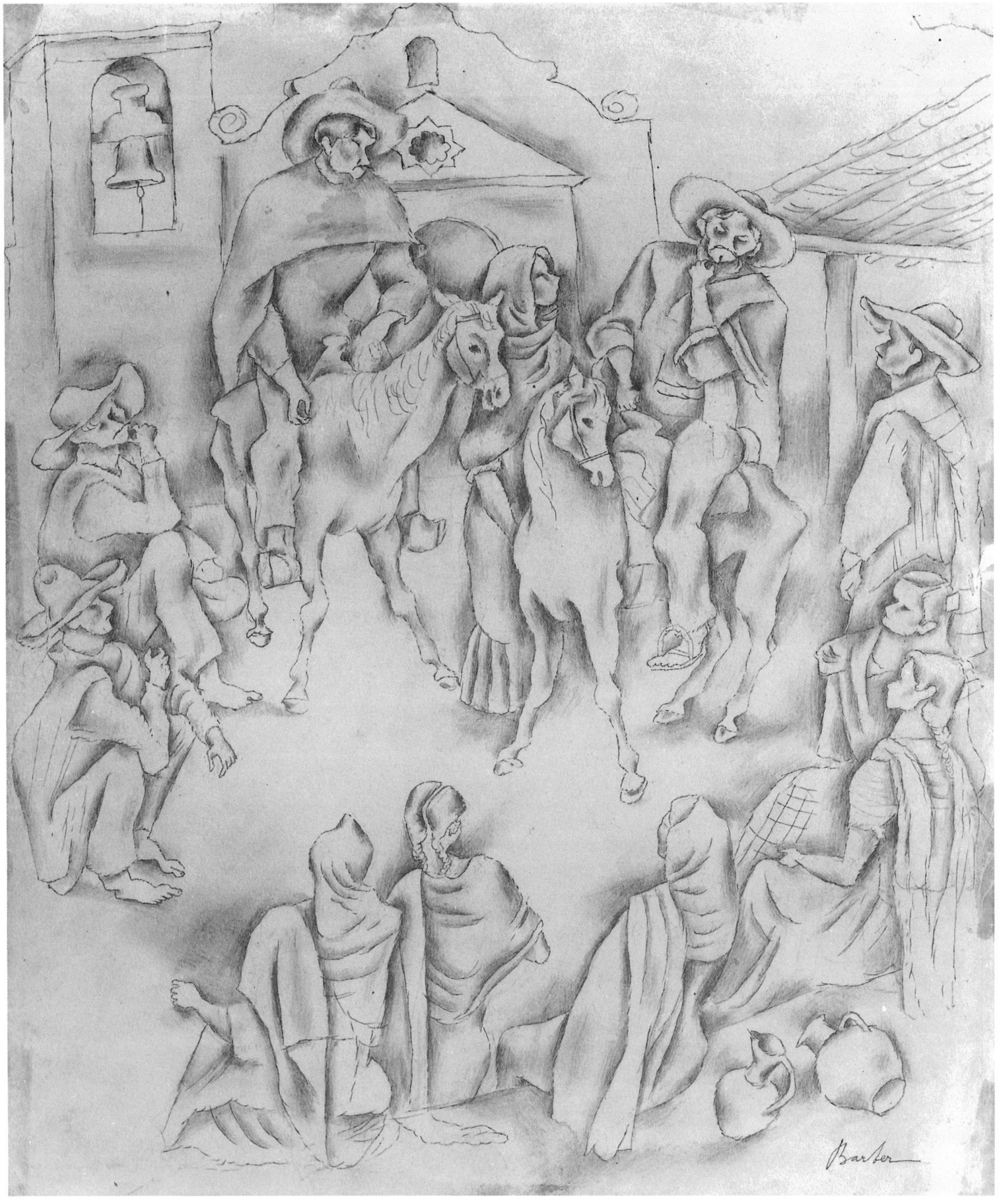

Fig. 84
John Barber
Before the Church
Graphite and ink, 15 x 12 $\frac{1}{8}$
Collection of Dr. Margaret De Ronde Barber,
on loan to The John Barber Memorial Collection,
Bayly Art Museum of the University of Virginia

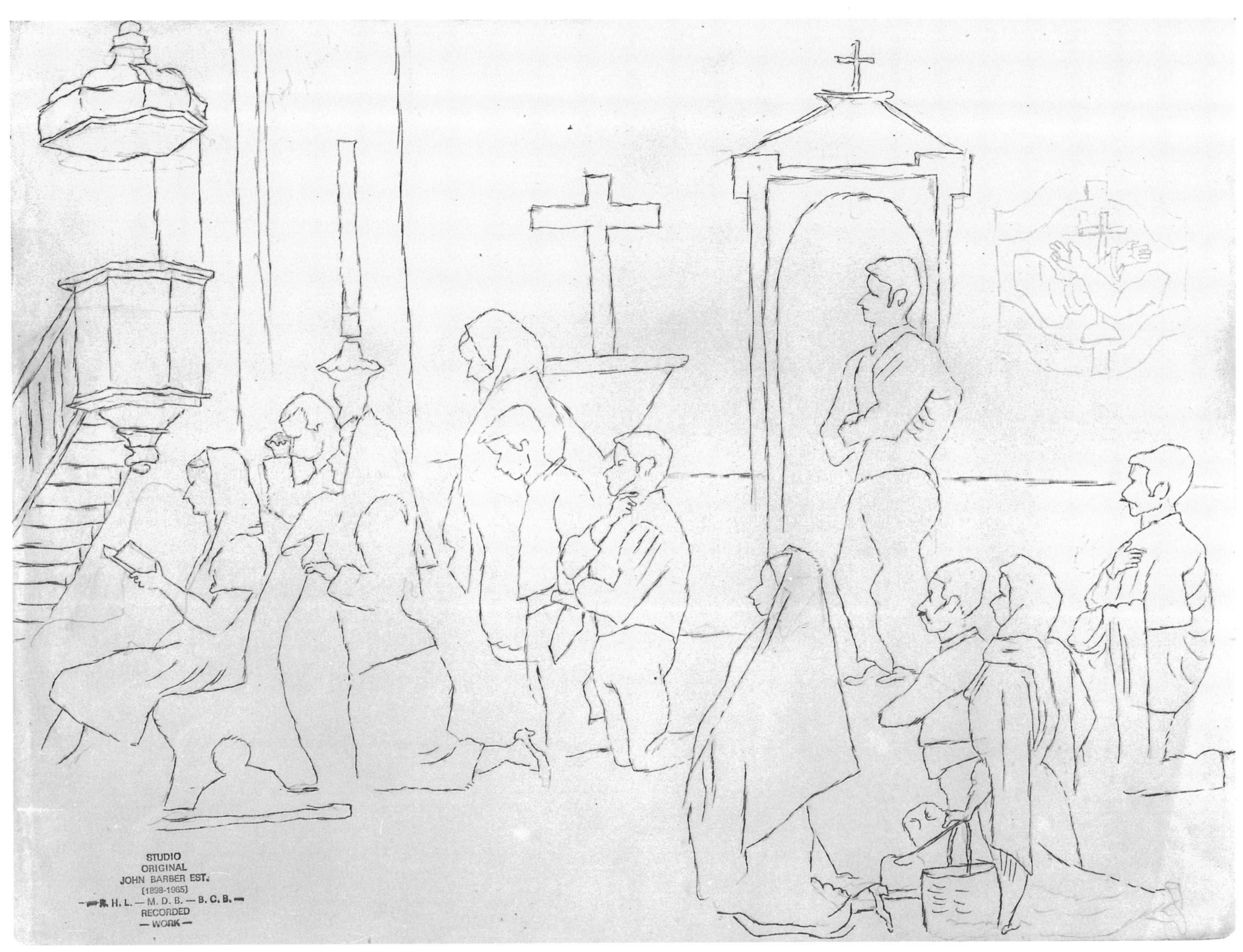

Fig. 85
John Barber
In a Church, Mexico
Graphite and ink, 9 1/8 x 12
Collection of Dr. Margaret De Ronde Barber,
on loan to The John Barber Memorial Collection,
Bayly Art Museum of the University of Virginia

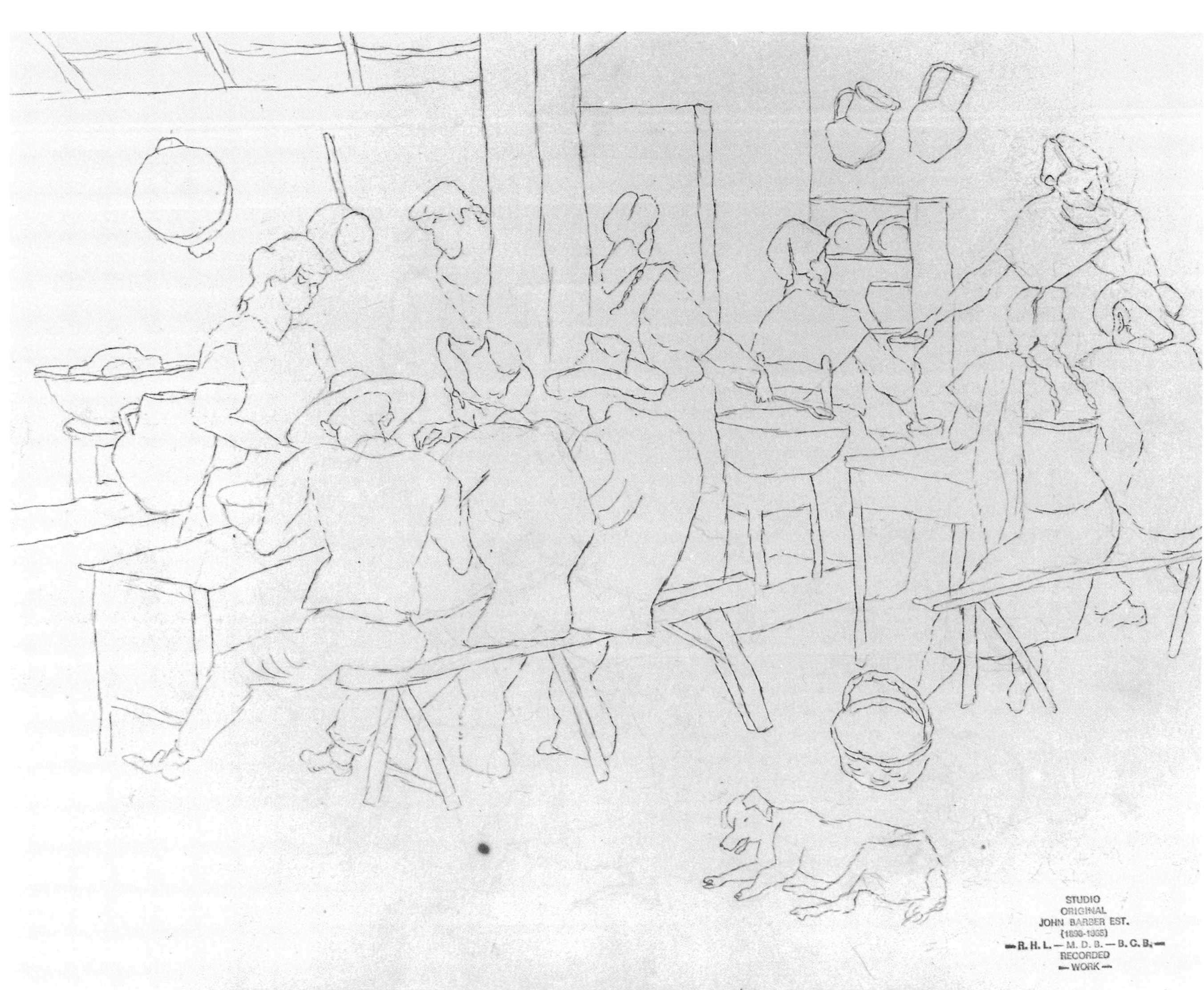

Fig. 86
John Barber
Mexican Kitchen
Graphite and ink, 9 ½ x 11 ½
Collection of Dr. Margaret De Ronde Barber,
on loan to The John Barber Memorial Collection,
Bayly Art Museum of the University of Virginia

172

Fig. 87
John Barber
Crucifixion with Saint Mary, 1949
Graphite and ink, 15 x 12 ¹/₈
Collection of Dr. Margaret De Ronde Barber,
on loan to The John Barber Memorial Collection,
Bayly Art Museum of the University of Virginia

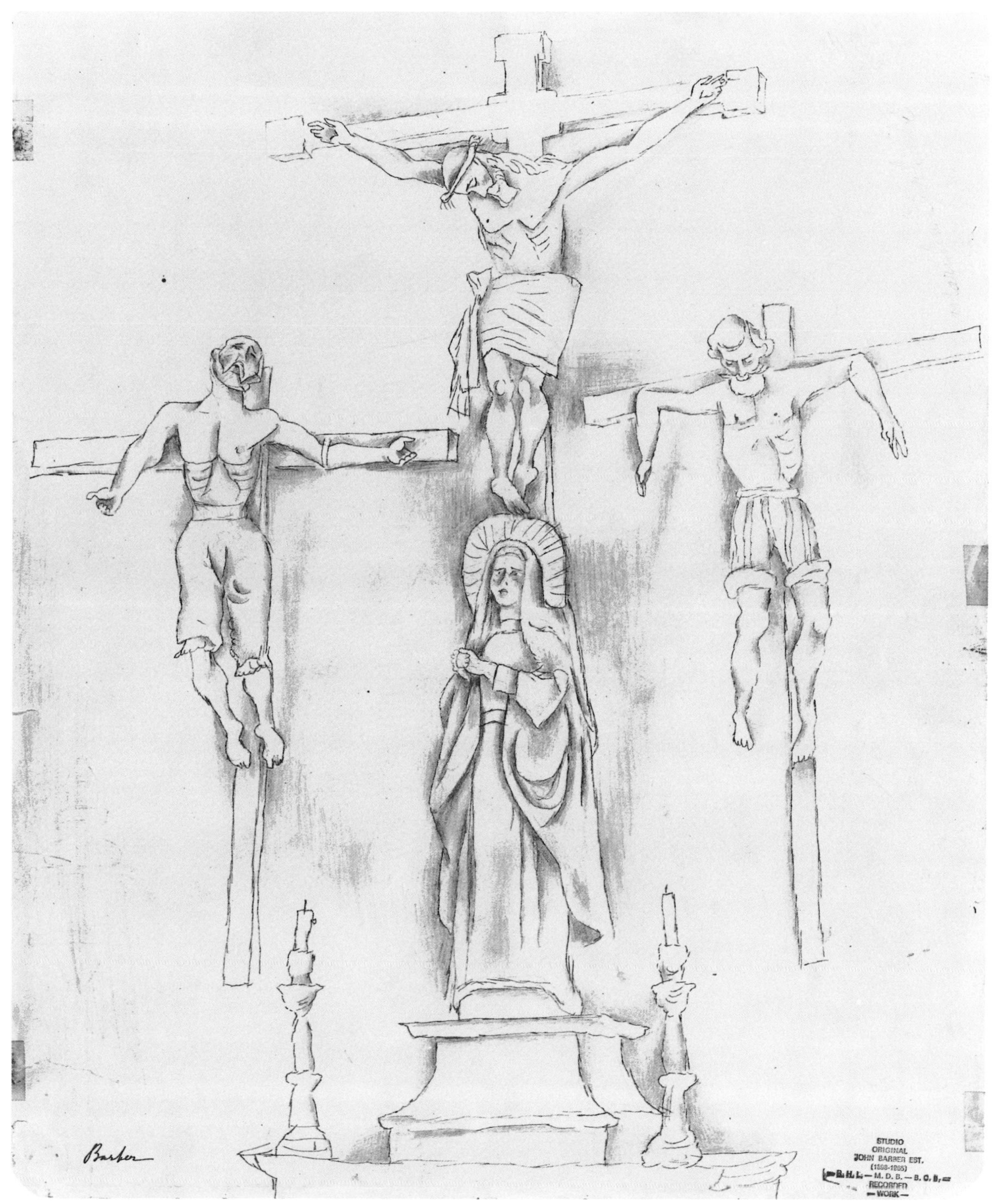

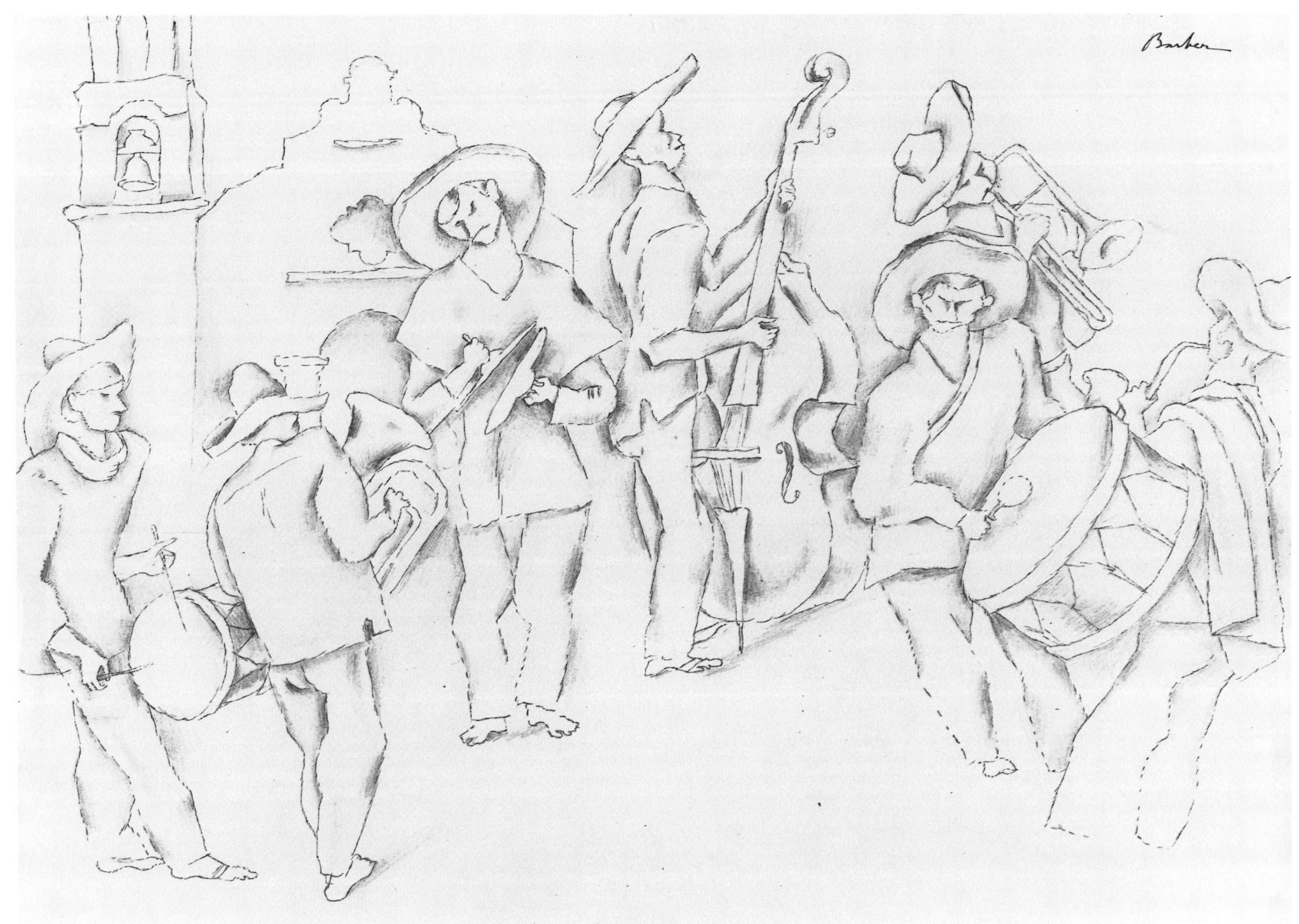

Fig. 88
John Barber
Street Band, Mexico
Graphite and ink, 11 x 15
Collection of Dr. Margaret De Ronde Barber,
on loan to The John Barber Memorial Collection,
Bayly Art Museum of the University of Virginia

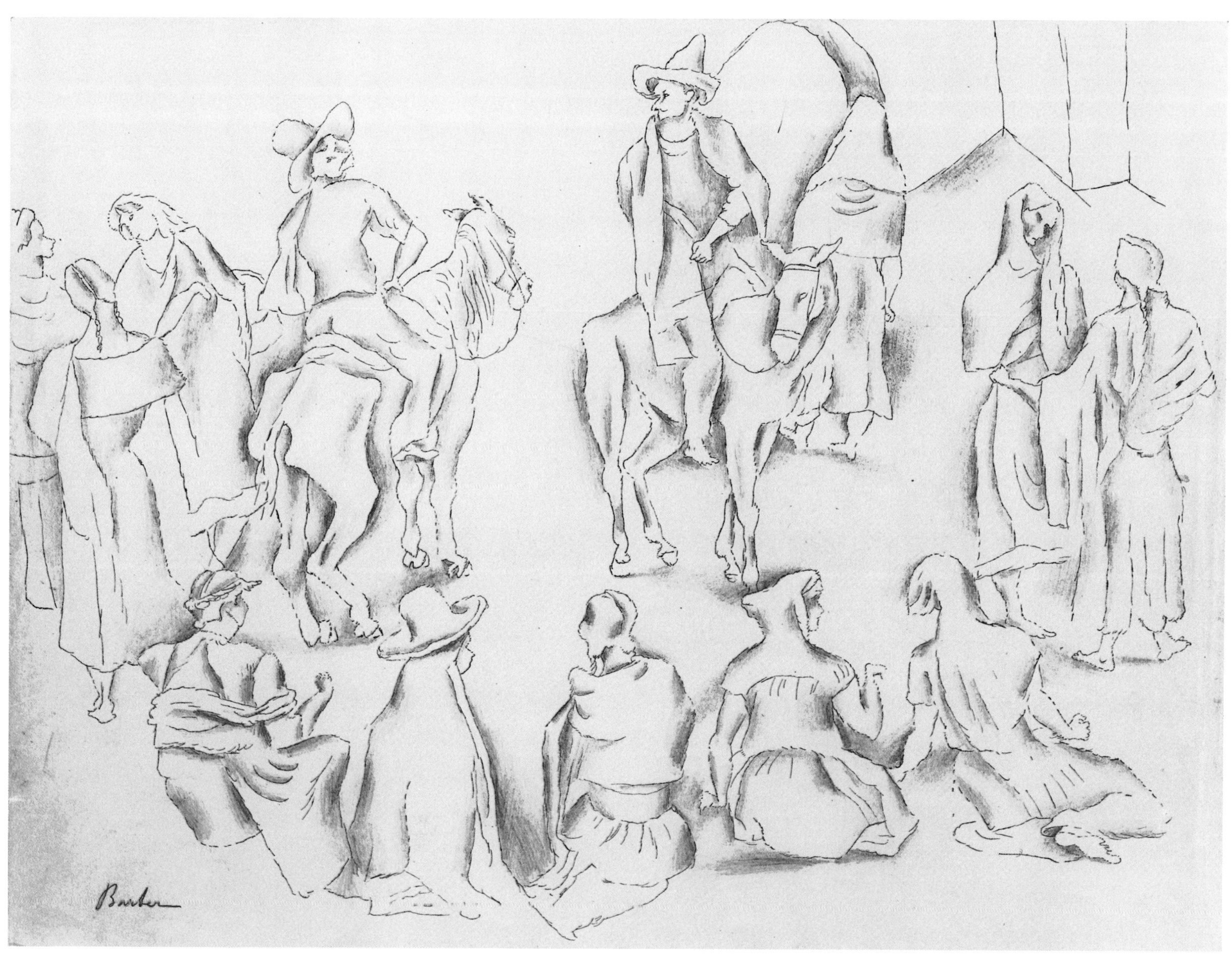

Fig. 89
John Barber
Horsemen and Women
Graphite and ink, 11 x 14
Collection of Dr. Margaret De Ronde Barber,
on loan to The John Barber Memorial Collection,
Bayly Art Museum of the University of Virginia

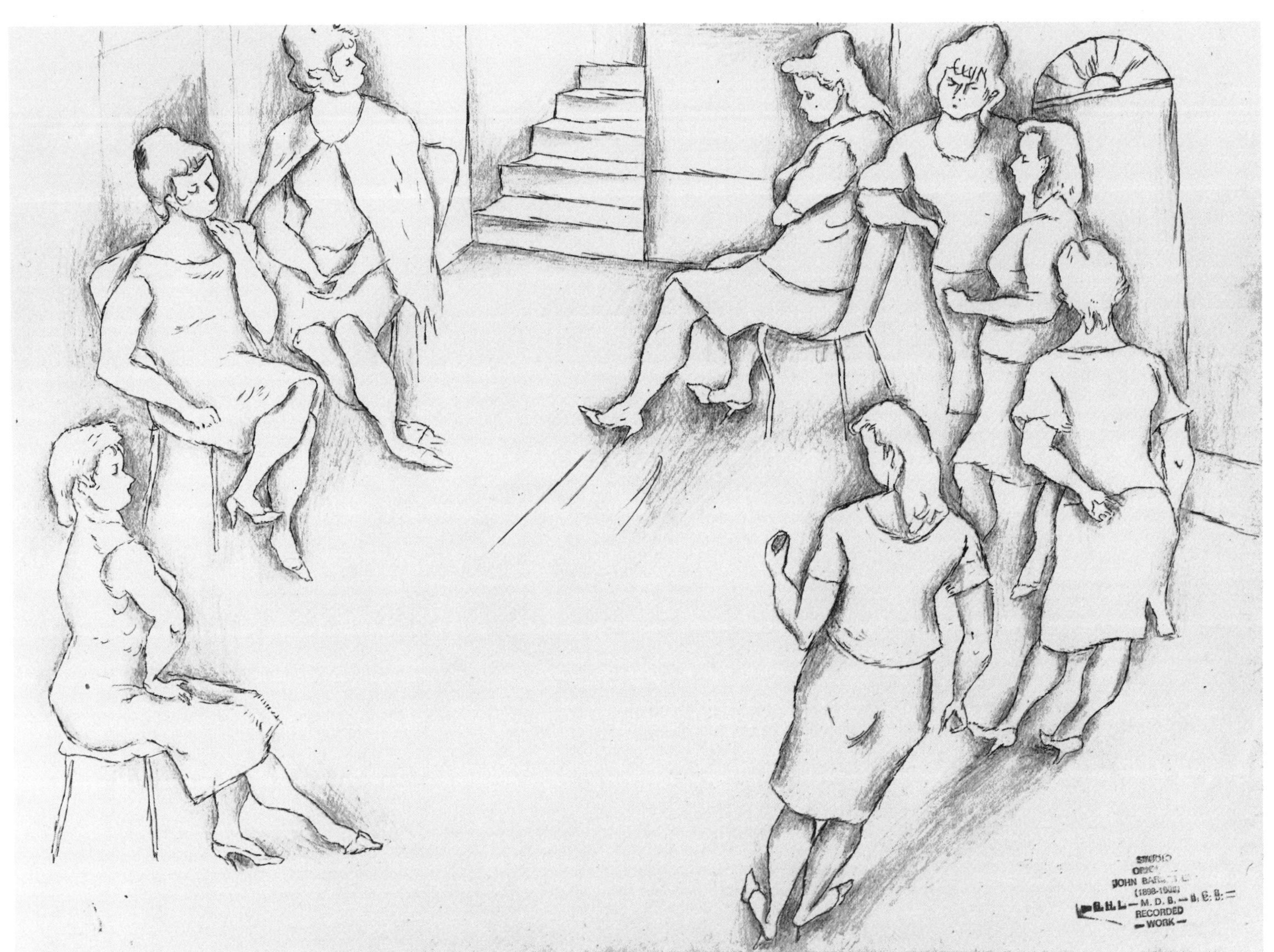

Fig. 90
John Barber
Women of Genoa, 1965
Graphite and ink, 9 1/2 x 12 1/2
Collection of Dr. Margaret De Ronde Barber,
on loan to The John Barber Memorial Collection,
Bayly Art Museum of the University of Virginia

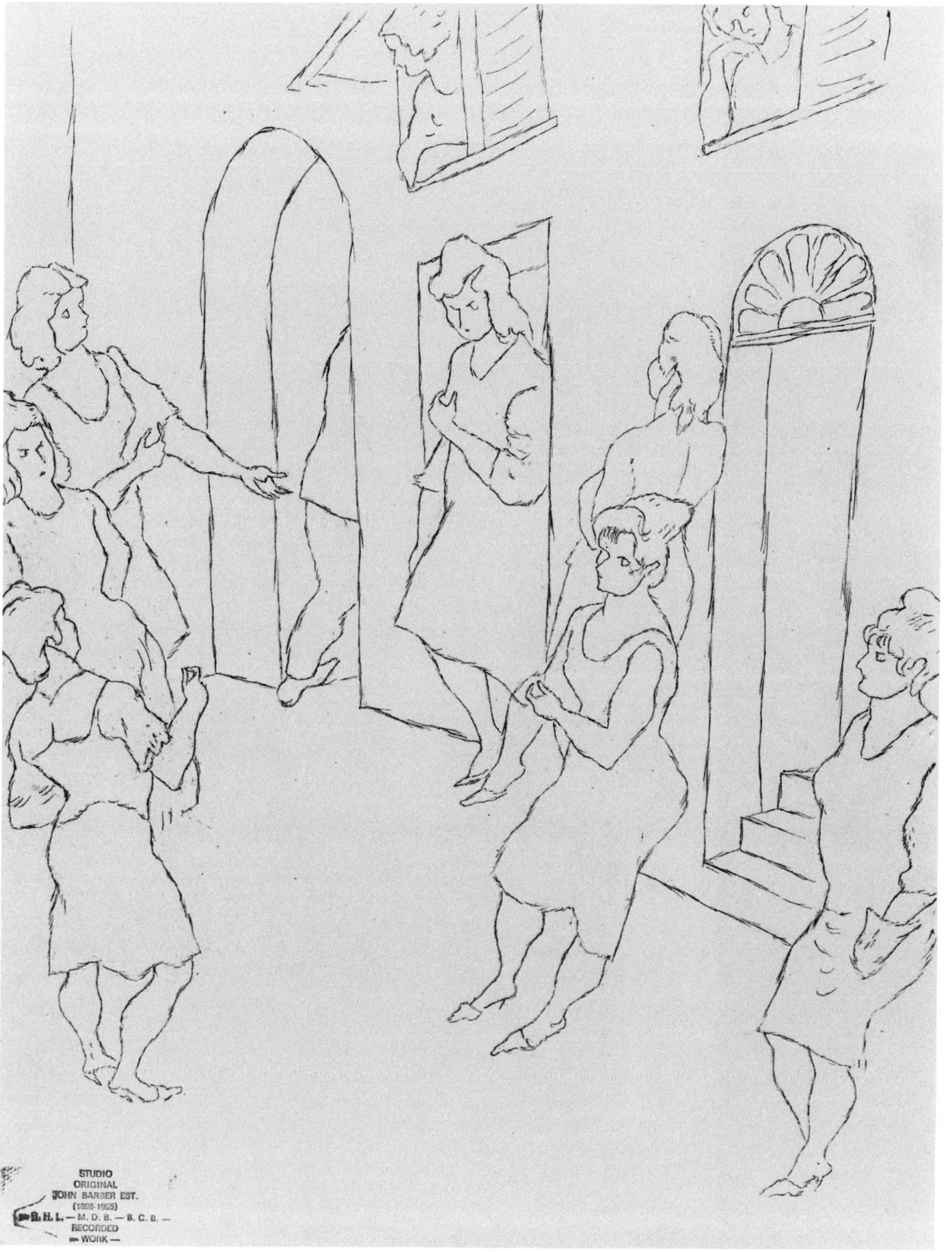

Fig. 91
John Barber
Women of Genoa, 1965
Graphite and ink, 12 $\frac{1}{2}$ x 9 $\frac{1}{2}$
Collection of Dr. Margaret De Ronde Barber,
on loan to The John Barber Memorial Collection,
Bayly Art Museum of the University of Virginia

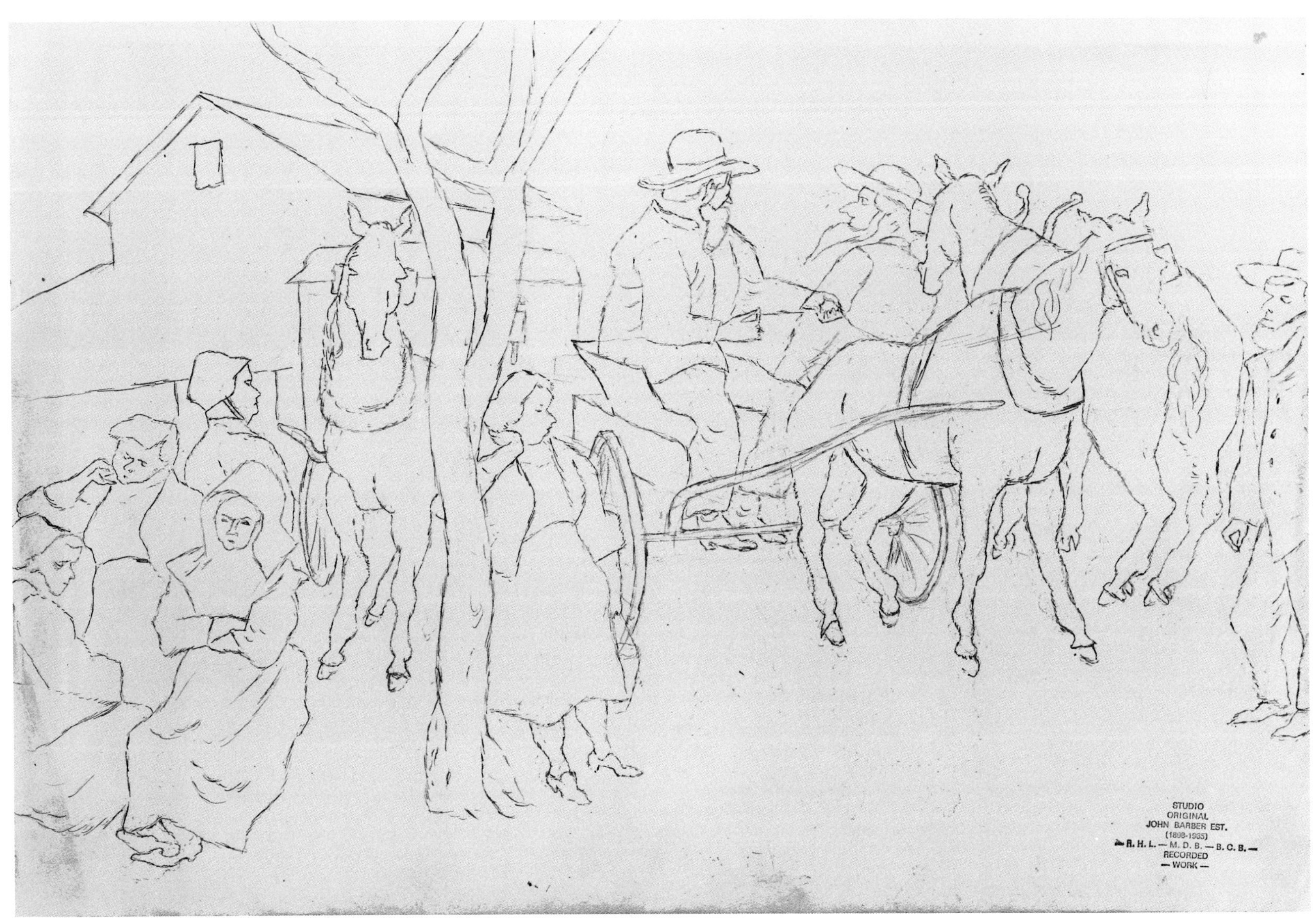

Fig. 92
John Barber
Amish
Graphite and ink, 9 3/4 x 14
Collection of Dr. Margaret De Ronde Barber,
on loan to The John Barber Memorial Collection,
Bayly Art Museum of the University of Virginia

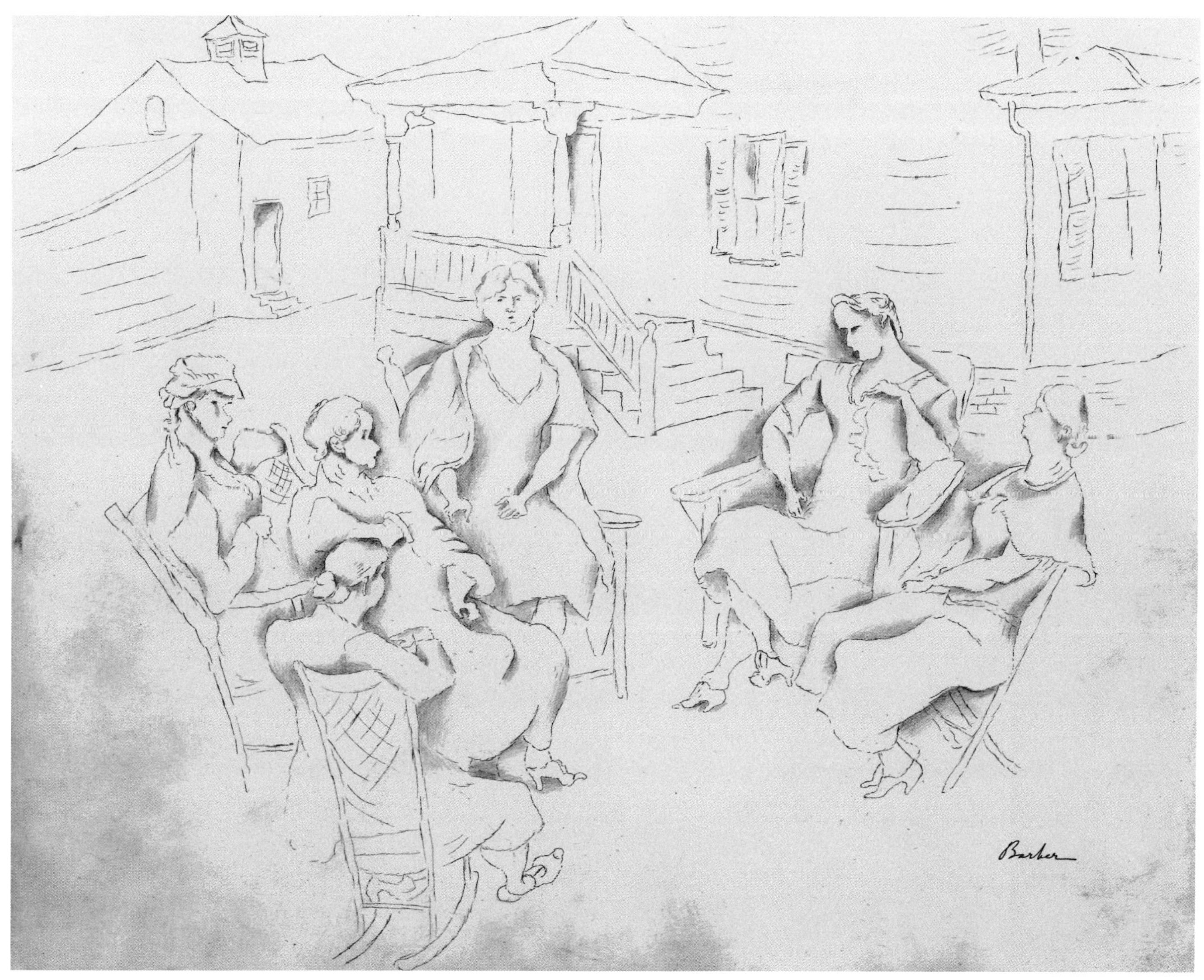

Fig. 93
John Barber
Neighbors
Graphite and ink, 12 ¹/₄ x 15
Collection of Dr. Margaret De Ronde Barber, on loan to
The John Barber Memorial Collection, Bayly Art Museum of the University of Virginia

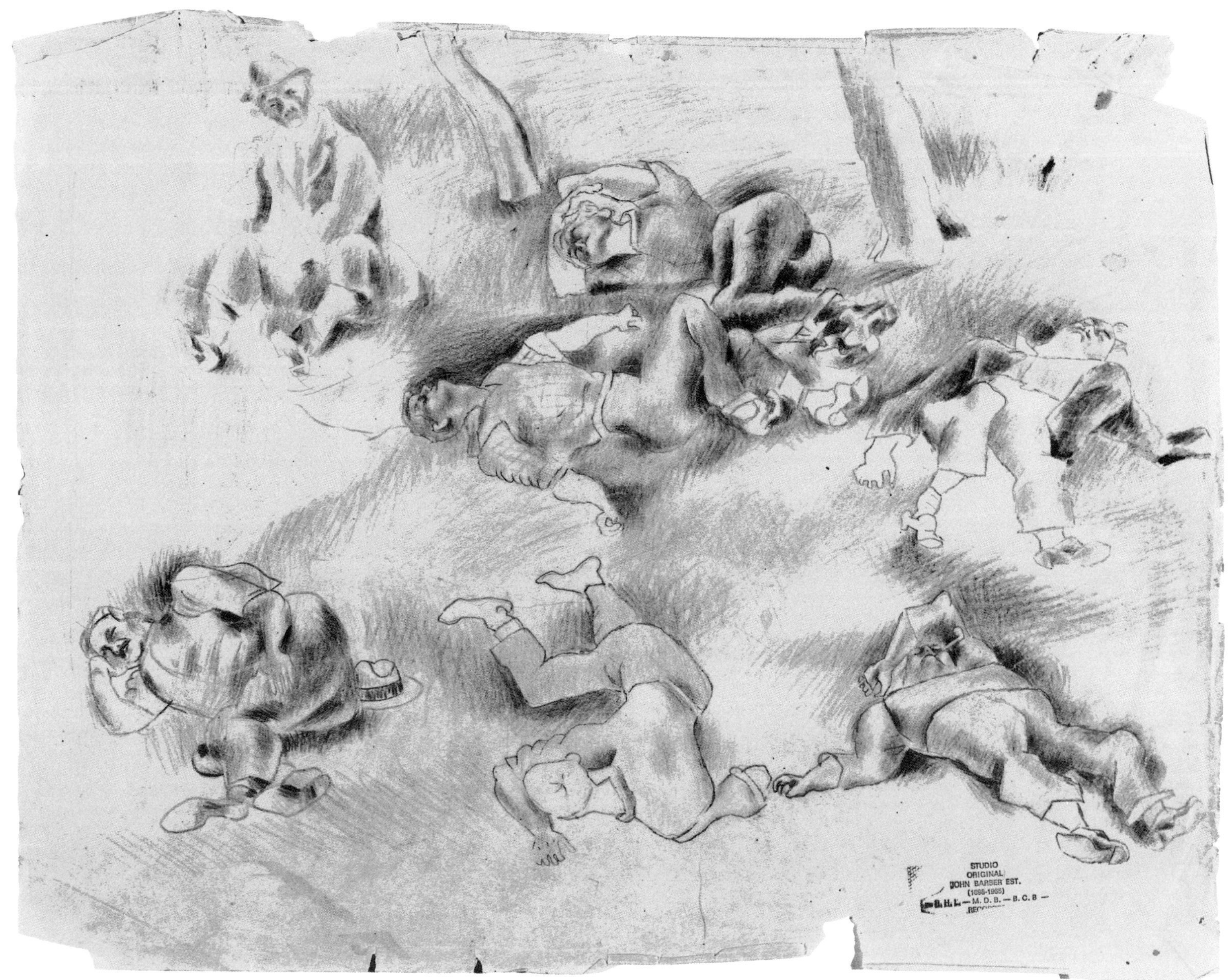

Fig. 94
John Barber
Sunday in the Park
Graphite and colored pencils, 12 x 14 $^3/_4$
Collection of Dr. Margaret De Ronde Barber, on loan to
The John Barber Memorial Collection, Bayly Art Museum of the University of Virginia

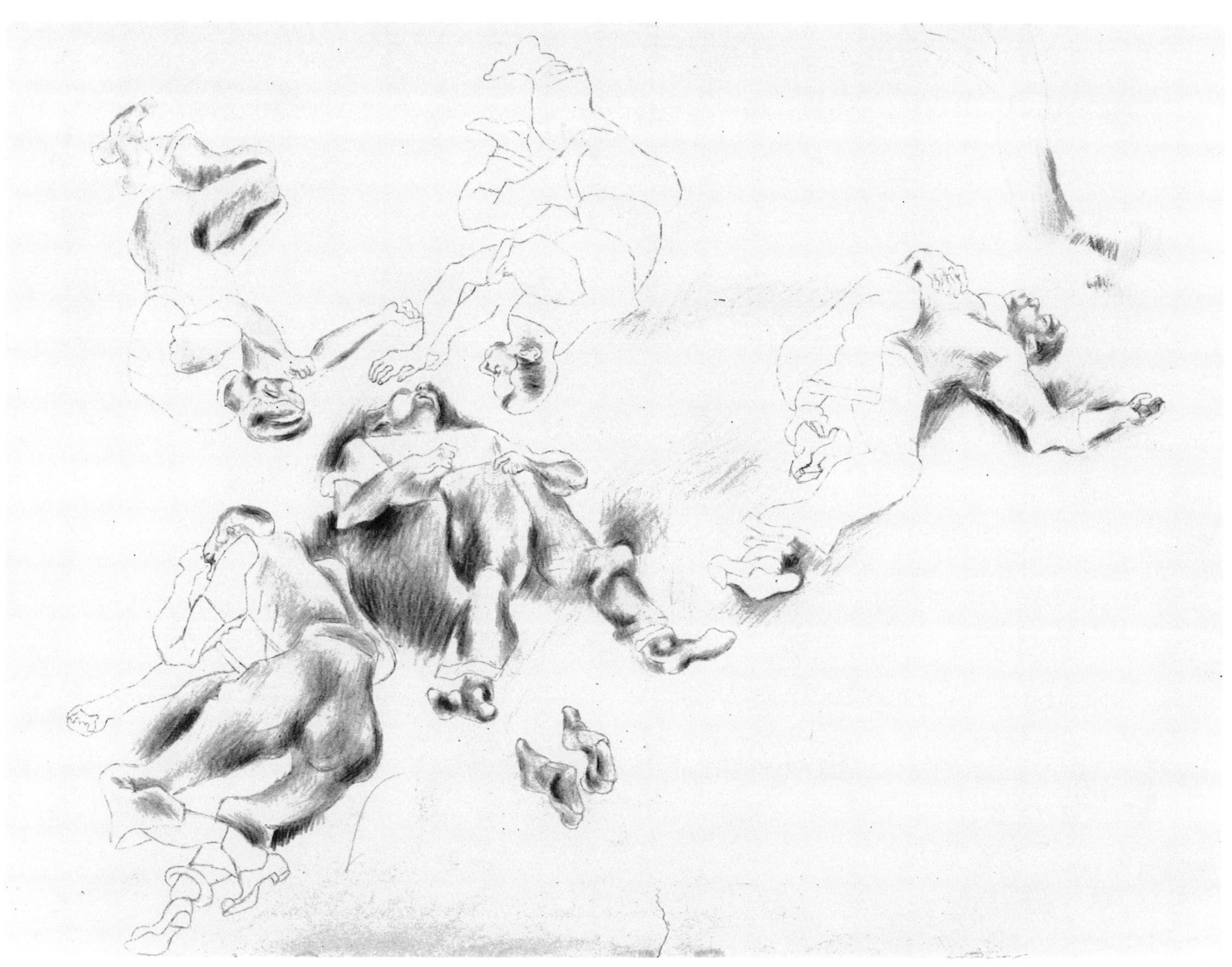

Fig. 95
John Barber
Sunday in the Park
Graphite and colored pencils, 11 3/8 x 14 3/4
Collection of Dr. Margaret De Ronde Barber,
on loan to The John Barber Memorial Collection,
Bayly Art Museum of the University of Virginia

XII. Paintings

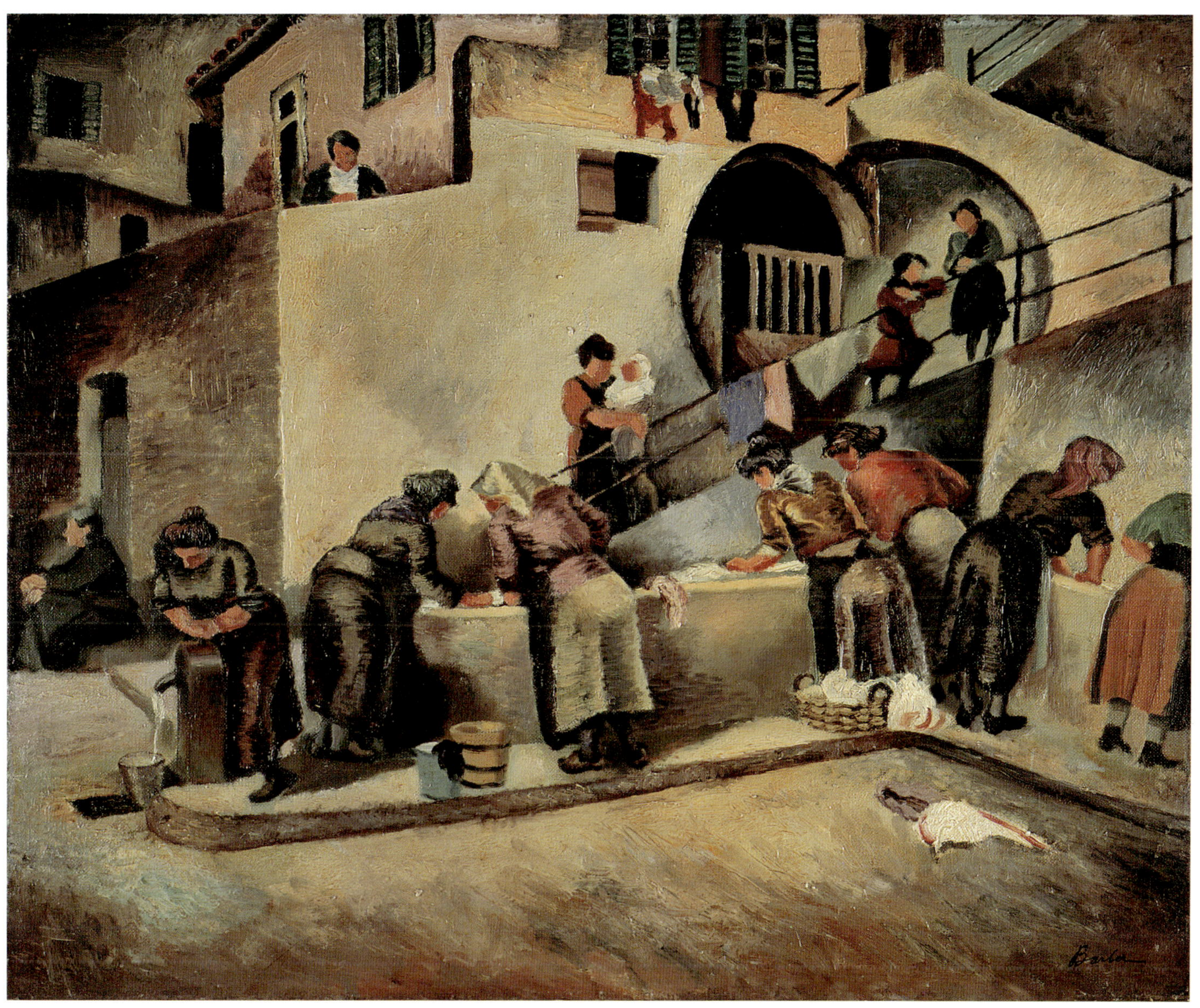

Pl. 1
Street Scene with Washerwomen, ca. 1922
Oil on canvas, 18 x 21 ³/₄
Gift of Dr. Margaret De Ronde Barber
to The John Barber Memorial Collection,
Bayly Art Museum of the University of Virginia,
1988.33.1

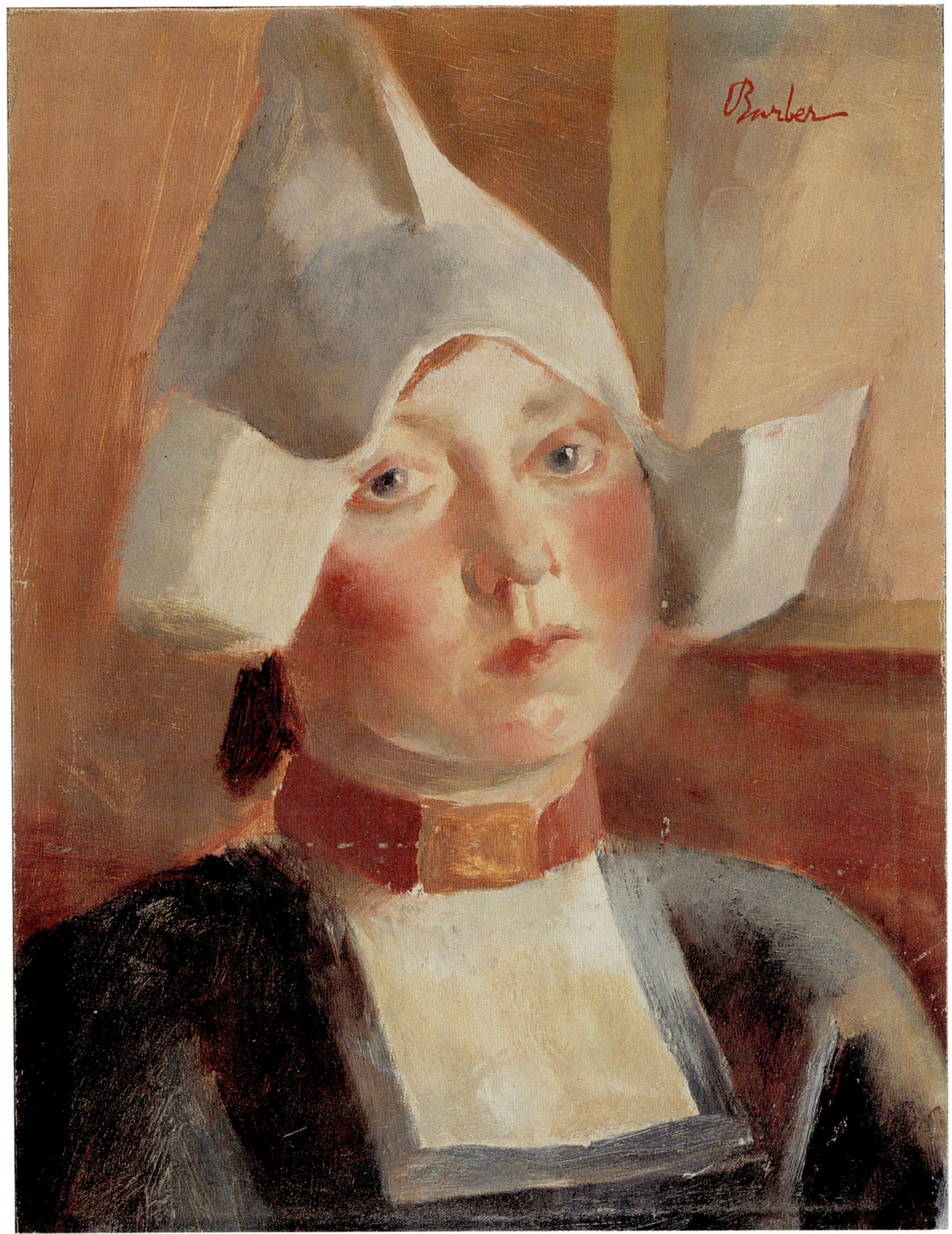

Pl. 2
Voldendam Girl
Oil on panel, 12 x 9
Gift of Dr. Margaret De Ronde Barber
to The John Barber Memorial Collection,
Bayly Art Museum of the University of Virginia,
1988.33.7

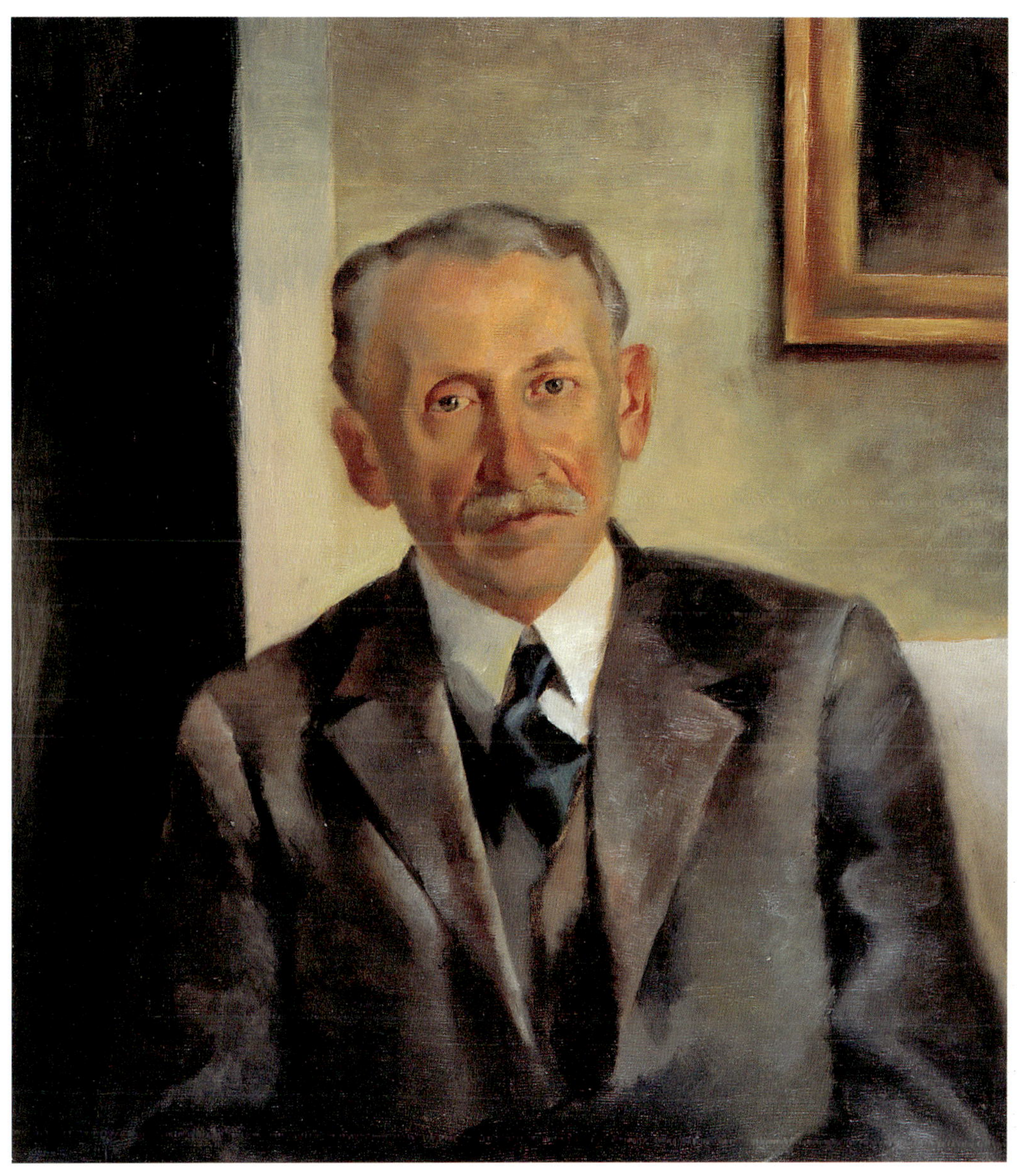

Pl. 3
Portrait of the Artist's Father, Frederick Barber, ca. 1922
Oil on canvas, 21 x 18
Gift of Dr. Margaret De Ronde Barber
to The John Barber Memorial Collection,
Bayly Art Museum of the University of Virginia,
1988.33.2

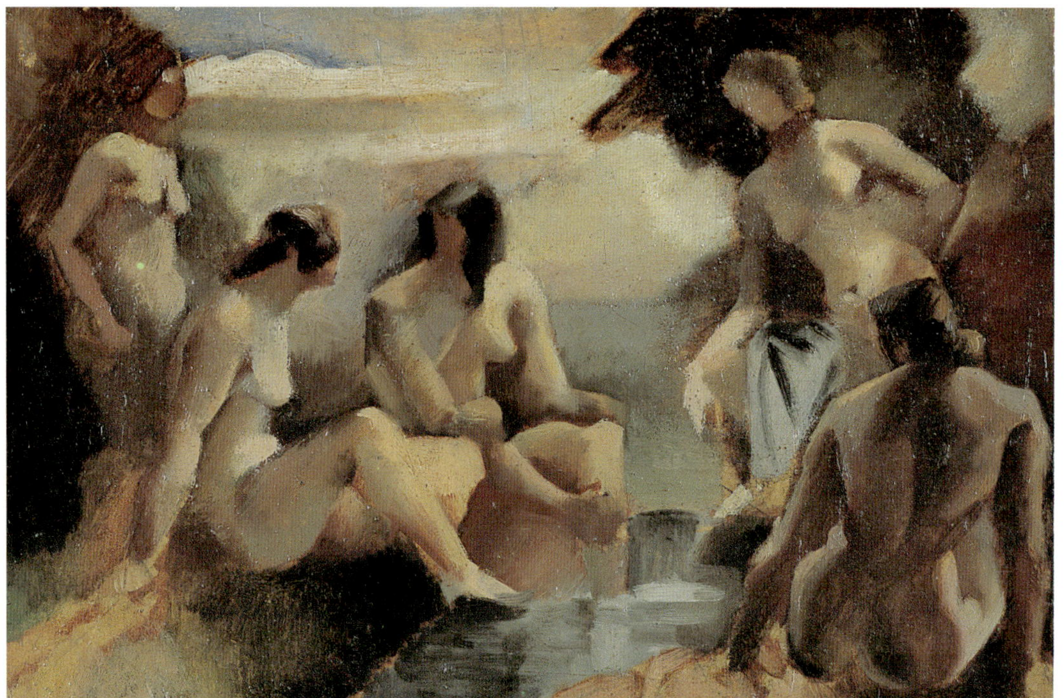

Pl. 4
Five Bathers, 1923
Oil on board, 8 1/2 x 12 1/2
Gift of Dr. Margaret De Ronde Barber
to The John Barber Memorial Collection,
Bayly Art Museum of the University of Virginia,
1988.33.4

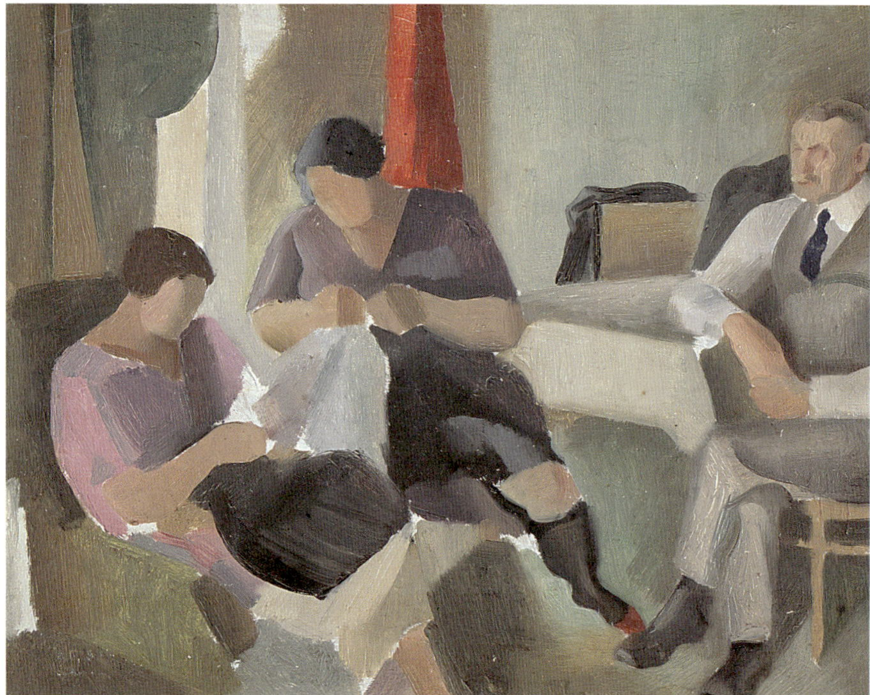

Pl. 5
Family of the Artist
Oil on board, 12 1/2 x 15 1/8
Collection of Dr. Margaret De Ronde Barber,
on loan to The John Barber Memorial Collection,
Bayly Art Museum of the University of Virginia

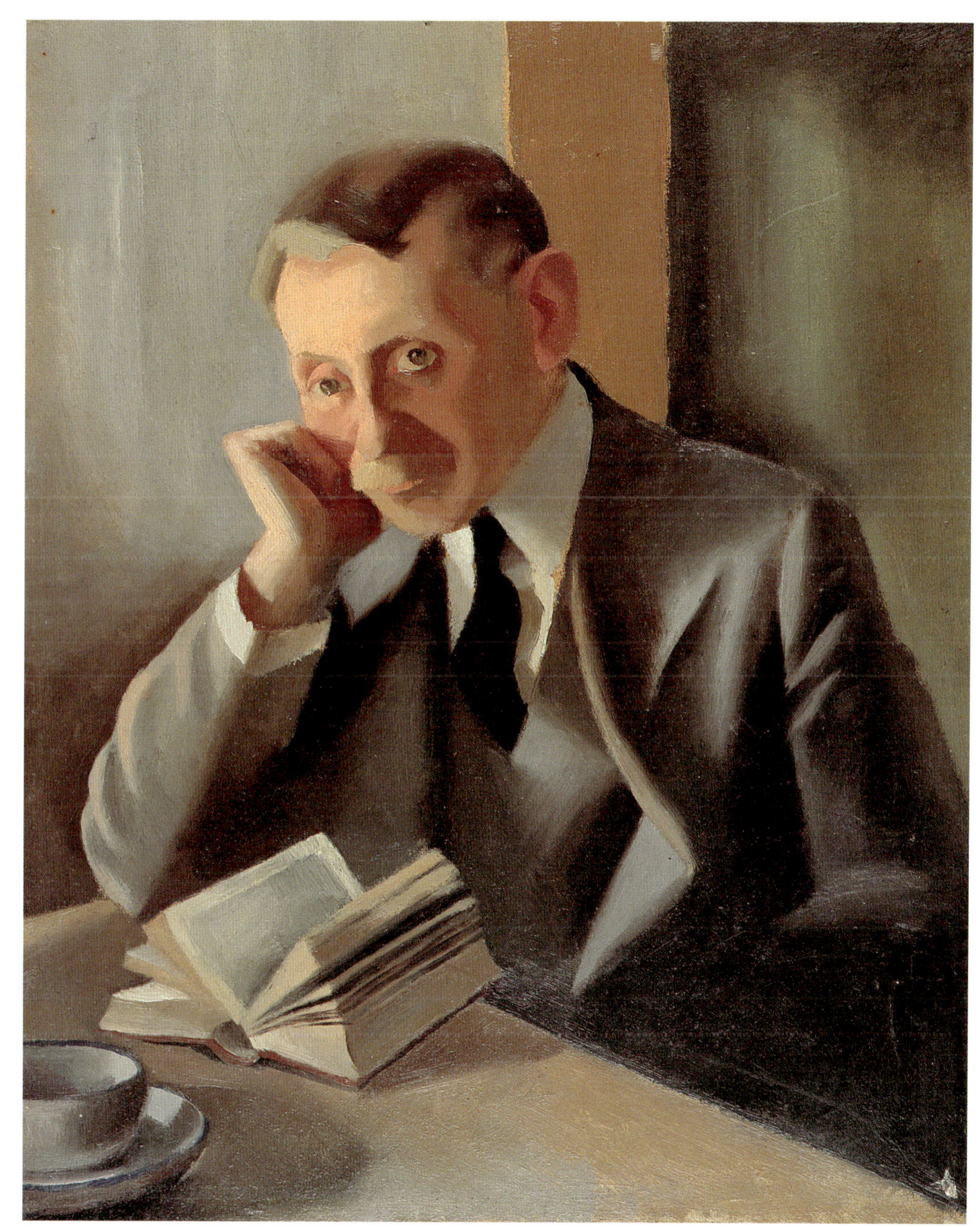

Pl. 6
Portrait of the Artist's Father, Frederick Barber, ca. 1923
Oil on board, 16 x 13
Gift of Dr. Margaret De Ronde Barber
to The John Barber Memorial Collection,
Bayly Art Museum of the University of Virginia,
1988.33.3

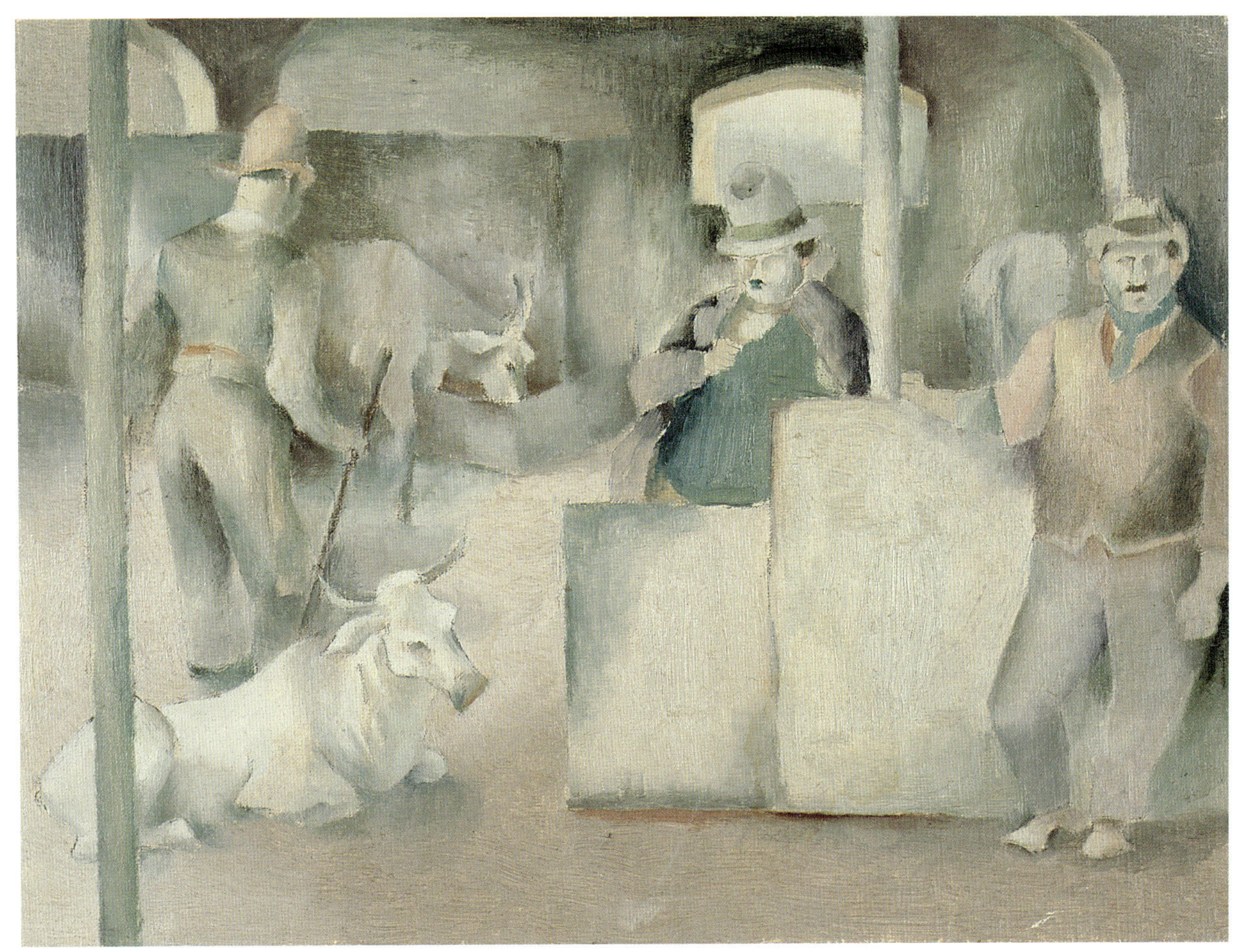

Pl. 7
Men in a Barn
Oil on canvas, 7 ³/₄ x 10
Gift of Dr. Margaret De Ronde Barber
to The John Barber Memorial Collection,
Bayly Art Museum of the University of Virginia,
1988.33.10

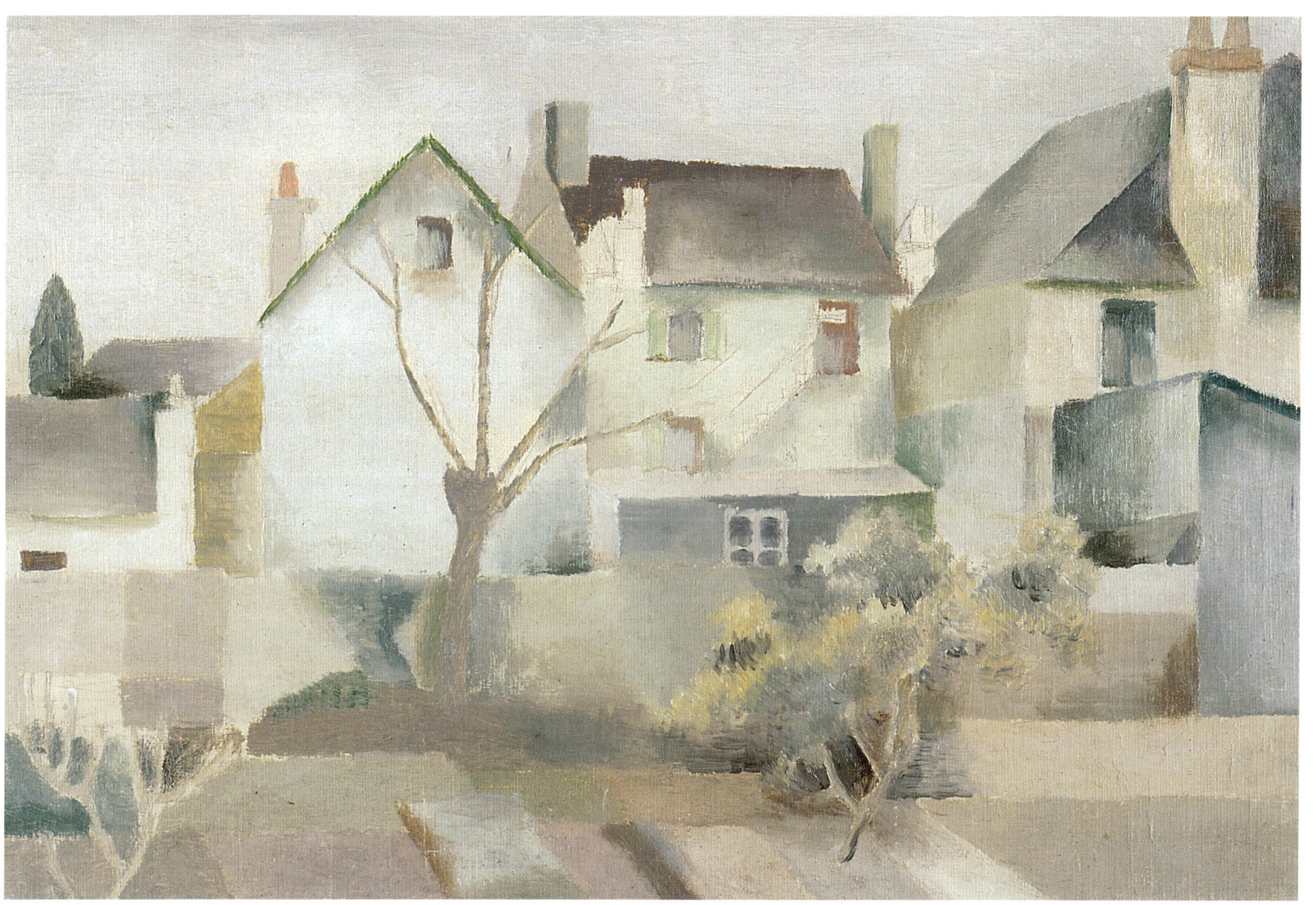

Pl. 8
Village Scene
Oil on canvas, 9 x 13
Gift of Dr. Margaret De Ronde Barber
to The John Barber Memorial Collection,
Bayly Art Museum of the University of Virginia,
1988.33.5

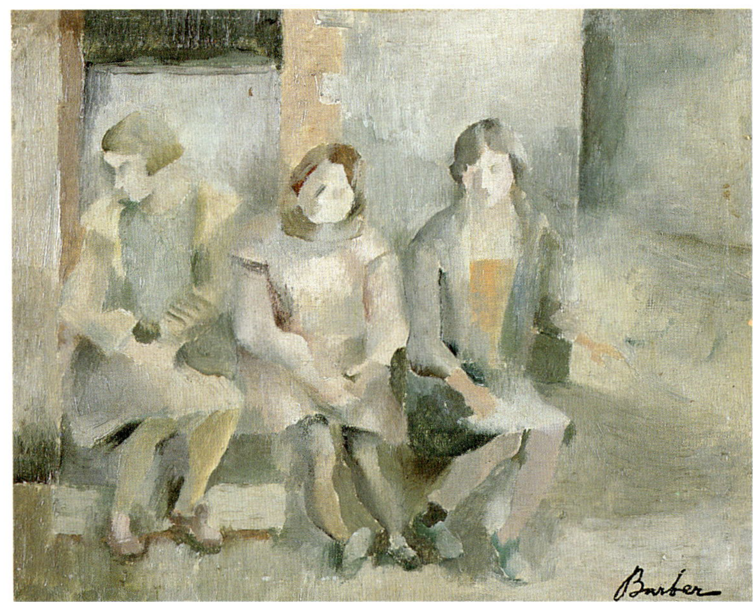

Pl. 9
Three Girls Seated
Oil on board, 7 x 8 $^5/_8$
Gift of Dr. Margaret De Ronde Barber
to The John Barber Memorial Collection,
Bayly Art Museum of the University of Virginia,
1988.33.11

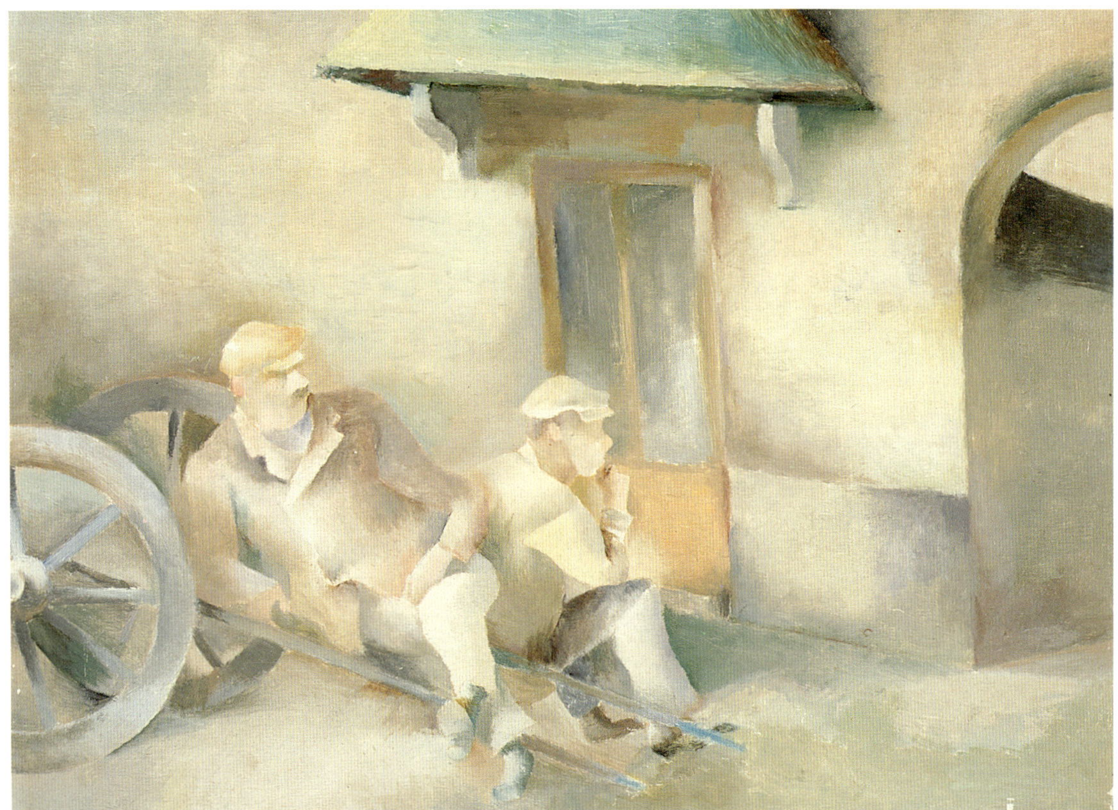

Pl. 10
Loafing
Oil on canvas, 10 $^1/_8$ x 13
Gift of Dr. Margaret De Ronde Barber
to The John Barber Memorial Collection,
Bayly Art Museum of the University of Virginia,
1988.33.12

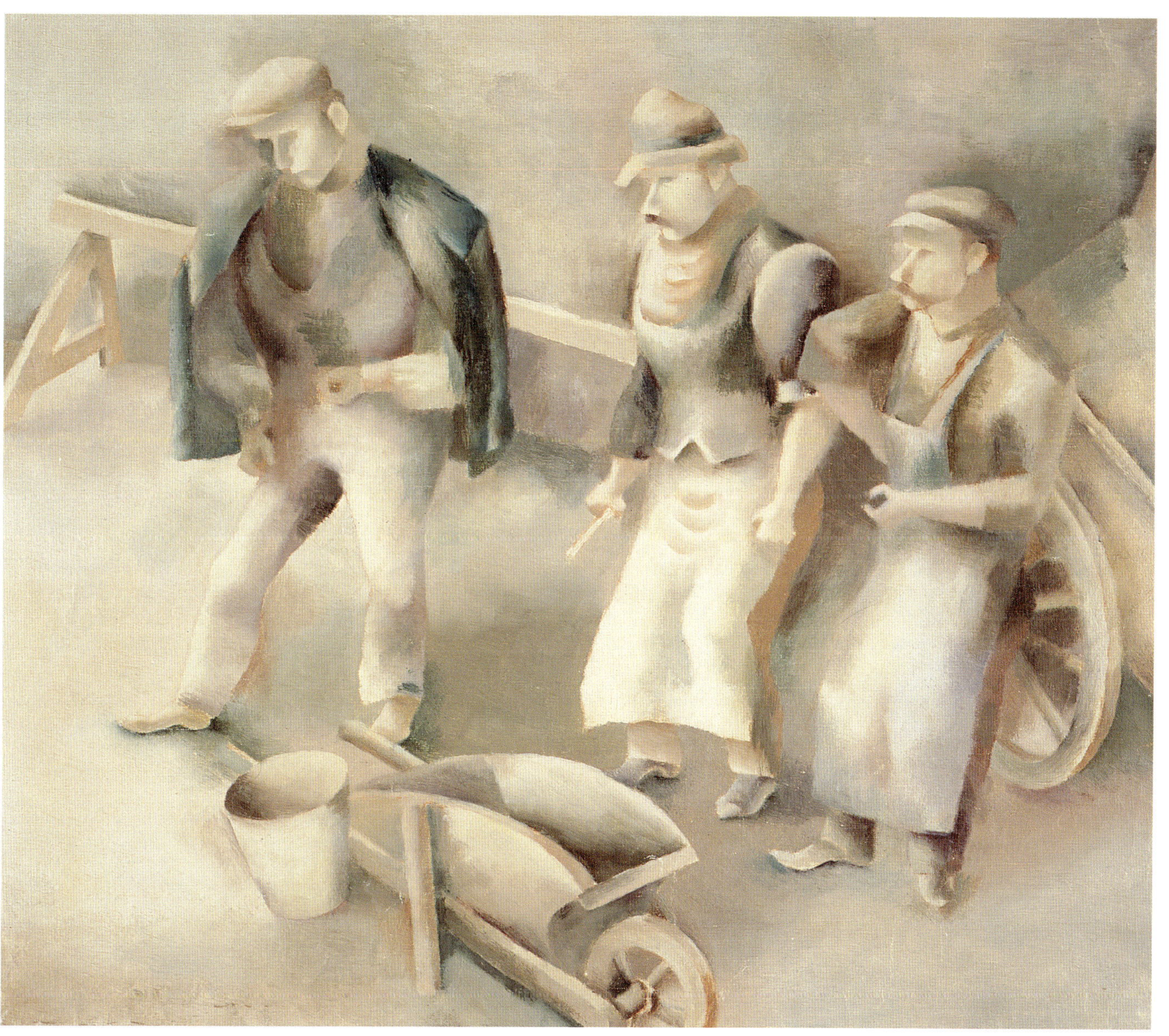

Pl. 11
Cement Workers
Oil on canvas, 14 x 16
Gift of Dr. Margaret De Ronde Barber
to The John Barber Memorial Collection,
Bayly Art Museum of the University of Virginia,
1986.16

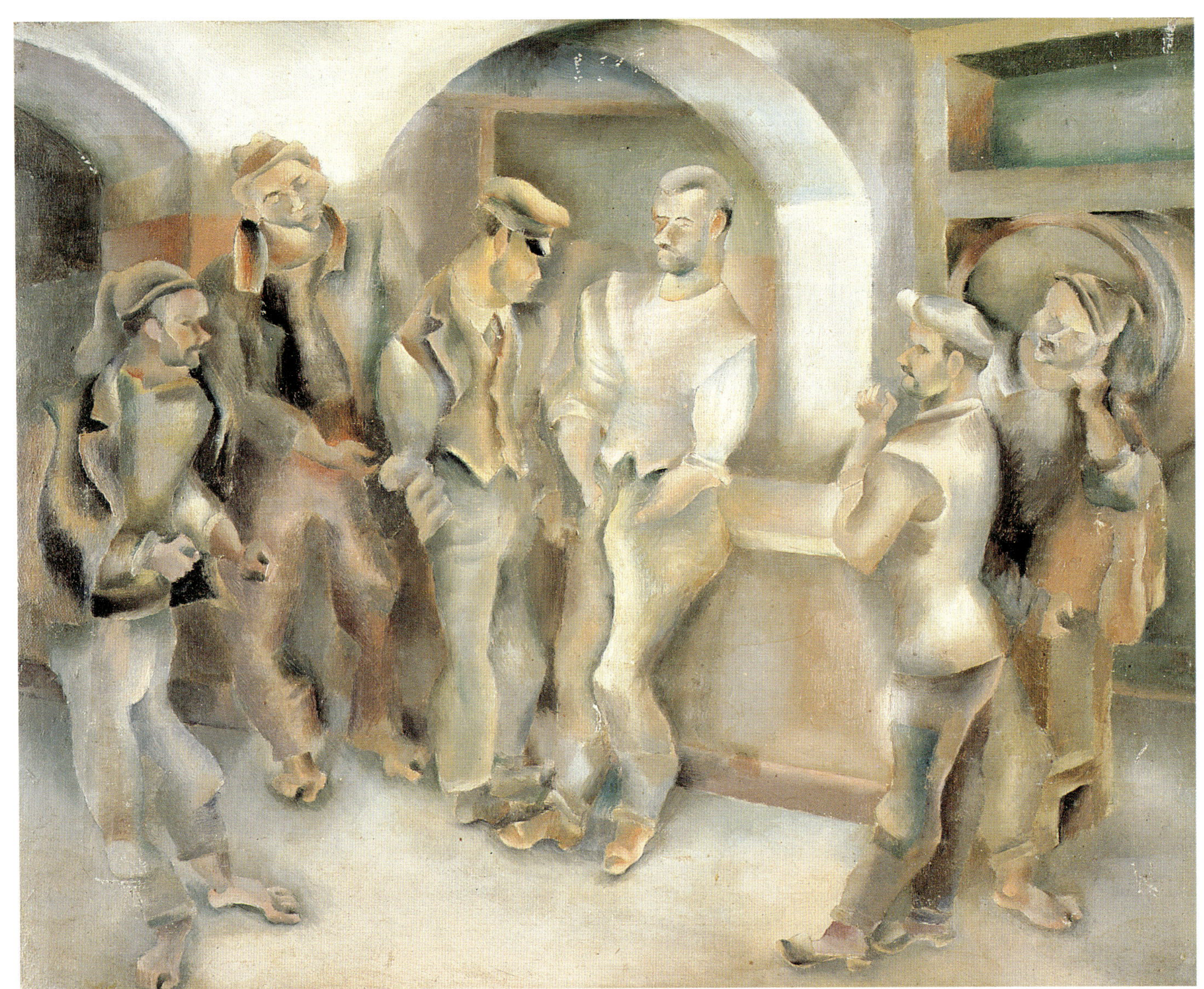

Pl. 12
At the Tavern, ca. 1936
Oil on canvas, 14 x 17 ¼
Gift of Dr. Margaret De Ronde Barber
to The John Barber Memorial Collection,
Bayly Art Museum of the University of Virginia,
1988.33.15

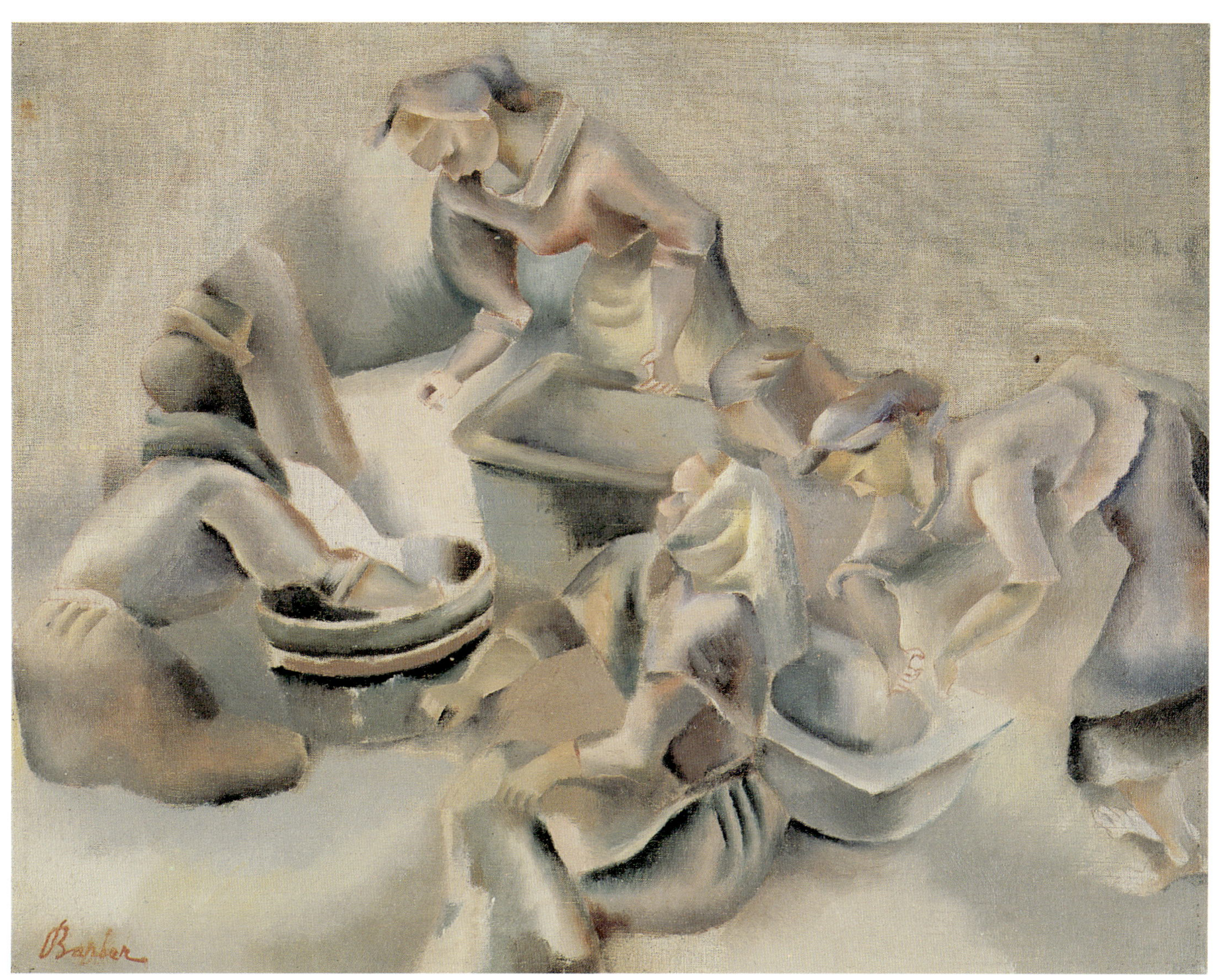

Pl. 13
Portugese Washerwomen, 1930
Oil on canvas, 12 x 15
Gift of Dr. Margaret De Ronde Barber
to The John Barber Memorial Collection,
Bayly Art Museum of the University of Virginia,
1988.33.9

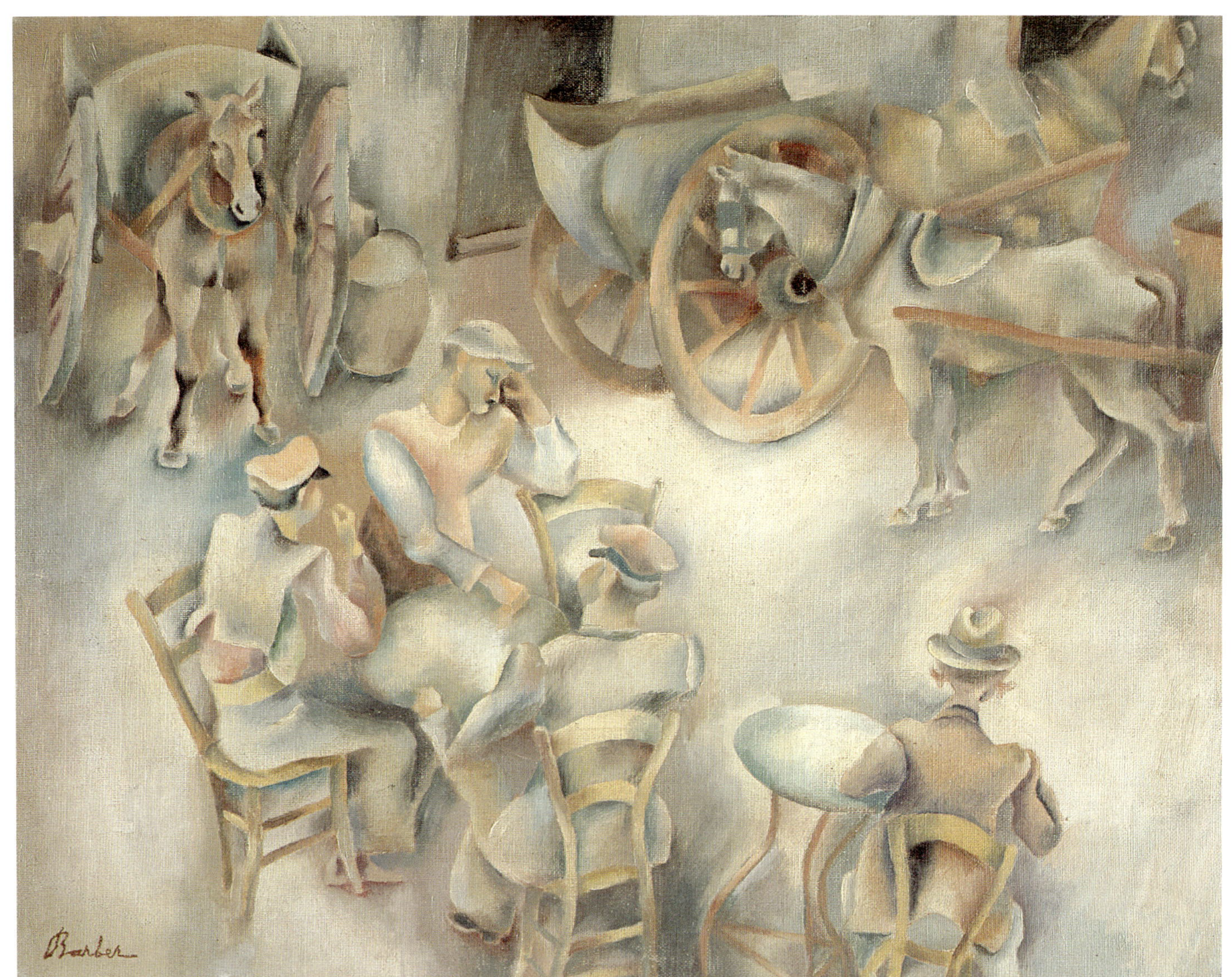

Pl. 14
Outside a Café, Portugal
Oil on canvas, 16 x 20
Gift of Dr. Margaret De Ronde Barber
to The John Barber Memorial Collection,
Bayly Art Museum of the University of Virginia,
1988.33.17

Pl. 15
Greek Pleasure Boat
Oil on canvas, 24 $\frac{1}{8}$ x 20 $\frac{1}{4}$
Collection of Dr. Margaret De Ronde Barber,
on loan to The John Barber Memorial Collection,
Bayly Art Museum of the University of Virginia

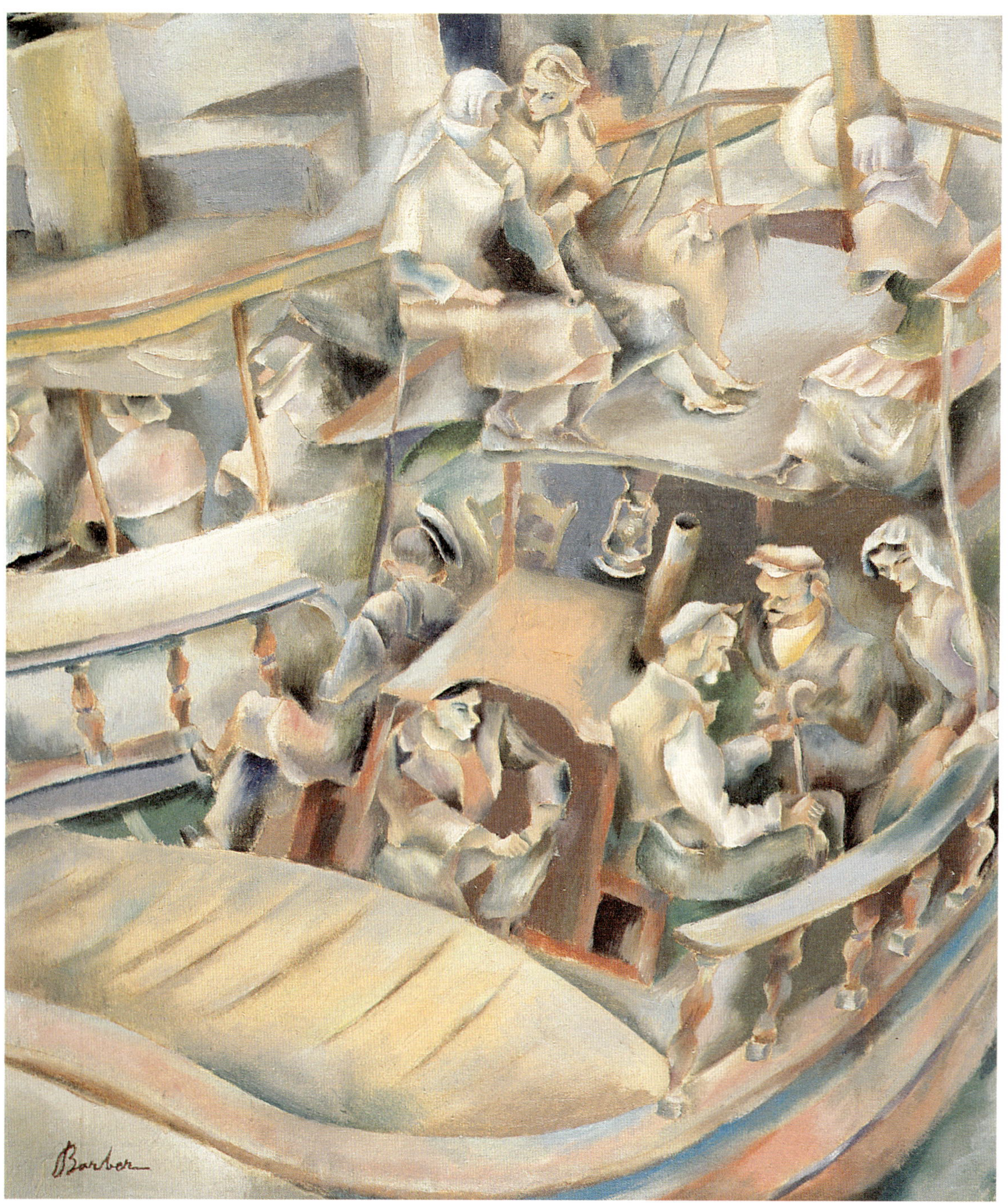

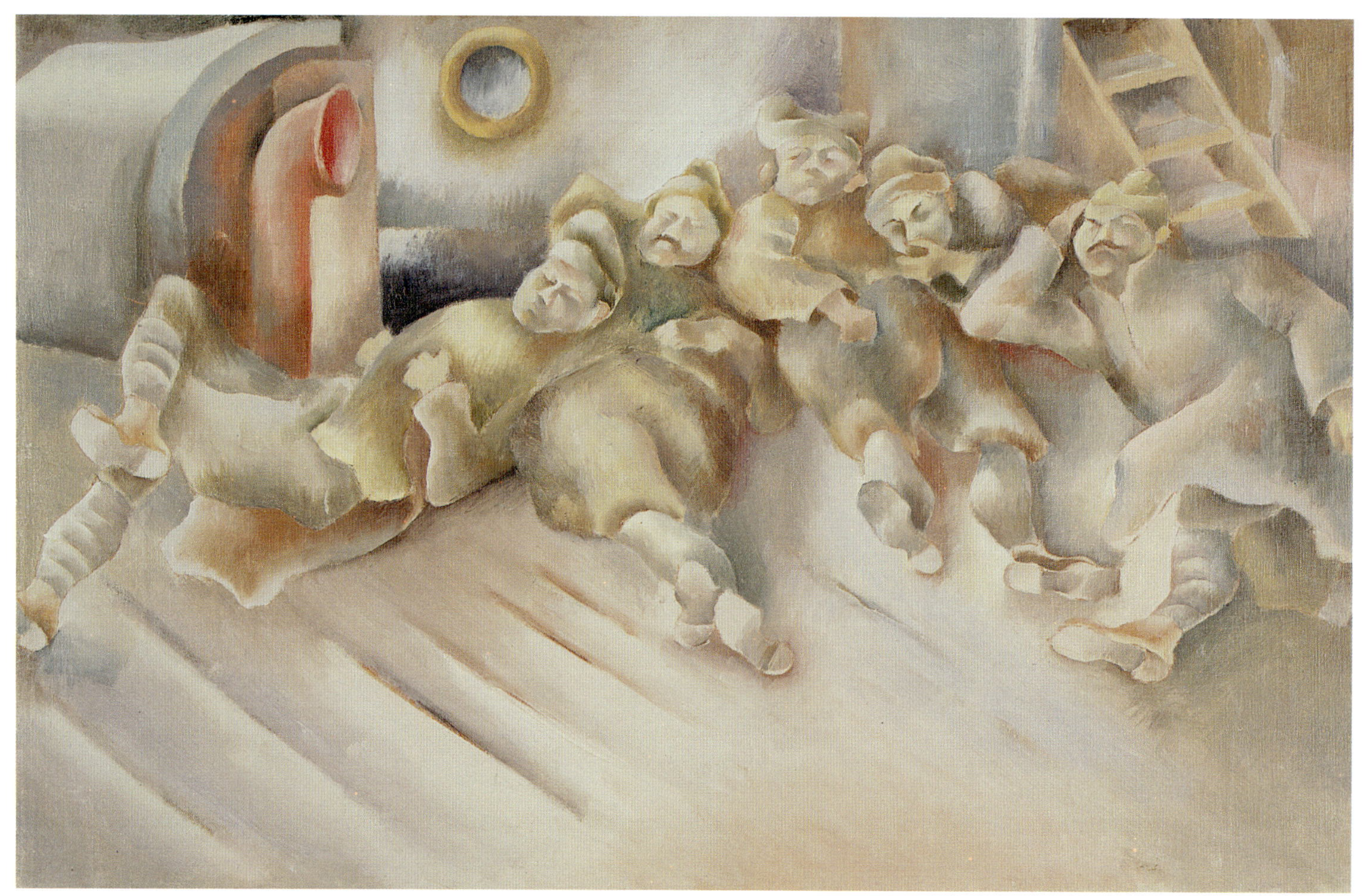

Pl. 16
Steerage, 1939
Oil on canvas, 12 x 18
Gift of Dr. Margaret De Ronde Barber
to The John Barber Memorial Collection,
Bayly Art Museum of the University of Virginia,
1988.33.14

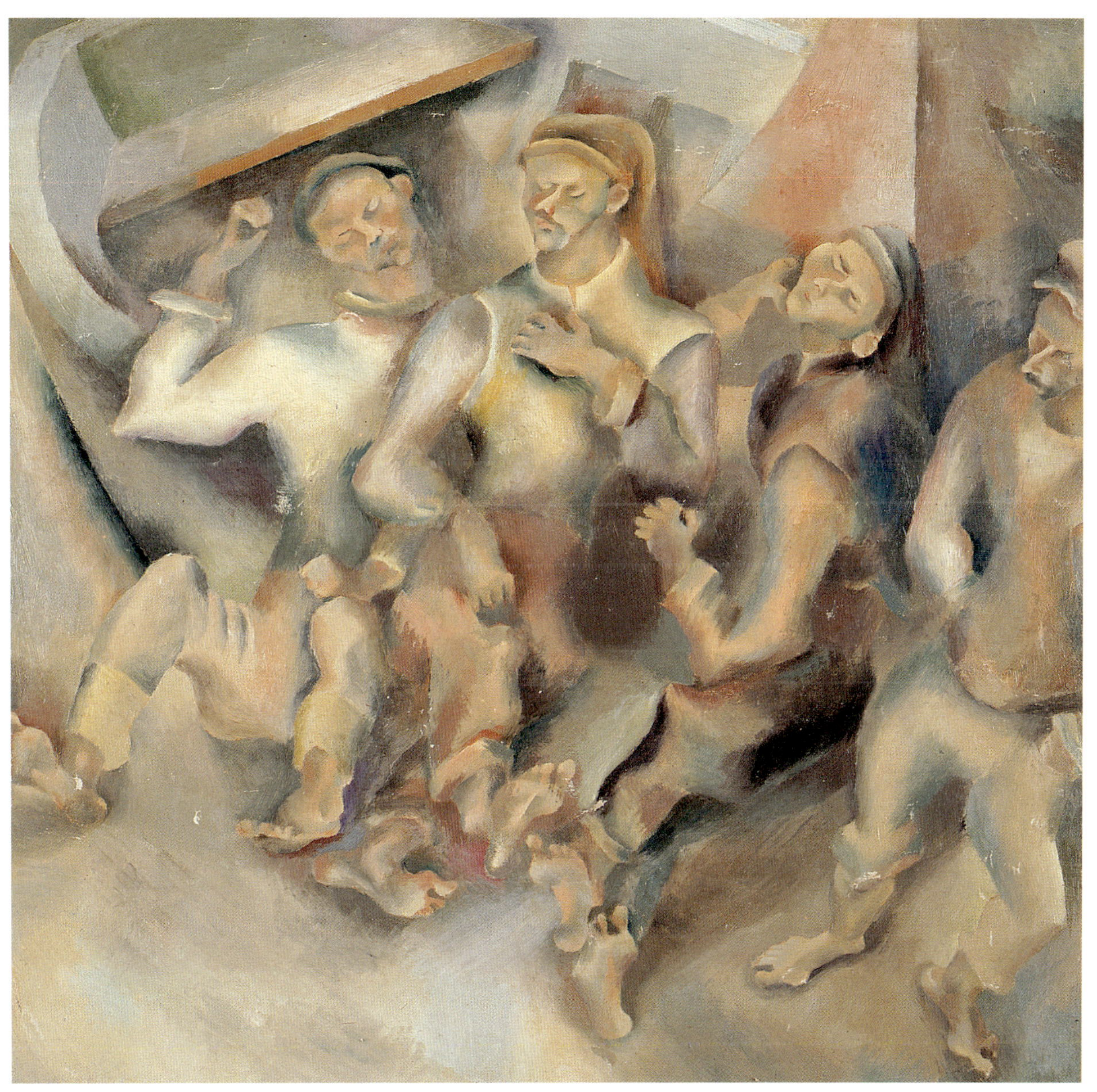

Pl. 17
Barefoot Greek Sailors
Oil on canvas, 15 ¹/₄ x 15 ³/₈
Gift of Dr. Margaret De Ronde Barber
to The John Barber Memorial Collection,
Bayly Art Museum of the University of Virginia,
1988.33.13

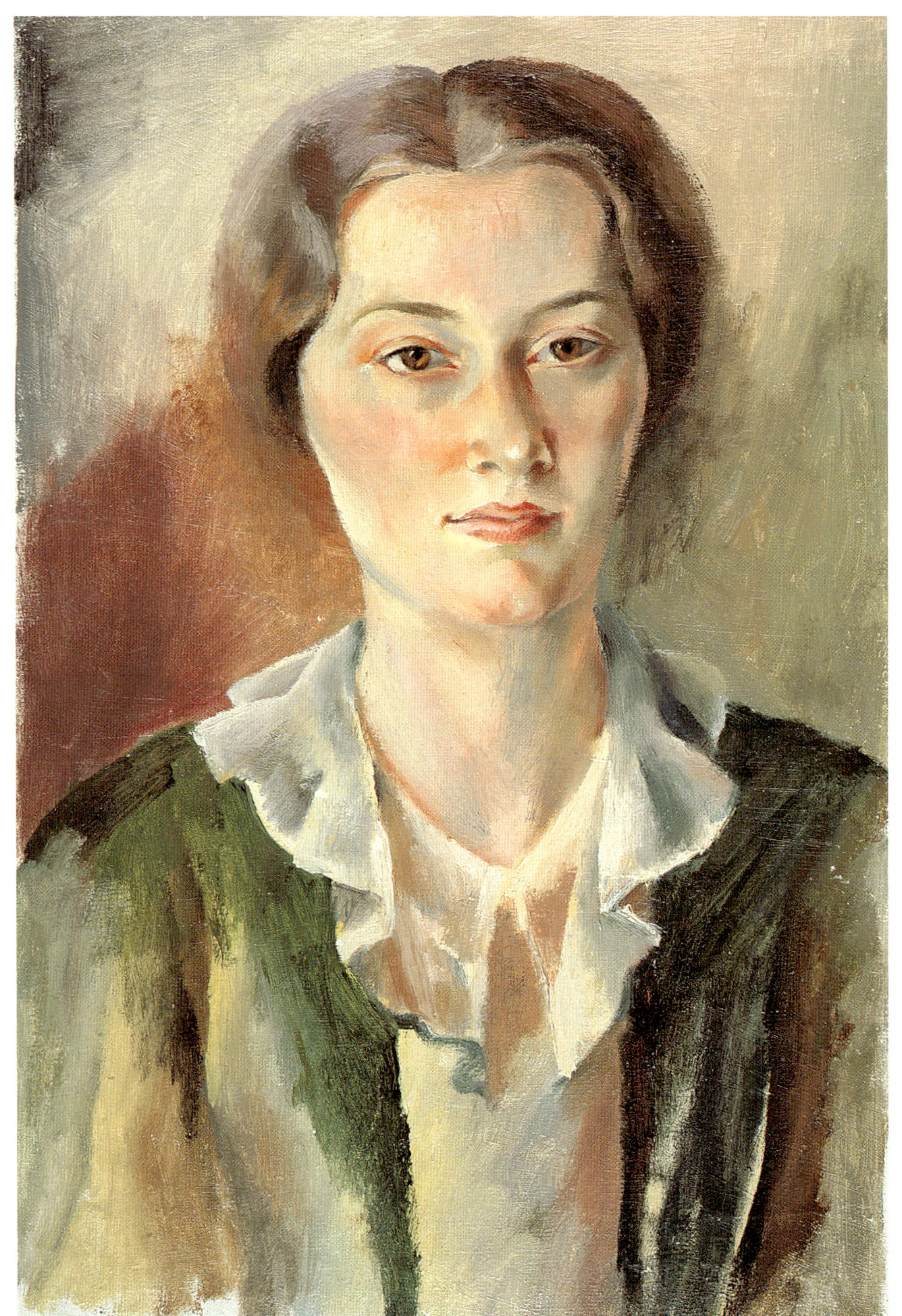

Pl. 18
Girl in Green
Oil on canvas, 15 x 10
Gift of Dr. Margaret De Ronde Barber
to The John Barber Memorial Collection,
Bayly Art Museum of the University of Virginia,
1988.33.8

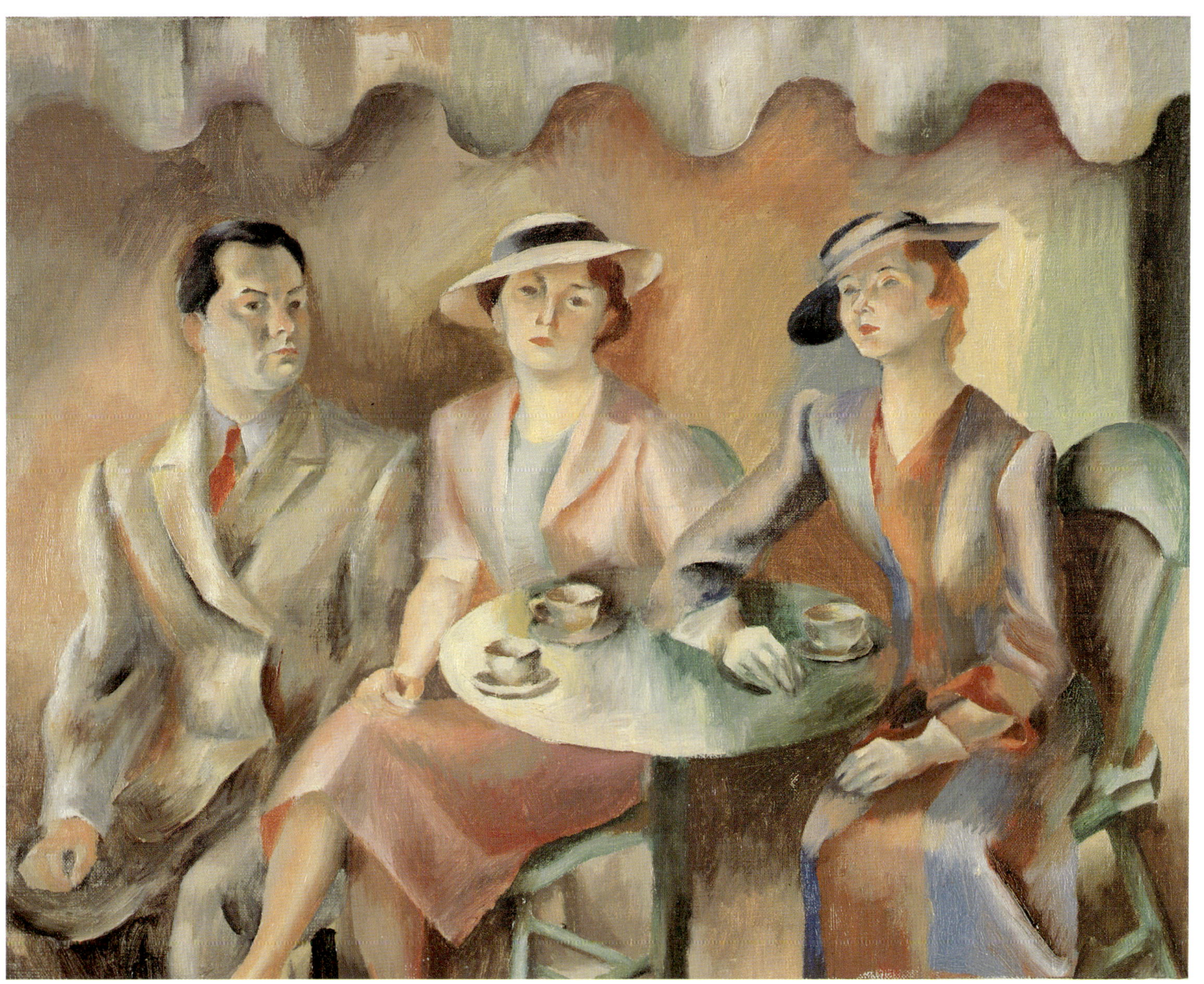

Pl. 19
Self Portrait, at a Café
Oil on canvas, 17 x 21
Collection of Dr. Margaret De Ronde Barber,
on loan to The John Barber Memorial Collection,
Bayly Art Museum of the University of Virginia

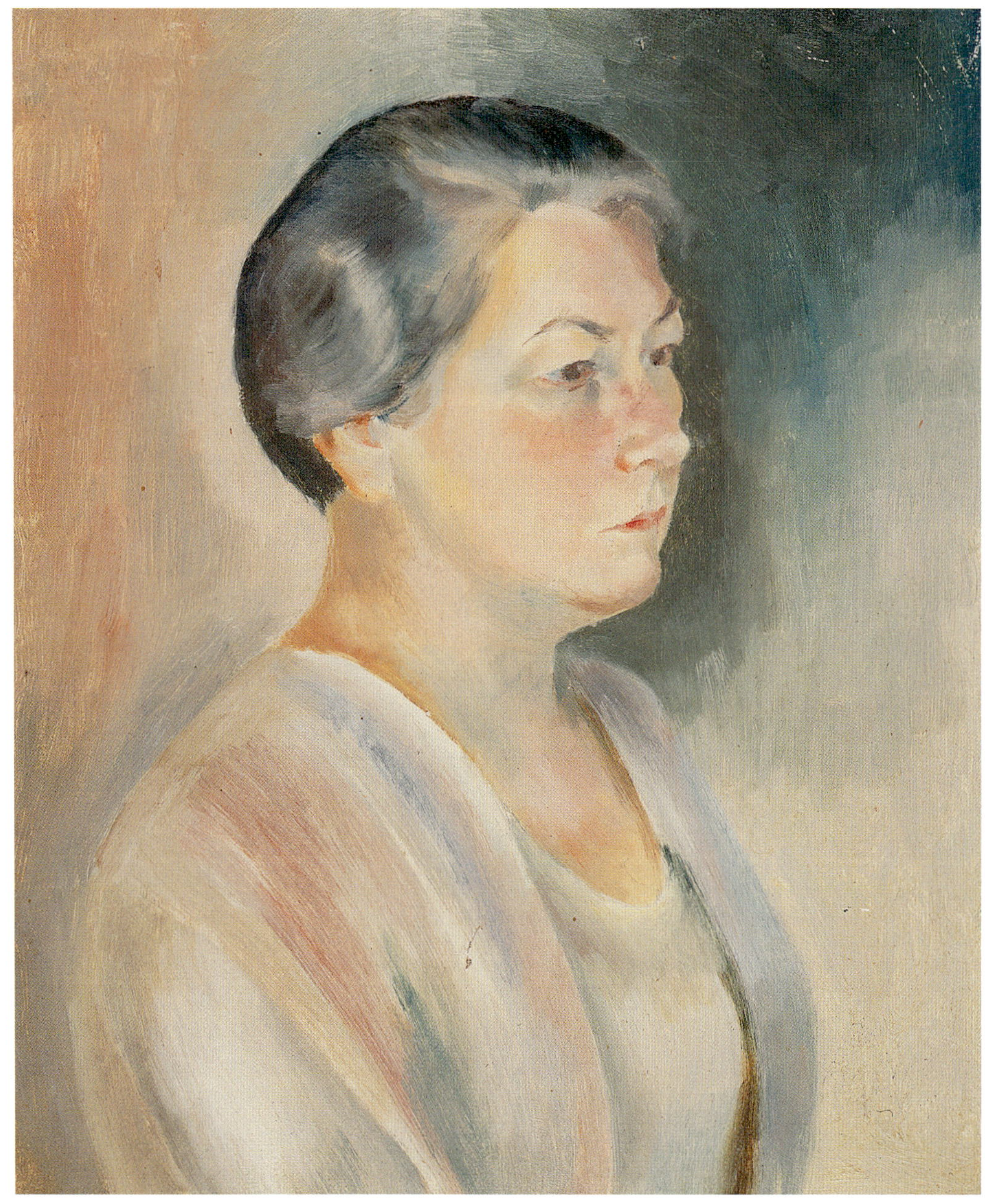

Pl. 20
Portrait of the Artist's Mother, Betty Barber
Oil on canvas, 10 3/4 x 8 3/4
Collection of Dr. Margaret De Ronde Barber,
on loan to The John Barber Memorial Collection,
Bayly Art Museum of the University of Virginia

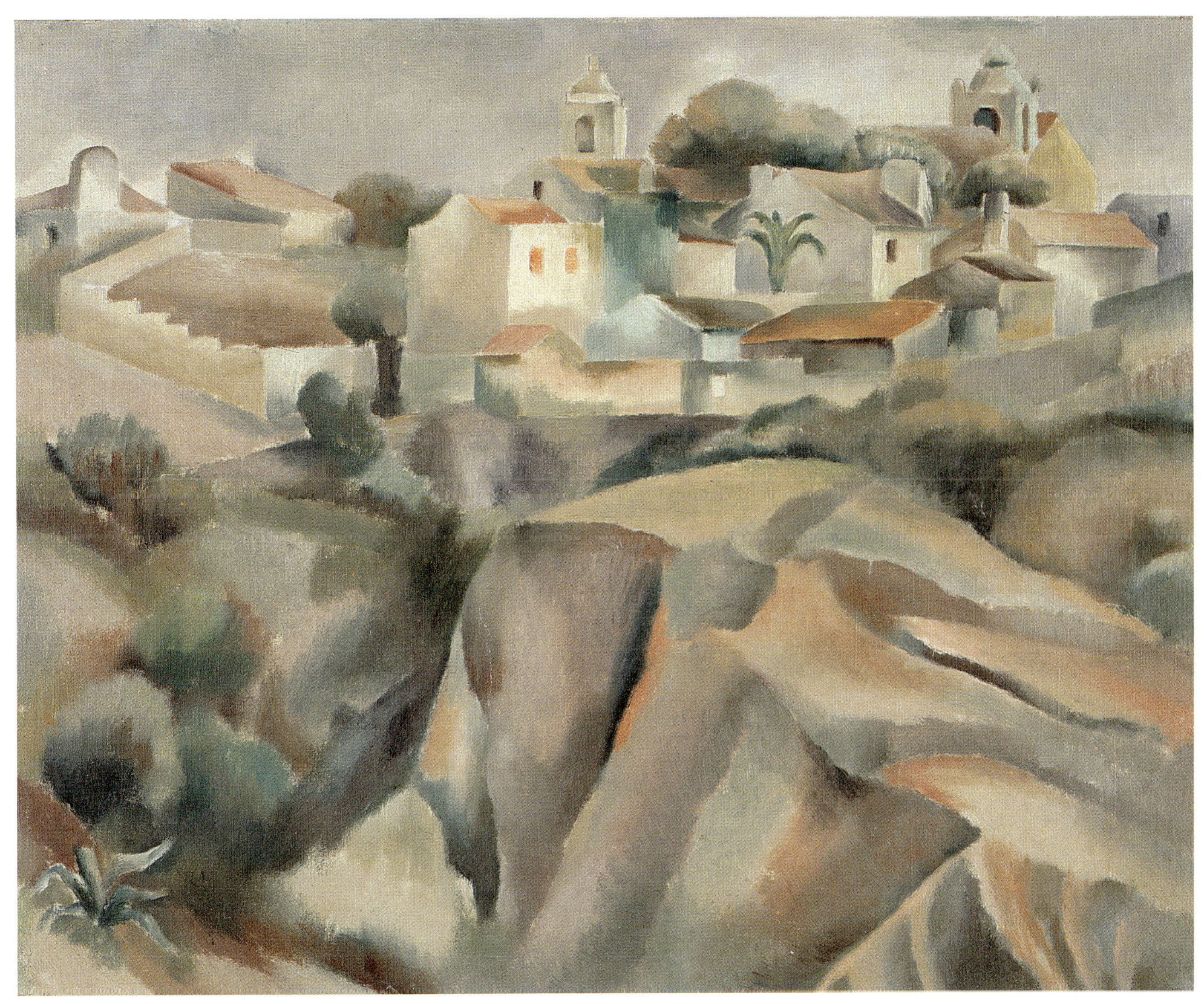

Pl. 21
Landscape Study, France, ca. 1923
Oil on canvas, 14 x 17
Gift of Dr. Margaret De Ronde Barber
to The John Barber Memorial Collection,
Bayly Art Museum of the University of Virginia,
1988.33.6

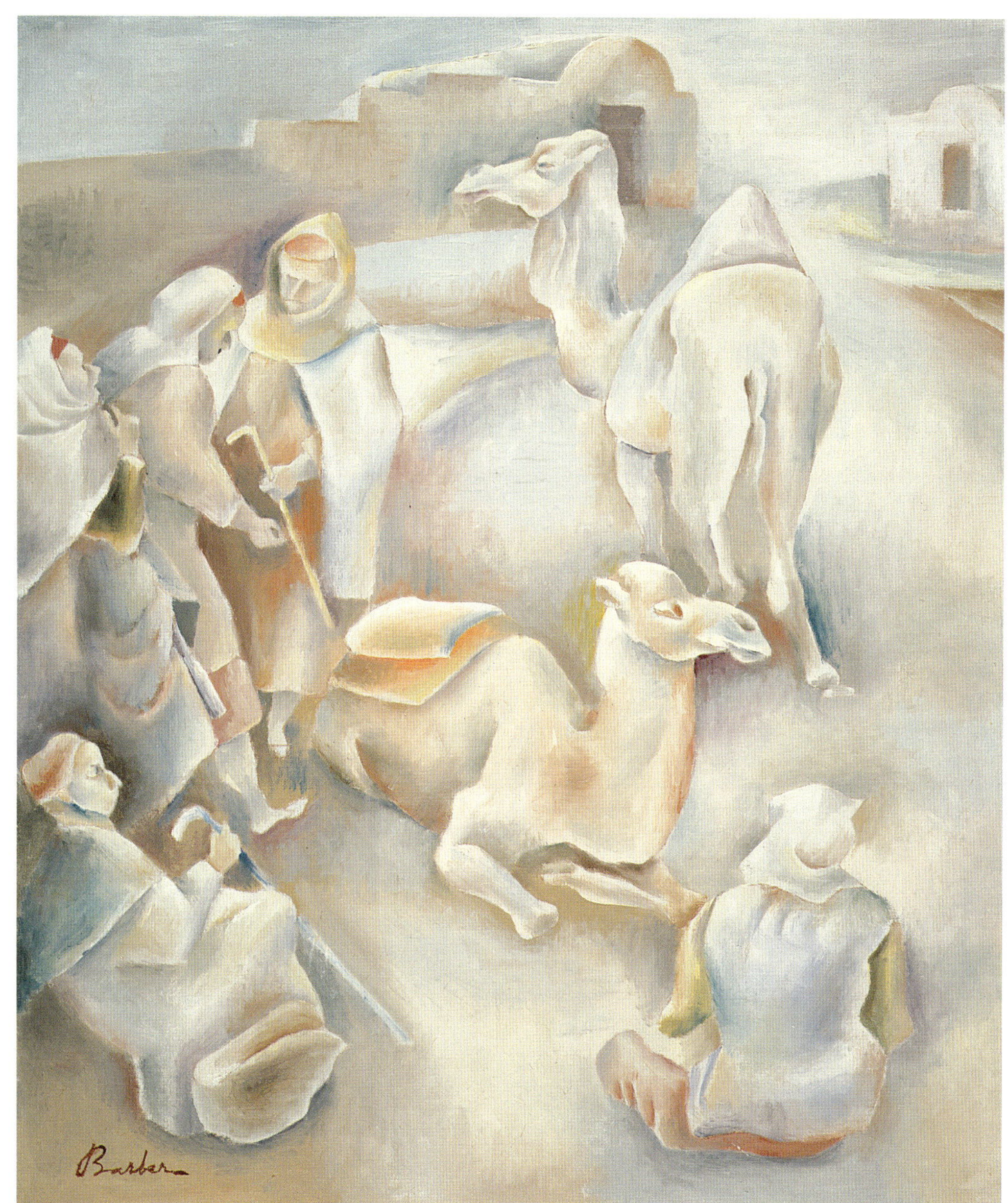

Pl. 22
Camel Exchange, 1948
Oil on canvas, 17 x 14
Gift of Dr. Margaret De Ronde Barber
to The John Barber Memorial Collection,
Bayly Art Museum of the University of Virginia,
1988.33.19

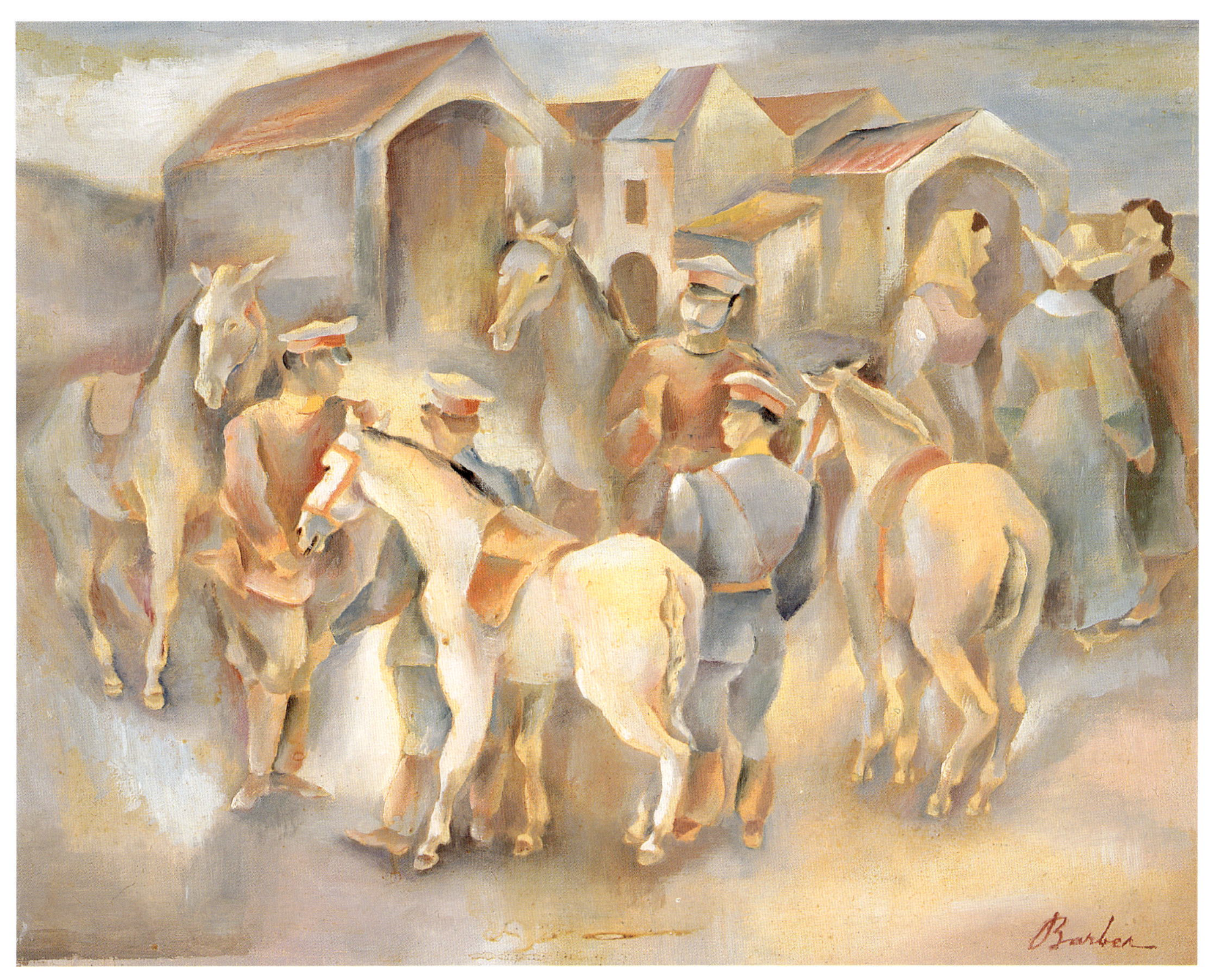

Pl. 23
Gendarmes Four
Oil on canvas, 17 x 14
Collection of Dr. Margaret De Ronde Barber,
on loan to The John Barber Memorial Collection,
Bayly Art Museum of the University of Virginia

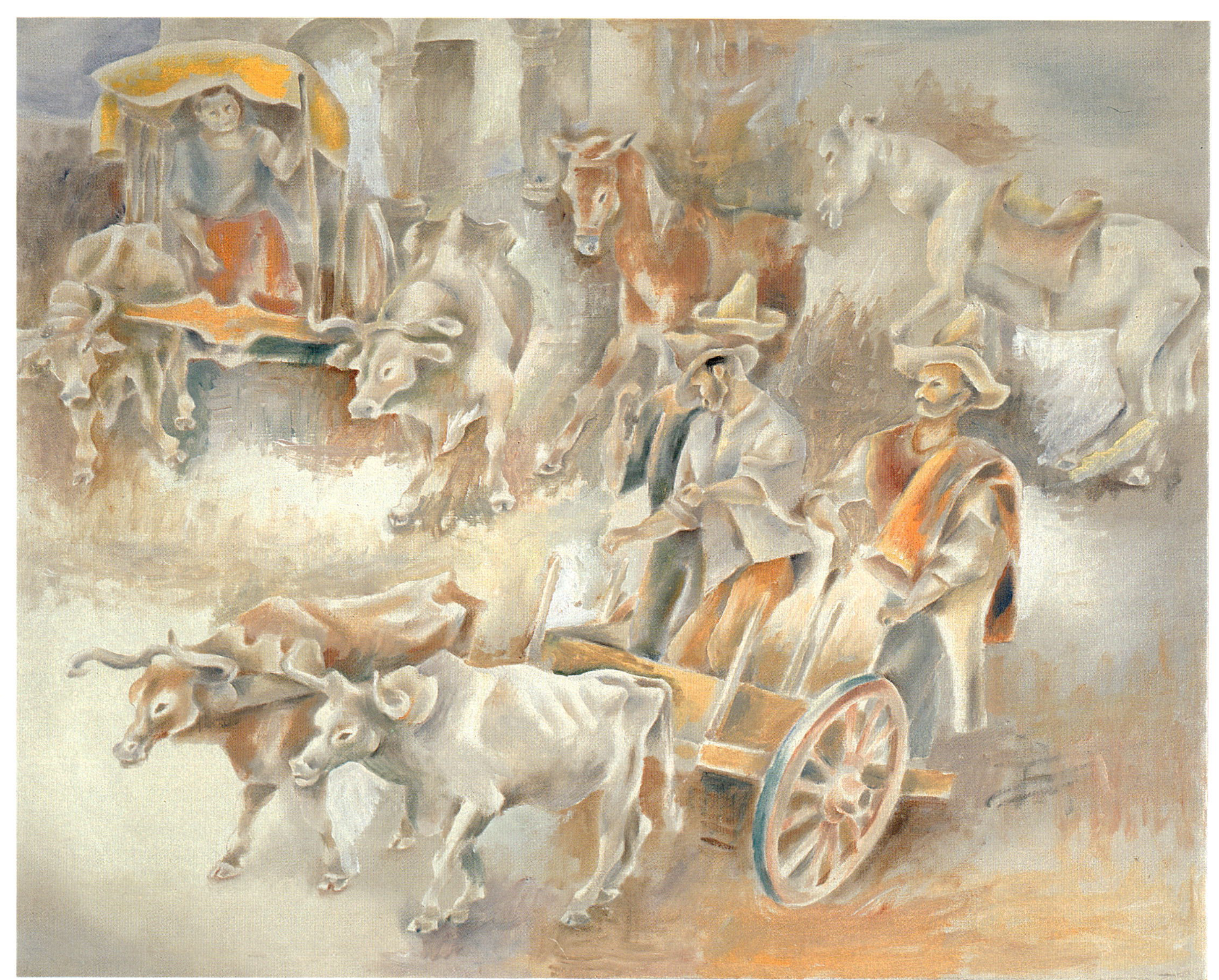

Pl. 24
Ox-Carts and Horses
Oil on canvas, 17 x 12
Collection of Dr. Margaret De Ronde Barber,
on loan to The John Barber Memorial Collection,
Bayly Art Museum of the University of Virginia

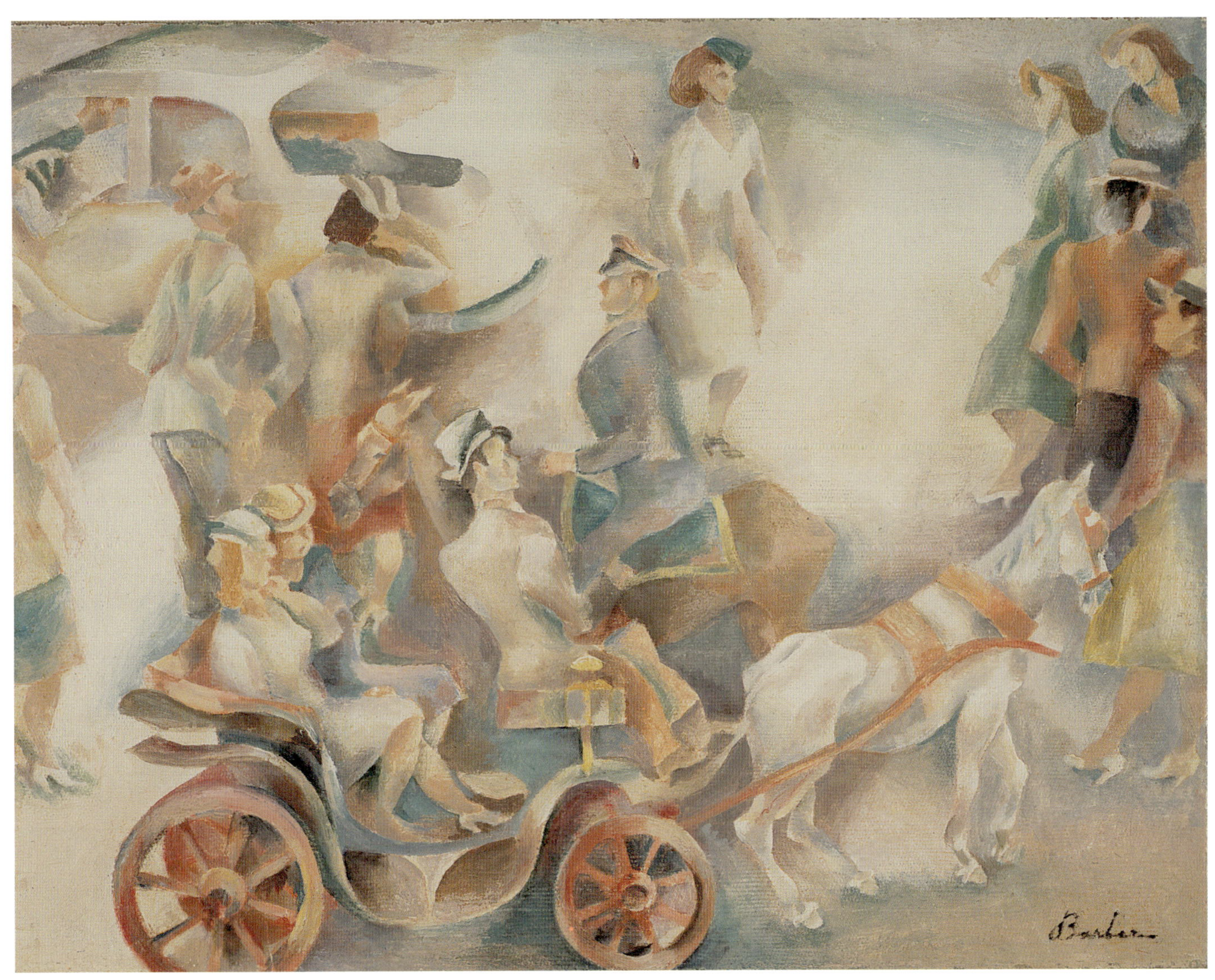

Pl. 25
Just off the Square
Oil on canvas, 11 3/4 x 14 3/4
Gift of Dr. Margaret De Ronde Barber
to The John Barber Memorial Collection,
Bayly Art Museum of the University of Virginia,
1988.33.16

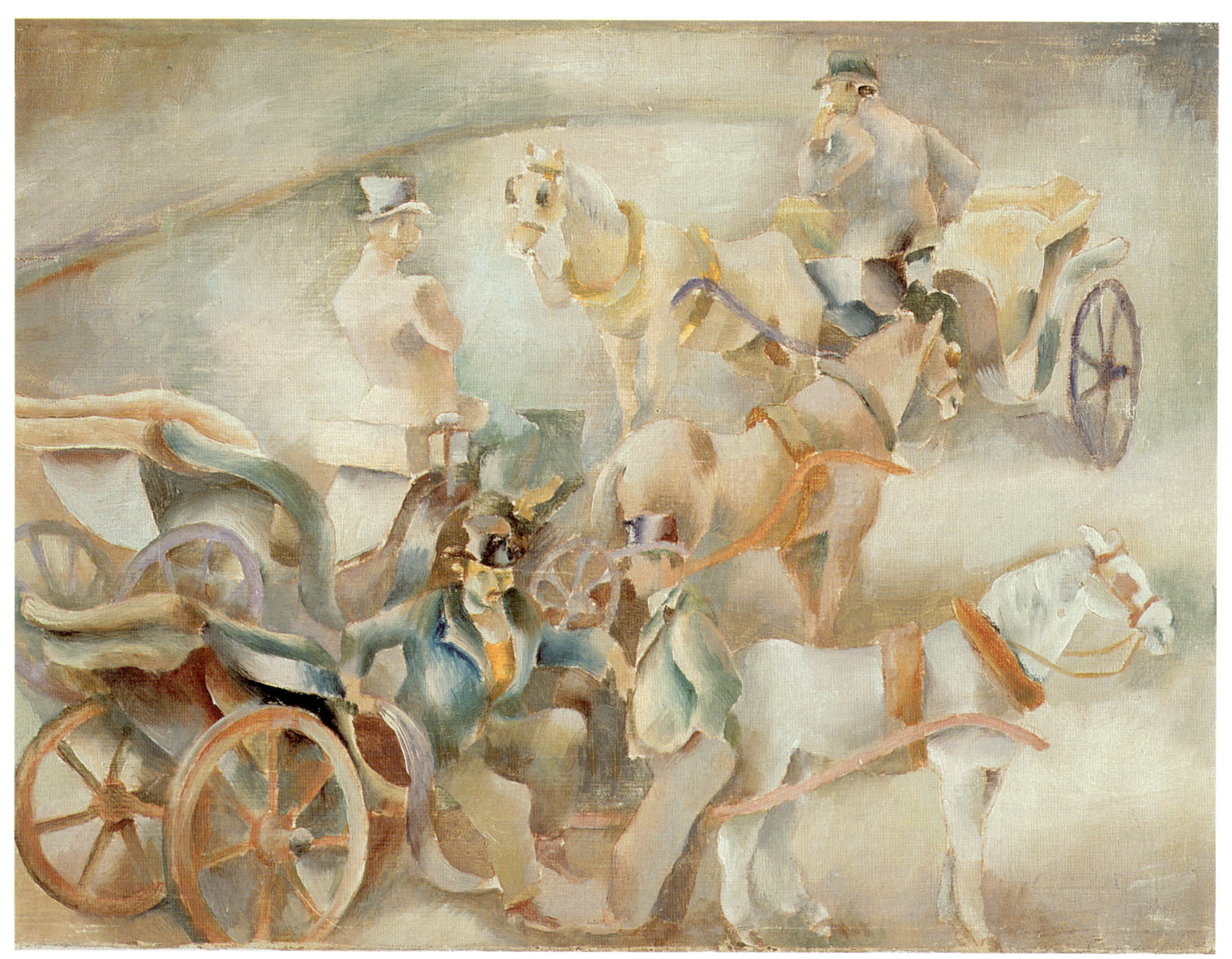

Pl. 26
Carriages and Drivers
Oil on canvas, 9 1/4 x 11 7/8
Gift of Dr. Margaret De Ronde Barber
to The John Barber Memorial Collection,
Bayly Art Museum of the University of Virginia,
1988.33.18

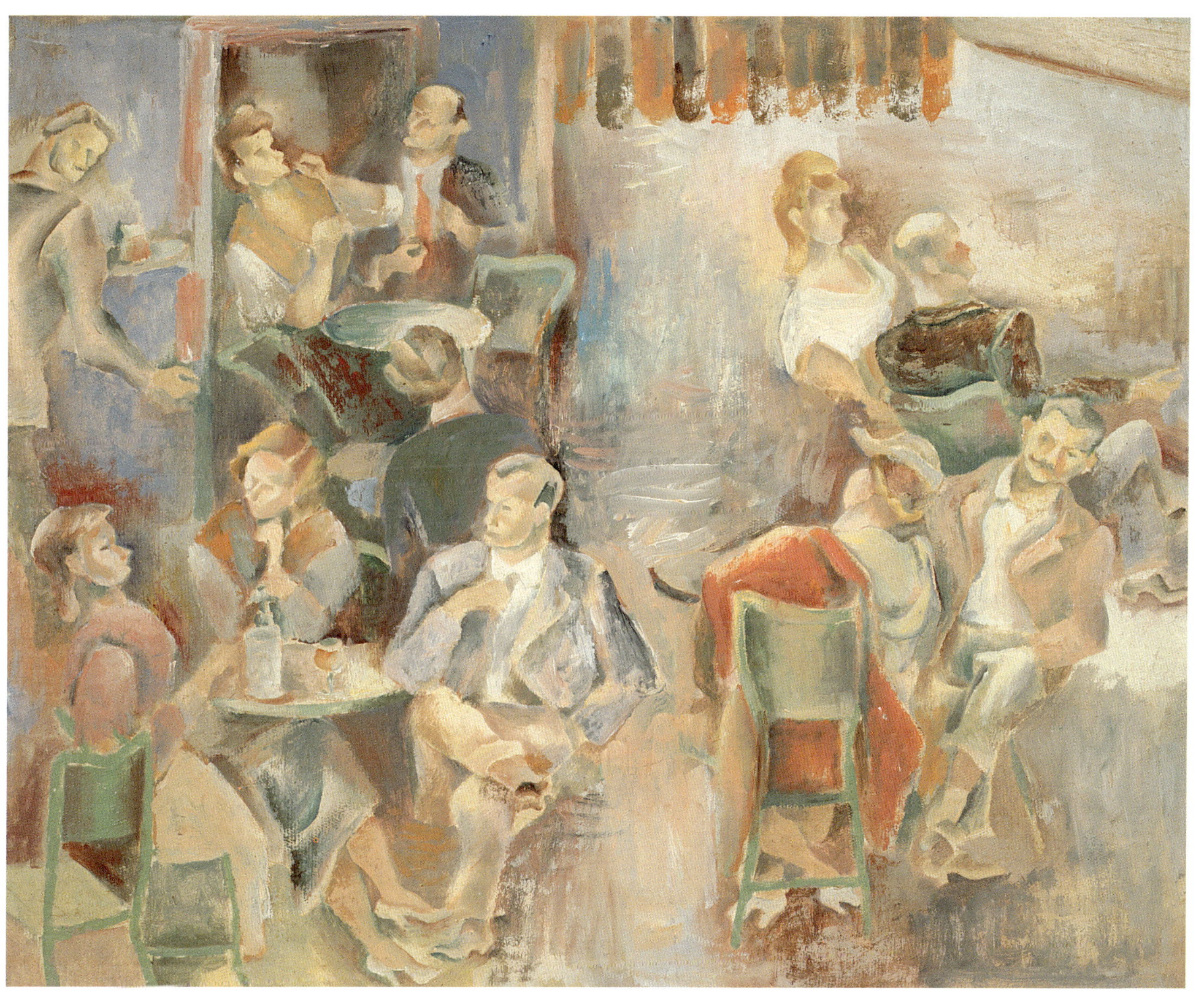

Pl. 27
Gin and Tonic, ca. 1948
Oil on canvas, 15 x 18
Collection of Dr. Margaret De Ronde Barber,
on loan to The John Barber Memorial Collection,
Bayly Art Museum of the University of Virginia
Photograph: Michael I. Price

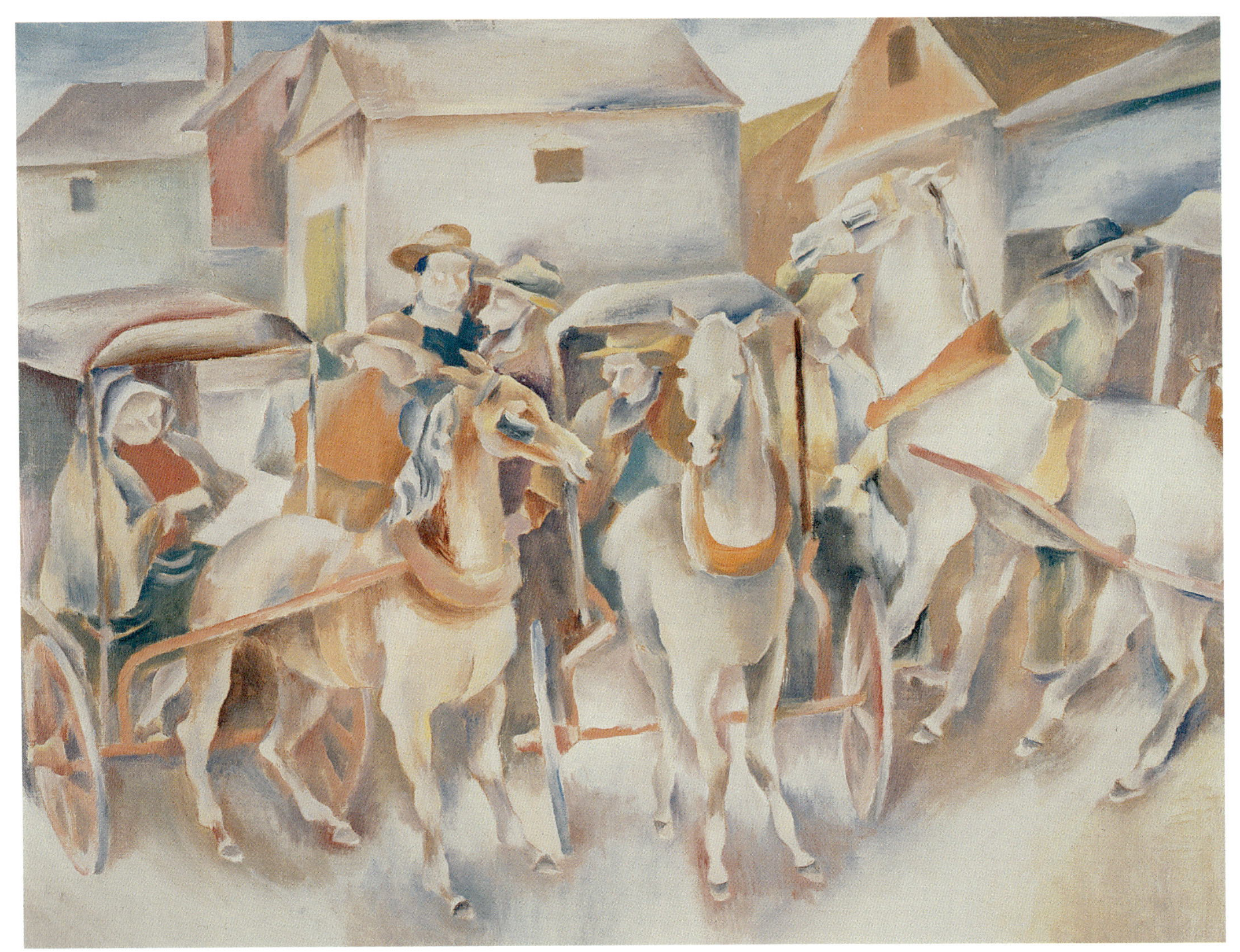

Pl. 28
Amish Parking, 1956
Oil on canvas, 14 x 18 ¹/₄
Gift of Dr. Margaret De Ronde Barber
to The John Barber Memorial Collection,
Bayly Art Museum of the University of Virginia,
1988.33.20

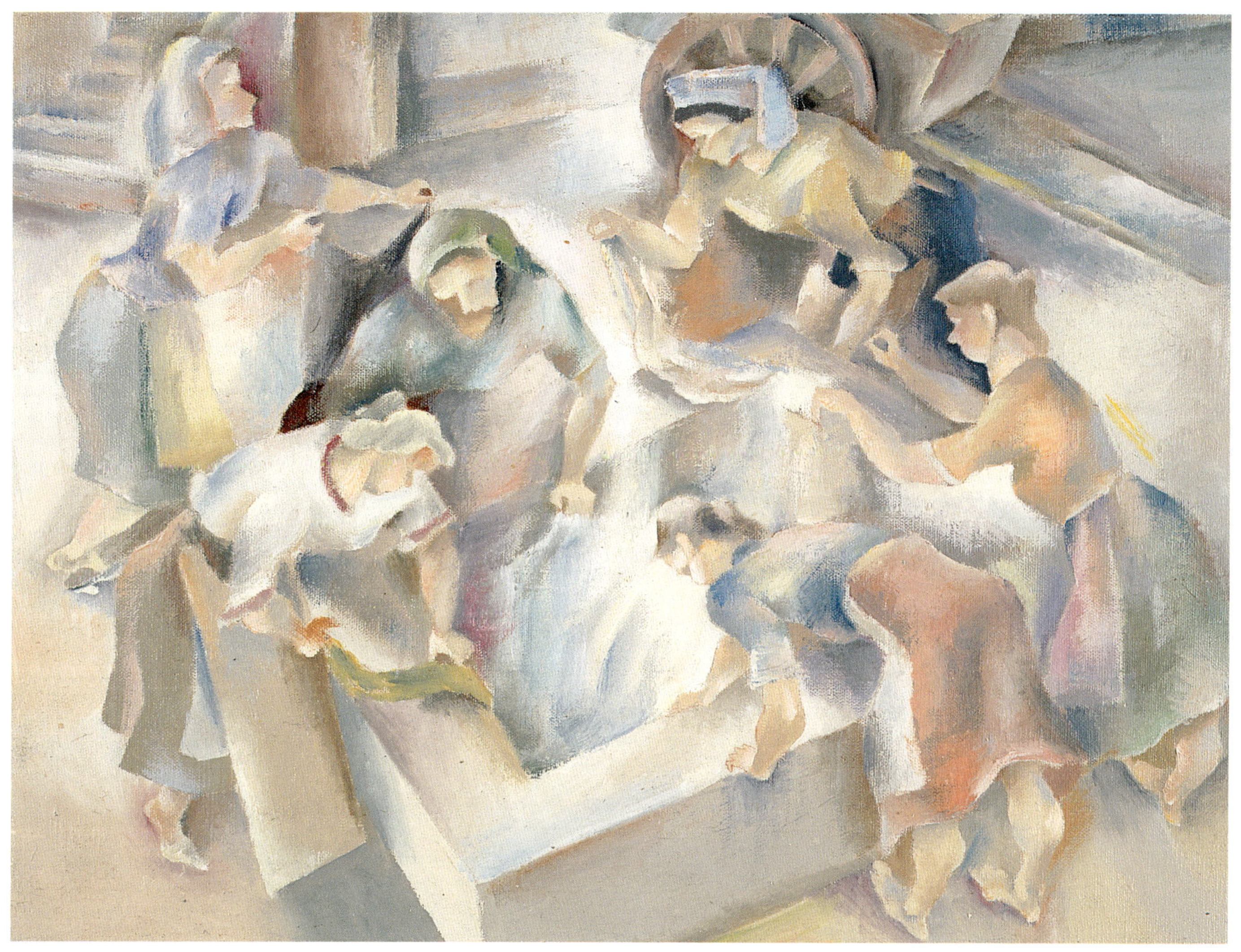

Pl. 29
Washerwomen at the Fountain
Oil on canvas, 10 x 13
Collection of Dr. Margaret De Ronde Barber,
on loan to The John Barber Memorial Collection,
Bayly Art Museum of the University of Virginia

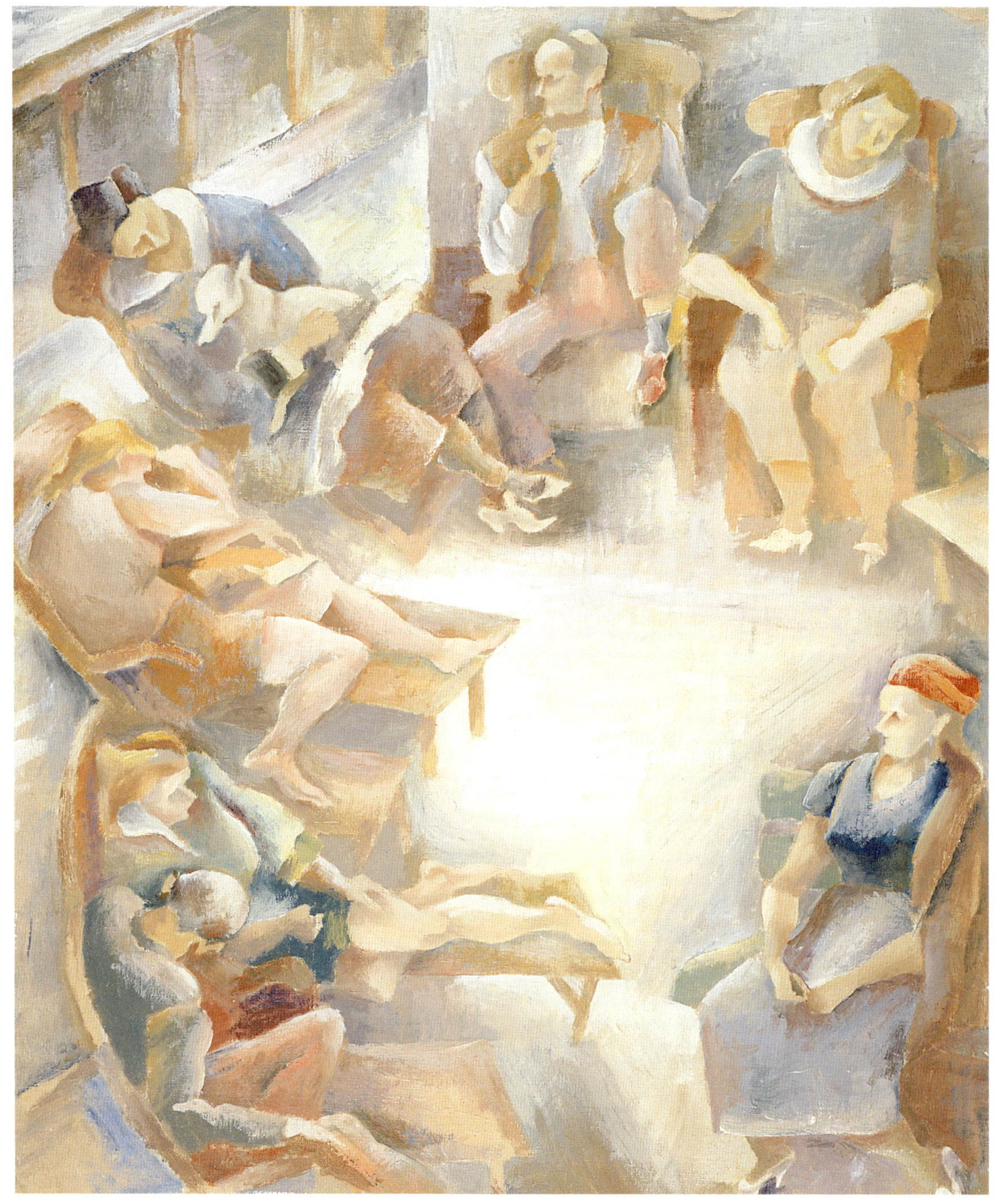

Pl. 30
Relaxing on Deck
Oil on canvas, 16 x 13
Collection of Dr. Margaret De Ronde Barber,
on loan to The John Barber Memorial Collection,
Bayly Art Museum of the University of Virginia

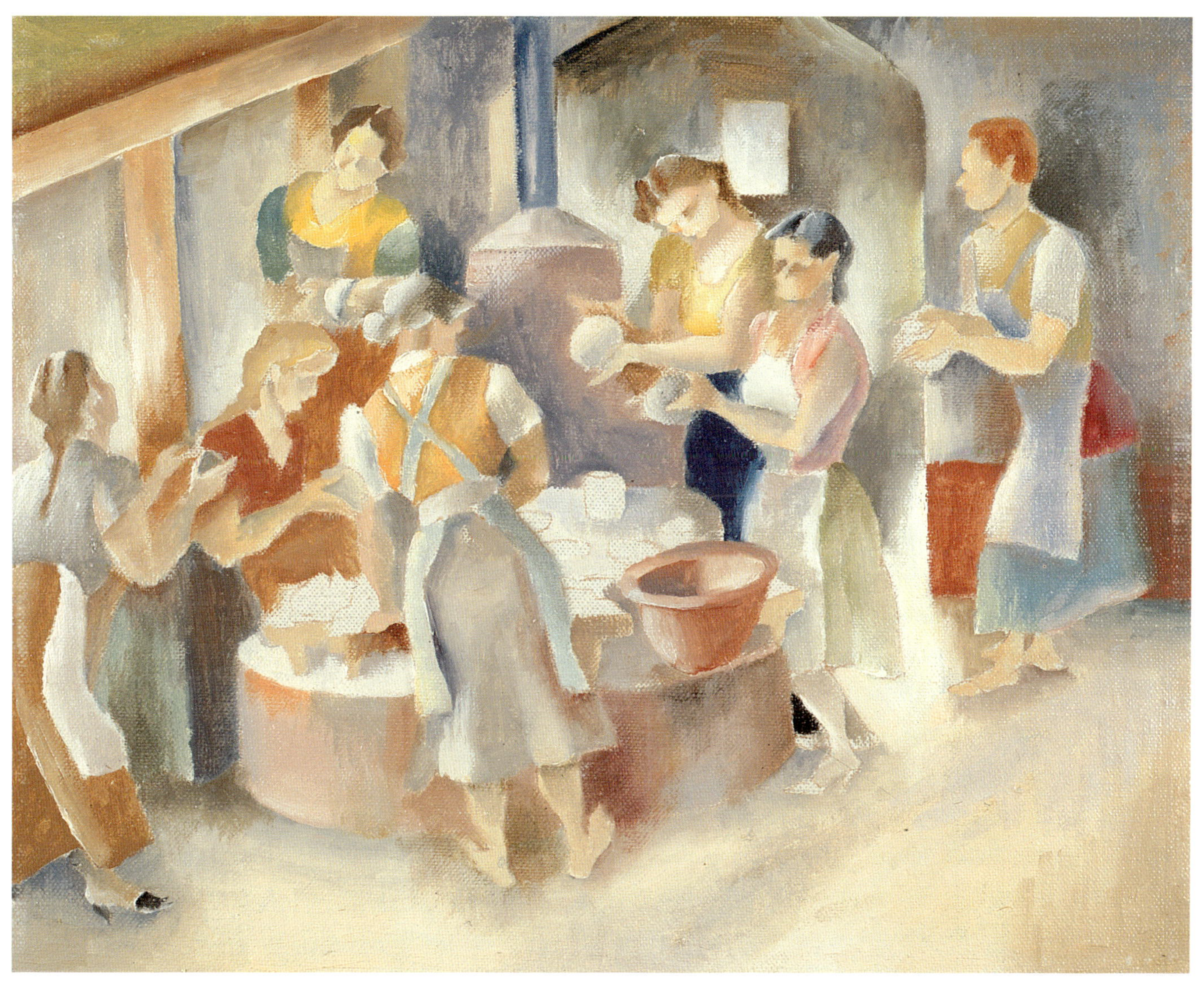

Pl. 31
Tortilla Making
Oil on canvas, 9 x 12
Collection of Dr. Margaret De Ronde Barber,
on loan to The John Barber Memorial Collection,
Bayly Art Museum of the University of Virginia

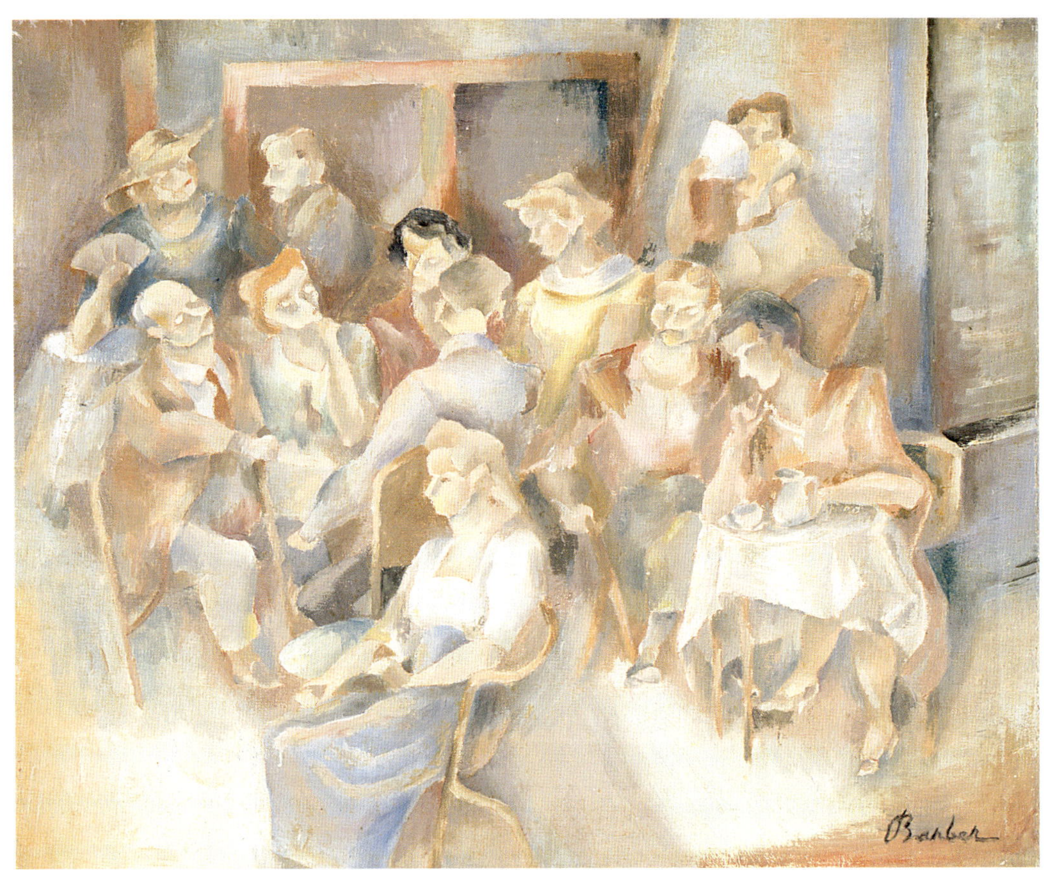

Pl. 32
At Dinner, 1953
Oil on canvas, 10 x 11 ³/₄
Gift of Dr. Margaret De Ronde Barber
to The John Barber Memorial Collection,
Bayly Art Museum of the University of Virginia,
1988.33.21

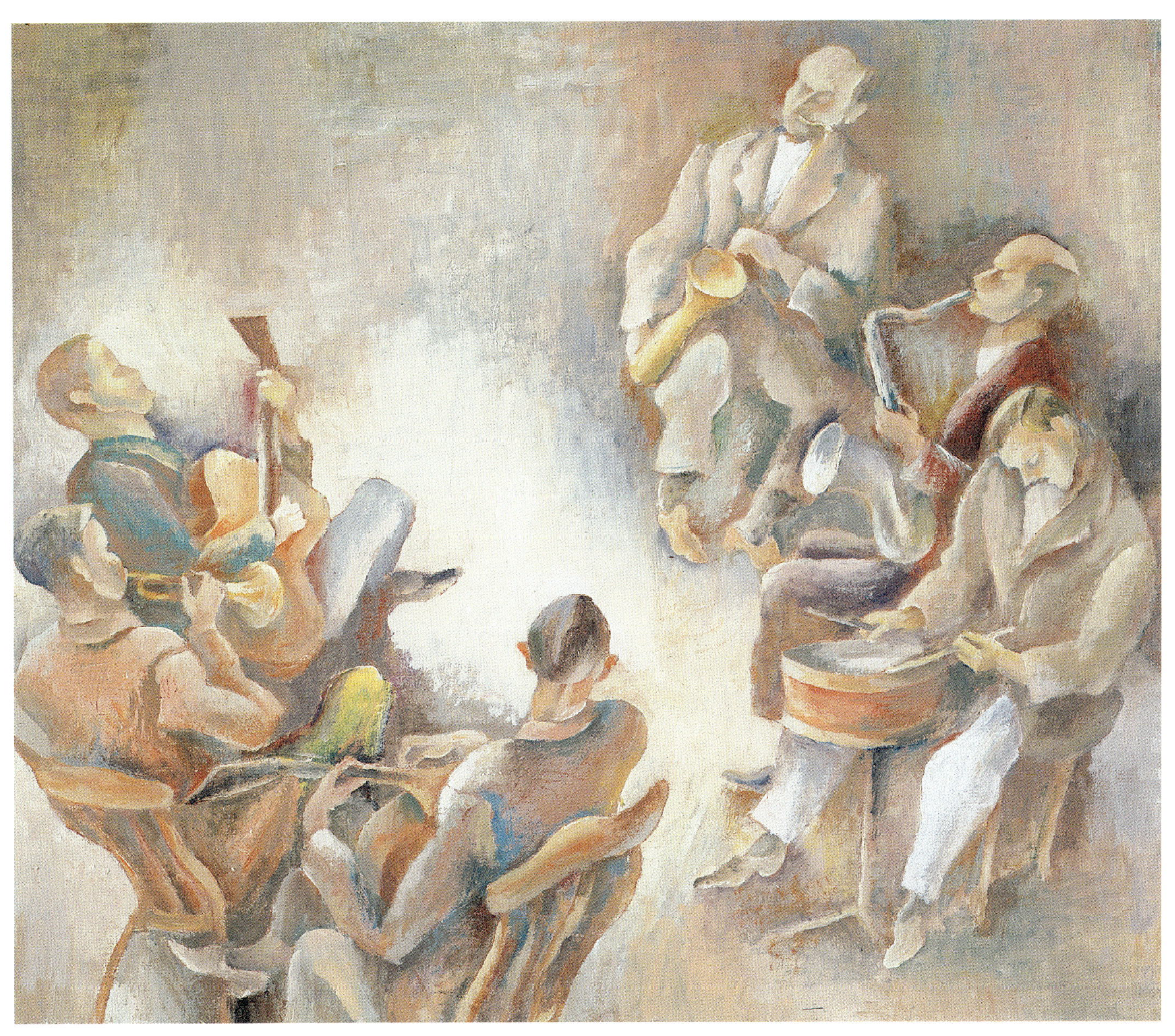

Pl. 33
Italian Jazz Band
Oil on canvas, 13 1/4 x 15 1/8
Collection of Dr. Margaret De Ronde Barber,
to The John Barber Memorial Collection,
Bayly Art Museum of the University of Virginia

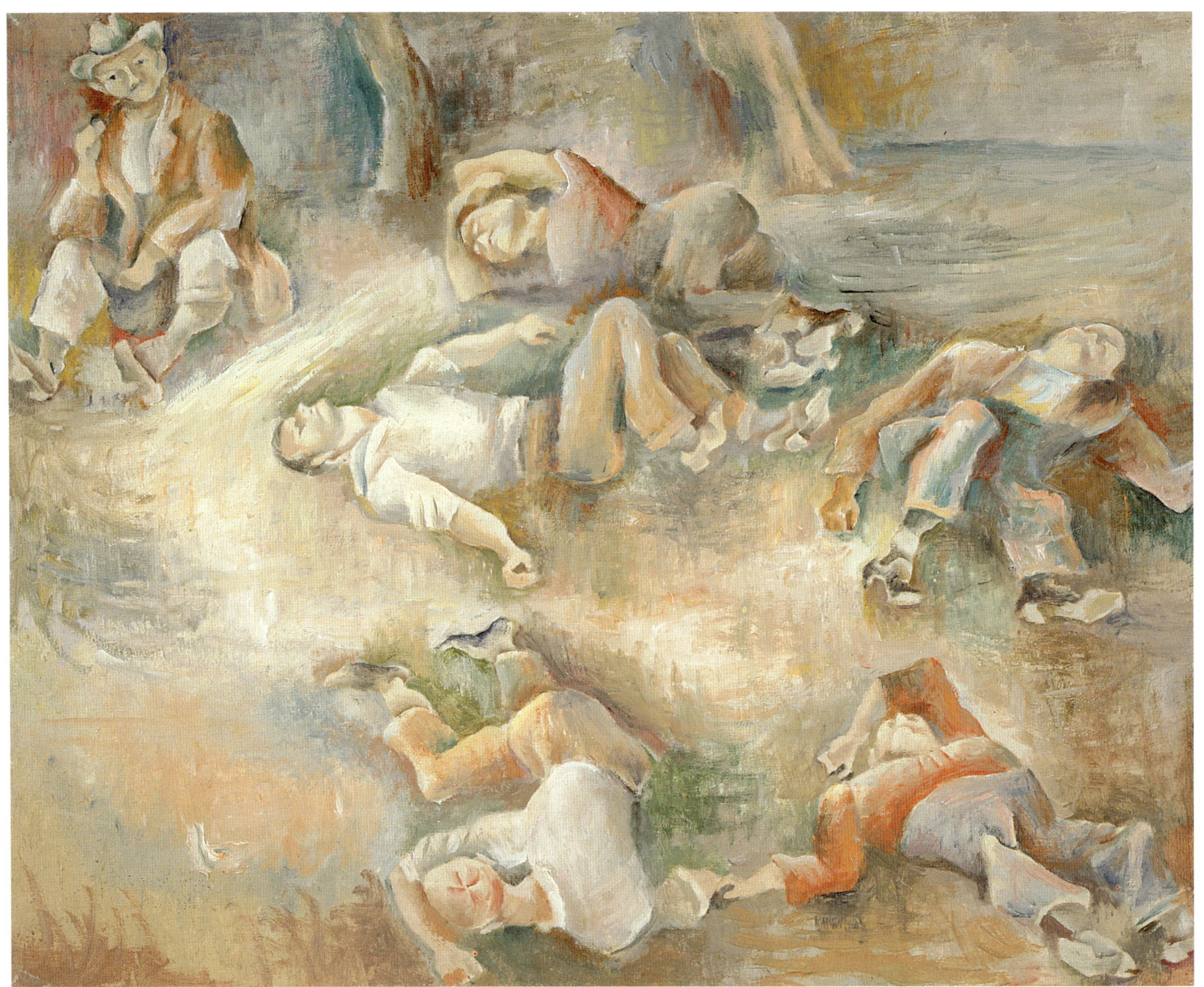

Pl. 34
Sunday in the Park
Oil on canvas, 14 x 17
Gift of Dr. Margaret De Ronde Barber
to The John Barber Memorial Collection,
Bayly Art Museum of the University of Virginia,
1988.33.22

Chronology

1893–1913
Born October 19 in Galati, Romania, to Frederick
and Betty Barber. Sister, Riviere (Rita). Grows up in
Romania; emigrates to the United States in his youth.
Becomes an American citizen. (His birth date is also
listed as 1898. Information on his Army discharge
document indicates a birth date of 1893.)

1914
In New York City contributes illustrations for publication to *The Masses,* a social reform magazine
which continued publishing into 1917. Has a drawing published in January 1915 issue.

1916
Becomes contributing art editor of *The Masses* in
July.

1917
Is drafted into the United States Army in September.

1918
Is court-martialed in France on April 18 and sentenced to two years in army prison for refusing orders
for medical treatment on the grounds that it is incom-
patible with his religious commitment as a Christian
Scientist. On June 20, is dishonorably discharged
from the United States Army; returns to New York
the following year.

1922
Travels to Europe; settles in Paris beginning in
February.

1923
Studies art with French painter André Lhote. Travels
to the Riviera and Italy with his mother in January.
In October, exhibits six etchings and paintings at the
Salon d'Automne in Paris. Is elected to the American
Art Association of Paris in November. *Vecko-
Journalen,* a Swedish illustrated magazine for which
he made drawings of Paris life, publishes an article
about John Barber in its December 9 issue.

1924
Exhibits in **L'exposition des cents dessins** at the
Galerie Devambez, Paris in October, having exhibited
there in April with the Vème Salon de l'Araignée, a
parody on official salons. In the November Salon
d'Automne in Paris, exhibits three paintings.

1925
Exhibits with American artists George Biddle, Paul
Burlin, Hunt Diederich, Marsden Hartley, Jules
Pascin, Maurice Sterne, and John Storrs at Galerie
Briant-Robert, Paris, January 19–February 19.
Travels to Italy in March. Exhibition of work by
seven of the eight Americans exhibited earlier in Paris
at Neue Galerie, Vienna, opened April 24. (John

Storrs did not show in Vienna.) Enjoys friendship of American artist Jules Pascin, who paints a full-length, seated portrait of John Barber in June.

1926
Travels to Holland and Germany in July and August. Father, Frederick Barber, dies November 6 in Marseille.

1927
Travels extensively beginning in January to Rome and Tunis, to Paris in May where his work is included in a group exhibition at Galerie Carmine, in June to Holland, and to New York City in December.

1928
Resumes contact with Jules Pascin, who is also living in New York. In February, travels again to Europe, first to Portugal, to Spain in March, to Palestine in May. Returns to Paris where he has one painting in a large group exhibition, **Les Invités**, from June 16–October 15 at Galerie Carmine. His work is shown in the Salon d'Automne in Paris in November.

1929
Travels to Italy in April. Work included in exhibitions in Paris at Le Salon des Tuileries in May and Galerie Zak in June. Galerie Zak mounts a one-man exhibition of paintings from October 25 through November 8. Exhibits in the Salon d'Automne in Paris in November.

1930
Exhibits in Paris in June at the VIIIe Salon des Tuileries and in November at the Salon d'Automne. In November, his painting *Portugese Women Baking Bread* is bought by the government of France for 800 francs for the Musée du Jeu de Paume in Paris. Jules Pascin dies June 2 in Paris.

1931
Trip to Germany in May.

1932
Exhibits with 32 artists in **Artistes Americains de Paris** at Galerie de la Renaissance, Paris, from January 18 through February 6. Travels in Spain and Portugal from March through June. Exhibits in the Salon d'Automne in Paris in October.

1933
Spends April through December in Portugal. In November in Lisbon exhibits at the Salaõ dos Independentes in **Exposicao de Pintura, Escultura e Arquitectura,** sponsored by the Sociedade Nacional de Belas Artes.

1934
In February, returns to the United States after seven years abroad. In April, a one-man exhibition of his work is shown at Grace Horne Galleries in Boston, his first American exhibition. In July, exhibits in the Gloucester (Massachusetts) Society of Artists' second annual summer exhibition.

1935
In January, exhibits at Hudson Galleries, Detroit. The John Herron Art Institute, Indianapolis, purchases etching, *Normandy Farmyard*. One-man exhibition, **Paintings of Portugal**, is shown at the New York gallery Ehrich-Newhouse, Inc. from March 11–23. Is invited to show in the **14th International Exhibition of Water Colors** at The Art Institute of Chicago. Travels to Portugal in November.

1936
In Portugal, exhibits at the Estúdio do Secretariado da Propaganda Nacional, Lisbon, in a two-man exhibition, **John Barber, paintings, and Hein Semke, sculpture**, opening January 25.

1937
In New York, exhibits at Ehrich-Newhouse, Inc. in March. One-person exhibition, **Mostly Portugal**, of 28 paintings at Grace Horne Galleries, Boston, in May.

1938
One-man exhibition of paintings at Marie Sterner Galleries, New York, January 29–February 12. Shows in the **One Hundred and Thirteenth Annual Exhibition** of the National Academy of Design, New York, March 26–April 13. In May exhibits with the American Artists' Congress at Wanamaker's Galleries, New York. In December travels to Tunis.

1939
Travels extensively, from Tunisia to France, Switzerland, Italy, Yugoslavia, arriving in Greece in February, where he visits Athens, Calamata, and Crete, continuing on to Paris in May, and returning to New York in June. Exhibits a painting, *Sardine Workers, Portugal,* in the American Section of Paintings, Division of Fine Arts, Golden Gate International Exposition, San Francisco, from February 18 through December 2.

1940
A painting is included in the **Second Biennial Exhibition of Contemporary American Paintings**, Virginia Museum of Fine Arts, Richmond, March 9–April 21. At the Town Hall Club, New York, exhibits paintings and gives a talk on "Modern Aspects of French Art," on March 31.

1941
Travels to Mexico in August, returning to the United States in December.

1943
Exhibits at Harcum Junior College, Bryn Mawr, Pennsylvania, while a faculty member in the Art Department.

1944
Serves as Head of the Art Department at Harcum Junior College.

1945
Is appointed President of Harcum Junior College in February, a position he holds through 1946.

1946
Sister, Rita, dies February 23 after a long illness. Meets Margaret De Ronde, a psychiatrist on the staff of the Institute of the Pennsylvania Hospital, University of Pennsylvania, Philadelphia, his future wife.

1947
Visits Rita's widower in Tunis with his mother, Betty Barber in September.

1948
In June the two move to Copenhagen for Mrs. Barber's health. Betty Barber dies June 21. He returns to the United States in October. Marries Margaret De Ronde; they reside in Merion, Pennsylvania.

1951
His painting, *Arab Horsemen,* is exhibited in **Annual Exhibition of Contemporary American Painting**, Whitney Museum of American Art, New York, November 8, 1951–January 6, 1952.

1953
Summer travel in Europe to Italy, Spain, Portugal, and Capri.

1955
Travels to Greece in August.

1957
One-man exhibition at The Philadelphia Art Alliance, February 12–March 3. Trip to Portugal in September.

1958
Exhibits with a group of American painters at Galerie Philadelphie, Paris, opening on April 30.

1959
Exhibits at F.A.R. Gallery, New York City, in January. Article on John Barber by Frederick Taubes is published in *The American Artist*, vol. 23, no. 6, June-July-August issue. Makes fall trip to Italy.

1960
A painting, *Mexican Horsemen,* is acquired by Musée National d'Art Moderne, Paris, in February.

1961
Travels to Sardinia from mid-August to mid-October. One-man exhibition at Penn Art Center Galleries, Philadelphia, November 15–December 15.

1962
A painting is exhibited in the Third Philadelphia Arts Festival, at the Philadelphia Museum of Art, June 9–24. Author of article "Creating Your Compositions" in *The American Artist,* vol. 64, no. 1, October issue.

1963
Travels to Italy. One-person exhibition at Fontana Gallery, Philadelphia, in June. Painting is included in **Exhibition of Contemporary Liturgical Art,** The Archdiocese of Philadelphia, Convention Exhibition Hall, Philadelphia.

1964
Exhibits at Reyn Gallery, New York, in September. Painting is included in the **Regional Exhibition: Paintings, Sculpture, Prints and Drawings by Artists of Philadelphia and Vicinity** at the Pennsylvania Academy of Fine Arts, Philadelphia, October 9–November 15.

1965
Exhibits at Reyn Gallery, New York, in February; in May at Vincent Price Enterprises, Los Angeles; in June at Galerie Fontainebleau, Inc., Miami Beach, Florida. Travels to Italy from July 15 to September 23. Work is included in the **First Regional Oil Painting Exhibit** at the Philadelphia Art Alliance from October 25–December 5.

Dies of leukemia December 8 at his home in Merion, Pennsylvania.

List of Illustrations

Index

List of Illustrations

FIGURES

COLOR PLATES

John Barber
1893–1965
Selections from the Archive

Designed by Franklin Street Communications, Inc.
Composed with Adobe Sabon using Aldus Pagemaker
Printed by Expert/Brown on Potlatch Mountie Matte
Case Bound by Advantage Book Binding with Holiston
Roxite Linen and Mohawk P/C text endsheets,
Soft Bound with International Springhill Cover